CRITICAL DIRECTIONS IN COMICS STUDIES

CRITICAL DIRECTIONS
—— IN ——
COMICS STUDIES

EDITED BY
THOMAS GIDDENS

UNIVERSITY PRESS OF MISSISSIPPI • JACKSON

The University Press of Mississippi is the scholarly publishing agency of
the Mississippi Institutions of Higher Learning: Alcorn State University,
Delta State University, Jackson State University, Mississippi State University,
Mississippi University for Women, Mississippi Valley State University,
University of Mississippi, and University of Southern Mississippi.

www.upress.state.ms.us

The University Press of Mississippi is a member
of the Association of University Presses.

First printing 2020
∞

Library of Congress Control Number: 2020939615
Hardback: 978-1-4968-2899-6
Trade Paperback: 978-1-4968-2900-9
Epub Single: 978-1-4968-2901-6
Epub Institutional: 978-1-4968-2902-3
PDF Single: 978-1-4968-2903-0
PDF Institutional: 978-1-4968-2904-7

British Library Cataloging-in-Publication Data available

CONTENTS

WELCOME AND ORIENTATION

Welcome to *Critical Directions in Comics Studies*, a collection of essays both textual and multimodal that aim to indicate and explore a diverse range of ways of thinking about comics. This collection is a consolidation and an opening up: consolidating some of the critical approaches within comics studies that have emerged in recent decades, and opening up to the potential for further examinations and reflections in the future. Each chapter indicates and performatively embodies a way of thinking about or approaching comics or comics studies that in some way seeks to go beyond or challenge or deviate from emerging assumptions within the discipline, notably around the primacy of semiotics or structural linguistics in the way we conceptualize or engage with the medium. Indeed, the project was inspired by an encounter with Hannah Miodrag's clarion call for an expanded critical approach to comics studies (see Miodrag 2013). But this "going beyond" is embodied in other ways, too; and these approaches are not codified—if such a thing is even possible—but instead left as provocations or indications as to the potential variety and expanse of comics thinking for the reader to navigate through their own interpretive endeavor.

The volume you are entering is intentionally fluid in its construction, expansive and indicative in its scope, and irresolute in its conclusions. Chapters are organized in a rough trajectory that runs from the encounter with the form, through its material production and contexts of appearance, to the revolutionary spirit that might be seen to animate critical as well as comics thinking more generally. But this trajectory is merely one possible imposition of meaning. The atemporal, multifaceted structure of the comics form is intentionally reflected in the atemporal and multifaceted structure of this volume, with a range of critical directions being indicated across and within and between the chapters articulated within it—not all of them explicit or intended by the volume's creators. Each chapter escapes the volume, suggesting a trajectory that moves beyond the collection itself, and that is often challenged or reframed by other chapters. It is a restless collection. In its totality it contains no answers, but in indicating directions is instead all about questions.

This preface is rhapsodic, like the volume it marks. Aphoristic. It lacks coherence and drive, it lacks single aim or purpose. It wanders. It meanders and surveys and suggests. It disagrees with itself. These words describe the volume, or the preface? Yes. An opening to alternative perspectives, alternative ways of doing comics thought, of thought in general, of performing the creative work of academic study. An intellectual and material space in which to get lost and find a way forward.

This preface welcomes you to this unstable environment, orienting by disorienting. The volume augured does not seek to follow expected editorial trajectories nor does it respect disciplinary boundaries. Text is ruptured by image, image by text (if such divisions exist); multiple perspectives, disciplines, perspectives, concepts, ideas, ideals, hopes, desires, and thoughts are traversed; and it is hoped that comics thinking is invigorated with the critical spirit that is emerging across the "discipline" (if we want to wed ourselves to such a limiting, white, male, European concept as "discipline"—a possibility provocatively represented in the first comics interlude in its characterization of disciplinary authority, and the disciplines it constitutes, as white men).

The volume has a narrative arc that can be traced, an intentional order to the chapters betraying a desire for revolution—or a movement toward the revolution that is always to come. (It has just been said the collection lacks structure; but was it not also indicated that the preface disagrees with itself?) A revolutionary ethos that operates at numerous levels: epistemic, disciplinary, political, emotional, pedagogic. A rupture and changing of the world through thought and image and word and discourse. A rupture that is always emerging, that characterizes critical work. How else could such a critically oriented volume be organized—if indeed it is organized at all and not instead a collection of disparate and divergent reflections—but in terms of revolution.

This preface hopes you feel welcome in this expansive realm, this landscape of potential. It hopes, also, that you feel suitably (dis)oriented to embark upon a journey across its topographies, a reduction and closure of its potential pathways in the journey you happen to take, a single traversing amidst a range of directions, your own personal and particular inhabiting and activation of the chapters that follow—just as one inhabits and activates the database aesthetic of the comics form (see Bukatman 2014).

THOMAS GIDDENS

6 APRIL 2019

References

Bukatman, Scott. 2014. "Sculpture, Stasis, the Comics, and Hellboy." *Critical Inquiry* 40 (3): 104–17.

Miodrag, Hannah. 2013. *Comics and Language: Reimagining Critical Discourse on the Form*. Jackson: University Press of Mississippi.

CRITICAL DIRECTIONS IN COMICS STUDIES

COMICS INTERLUDE #1

Critical Comics Studies
An Origin Story

BY THOM GIDDENS

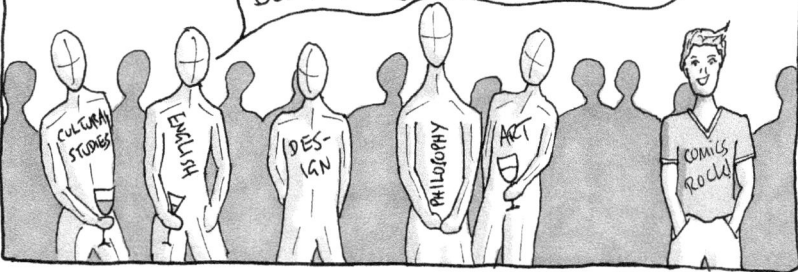

And so comics studies became critical comics studies, and never again took anything as given

Accordingly, as a tentative example of **critical comics studies,** the book you are (virtually?) holding seeks to *break* from emerging assumptions and sedimentations in comics discourse and instead to roam free in its encounter with **Comics** in its various and expansive emanations

And here, in their authors' own hands, are...

The Chapters!

...which make up this book—free from the tyranny of section headings and imposed themes!

I'm Chris Pizzino. My chapter explores the relationship between comics reading, as a phenomenological experience, and delinquency.

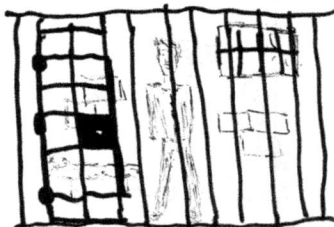

Lisa DeTora
Associate Professor at Hofstra University

I'm interested in how health humanities balances theory and medical practice. My essay examines articulation and augmentation in graphic narratives by medical illustrators

Why are you wearing a Deadpool mask? And why are you dancing to Saturday Night Fever?

I'm shy, and I'm not good at drawing. Now, shh!

I'm Yasemin, I'm a philosopher at St Mary's University, and my chapter is about Deadpool. Did the mask give it away? It's about fourth wall breaking, why Deadpool is an existential antihero, and how life might be meaningless. Enjoy!

Hi! My name is Tim Peters. I'm a cultural legal scholar at the University of the Sunshine Coast, Queensland, Australia

Drawing on the work of Merleau-Ponty, my chapter elaborates a phenomenological analysis of comics as a form of 'critical seeing' via a consideration of the blind superhero Daredevil.

P.S. I can't draw, so my lovely wife drew this for me. Thanks Chantelle!!

Comics Interlude:
Let's Get Critical!

My chapter looks at the Birmingham Arts Lab as a site of comics production and how struggles over creative labor and the value produced are inscribed in the comics made

HI! I'm MAGGIE GRAY. I'm A COMICS ART HISTORIAN TEACHING AT KINGSTON UNIVERSITY

Hi my name is Lydia Wysocki, I'm a researcher in Education

Join me for a deep dive into what's REALLY - ACTUALLY - EMPIRICALLY going on in British comics

PAUL F. DAVIES

My chapter explores DIALOGISM and HETEROGLOSSIA in comics...

Yeah!

...How comics comprise MULTIPLE VOICES at a range OF LEVELS!

I did my PhD at the UNIVERSITY of SUSSEX and I teach at EAST SUSSEX COLLEGE, Lewes.

I'm Nicola Streeten, graphic novelist, comics scholar and Co-founder of Laydeez Do Comics

My chapter shows how Simone Lia's "Fluffy" uses humor to challenge gendered assumptions about parenting

teacher

HI! I'M VLAD MAKSIMOV, AND MY CORE INTEREST IS THE ANALYSIS OF GOVERNANCE PROCESSES AT ALL LEVELS OF SOCIAL ORGANIZATION. IN MY CHAPTER I ATTEMPT TO USE GEORGIO AGAMBEN'S TOPOLOGY OF SOVEREIGN POWER AND BARE LIFE TO ARGUE THAT THE STORY OF V IS A TALE OF THE DYNAMICS BETWEEN SOVEREIGN VIOLENCE AND ITS UNINTEDED CONSEQUENCES.

Comics Interlude:
The Nested Text

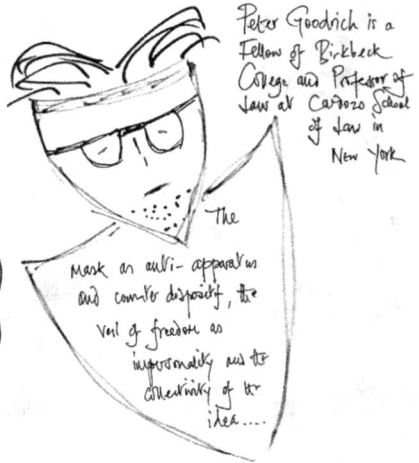

1

On Violation

Comic Books, Delinquency, Phenomenology

CHRISTOPHER PIZZINO

The time is the mid-1950s; the place, any town in the United States. A group of boys meet in the woods to read and swap comic books. Fixating on stories that show violence tinged with sex, they scan pages with interest and then with excitement. One boy leaves the ragged circle of his fellows. Producing a pocketknife, he begins to stab a tree, grimacing in agitation as thrust follows thrust. A second boy rises and, grabbing a broken brick, smashes it against a rock; moments later, he considers using it to crush a third boy's head. No adults are present to witness this scene of savagery and social collapse—only the kids and the comic books that seem to be destroying them.

There were, of course, quite a number of adults on hand for this moment, since they were filming it, using child actors, for a segment of the news show *Confidential File* (Kirshner 1955). This well-known instance of anticomics propaganda was broadcast a year after the 1954 Congressional hearings on comic books as a cause of juvenile delinquency, which had resulted in the formation of a new Comics Code Authority.[1] The segment's effect on existing anticomics stigma may have been minimal. What *Confidential File* put on film already existed in the writings of midcentury anticomics crusaders, and thanks to the extensive strictures of the new Comics Code, the fate of comic books in the United States had already been sealed. Yet this scene offered a concentrated image of widespread fears about the comic book's power to take hold of the mind and the body, and to make the comics-reading subject delinquent.

Comics studies has not yet grasped what this infamous tableau of savage young comics fans could reveal about comic book reading today.

I offer this scene as a powerful image of the phenomenology of comic book reading—and it is revelatory, in part, because it is paranoid and distorted. The distortion, which links comics reading to delinquency, has not been and currently is not correctable by a simple adjustment of terms, nor by more seemingly respectable categories of comics such as the literary or highbrow comic, the graphic novel, and so on. Perceptions of comics as delinquent have certainly diminished over time, but separate names for more "literary" comics will not end such perceptions. To understand why this is the case, we must grasp the medium's link to delinquency with a fuller sense of how it touches, and is touched by, phenomenological experience specific to comics.

I employ those aspects of phenomenology most concerned with sense experience and its relation to embodied subjectivity, as explored by Maurice Merleau-Ponty ([1945] 2012). Although phenomenological studies (in the sense just delimited) of the visual arts are numerous, their focus is almost invariably on fine arts expression, and there has been no sustained investigation of the phenomenology of comics reading. In beginning a pursuit of this fugitive concern, scholars can, I hope, be excused for paying serious attention to anecdotal evidence. Pascal Lefèvre (1998) takes this approach in his paper "Recovering Sensuality in Comic Theory," which cites, among several striking recollections from comics readers and creators, this anecdote from Thierry Smolderen concerning his childhood experience with a sequence from the Franco-Belgian Western comic *Blueberry*:

> I spent hours reading and reading again the whole sequence. . . . I almost felt the comic book vibrating in my hands . . . my eye perceived this image, my body received it like a whiplash, but my mind stayed paralyzed. . . . What drives me to scrutinize the images of contemporary comics is [. . .] the palpitating perspective to understand intellectually one day what seems to be by essence destined to escape me forever. (2, bracketed ellipsis in original)

The susceptible viewer of *Confidential File*'s segment on comics might, of course, take this anecdote as further proof of comics' destructive effects. But I see the disturbance young Thierry Smolderen felt as the emergence of a robustly embodied reading experience, a "palpitating perspective" found not in the "vibrating" comic book itself but in its phenomenological relation to the eye, body, and mind of the reader—most especially in the context of comics as an illegitimate art.

One of the reasons discussion of phenomenological matters has not been copious in comics studies is that, as Ian Hague (2014) notes, "materiality as a whole remains a relatively neglected area of comics scholarship" (23). In its earliest years, comics studies made little space for phenomenological approaches to comics, though the occasional revelatory excursus—notably from Charles Hatfield (2005, 58–64) and from Roger Sabin (1993, 52)—indicated possible approaches to comics reading as embodied experience. More recently, the issue of embodiment has been more likely to arise in relation to comics creatorship, often with an eye to the way comics can be read as traces of bodily marking.[2] This newer inquiry does not necessarily exclude the question of reading; indeed, its discussion of how readers experience comics as traces of a creator's body can offer better understanding of cycles of comics creation and consumption.[3] Thus far, however, this line of investigation has not prompted much consideration of even basic haptic aspects, tactile and visual, of comics reading as such.

When such consideration does arise, there is a persistent focus on sites marked as haptic in the narrow sense, i.e. clear visual references to the tactile, such as images of the author's hand in autobiographical or other nonfiction comics.[4] Such sites often are indeed revealing vis-à-vis questions of embodied reading; I will presently discuss a related kind of haptic self-reflexivity in Kyle Baker's *Nat Turner* (2008). But our understanding of the significance of such sites is likely to be limited if not made part of a larger surround so that many aspects of comic book reading can be understood phenomenologically. Karin Kukkonen's (2015) brief discussion of page design in relation to the reader's body schema points in this direction, but a more thoroughgoing approach is needed (61–63). My object of focus here is the reader holding and held by her comic book, fixed in a disciplinary gaze that cares little how the comic was produced, or by whom, but that is certainly ready to treat the reader with suspicion. We must conceive of comics reading in terms of ongoing phenomenological processes that do not necessarily originate in creatorship, that do not need clear visual denotation to be in effect, and that are strongly tied to comics' delinquent status.

To bring this conjunction of phenomenology and status concerns into focus is to discover hitherto unseen complexities in the dynamics of comics reading. The new critical direction offered here for comics studies offers a deeper—and hopefully less defensive—understanding of how comics reading can be affected, continuously and intimately, by the problem of illegitimacy. This latter problem is quite familiar to comics studies, but typically it is detached from phenomenological concerns, not least because scholarly understanding of comics history has, for the most part, developed separately from understanding of comics form. Early theorists of comics in the United States knew well that the medium as it has existed historically—loved by fans but often disrespected, infantilized, treated as disposable, and threatened with censorship—and comics form in the abstract might productively be seen as unrelated matters. In his founding theoretical work *Understanding Comics* (1993), Scott McCloud addresses this difficulty while discussing his own thought process as he developed his ideas about the medium: "Sure, I realized that comics were usually crude, poorly-drawn, semiliterate, cheap, disposable kiddie fare . . . but—they don't have to be!" (3). Such an approach is scarcely neutral in relation to status questions, since it asserts that comics deserve to be taken seriously, if only for their often-unrealized potential. But drawing out this potential, for McCloud, means valorizing comics form as largely separate from comics history.

History and form have sometimes been in conversation with one another in the work of later scholars. In some cases, their purpose has been to shed light on the historical roles that particular kinds of comics have played; in other cases, the goal has been to understand how the particular formal mechanisms of comics emerged historically and developed over time. Both projects have tended, directly or indirectly, to reiterate McCloud's assertion that the medium deserves respect—though now for the historical roles it has played as well as for its artistic power. Thus, for comics theorists, questions about the relations between form and history have been shadowed by status concerns that are difficult to avoid and that affect not only terms and concepts but also basic orientation to the object of study. In short, the goal of understanding comics' specific historical conditions and formal manifestations is subject to the constant gravitational pull of another goal: making comics less illegitimate.

What I am describing is arguably endemic to the study of illegitimate genres and media, and it strongly distinguishes the history of comics studies from that of scholarship devoted to more legitimate art forms. Studies of major modern literary genres such as the novel, or of dominant modern media such as film, tend to assume that questions of history and of form naturally enrich one another—indeed, that historical trajectory and form are a fated match. When first developing a sense of the novel's identity as a genre, scholars readily perceived the growth of the novel in the volatile conditions of modernity and its highly self-reflexive formal qualities as mutually complimentary; much the same can be said for the rapidly changing historical conditions in which film emerged relative to its particular technological and formal properties. Such understandings of history and form are, of course, inseparable from the legitimacy of the object of study.

A theorist of comics might well envy this state of affairs, since the relation between the medium's history and its formal and material features is fraught wherever comics have been harshly condemned and designated culturally "low," as in the United States.

Indeed, comics history and theories of comics form are mutually implicated around dynamics of *violation*—of literary and artistic norms, and of morals and laws—quite different from the principles of social and political coordination typically believed to be in effect for the novel or film. When phenomenological concerns enter the picture, these dynamics only become stronger because, as will be increasingly clear, comics violate the mind-body relations considered normative for the act of reading. In focusing on this dynamic of violation, I consider the comics reader as a subject whose body, since the advent of the comic book, has a primary place in the history/form relation. I do not consider comics history in terms of an abstract timeline of economic, formal, or stylistic changes; nor, obviously, do I consider comics form apart from its relation to the act of reading. Rather, both history and form here take their primary orientation from the fact that the comic book reader has a richly embodied relation to the comic book itself, and a likewise complex, and more troubling, relation to the disciplines and institutional forces that have designated comic book reading as suspect. In other words, the comics-reading subject exists at the intersection of immediate sensory experience and large-scale disciplines and structures of power—of phenomenology and Foucauldian concerns, as it were—in ways that are specific to this medium and to its history.

Let us then confront a single difficult fact that remains mostly unaddressed in discussions of the history/form relation: when the medium was most embattled in the middle of the twentieth century, anticomics discourse seized upon its material features and its distinct way of interacting with readers' bodies as fundamental to its damaging effects. In short, the phenomenology of comics reading was central to the medium's delinquency. Most attentive to this fact thus far has been Jared Gardner (2012), who emphasizes the open, participatory nature of comics reading, which was objectionable to midcentury critics of literature and the fine arts alike. "Within postwar art criticism," Gardner observes, "the emerging aesthetic ideal privileged the work as complete . . . appealing to the viewer's logic and not to bodily experience or personal emotions. . . . The comic, with its formal and inescapable demands for active completion by the reader, is therefore a most predatory

aesthetic object" (80). For New Critics and most other midcentury intellectuals discussing the comic book, its "predatory" tendencies were incurable; "The
popularity of the comic book certainly suggested some kind of mass mind
control, which the well-made poem and the well-tuned critic stood ready
to resist" (81). To understand the depth of New Critical aversion to comics
reading, we must trace the relation of this "mind control," as understood
by anticomics discourse, to the specific "bodily experience" of holding and
reading a comic book.

The attitudes of postwar art critics Gardner discusses were, in some ways,
simply a concentrated version of the animosity that had arisen in response
to comics almost from the start. For most of the twentieth century, con-
tempt for comics trumped sincere scholarly curiosity about them; attempts
to understand the medium were often inseparable from beliefs that comics
contributed to illiteracy, or criminality, or various kinds of delinquency. This
explains why psychologist Fredric Wertham, the most influential anticomics
crusader of the twentieth century, has sometimes been named a key early
theorist of the medium; Wertham's focus on how young people read comic
books was, if strongly biased, at least serious inquiry of a kind. But as we will
see, Wertham's writing also expresses the revulsion that motivated even—or
especially—the most intellectually respectable anticomics discourse, and that
shaped the ways it figured or imagined comic book reading.

An additional glance at the anticomics segment of *Confidential File* will
begin to indicate the precise target of this revulsion. In the staged scene
discussed earlier, there is a strong focus on the haptic nature of comic book
reading; several close-ups show the boys' hands swapping books with eager-
ness and agitation prior to the climactic moments of potential violence. The
rapidity with which the boys swap their comics parallels the swiftness with
which they translate violent images into action, and the scene as a whole
suggests exactly how the "mass mind control" feared by critics was seen to
work (Gardner 2012, 81). Comics were perceived as transmitting a kind of
zombie plague, seizing control of motor function and consciousness and then
propagating, in the real world, the violence their pages displayed.

Such an image of comics was not randomly sensational. In fact, it was
quite well attuned to a key factor that likely made midcentury intellectuals
more opposed to the comic book: its intentional, coordinated activation of
eye and body in the act of reading. As Garrett Stewart (2010) notes in his discussion of book theory, the "routinization of books as objects of consciousness" in modernity has become so complete that reading—a physical process
involving sustained interaction with a fairly complex material thing—can

be understood as a purely mental activity; for the modern reader, works of printed literature seem oddly to "inoculate against response to their own physical format" (437). For midcentury New Critics, as Gardner (2012) argues, such inoculation was crucial to the project of training and cultivating the reader's consciousness. The material book as such was ostensibly the mere instrument—necessarily ignored by critic and reader alike—of an elaborate intellectual, social, and moral discipline.[5] The comic book violated the basic terms of this arrangement, offering a reading experience unmistakably rich in material and sensory awareness.

Here it is important to distinguish between the mental processes intrinsic to comprehending a comic, which will be discussed shortly, and the broader phenomenology of comics reading in material forms such as the comic book. Phenomenologically speaking, what distinguishes the reading of a comic book is not merely that, ordinarily, the subject both looks (at pictorial elements) and reads (verbal elements). Regardless of how much visual scanning or verbal parsing a particular comic book invites, the reading experience as a whole typically has bodily and sensory aspects that are quite distinct, and that are both enabled and demanded by the material and spatial qualities of the medium. In terms of its use of space, the comic book is, as Hillary Chute (2013) observes, "a *site-specific medium*" that "can't be re-flowed, re-jiggered on the page"; usually, its elements are arranged in precise relation to one another, page by page, for the reader's consumption (379–80, italics in original). Any book requires coordinated movements of the reader's eyes, head, neck, torso, arms, wrists, fingers, and other body parts—for readers with disabilities, possibly by prosthetics as well—needed to touch, and to turn, pages and read (visually and/or verbally) the pages' spatially displayed content. In the case of a comic book, and in strong contrast to the print novel, such coordination is synched to, and kinesthetically inseparable from, attention to the specifics of spatial arrangement, which themselves make the act of scanning the material book inseparable from the act of scanning the narrative and thematic elements that are spatially displayed.

It may seem there is little at stake in the distinctions I am making beyond the general difference between the affordances of conventional print fiction, which can at best offer what Joseph Frank (1991) terms the spatial form common to literary modernism, and the affordances of plastic visual arts. To be sure, the comics reading experience could scarcely be more different from that of a printed text whose spatial arrangements, under the hand and eye of the reader, feel mostly or entirely incidental to the flow of discourse. This is a key aspect of print reading without which a New Critical approach to print literature might have been impossible—and that anyone can now confirm as a norm for print discourse by opening the average classic realist or modernist novel in an e-reader and scanning passages while altering the pagination and/or the size of the font. However, the phenomenology of comic book reading is also usually not offered by fine arts arranged in conventional museum space, where works remain in fixed places while the viewer's body moves among them without physical contact with them. In contrast to the art museum, comic book reading is spatially contained within an elaborate set of discrete movements that are both intrabodily and keyed to the material text, while in contrast to the printed book, these movements can be far less routinized. As Thierry Groensteen (2007) notes, "Every comics reader knows from experience that, in practice . . . the eye's movements on the surface of the page are relatively erratic and do not respect any precise protocol" (47). But in being thus "erratic" and resistant to a specific "protocol," such movements are richly intentional in their traversal of the space of the page. The comic book reader's body continually makes multivectored, often nonroutinized, comprehension-driven new movements to manipulate and reposition the text. By requiring these movements, the comic book activates the mind-body relation through distinct phenomenological processes, centered on a self-contained tactile opening of body to book, and of book to body.

It could be argued that comic book reading is located somewhere "between" the experience of fine arts in the context of the museum and the kind of reading elicited by a print text that does not foreground its phenomenological valences—that, for instance, the comics reader is more visually stimulated, more set loose from verbal routine, than the consumer of a print novel while being more confined to intrabodily experience, to a more tightly woven or layered array of possibilities, than museum-goers (even if they are encountering framed art in the European tradition of oil painting rather than newer traditions that more readily evoke mobile subjective embodiment). But this notion of betweenness so often evoked when comics are discussed in relation to literature and fine art—a notion tied to the fact that comics typically combine verbal and visual elements—strikes me as misleading. It does not account for the strangely non- or antidisciplinary frisson that, as Smolderen's anecdote suggests, can accompany comic book reading and that depends on its "palpitating" quality—which, while it is always extrabodily, connected as it is to the book, is also always intrabodily, activating the relation of parts of the body and its senses to one another (Lefèvre 1998, 141). Comics offer an involution of the act of reading, an enrichment of intrasubjective experience, precisely through material and bodily awareness. This is not reading "between" print and the museum, but rather deinstitutionalized reading provided for neither by the disciplinary routines of print nor by infrastructural controls of the art world. To either the New Critical mind or the mind of the Greenbergian art critic, it is a kind of savage reading, done in the woods alone (or at most with other savage readers), set loose not merely from routine but from civilization.

The simultaneously extra- and intrabodily nature of this reading has thus far been underestimated relative to other aspects of comics consumption. Gardner (2012) attends to the participatory nature of comics reading in general but asserts that the medium's segmented nature—the separation of its images by the blank space of gutters—is most central to its stimulation of reader experience. When Gardner speaks of comics' "formal and inescapable demands for active completion by the reader," he supposes it is this alternation of presence and absence, panel and gutter, that demands the "active completion" in question (80). Yet as recent research led by linguist Neil Cohn has demonstrated, the mind of the comics reader usually processes relations among panels and gutters as mere conventions, much as it processes the spaces between words in a printed text. At the levels of basic visual processing and narrative comprehension, Cohn's numerous studies have shown, we read comics as a language, structured by an unconscious grammar that requires neither more nor less "active completion" than the grammar(s) structuring traditional print discourse.[6] Given this discovery, it seems even more likely that what distinguishes the reading of a printed comic, especially a multipage comic book, as distinctly participatory is its intra/extra, multivalent way of engaging the body.

Thus we can distinguish the phenomenological sense of the comic book before the reader's eyes and within the reader's grasp from the mental act of reading. "Common experience," Merleau-Ponty ([1945] 2012) asserts, "establishes a difference between sensing and knowing that is not the difference between the quality and the concept" (52). Applying this difference to comic book reading, we can distinguish knowing—the mental routines readers acquire for absorbing comics' grammatical utterances, as investigated by Cohn—from sensing, which involves absorption of the comic book as a rich material object and not merely a platform or medium for conveying such utterances. Following Merleau-Ponty, we can further assert that such sensing apprehends no mere "quality" separate from, or incidental to, the putatively conceptual information conveyed through comics' grammar. Admittedly, the latter does constitute a kind of routinized knowledge that is provisionally separate from the "sense" of the comic book in its interaction with (that is, its mutual activation by and activation of) the embodied reader. Yet we must not set aside, or render secondary, this larger sense of the comic book relative to the grammar of its utterances—not least because comics do not typically offer themselves to readers on the basis of such a distinction. As Hatfield (2005) rightly observes, "many comics make it impossible to distinguish between text per se and secondary aspects such as design and the physical package, because they continually invoke said aspects to influence the reader's participation in meaning-making" (60). From the structure of its grammar to the putatively contingent features of its material form, the comic book, as it is read, retains contact with distinct phenomenological valences.

With a keener sense of these valences, we can see more clearly how midcentury critics assumed the mind of the comics consumer was not really reading precisely because that consumer's senses and motor functions were so strongly engaged. Zombie-like, delinquent comics "readers" moved without thinking—more precisely, they did not think because, as readers, their eyes and bodies were in such active motion. In his book *Seduction of the Innocent* (1954), Fredric Wertham repeatedly contrasts the thoughtless consumption of comic books with the intellectual and cultural benefits of literature, and provides several anecdotes of weaning kids from their comics by providing them with "good books" to read. Wertham clearly believes that comics consumers are not actually readers at all—one gets the sense that he believes reading comics is no more like reading literature than hearing profanity is like listening to a symphony—and contrasts the two activities constantly, at one point counseling a child thus:

> "If later on you want to read a good novel it may describe how a young boy and girl sit together and watch the rain falling. They talk about themselves and the pages of the book describe what their innermost little thoughts are. This is what is called literature. But you will never be able to appreciate that if in comic book fashion you expect that at any minute someone will appear and pitch them out of the window." (65, quotation marks in original)

Wertham habitually assumed that portrayals of violence were central to comics, but here he also indirectly references the physical volatility of engagement with comic books as objects, which is presumed to destroy the interior stillness of proper reading experience. In this anecdote, such experience is certainly that of literary modernism with its exploration of "innermost little thoughts," providing the strongest possible contrast with the comic book's phenomenology, which Wertham could perceive only as vulgar, even brutish, physicality.

In Wertham's view of the effect of comics reading on literacy we find, very precisely expressed, the concept of delinquency as discussed by Foucault in *Discipline and Punish* (1977). This work is best known for its discussion of questions of surveillance and bodily discipline, but equally if not more important is its tracking of the emergence of delinquency as a social, institutional and legal category in modernity. To prosecute and issue a sentence for a crime, Foucault notes, is merely to address the crime itself in a narrow sense; to carry out and enforce the sentence, however, it is necessary to manufacture a narrative about the individual who committed the crime. "The legal punishment bears upon an act; the punitive technique on a life"—and the latter is thus "a biographical knowledge and a technique for correcting individual lives" (252). And once such biographical knowledge and technique begin the work of delinquency assignment, they can shape and predispose the operation of the law, expanding disciplinary regulation of action and behavior. As the biography of an individual—both what has occurred and what is predicted—can be used to establish the course of delinquency, that individual can be judged delinquent prior to the commission of any particular criminal wrongdoing. In the anecdote from *Seduction of the Innocent* related above, Wertham applies (albeit gently) a punitive technique by explaining to the child the culturally (if not quite criminally) delinquent state she will enter, or is already entering. The act of reading comic books is preindicted by default, since the "Innocent" of Wertham's title, once seduced by the comic book, are delinquents regardless of any crime they do or do not eventually commit.

How might this tendency to assign delinquency affect comics readers' experience? To read a comic book while surrounded by the stigma Wertham encourages the girl to internalize is to feel *both* the grip of the comic book's sensory valences, eliciting one's attention and activity in relation to the pages in one's hands, *and* the pressure of disciplinary rules marking this activity as suspect. These two forces converge on the act of comics reading so that its phenomenology is subject to a punitive tactic that renders it potentially delinquent. Against the background of midcentury anticomics discourse, the opening of comic book to body and of body to comic book violates—in several senses, from loss of innocence, to breakage of boundaries, to transgression of norms—the parameters of literary reading. At the same time, the assignment of delinquency to comics reading violates the reader's intra- and extrabodily communion with the comic book by disrupting its sense of its own self-fulfillment and sufficiency. Thus it is that the destiny of comics form, with its distinct phenomenological valences, is distressingly intertwined with the history of the disciplines that rendered the physical act of comics reading delinquent.

To trace this troubling relation of history to form is not to claim that comic book readers today require special political protection or ethical care; I pursue no human rights claim, except perhaps a modest claim to the right to read comic books. I also forego familiar arguments for the legitimacy of comics as a medium separate from, but equal to, others. Rather, I offer comics as a kind of laboratory and toolset with specific affordances, quite different from those of conventional print, for thinking about the relationship of the arts to the body under what Foucault would term the disciplines, and more broadly for thinking about cultural policing and related mechanisms for delinquency assignment that occupy a prominent place in modern categories of subjectivity and legitimacy. The point of such experimentation is not to prove how useful the medium can be; comic books ought not be tested for positive qualities that can somehow offset their alleged historical delin-quencies. Rather, comic books can test our conceptions of delinquency and legitimacy. This is, no doubt, a valuable affordance, but the point is to take advantage of it. Thus, before concluding with a glance at a case study, I turn to a more specific question of history/form relations. Employing the sense of comic book reading for which I have argued here, let us test our concep-tions of literary legitimacy in relation to modernity's central genre, the novel.

As Gardner's discussion of midcentury anticomics discourse makes clear, the comic book emerged at a time when the novel purported to offer ut-terances wholly separate from its medium. Novelistic discourse had long trafficked in claims of truthfulness and verisimilitude that, while compatible with a focus on subjective experience (including, in many early novels, the experience of writing itself), tended over time to treat the medium of print as a mere delivery device. The modernist ideas Wertham tried to teach one young comics reader simply carried the novelistic tendency to conceive of reading experience as wholly separate from medium to its logical conclu-sion. When we observe this conclusion next to the emergence of the comic book, however, we can see more clearly its tie to cultural legitimacy. The novel had come to wield great moral and cultural authority—as well as un-limited capacity to explore interior life—at a moment when it was marked as phenomenologically neutral, a mere set of printed surfaces to which the reader's body was supposed to remain indifferent. At this historical coinci-dence of nonreactive medium and authoritative discourse, the novel was also arguably at a peak of formal and aesthetic freedom, a moment when what Georg Lukàcs ([1920] 1971) understood as the genre's formlessness—more particularly its tendency to turn the act of form-seeking into its content—was vigorously exercised. It thus seems likely that the novel attained bodilessness (in the minds of New Critics and opponents of comic books) as one condition of its aesthetic freedom and moral authority.

This exchange is also one possible contributor to the novel's capacity to wield a political, even quasi-legal authority to adjudicate claims to justice and human rights, an aspect of the genre discussed at length by Joseph Slaughter (2007). Though this possibility is not indicated in Slaughter's argument, the seeming phenomenological nonreactivity of the novel at the level of its medium—further reinforced, as I suggested earlier, by the emergence of new print delivery devices such as the e-reader—would seem to increase its shadowy resemblance to the law itself, expressed in printed words that, through their very "neutrality" vis-à-vis medium, announce the authority of law as discourse. We have here, if not a rule, then at least a notable drift in the cultural priorities that underwrite the legitimacy of the novel: the authority and legitimacy of its utterances is buttressed by their putative separation from the supposedly neutral conveyance of their medium. Completing this picture, we should note as well that in the context of the novel, modernist "spatial form" is actually an absorption of the dynamics of plastic arts into a reading practice that is supposed to be purely mental (Frank 1991, 60–61).

Such an arrangement of medium (the novel as phenomenologically neutral and nonreactive) and legitimacy (the novel as culturally, even politically authoritative) amplifies the novel's adjudicatory power, its capacity to intervene in human affairs freely, flexibly, and continuously. Seemingly unengaged with its medium, the novel can be openly form-seeking, and it can continually seek the forms through which it can be legitimately engaged with social, political, and other matters. The comic book, forever tied to its medium, cannot be "transparently" form-seeking in this way. This is not to say that comics tend to be politically or culturally unengaged or that they are somehow uninterested in questions of form, only that their mode of engagement and their exploration of form can perforce never present themselves as separate from their material, phenomenologically reactive medium.

What does this fact mean in a culture where the novel, discursively authoritative more or less in proportion to its supposed phenomenological nonreactivity, is a standard-bearer of cultural legitimacy? Any political, social, or moral utterance in a comic book is linked to—and thus intruded upon and (from the point of view of a descendant of Fredric Wertham, or other likeminded critics discussed by Gardner) diminished by—bodily interaction with a "spatial form" wholly different from that of literary modernism. The comic book reader is denied unmediated access to cultural or political discourse, and must continuously interface with tactile discursive surfaces in mutually open relations to the reader's body—relations that, as they change page by page, activate continuously changing mind-body interactions. The comic book offers a phenomenological and discursive encounter in which it is the reader, not the text, that seeks. What the reader seeks is not the form of a given content (the two being joined, in the comic book, in a way unavailable to the novel) but the relation—always mediated and therefore always disrupted, troubled, violatory, potentially if only distantly delinquent—of reading to narrative, thematic, political, or social content. It is possible to argue that such reader activity is the sign that anticomics discourse has always been mistaken about the zombifying power of the comic book, and that its reader is a fully agentive subject. But the activity in question retains, even now, shades of its midcentury delinquency, precisely because of its strong contrast to the still-existing tie between the novel's legitimacy and its supposed bodilessness.

This line of reasoning may seem outdated now that postmodern fiction has long since made print instantiations of what Espen Aarseth (1997) calls ergodic literature—which encompasses play with typography, page design, diagrams, and some pictorial elements—familiar to us. But to this comic book reader, at least, the typographic and other design-forward qualities of the ergodic print novel feel as if they exist within a larger claim to bodiless legitimacy. The print novelist can *cite* ergodic qualities—for the length of an entire book, if desired—within a larger surround that has, in the last instance, the novelistic quality of seeming unmediated. To speak of the ergodic comic book, however, is simply to speak of the comic book as such. Thus it is that the comic book's birthright is not discursive adjudication but violation—of the reader's "proper," seemingly unmediated relationship to political, cultural, and other discourses. A comic book may or may not overtly thematize this birthright, though of course nothing is more familiar, at least in the United States, than comics that resist respectability, reverse cultural priorities, or otherwise refuse to behave properly. But I speak here in the broadest terms of a deep difference between the alleged tendencies of the novel and those of the comic book, of the level at which the comic book body seems intrinsically troubled and troubling, as the bodiless novel does not.

The great theme of the novel is seeking, as Lukàcs argues, and this theme is consonant with the form. But the novel seeks out its form, I am suggesting, so as to legitimate its relation to the social, moral, and political questions it engages. In the fullness of its legitimacy in modernity, the novel is on the side of the law and of legitimacy, not necessarily in the sense of being conformist, but in the sense of addressing itself to social and political matters with an unquestioned sense of its capacity to do so. But because of the overtly "mediated" quality of the comic book, its great theme is violation, across a range of this term's meanings: transgression, division, breakage, inconsistency, shortfall, excess, interruption. What the comic book seeks is not its form but rather the possible meanings of the fact that its form violates a properly "transparent" relation to discourse—and, again, it necessarily seeks out such meanings in phenomenological terms interfaced with the reader's intra- and extrabodily reading experience.

To pursue this discussion one step further: the question of medium, and its phenomenological valences, should prompt us to ask if characterological differences between comic books and novels are more than coincidental. The protagonist of a novel is likely to be offered to the reader in terms of her possible development—its likelihood, course, and meaning—in a manner that ties biography to legitimation. The protagonist of a comic book is more likely to be a character who, in some way or other, does not obey developmental laws, confronting instead a divided self, a set of parallel destinies, a cyclical existence resistant to linear development, or some other, less legitimate path. Here the superhero ceases to be a contingent fact of comics history, and this genre's prominence, at least in the United States, can be compared (rather than, as is often the case, contrasted) to the rise of autobiographical comics that rarely traffic in conventional narratives of personal development. Here I turn to a case study, Kyle Baker's *Nat Turner* (2008), which has some qualities of both the superhero story and the memoir and will flesh out my concept of violation. I stress, however, that my goal is not the full reading this work deserves, but a more preliminary consideration that asks what is at stake in its medium-specific qualities.

Baker presents the life of Nat Turner in the larger context of the history of slavery. The book opens not with Turner's own experience but with a portrayal of the overall process of enslavement, from kidnap to Middle Passage, focused on one female protagonist who, Baker strongly implies, is Turner's mother. In a climactic moment, while confined on a slave ship, she watches as a fellow slave attempts to throw his newborn child overboard. A violent struggle ensues; slavers attempt to stop him but he finally succeeds in delivering his child from the experience to which he is condemned. *Nat Turner* as a whole is obsessed with hands; almost every plot event is keyed to their

Figure 1.1: Photograph of the author holding *Nat Turner*, 2008, open to pages 52 and 53. *Nat Turner* © Kyle Baker. Photo credit: Amanda Madden.

presence, from the hands of slaves beating drums for communication—and later severed as punishment—to the hands of the titular protagonist holding a book as he learns to read. But in this early climactic moment of struggle, the critic interested in comics' haptic qualities will note how they reach a peculiar degree of intensity as various hands struggle to grasp, and determine the fate of, the child.

At this precise moment in the narrative, Baker provides a fascinating instance of site-specific haptic self-reflexivity: one panel showing the child, floating but within the grasp of competing hands, is canted so that its upper left corner is notably further from the outer edge of the page than the lower left. While no comics maker can predict exactly where readers might choose to put their hands as they read, it would scarcely be unlikely for a reader's thumb to occupy this empty space created by the canted panel, generating an overtly mediated relation of readerly grasp to graphic design, as shown in figure 1.1. This relation is reinforced by the panel's content; the wakeful reader is prompted to compare the hands struggling over the child's fate, as imaged in the panel, and the seeming displacement of this image's proper place on the page by the reader's hand.

Certainly questions of historical witness arise here; the page indicates that the act of witness shifts and transforms what it witnesses. The panel seems uncannily to react to our reading it, floating out of our grasp, though it thereby underscores our phenomenological relation to the comic book. Other numerous layers of meaning arise as well, not least that of racial identification; this writer for instance, who posed for figure 1.1, got fresh reminders of some possible meanings of his skin color. But whichever meanings we might choose to explore, they are made possible by the fact that this is no mere "image" of a relationship between reader and textual content; it is a clearly phenomenological relation that cannot be divorced from its medium-specific aspects.

Viewed in light of the concept of comic book reading I have espoused here, however, such overt haptic moments, dependent on specific image and design, are also simply elements of the general condition of comic book reading, a condition in effect even in the absence of such obvious material evidence. Every passage in *Nat Turner* is—and is implicitly if not explicitly readable as—"up for grabs" in the manner of the child at the center of the struggle between masters and slaves. And while, in the case of this comic book, this struggle has unavoidable historical, moral, and political stakes, what makes *Nat Turner*, as a comic book, different from any novel on the same subjects is the intrusive manner in which, as a phenomenologically rich reading experience, it seems constantly to violate proper relations to these subjects. There are obvious tonal moments that highlight this violation, such as a disruptively humorous image of a slave, during Turner's revolt, beheading the child of his master (the precise inversion of the child's head, and its vacant smile, strike a note reminiscent of the more daring strains of humor found in midcentury satirical comics magazines [Baker 2008, 135]). I mention this moment not to read it in detail, but simply to observe that, as with the question of overt site-specific haptic imagery, it is a concentrated, explicitly referential instance of what is, throughout the book, a continuous discursive disruption. The same is true of the various, often clashing styles of Baker's figure drawing (sometimes fairly realistic, sometimes outsized and exaggerated in the manner of some superhero comics) and the wide range of references to technologies of image reproduction (some images are made to look like photographs, others like drawn illustrations, others like plate prints of various kinds). Whatever specific mode, obvious or subtle, such disruption takes, its existence and meaning are decisively affected by the comic book's phenomenologically reactive material form.

Returning to the canted panel of the child and the struggling hands in figure 1.1, I note that while it underscores the reader's disruptive, improper relationship to the struggles of the Middle Passage, it scarcely interferes with Baker's attempt to position these struggles as key to Turner's later rebellion. The young Nat Turner is shown as knowing about this incident as a child despite having never been told of it; a talk balloon ascribed to him is filled not with words, but with an image, shown on a previous page, of the child falling into the mouth of a shark—and since this image is one of the last in the Middle Passage sequence, the entire sequence is retroactively cast as young Nat's uncannily knowing utterance (57). This linking of Middle Passage to Turner's life attempts to contextualize and justify Turner's revolt, a point well expounded by Qiana Whitted (2014, 87), and it is central to Baker's vision of black history after slavery as revolutionary, as argued by Michael Chaney (2016, 76–80). Yet this potential relation of cause to effect, and of supernatural vision to revolutionary action, never fully establishes Turner as a legitimate agent. Chaney argues that Turner is often shown as ethically troubled, caught between differing images of past or potential violence that make incommensurable moral demands, so that his "politically conscious form of living through and beside history mirrors the position of the reader of comics, who likewise scans an image for affect and meaning in the presence of proximate images vying for attention" (81). Here I differ only with the claim that there is a mirroring of Turner and the reader—not surprisingly, since the central concept I am pursuing is not reflection but violation. In a more general sense, however, the violation of a straightforwardly revolutionary narrative with a fully legitimate protagonist and the constantly "up for grabs" quality of *Nat Turner*'s presentation of its content are, if not reflections, then at least mutually reinforcing indicators. And what they indicate is the unstable, illegitimate status of the comic book reader in relation to the discourse or content with which she is engaged. Nat Turner, as a figure in a comic book, cannot quite lay legitimate claim upon us; and—in a manner not reflective but certainly telling—we cannot fully lay claim to him. He eludes our all-too-present grasp as the fated, messianic, and tragic seamlessness of his story is violated by the inescapable phenomenology of its presentation.

I trust it is clear that the reading approach to *Nat Turner* I am suggesting can go much further and into considerably more detail (both discursive and phenomenological) than I have managed in this brief excursus. Here I simply repeat that any specific moment of "obvious," self-reflexive haptic reference in a comic book, such as the canted panel in *Nat Turner*, is always part of its overall phenomenology. And thus, for the reader already familiar with the subject matter of *Nat Turner*—and familiar as well with questions of historical mediation, witness, trauma, and other obviously relevant concerns—this comic book, by virtue of its very properties *as* a comic book, seems to test what we think we know about the proper way to tell a story of slavery. In *Nat Turner*, Baker tries to put this weighty subject up for grabs in a fashion that, for some readers, will likely be seen as either delinquent or as excusably disruptive. If judged delinquent, the violations *Nat Turner* commits might be attributed either to the insufficiency of the medium (let there be no cartoonish images of slavery, some might say—or sensational and whimsical images of the murder of children, others might claim) or to wrong choices on the creator's part. If the book is judged excusably disruptive, the creator himself will almost certainly be credited, and not his chosen medium—as if only a certain quality of creative mind can elevate what must otherwise be judged illegitimate. But what animates *Nat Turner*'s disruptive approach to its subject, an approach forever in danger of being judged delinquent (and then, perhaps, rescued from this charge by reference to the creator as auteur), is precisely its medium-specific qualities.

Of the two likely critical responses I have suggested—to indict the book as delinquent, or to excuse its disruptiveness—quite a number of scholars have chosen the latter, as Marc Singer (2018, chapter 6) explains in detail. Singer shows that some critics credit the book with much more historic accuracy than it evidently possesses, bolstering the legitimacy of Baker's work (incorrectly, as Singer demonstrates at length) in quite another fashion (206–24). For the most part, Singer himself sees Baker's project as delinquent. He targets precisely the disruptive and incomplete presentation of Turner's rebellion, arguing that it is at odds with (though subtly abetting) Baker's portrayal of Turner as a hero, and with Baker's justification of the rebellion through "retributive causality," which presents the murder of slave owners and their families as the inevitable consequence of slavery (229). I trust it is clear that my approach attempts to move away from this range of possible readings. I see Baker as putting the worth of Turner's rebellion up for grabs in a way that destabilizes both a fragmentary past and a morally uncertain present, denying the reader's body and perceptions any "proper" relationship to slavery while insisting that many necessary relations, however unstable, do exist. Such an approach is best seen as fiction, not proper history, and it does not lend itself to familiar kinds of moral litigation. To this extent, the book remains wide open to Singer's critique. But I see *Nat Turner* as a phenomenological presentation of the state of our grasp of slavery, and insofar as Baker pursues such a presentation deliberately, the book has quite a different aim than many readers seem to have expected of it. The degree to which the book fulfills this aim I leave as an open question.

The skeptical reader could argue that there are many comic books, whether they are called graphic novels or not, that do not violate proper approaches to their subject matter in the way *Nat Turner* seems purposely designed to do. And to be sure, it is possible to construct a comic book that does not engage such elements so actively, or even suppresses them. But such comics—likely easier to gentrify under the heading of the graphic novel than *Nat Turner* is—are roughly the inverse of the ergodic novel. They may *cite* a kind of novelistic transparency and discursive legitimacy, but it is not their birthright. I make this point not to condemn any comics creator who chooses such an approach (though few do, in my observation), but to assert, finally, a point about the phenomenology of media at which I have hinted throughout this discussion: relations among media are shot through with questions of legitimacy that cannot be done away with by simple recategorization (as when a well-meaning literary critic says of his favorite comic, "This isn't a comic book; it's a graphic novel"). And these questions are persistent because they exist not merely in a cultural field, but in specific relations to the reader's body, and to that body's historical position in an array of disciplines much more resistant to change than the abstract terms attached to them.

The inherited notions of literary legitimacy we possess at present call for transparent, seemingly unmediated utterance that the comic book cannot make. This fact, while inconvenient, should be folded into our understanding of comic book reading henceforth. It does not stop particular comics creators, or even comics in general, from refusing novelistic discursive transparency and yet, in an increasing number of cases, still gaining some artistic and political authority. And this authority may derive from the very qualities that first made comics delinquent. Indeed, Hillary Chute's (2016) recent study of comics as a form of witness argues that the comic book's overtly mediated quality, and the openness of its address to readers, is central to its effectiveness. Such truths may, or may not, permanently alter the terms of legitimacy in time.

Meanwhile, the savage children pictured in the anticomics segment of *Confidential File* are lost to us; we cannot intervene in their fate. We can, however, admit to being their peers, and to being under a kind of discipline, if not surveillance, as we grasp our comic books (whatever they are called). This may no longer be a threatening truth; some will argue, depending on how lightly they take the damage done by anticomics crusades, that it never was. Yet it is a truth still joined to our skin and sealed to our eyes. I doubt the transformation for which comics scholars and fans might hope, the long-awaited day of unquestioned legitimacy, will be hastened if we ignore what, as comics readers, our bodies know.

Notes

1. For an account of the Code's formation and some discussion of its aftermath, see Nyberg (1998).

2. See for instance Chute (2016) and Baetens (2001), as well as the discussion of Gardner (2012) in the current essay.

3. See particularly the discussion of Philippe Marion in Baetens (2001). At present, in the absence of an English translation of Marion, Baetens provides a clear account of the latter's now-classic discussion of comics readers' experience of embodied marking. For a recent further discussion of cycles of comics consumption and creation, see also Crucifix (2017).

4. See for instance Watson (2008, 39–41) and Chaney (2016, 110–12).

5. This concept of the book as neutral conveyance of interior reading experience was, of course, more mythical than actual. Postwar publishing culture encouraged readerly attention to print quality as complement to, if not enhancement of, literary value; see Rasula (1990, 53–54).

6. See particularly Cohn (2010) and Cohn et al. (2014).

References

Aarseth, Espen. 1997. *Cybertext: Perspectives on Ergodic Literature*. Baltimore: Johns Hopkins University Press.

Baetens, Jan. 2001. "Revealing Traces: A New Theory of Graphic Enunciation." In *The Language of Comics: Word and Image*, edited by Robin Varnum and Christina T. Gibbons, 145–55. Jackson: University Press of Mississippi.

Baker, Kyle. 2008. *Nat Turner*. New York: Abrams.

Chaney, Michael A. 2016. *Reading Lessons in Seeing: Mirrors, Masks, and Mazes in the Autobiographical Graphic Novel*. Jackson: University Press of Mississippi.

Chute, Hillary. 2013. "Secret Labor." *Poetry* 202 (4): 379–81.

Chute, Hillary. 2016. *Disaster Drawn: Visual Witness, Comics, and Documentary Form*. Cambridge, MA: Harvard University Press.

Cohn, Neil. 2010. "The Limits of Time and Transitions: Challenges to Theories of Sequential Image Comprehension." *Studies in Comics* 1 (1): 127–47.

Cohn, Neil, Ray Jackendoff, Phillip J. Holcomb, and Gina R. Kuperberg. 2014. "The Grammar of Visual Narrative: Neural Evidence for Constituent Structure in Sequential Image Comprehension." *Neuropsychologia* 6 (4): 63–70.

Crucifix, Benoît. 2017. "Rethinking the 'Memorable Panel' from Pierre Sterckx to Olivier Josso Hamel." *European Comic Art* 10 (2): 24–47.

Foucault, Michel. 1977. *Discipline and Punish: The Birth of the Prison.* Translated by Alan Sheridan. New York: Vintage.

Frank, Joseph. 1991. *The Idea of Spatial Form.* New Brunswick, NJ: Rutgers University Press.

Gardner, Jared. 2012. *Projections: Comics and the History of Twenty-First-Century Storytelling.* Stanford, CA: Stanford University Press.

Groensteen, Thierry. 2007. *The System of Comics.* Translated by Bart Beaty and Nick Nguyen. Jackson: University Press of Mississippi.

Hague, Ian. 2014. *Comics and the Senses: A Multisensory Approach to Comics and Graphic Novels.* London: Routledge.

Hatfield, Charles. 2005. *Alternative Comics: An Emerging Literature.* Jackson: University Press of Mississippi.

Kirshner, Irvin, dir. 1955. "Horror Comic Books." *Confidential File.* KTTV Los Angeles.

Kukkonen, Karin. 2015. "Space, Time, and Causality in Graphic Narratives: An Embodied Approach." In *From Comic Strips to Graphic Novels: Contributions to the Theory and History of Graphic Narrative,* 2nd ed., edited by Daniel Stein and Jan-Noël Thon, 49–66. Berlin: De Gruyter.

Lefèvre, Pascal. 1998. "Recovering Sensuality in Comic Theory." *Academia.edu.* https://www.academia.edu/660772/Recovering_sensuality_in_comic_theory.

Lukàcs, Georg. (1920) 1971. *Theory of the Novel.* Translated by Anna Bostock. Cambridge, MA: MIT Press.

McCloud, Scott. 1993. *Understanding Comics: The Invisible Art.* New York: HarperPerennial.

Merleau-Ponty, Maurice. (1945) 2012. *Phenomenology of Perception.* Translated by Donald A. Landes. London: Routledge.

Nyberg, Amy Kiste. 1998. *Seal of Approval: The History of the Comics Code.* Jackson: University Press of Mississippi.

Rasula, Jed. 1990. "Nietzsche in the Nursery: Naive Classics and Surrogate Parents in Postwar American Cultural Debates." *Representations* 29 (Winter): 50–77.

Sabin, Roger. 1993. *Adult Comics: An Introduction.* London: Routledge.

Singer, Marc. 2018. *Breaking the Frames: Populism and Prestige in Comics Studies.* Austin: University of Texas Press.

Slaughter, Joseph R. 2007. *Human Rights Inc.: The World Novel, Narrative Form, and International Law.* New York: Fordham University Press.

Stewart, Garrett. 2010. "Bookwork as Demediation." *Critical Inquiry* 36 (1): 410–57.

Watson, Julia. 2008. "Autographic Disclosures and Genealogies of Desire in Alison Bechdel's *Fun Home.*" *Biography* 31 (1): 27–58.

Wertham, Fredric. 1954. *Seduction of the Innocent.* New York: Rinehart.

Whitted, Qiana. 2014. "'And the Negro Thinks in Hieroglyphics': Comics, Visual Metonymy, and the Spectacle of Blackness." *Journal of Graphic Novels and Comics* 5 (1): 79–100.

2

Articulating Health Humanities in Graphic Narratives by Medical Illustrators

LISA DeTORA

Introduction

Health humanities evolved from an initial need to humanize a medical profession that lost sight of bedside manner—the way to treat people, both medically and personally—amidst the exigencies of technology. Hence, health humanities modes like narrative medicine use literature and culture to enrich clinical practice and reduce physician burnout (Jones et al. 2014). Graphic medical memoir has become an important area of research, as evidenced by a burgeoning field of scholarly endeavor (Graphic Medicine 2007–2019; Willberg 2018). Indeed, a field of graphic medicine, identified by Jenell Johnson in *Graphic Reproduction: A Comics Anthology* (2018) among others, has also been cited, as by several scholars (Lewis 2011; Shapiro 2012; Shapiro et al. 2009) as a means of building more empathetic physicians. Within these contexts of health humanities an area deserving of further inquiry are works like Héloïse Chochois's *La Fabrique des corps: Des premièrs prothèses à l'humaine augmenté* (2017) or Kriota Willberg's *The Wandering Uterus* (Furor Uterensis) *and Contemporary Applications of Ancient Medical Wisdom* (2016). These graphic narratives can be seen as a site of representation and inquiry relevant to both domains of the health humanities.

This essay presents a critical study of comics by examining the means of articulating two domains of health humanities inquiry, medical education and humanistic critique, in graphic narratives by medical illustrators, which is an under-examined area in both comics studies and health humanities. Consistent with the general aims of the present volume, this essay avoids semiotic approaches to such inquiry—the ways that comics are or are not hybrid forms or how they convey symbolic meaning—and instead treats graphic narratives as though they are already worthy of study.[1] In doing so, I forward Hannah Miodrag's critique (2013) that comics studies can be hampered by defensiveness and a need to assert its legitimacy. Instead, I approach critical comics inquiry by placing specific books within the intellectual context of health humanities and treating both as objects worthy of specific consideration and study.

Importantly for the current discussion, health humanities itself is somewhat fragmented in part because, simultaneous with moves to humanize medicine, the humanities have sought to make sense of posthumanity—or how theoretical constructions of humanity entwine with the technological to augment and define identity. Deepening connections between technology and humanity afforded what Donna Haraway (1991) termed *cyborg* identities that trouble accepted categories of human embodied experience. Rhetorician Nathan Stormer considers the cyborg as a means of situating a model of what he calls prosthetic thinking (as rhetorical *taxis*) that elucidates the connections between bodies of knowledge, material bodies, and words. Beginning with an explanation of rhetorical articulation and prosthesis and moving to a reading of two graphic narratives that articulate humanistic inquiry and medical education, I suggest that prosthetic inquiry, figured through rhetorical theory, is an interesting critical approach to comics studies that is accessible to both domains of health humanities.

Articulation as Prosthetic Inquiry in Health Humanities

In "Articulation: A Working Paper on Rhetoric and *Taxis*" Stormer (2004) argues that a gap between words (rhetoric) and things (materiality) is cultural performance. For Stormer, *taxis*, "the linkage of elements within a text" (260) reflects and constructs rhetorical practices. Stormer, who calls for situated ways of knowing that account for historical circumstances (257), grounds his theory of articulation within a discourse of posthuman inquiry, drawing on Haraway, Gilles Deleuze, and Bruno LaTour, each of whom troubles empirical thinking and offers disruptive ways of understanding various linkages of words, things, and ideas. By tracing the term *prosthesis* back to its original, linguistic, meaning, Stormer shows that current embodied and material notions of prosthetics participate in a longer tradition of augmentation than current medical technology, or even postmodern theory (see Roberts 2005), might suggest. Interpretations of Stormer's work (Lynch 2009) suggest that articulation can apply to different discursive registers, a model I follow below.

It is important here to note that the current paper does not pretend to give an account of all cultural and theoretical modes of considering prosthesis—notably, this paper does not address questions about what Bernard Stiegler called "the invention of the human" (Roberts 2005, n.p.). Rather, I seek to identify a theoretical register for producing discernible linkages between medical-humanities-as-medical-education and medical-humanities-as-humane-endeavor in lived practice. In other words, the idea of prosthesis in the current essay, as for Stormer, is a means of reading cultural performances that are already historically and culturally constituted rather than attempting to interrogate the means by which they came to be so constituted. This is not to say that a critical comics studies should not take up such questions, but rather that such an endeavor should be the object of its own paper. Returning to the aims of the current paper, the goal is to find sites where the dual foci of health humanities are more or less effectively articulated.

Medical humanities was created to manage a gap between the personal and the empirical in patient-physician interactions. As Chiapperino and Boniolo (2014) note, scientific discovery far outpaced philosophical endeavors to humanize it and Therese Jones et al. (2014) see medical humanities as arising from the need to impart ethical education to medical students. As K. Danner Clouser observed, both humanities-based medical intervention and humanistic inquiry into medicine were necessary to recuperate physicians self-selected on the basis of scientific aptitude rather than a desire to interact with the sick (Jones et al. 2014). Of note, Clouser's model of medical humanities parallels eighteenth-century tensions between humanistic medical training and surgical apprenticeship models, which were reconciled by enhancing general education for surgeons (see Jones et al. 2014; Foucault [1963] 1994). Health humanities expands these considerations beyond physicians to account for further viewpoints and perspectives (Jones et al. 2014; Katz 2014).

Currently, health humanities proliferates within interdisciplinary subfields—gender studies, disability studies (see Couser 2011), literature and medicine, theories of embodiment, as well as social sciences and rhetorics of medicine. As humanities no longer aims to make better people, a significant shift since the 1960s (Hawthorn and Lothe 2013; Jones et al. 2014; Shapiro et al. 2009), approaches like narrative medicine (see Charon 2001a) that use fiction in applied clinical or bioethical practice raise questions for literary and cultural scholars. This is particularly important given that, as Atkinson et al. (2015) observe, humanistic theoretical perspectives in current scholarly practice seem absent from medical-humanities-as-medical-education. (This is one reason that the broader philosophical questions taken up by

Roberts, Stiegler, or Derrida [Roberts 2005, n.p.], are not considered within the scope of the current essay.) Ironically, the type of posthuman theory that Stormer considers in his model of articulation examines how technological advancements inhibit affective emotions (Dinello 2005), forming an interesting parallel for scientific medical practice. Cyborg identities, while affording a possibility for postgendered experience, may elide the feelings that inform humanity itself. Thus, potentially irreconcilable paradoxes may result from articulating posthuman discourses within the health humanities, since the very modes of inquiry intended to impart humanity may simultaneously undercut it.

Graphic Narratives as a Site of Articulation

If, as Stormer suggests, the gap between words and things is a cultural performance, then graphic narratives, by placing words and images together on a page—what Thierry Groensteen (2008; 2013) refers to as arthrology—may provide a site for hybrid performances that can recuperate the potential paradox of combining posthuman theory and humanistic medicine. The current discussion accepts Groensteen's impulse to unify graphic narrative forms under a single term (2008), using "graphic narrative" broadly. His description of "simultaneous mobilization" (2013, 89), or the operation on the page of multiple elements at the same time (89), and "arthrology," or the articulation of elements on the comic page (96), are the basis for semiotic readings of graphic narrative. Yet, simultaneous mobilization, like Stormer's model of articulation, may be read as a performance that can be better understood once properly situated. That is, semiosis itself, like rhetorical *taxis*, is constrained by its situation in history and culture. The intention of the current chapter, as with other entries in the current volume, is to present a critical comics study that does not rely exclusively on semiotic theory. The current discussion thus acknowledges semiotic study and considers its positions as compatible with Groensteen's theoretical model of graphic narrative, yet seeks to propose another mode of critical inquiry.

In situating the two graphic narratives *La Fabrique des corps: Des premièrs prothèses à l'humaine augmenté* (Chochois 2017) or *The Wandering Uterus* (Furor Uterensis*) and Contemporary Applications of Ancient Medical Wisdom* (Willberg 2016), I draw on the idea that the combined operations of words and images makes the graphic narrative an opportunity for representing experiences that defy language. Hillary Chute (2016) links a witnessing function of graphic narratives to their international importance as documentary and journalistic forms, noting that the interaction of text and image allows for multiple modes of experience and knowing, taking a similar position to that of Harriet Earle (2017), who considered the connections between trauma, war, and comics. Chute (2017) describes comics as a site of hybridity that does not merely allow for an articulation between words and things but also provides a space in which the formerly unarticulable can be expressed. In *Why Comics: From Underground to Everywhere* (2017), Chute takes up disability and illness in comics, noting that the medium's "immediacy and its diagrammatic ability to display otherwise hard-to-express realities and emotions" (241) inform the burgeoning field of graphic medical memoir and fictional forms in traditional publishing platforms as well as a growing trend for web comics and self-publishing. In general, these comics concentrate on personal experiences, engaging in a type of witness bearing that allow access to difficult emotions.

Works like *La Fabrique des corps: Des premièrs prothèses à l'humaine augmenté* (Chochois 2017) or *The Wandering Uterus (*Furor Uterensis*) and Contemporary Applications of Ancient Medical Wisdom* (Willberg 2016), drawn and written by professional medical illustrators, negotiate a unique space as graphic narratives and medical humanities texts. Medical illustrators have advanced training in life sciences and visual communication, often from specialized programs (Association of Medical Illustrators 2017). Monique Guildersen (2002) notes that medical illustration continues visual discourses originating in sixteenth-century works of Andreas Vesalius, who drew the "first anatomical atlas based on human models" (see figures 2.1 and 2.2.). For Guildersen, who sees medical illustration as a combination of "the world of art and medicine," "a medical illustrator creates artwork that is visually pleasing as well as being medically and scientifically accurate." Guildersen describes multiple competencies—scientific, medical, artistic—that support clinical accuracy. In contrast to the efforts of medical practitioners and scholars whose work contributed to the *Graphic Medicine Manifesto* (Czerwiec et al. 2015), *Graphic Reproduction* (Johnson 2018), or the works Chute or Earle just described, graphic narratives by medical illustrators articulate two distinct preexisting sites of hybridity. What remains to be seen is how medical illustration translates to graphic narrative and health humanities, whether medical illustrators will reflexively articulate the humanism necessary for medical education, posthuman theory, both, or neither.

A critical reading of graphic narratives that present medical educational materials should consider their relationship to empirical modes of seeing.[2] In

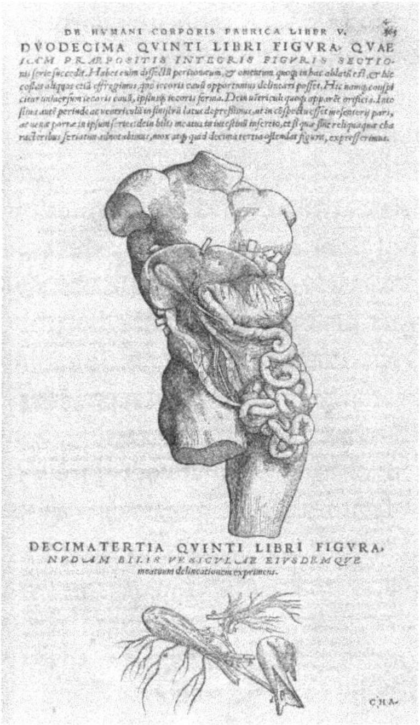

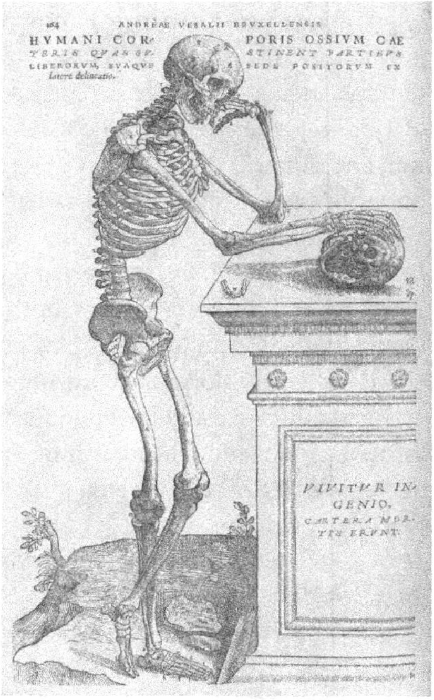

Figure 2.1: Human torso with digestive system. Andreas Vesalius, *De humani corporis fabrica libri septem*, 1543, 465. Available at: https://www.nlm.nih.gov/exhibition/historicalanatomies/vesalius_home.html.
Figure 2.2: Human skeleton. Andreas Vesalius, *De humani corporis fabrica libri septem*, 1543, 164. Available at: https://www.nlm.nih.gov/exhibition/historicalanatomies/vesalius_home.html.

Birth of the Clinic: An Archaeology of Medical Perception ([1963] 1994), Michel Foucault describes a medical or clinical gaze as a site of coalescence, the moment that visual perception (*regard*) can be transformed into language. "The paradoxical ability to *hear a language* as soon as it *perceives a spectacle*" (108) allowed for a new mode of perception that incorporated hitherto un-recognizable phenomena, like disease, into the realm of knowledge. Foucault describes a system in which the ability to exchange knowledge through language creates and drives perception, effectively changing the very visibility of material reality. Foucault's further work, on the archaeology of knowledge (1982), expanded his theory that language differentiates knowledge from simple experience; these ideas underpin Judith Butler's construction of bodies that matter (1993) and her notion that certain types of "abject, unlivable" bodies haunt the edges of knowledge (xi). The abject can be seen as a way of situating knowledge and experience, a necessary cognitive category that requires an articulation of language, ideas, and materiality. When considering critical studies of graphic narratives that present medical information, this type of articulation should be held in tension with the site of rhetorical practice that Stormer considers.

At its core, the medical gaze is a site of articulation that creates knowledge at the nexus of language and spectacle, creating the possibilities for the type of rhetorical articulation discussed by Stormer. The medical gaze is a useful frame for understanding comics as a hybrid form that presents otherwise difficult-to-render experiences (one that Chute does not mobilize in her consideration of illness). In fact, Foucault's medical gaze can also be theorized as a sort of rhetorical performance, one that shifts the focus from an individual patient's illness to the underlying knowledge of disease that enables the delivery of biomedically based healthcare. Especially insofar as Foucault cites language as a necessary delivery mechanism for knowledge (as opposed to experience), the medical gaze can serve as a means of understanding not only the representation of materials in graphic narratives but also the possibility for such narratives to inform the different domains of health humanities.

Fabricating Bodies

Héloïse Chochois's *La Fabrique des corps: Des premièrs prothèses à l'humaine augmenté* (2017) draws on the artist's background in scientific illustration to produce a complex graphic narrative for younger audiences. Chochois holds degrees in science and scientific education and produces medical illustrations and didactic materials in English and in French (2018). Her early works include "Promenade" (2012), which illustrates the muscle movements of a horse and rider for children as well as a series of illustrations for the magazine *Thinkovery* (2015). Each of these works employs a characteristic *bande desinée* style, accessible, cartoonish, in colors emphasizing rusts, fleshtones, browns, and soft greens. The evident aim of these illustrations, similar to Guildersen's description, is to present graphically appealing, yet medically and scientifically accurate information.

La Fabrique des corps, Chochois's first graphic narrative, adopts her characteristic style; however, the overall aims of the book appear quite different than straightforward illustrations like "Promenade." In fact, the graphic novel is described on the Delcourt website as a fantastic tale, a fiction that might operate within the context of posthuman visions that Dinello describes.

Un postulat joliment absurde qui met en scène, sans pathos ni péda-
gogie outrancière, le récit intime et l'aventure scientifique dans une
fiction fantastique sublime et étonnante !

[An entertainingly and beautifully absurd tale that presents, without
pathos or overt pedagogy, an intimate narrative and scientific adventure in a sublimely astonishing fictional fantasy!] (Editions Delcourt
2015)

Chochois presents an individual experience of everyday trauma and recovery
as well as a history of prostheses and a vision for the future of humanity. These
are complex and lofty aims, which Chochois achieves with seeming ease.

Chochois's illustrations of medically correct information contribute to two
separate, yet intertwined, narrative threads, interrupted by two explanatory
scientific "interludes." In the first of these narrative threads, an unnamed
young man, who appears to be a student, loses an arm in a motorcycle crash.
This largely wordless sequence, illustrated for the most part in black-and-
white, spans the book, illustrating the trauma and recovery of losing a limb
unexpectedly and serving as a series of four chapter introductions and an
epilogue. In the second narrative, which is broken into discrete, titled chapters ("Amputation," "Membre fantôme," [phantom limb] "Prothèses," and
"Transhumanisme"), the unnamed sufferer follows father of amputation
Ambroise Paré on historically informed journeys that see him through each
stage of his recovery and on toward the possibility for transhuman transcendence by means of technological augmentation. This second narrative
punctuates and propels the first, in images of reds and oranges ("Amputation"), then blues ("Membre fantôme"), then greens ("Prothèses"), and
finally a future-looking section ("Transhumanisme") that incorporates all the
tones used across the book. Like the ghosts in Dickens's *A Christmas Carol*
or Dante's guides through the Divine Comedy, Paré ushers the unnamed
amputee through the history of amputation, the neurological understanding of phantom limbs, the history of prosthetics, and finally the conceptual
affordances of transhumanism. Chochois offers a rich terrain for theoretical
inquiry. By explicitly addressing the idea that humans augment their bodies
to continue their evolution, she presents the unnamed sufferer as victim yet
transcendent human, a tension that is never quite resolved.

Significantly, the overall trajectory of the two intertwined narratives mimics psychiatric approaches to trauma and recovery, which require the formation of a coherent narrative. Judith Herman, in *Trauma and Recovery* (1992),

describes a key feature of trauma as preventing the sufferer from framing the experience in coherent language, a circumstance that has been folded into current descriptions of posttraumatic stress disorder. A person who experiences trauma cannot fully recover until s/he can articulate the traumatic event in language and rearticulate their day-to-day lives to overcome the physical and psychological aftereffects of a damaging incident. This type of articulation is of interest both as rhetorical *taxis* and as the integration of personal experience with medical science, and parallels comics as a means of representing experiences that are difficult to frame in language, as might be seen in Chute's and Earle's work. *La Fabrique des corps* also articulates historical, medical, and personal details into an overarching journey of education for the reader. Chochois historically situates a trauma narrative, building medical context and subject formation together. The narrative places reader needs, such as education, against storytelling, which appears to reconcile many aims of health humanities.

Yet, while Chochois's text ably combines elements that honor medical history and education as well as a theoretical position that grounds these aims against the relationship between technology and humanity, the book also incorporates problematic elements. For example, its humor undercuts the seriousness of the physician-patient encounter and creates an impression of medical practitioners as callous and insensitive. Medical humanities education, like narrative competence (Charon 2001b) or narrative humility (DasGupta 2014), trains physicians to honor the stories of illness and admit the limitations of medical practice. *La Fabrique des corps* does not really meet these ends, largely because of Paré's behavior as a narrator and physician. As the protagonist realizes that his arm is missing above the elbow, Paré leaps from an image on the hospital wall. He does not ask the patient's name, makes insensitive puns about the young man's missing limb—"un coup de main" (13)—and launches into an account of his own medical prowess, enacting the very opposite of narrative humility. By introducing himself as the father of amputation ("père de l'amputation," 13), Paré aggrandizes himself.

Throughout the book, visual cues and the text remind the reader that Paré views the patient as interesting only as audience and amputee. The patient's namelessness is underscored by historical accounts peppered with the names of gods (Odin, Haephestus, Tyr) and early physicians Hippocrates and Celsus, but not real-life patients, which further emphasizes a division between patients-as-objects and others-as-persons. Images at the end of chapter 1 ("Amputation") and beginning of chapter 2 ("Membre fantôme") clearly show the amputee protagonist descending into a deep depression and suffering from phantom limb pains, yet Paré, unlike practitioners of narrative medicine, shows no real empathy. After a quick "je vois" [I see], Paré responds to the patient's distress by propounding an anatomical and clinical explanation of the nervous system. At the end of the chapter, much like the end of chapter 1, the protagonist's body is used as the model for many possible clinical outcomes. Although the visual narrative hints that Paré's information aids in the healing process, this connection remains unclear as the interludes illustrate the patient engaging in everyday activities like dancing, and seeking comfort from his girlfriend. Chochois articulates a visual narrative of healing within a more complex series of chapters that recount important medical information, potentially sublimating the patient's experience into a series of medically informative images.

This objectification extends beyond the diegesis and past the comic frame. Chochois provides visual cues that situate the patient as a medical illustration, including a definition of amputation superimposed on the top right corner of the frame in which the patient first sits up. The patient is articulated within a series of narratives available to the reader, but not to him, further marginalizing his experience. Further, many of the book's images render the unnamed patient's body into an object—the illustration of medical procedures, which, combined with the absence of a name, dehumanizes the protagonist, distancing the work from what might be understood as the humanizing function of health humanities. These circumstances suggest that *La Fabrique des corps* serves primarily to provide educational information. In fact, the visual narrative casts the unnamed protagonist as every amputee within Paré's explanation of the rise and fall of medical knowledge. Illustrations in chapters 1, 2, and 3 use the figure of our unnamed protagonist as the model for contemporary forms of amputation, the charts of possible injuries and corresponding amputations (figures 2.2 and 2.3), different possible manifestations of phantom limbs, and various prostheses. This visual trajectory continues throughout each of the titled chapters. The patient, by serving as the visual example, becomes both survivor and victim, yet never attains the position of a true subject. In contrast with Paré, then, the patient is never fully humanized, occupying a body that is at once a site of recovery and abjection.

It is easy to lose this narrative thread in the sheer talent exhibited in *La Fabrique des corps*. Chochois's skills as a medical illustrator are evident throughout. In "Amputation" the specifics of historical and current surgical amputations are illustrated in careful stages, using the unwilling patient as model. In "Membre fantôme," the patient serves as the model for various

Figure 2.3: The image shows the protagonist as a model for various types of amputation. The bearded figure on the right of the first panel is a depiction of Ambroise Paré. Chochois 2016, 30–31. © Éditions Delcourt.

manifestations of phantom limbs and nervous system function. The remainder of the book presents the protagonist's recovery, acquisition of his prosthetic limb, and the affordances of transhumanism—an unproblematic evolution of human progress through technology rather than the more nuanced readings that Stormer's theoretical matrix, Focauldian theory, or the work of Earle and Chute might have afforded. As the novel progresses, the protagonist slowly recovers good spirits and regains his ability to engage in everyday activities, increasingly asking Paré questions, and paralleling the process of recovery from trauma Herman describes, yet without presenting his story in words.

Further, the book presents ethically troublesome practices in an unproblematized way. In one example, modern practices of amputation derive from Paré's research on nonconsenting soldiers, half of whom died. While these practices led to hygienic surgical theaters like the one that saved the protagonist's life, the means of attaining this good practice would be considered suspect today. The unproblematic portrayal of nonconsensual medical experimentation is joined in the book by an uncritical view of transhumanism, which, unlike the posthuman theories described above, has ties to eugenics and ethnic cleansing as a means of human progress. Further, Paré, the logical witness to the patient's experiences, does not exhibit any of the ideal qualities of health humanities, narrative humility, or narrative competence. He makes insensitive jokes, lectures, ignores the patient's stated preferences, and proudly recounts his own unethical research practices. Although the final chapter, "Transhumanisme," ends with the Paré asking his companion about the future, Paré disappears just as the unnamed young man begins to speak. The reader never has access to the patient's experiences or emotions, just his questions.

In fact, many of Chochois's narrative choices hint at an emphasis on historical and empirical accuracy that are at odds with the human and ethical concerns that led to the development of medical and later health humanities. Although the narratives within *La Fabrique des corps* allude to technological augmentation as a future, positive expansion of humanity, they do not highlight important limitations in that "transhuman" thinking. In effect, the nameless protagonist is embedded into a dehumanizing and universalizing narrative of progress and evolution. Given the didactic nature of the book and its ties to accurate medical information, it would appear that concentrating on the technical elements of amputation and prostheses mimicked the focus on science that led to medical and health humanities in the first place. Thus, this narrative, despite its attempt to incorporate theoretical material, offers little vantage for a deeper examination of prosthesis as human invention (following Stiegler: see Roberts 2005) because of the work needed to reconcile the ideologically constructive and unconstructive elements. While it could be argued that Chochois successfully mobilized the hybrid functions of the comics genre to present an as-yet-unarticulated version of the protagonist's experiences, still the integration of art and empiricism is limited in terms of its attempts at theoretical inquiry. Given Chute's observations about the functions of comics as hybrid forms, this may be natural, or even intentional; however, as a full solution to the problem of articulating the domains of health humanities, *La Fabrique des corps* is insufficient on its own.

Wandering Organs

Chochois's stunning performance hints that the mere connection of arts and medicine may not meet all the goals of health humanities. *The Wandering Uterus (Furor Uterensis) and Contemporary Applications of Ancient Medical Wisdom* by Kriota Willberg (2016) offers an alternative example of graphic narrative by a medical illustrator. Willberg, the inaugural artist in residence at the New York Academy of Medicine, actively contributes to the field of graphic medical memoir (see Willberg 2018). According to her blog *Kriotawelt* (2018), Willberg's professional identity mixes art and medical education:

> [she] uses comics, needlework, historical studies, bioethics, and her experiences from her career as a massage therapist and health science educator to explore body/science narratives. Combining this history with her background as an artist and educator, she has been creating comics and teaching artists about injury prevention through panels, workshops, and a series of minicomics.

Willberg's training includes experience and education as a massage therapist in addition to her artistic practice and training as a medical illustrator. She also encourages students to make literal art on bodies, to illustrate the function of muscles and tendons. Her blog showcases work in anatomy, biography, graphic medicine, self care, and teaching, as well as a series of "Pathology laffs" minicomics that present humorous accounts of various illnesses and medical interventions. *The Wandering Uterus* is a seven-page "Pathology laffs" minicomic that takes on an explicit question of interest to medical practitioners and humanists alike: do "traditional" medical remedies actually work and are they superior to current medical information?

Unlike *La Fabrique des corps*, *The Wandering Uterus* begins with a site of clearly stated intellectual, historical, and medical articulation. The artist's in-comic persona is suffering from a headache. Under the banner of "ANCIENT MEDICAL WISDOM," Willberg illustrates herself holding a bag of ice on an aching head. Speech bubbles outline the problem situation: not wanting to see a doctor for the headache and being told by friends to seek Ancient Wisdom. Willberg, then, begins with a common medical situation, a headache, and poses her question, which is seemingly answered by visual elements across the page. A banner provides an answer when she wonders if this is a helpful model for curing headaches: "YES! LOOK NO FURTHER THAN YOUR UTERUS!" (2016, I). The lower portion of the page features the uterus in multiple poses, one of which announces its mobility, "I can literally move around your body" (I), while others appear to be reading the information panels. Beginning with the idea that women do not need a "scientific diagnosis" (I), Willberg opens with a default hypothesis, that ancient medical wisdom defied logic by treating women as only receptacles of reproductive organs. The ironic presentation of images and text strongly suggests, but does not come out and state, that the "wandering uterus" is a highly improbable medical explanation

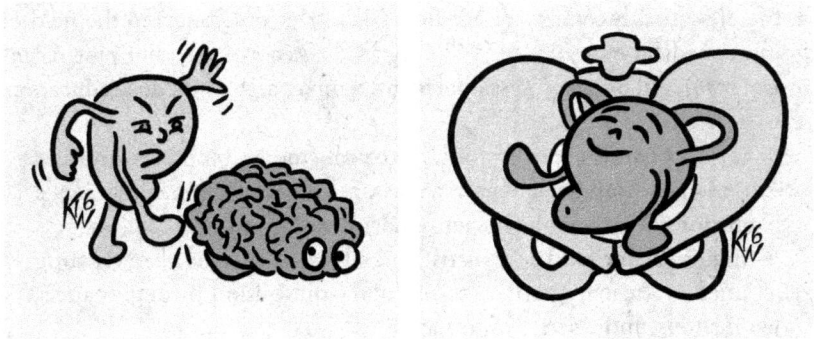

Figure 2.4: The angry uterus kicking a hapless brain, 2016. © Kriota Willberg. Image provided courtesy of Kriota Willberg and reproduced with her permission.
Figure 2.5. A contented uterus, nestled in the pelvis, where it belongs, 2016. © Kriota Willberg. Image provided courtesy of Kriota Willberg and reproduced with her permission.

for a headache. The comic thus signals a serious, yet unstated, problem with Ancient Wisdom, preventing an entry of this experience into Foucauldian knowledge.

Willberg presents her question in historical and medical terms, which lends to a reading through rhetorical articulation. An adaptation of medieval feminine anatomy outlines the specific illnesses caused by the wandering uterus, including migraines, fainting, palpitations, foot pain, and digestive problems (II). The bulk of the comic traces the origin of the fallen or wandering uterus idea to ancient Egyptian and Hippocratic medicine (III–IV), linking this concept to currently accepted modes of Platonic thought. In fact, Plato identified the womb as an angry animal that required pregnancy to be placated (IV; see figures 2.4 and 2.5). Although the overall trajectory of the book undercuts the legitimacy of the wandering uterus, the primary dissenting comment is a disapproving "hmmm" from an unnamed woman in ancient Egypt. Rather than offering an explicit critique, then, Willberg's narrator maintains an ironic tone, insisting that any medical "system in use for centuries" (III) must be reliable and, thus, requiring the reader to see past surface meaning and to uncover an unarticulated meaning.

The minicomic then walks the reader through empirical practice as the narrator tries ancient and medieval cures for the wandering uterus, such as inhaling foul smelling odors while fumigating the vagina with enticing scents to lure the errant organ back into place, or vigorous sexual activity to create a fetus (VI). Unsurprisingly, these remedies fail to do anything except frighten the narrator's cat. Despite the largely failed attempts to cure a headache, the narrator does not describe her emotional state or dwell on the experience of pain. Instead, and like the protagonist of *La Fabrique des corps*, the patient maintains a stance of questioning, seeking medical wisdom. It would appear, then, that *The Wandering Uterus* is not intended to serve as a medical memoir or an expression of personal experience, but rather as a frame for interrogating statements about medical practice. *The Wandering Uterus* articulates a response to the idea of Ancient Wisdom by vexing it as a category—tellingly, the next step on the narrator's unresolved journey of healing is acupuncture, which signals a shift not away from ancient medicine but from its Western tradition.

While Willberg's narrative merely demonstrates the inefficacy of ancient remedies for women, hinting at the absurdity of such notions, without direct commentary, an epilogue grounds the minicomic against Laurinda Dixon's humanistic critique of the wandering uterus in *Perilous Chastity* (1995). As with the rest of the narrative, Willberg's book relies on the reader to link this feminist reading to current medical practice, leaving open the possibility for a rhetorical articulation of theoretical and feminist concerns. Although a surface interpretation might suggest that *The Wandering Uterus* is less successful in incorporating the domains of health humanities than *La Fabrique des corps*, it ultimately promotes the precise types of critical thinking that inform both domains of the health humanities. Willberg's narrative enacts a series of practices generally in keeping with the medical educational goals of narrative humility and health humanities, and hints that one way of achieving insights to medical practice is through scholarly work in the humanities. By explicitly articulating historical elements as well as an academic humanities register (via Dixon), Willberg presents a site that can account for the unlivable conditions created by Ancient Wisdom as well as the realms of scientific and academic knowledge. In the end, this minicomic does more than examine the problems of the wandering uterus; it offers a model for examining the truth or consequences of medical beliefs more generally. That it does so without stating its intentions provides a fertile ground for critique.

Conclusions

La Fabrique des corps and *The Wandering Uterus* each present a site for articulating the humanistic and educational domains of health humanities. Both books ground their narratives in antiquity, situating current discussions against older practices while offering an intriguing opportunity for examining the relationships between visual and textual elements and their ability to frame medical knowledge and human experience. Significantly, these graphic narratives present a coalescence of spectacle and language that mirrors Foucault's medical gaze, the specific experience that allows new biomedical information to enter into the realm of knowledge. Both authors offer a site for the type of prosthetic posthuman inquiry that Stormer describes conjoined with the elements of hybridity that Hillary Chute and Jenell Johnson place within the field of graphic medicine. While Willberg's text is more successful in bridging the domains of the health humanities, neither book engages in the explicit critical reflection that characterizes Stormer's work or posthuman inquiry, let alone the deeper concerns highlighted in theoretical work on prosthesis as a means of locating the invention of humanity. Thus, although graphic narratives by medical illustrators provide a space for a critical study of comics in healthcare delivery (see Willberg 2018) as well as humanistic inquiry, the mere combination of art and medicine is not adequate to address all theoretical concerns within the health humanities, leaving a gap similar to the one Atkinson et al. (2015) describe: a space for the operation of theoretical perspectives. Yet these narratives show an awareness of such intellectual practice; it is telling that both Chochois and Willberg elected to include a specific reference to a more broadly theoretical approach to their topics. While Chochois cites transhumanism, which could have been an opportunity for such posthuman inquiry, the association with eugenics hints that this inclusion serves primarily to introduce a narrative of progress, rather than to critique that narrative.

Both narratives also leave room for further critique or examination of the limitations of ethics, bedside manner, and human experience. In fact, neither narrative presents the type of patient-centric experience that is a major focus of much graphic medicine. While Willberg's commentary appears more pointed, in fact, the function of bedside manner, the way to treat patients, remains largely implicit, as does an overt expression of the patient's emotional state. Nevertheless, Willberg and Chochois each illustrate the limitations of past and current medical care: leaving the reader to piece together the idea that medical practitioners might be able to do better, and offering few if any suggestions as to how, might be seen as an embedded educational frame, a means of encouraging readers to engage with medical practice rather than passively accepting information. While these books offer a means of reconciling certain theoretical and conceptual differences between medical accuracy and health humanities, the critical engagement with humanistic theory that characterizes posthuman inquiry appears to be a needed augmentation for these productions as medical representation. Ultimately, then, graphic narratives by medical illustrators remain an object of interest, which can be seen as distinct from other types of graphic medicine, and therefore deserving of increased attention.

Notes

1. See the chapter by Paul Fisher Davies in the current volume for a focused discussion on the structural form of comics from a critical linguistics perspective, including the limits of semiotic approaches to the comics form.

2. For a more phenomenological and theological account of seeing in comics, Timothy D Peters's chapter in the current volume may be of interest.

References

Association of Medical Illustrators. 2017. "About." Accessed November 20, 2018. https://www.ami.org/medical-illustration/learn-about-medical-illustration.

Atkinson, Sarah, Bethan Evans, and Angela Woods. 2015. "The 'Medical' and 'Health' in a Critical Medical Humanities." *Journal of Medical Humanities* 36: 71–81.

Butler, Judith. 1993. *Bodies That Matter: On the Discursive Limits of Sex*. New York: Routledge.

Charon, Rita. 2001a. "Narrative Medicine: A Model for Empathy, Reflection, Profession, and Trust." *Journal of the American Medical Association* 286 (15): 1897–902.

Charon, Rita. 2001b. "What Narrative Competence Is For." *American Journal of Bioethics* 1 (1): 62–63.

Chiapperino, Luca, and Giovanni Boniolo. 2014. "Rethinking Medical Humanities." *Journal of Medical Humanities* 35: 377–87.

Chochois, Héloïse. 2012. "Promenade." Accessed November 20, 2018. http://heloisechochois.tumblr.com.

Chochois, Héloïse. 2015. Illustrations for *Thinkovery*. Accessed November 20, 2018 http://heloisechochois.tumblr.com.

Chochois, Héloïse. 2016. *La Fabrique des corps: Des premièrs prothèses à l'humaine augmenté*. Paris: Delcourt.

Chochois, Héloïse. 2018. "À Propos." Accessed November 20, 2018. http://heloisechochois.tumblr.com/CV.

Chute, Hillary. 2016. *Disaster Drawn: Visual Witness, Comics, and Documentary Form*. Cambridge, MA: Harvard University Press.

Chute, Hillary. 2017. *Why Comics: From Underground to Everywhere*. New York: Harper.

Couser, G. Thomas. 2011. "What Disability Studies Has to Offer Medical Education." *Journal of Medical Humanities* 32: 21–30.

Czerwiec, M. K., Ian Williams, Susan Merrill Squier, Michael J. Green, Kimberly R. Myers, and Scott T. Smith. 2015. *Graphic Medicine Manifesto*. University Park: Penn State University Press.

DasGupta, Sayantani. 2014. "Narrative Medicine, Narrative Humility." *Creative Nonfiction* 52. https://www.creativenonfiction.org/online-reading/narrative-medicine-narrative -humility.

Dinello, Daniel. 2005. *Technophobia! Science Fiction Visions of Posthuman Technology.* Austin: University of Texas Press.

Dixon, Laurinda. 1995. *Perilous Chastity: Women and Illness in Pre-Enlightenment Art and Medicine.* Ithaca, NY: Cornell University Press.

Earle, Harriet H. 2017. *Comics, Trauma, and the New Art of War.* Jackson: University Press of Mississippi.

Editions Delcourt. 2015. "*La Fabrique des corps: Des premièrs prothèses à l'humaine augmenté.*" Accessed November 20, 2018. https://www.editions-delcourt.fr/serie/fabrique-des-corps -des-premieres-protheses-a-l-humain-augmente.html.

Foucault, Michel. 1982. *The Archaeology of Knowledge: And the Discourse on Language.* Translated by A. M. Sheridan Smith. New York: Vintage.

Foucault, Michel. (1963) 1994. *The Birth of the Clinic: An Archaeology of Medical Perception.* Translated by A. M. Sheridan Smith. New York: Vintage.

Graphic Medicine. 2007–2019. Accessed November 20, 2018. https://www.graphicmedicine .org.

Groensteen, Thierry. 2008. "A Few Words about *The System of Comics* and More." *European Comic Art* 1 (1): 87–93.

Groensteen, Theirry. 2013. *Comics and Narration.* Translated by Ann Miller. Jackson: University Press of Mississippi.

Guildersen, Monique. 2002. "I Am a Medical Illustrator." *Science*, May 24, 2002. http://www .sciencemag.org/careers/2002/05/i-am-medical-illustrator.

Haraway, Donna. 1991. "A Cyborg Manifesto: Science, Technology, and Socialist-Feminism in the Late Twentieth Century." In *Simians, Cyborgs, and Women: The Reinvention of Nature*, 65–105. New York: Routledge.

Hawthorn, Jeremy, and Jakob Lothe. 2013. "The Ethical (Re)Turn." In *Narrative Ethics*, edited by Jeremy Hawthorn and Jakob Lothe, n.p. Amsterdam: Brill Academic Publishers.

Herman, Judith. 1992. *Trauma and Recovery: The Aftermath of Violence—from Domestic Abuse to Political Terror.* New York: Basic Books.

Johnson, Jenell. 2018. *Graphic Reproduction: A Comics Anthology.* University Park: Penn State University Press.

Jones, Therese, Delese Wear, and Lester D. Friedman. 2014. "The Why, the What, and the How of the Medical/Health Humanities." In *Health Humanities Reader*, edited by Therese Jones, Delese Wear, and Lester D. Friedman, 1–12. New Brunswick, NJ: Rutgers University Press.

Katz, Joel T. 2014. "Applied Medical Humanities: Addressing Vexing Deficits, Promoting Enduring Skills." *American Medical Association Journal of Ethics* 16 (8): 610–13.

Lewis, Bradley E. 2011. "Narrative Medicine and Healthcare Reform." *Journal of Medical Humanities* 32: 9–20.

Lynch, John. A. 2009. "Articulating Scientific Practice: Understanding Dean Hamer's 'Gay Gene' Study as Overlapping Material, Social and Rhetorical Registers." *Quarterly Journal of Speech* 4 (9): 435–56.

Miodrag, Hannah. 2013. *Comics and Language: Reimagining Critical Discourse on the Form.* Jackson: University Press of Mississippi.

Roberts, Ben. 2005. "Stiegler Reading Derrida: The Prosthesis of Deconstruction in Technics." *Postmodern Culture* 16 (1): n.p.

Shapiro, Johanna. 2012. "Whither (Whether) Medical Humanities? The Future of Medical Humanities and Arts in Medical Education." *Journal for Learning through the Arts* 8 (1): n.p.

Shapiro, Johanna, Jack Coulehan, Delese Wear, and Martha Montello. 2009. "Medical Humanities and Their Discontents: Definitions, Critiques and Implications." *Academic Medicine* 84 (2): 192–98.

Stormer, Nathan. 2004. "Articulation: A Working Paper on Rhetoric and *Taxis*." *Quarterly Journal of Speech* 90 (3): 257–84.

Willberg, Kriota. 2016. *The Wandering Uterus (*Furor Uterensis*) and Contemporary Applications of Ancient Medical Wisdom.* New York: Birdcage Bottom Books.

Willberg, Kriota. 2017. "Get a Grip! How Graphic Medicine Is Changing the Landscape of Medical Care." *The Beat: The News Blog on Comics Culture*, December 6, 2017. Accessed November 20, 2018. http://www.comicsbeat.com/column-get-a-grip-give-yourself-a-dose-of-graphic-medicine/.

Willberg, Kriota. 2018. *Kriotawelt.* Accessed November 20, 2018. http://kriotawelt.blogspot.com.

3

"There Is a Man . . . with a Typewriter"

Deadpool as Existential Antihero, Breaking the Fourth Wall of Meaningful Existence

YASEMIN J. ERDEN

Frankly, if I'd known Deadpool was such a creep when I agreed to write the mini-series, I wouldn't have done it. Someone who hasn't paid for their crimes presents a problem for me.

—MARK WAID, QUOTED IN HAMILTON

"Do I still think in those little yellow boxes?" (Simone 2003, n.p.) asks Deadpool (see figure 3.1). The fourth wall is broken; the comic strip is just that (Thoss 2011, 554), and like a soliloquy, the reader enters Deadpool's inner life. But unlike the peek behind a curtain that some other literary devices may offer, Deadpool's fourth wall-breaking smashes both the security of his world and ours. The structure and identity of the work is compromised; the audience's passivity confronted. In this chapter I explore these ideas in relation to existentialism and make the following three arguments. That Deadpool's fourth wall-breaking makes the audience complicit with his actions and behavior. In so doing we are confronted with our own existential existence. For these reasons, among others, Deadpool is an existential antihero. In our experiences both in and out of the pages we are free to choose and to act, and are responsible. Yet we also face the possibility, or likelihood, that there may be no meaning and no certainty for any outcomes that may follow. That life, in both the comic world and in our own, is laughably, painfully, profoundly, yet also trivially meaningless. Before I can explain why, we first must meet our protagonist, in all his dreadful glory.[1]

Figure 3.1: Little yellow box asks, "Do I still think in those little yellow boxes?" From *Agent X #15: Deadpool Walkin' Part 3*. Gail Simone 2003, © Marvel Comics.

Who Is Deadpool?

> The foul-mouthed mercenary now known as Deadpool was once little more than medical waste, written off as a miscarriage of science and technology by the directors of the Canadian government's enigmatic Weapon X project. (Marvel Directory, n.d.)

Williams describes Deadpool as:

> a mercenary, a preternatural martial artist, tactician, swordsman and marksman—his unkillable cancer doesn't get in the way of that—and he's aware he's a character in a comic, so he's been known to gain information by reading back-issues. He is a fast-talker and piss-taker (hence "The Merc with a Mouth"). He killed his parents but doesn't know it. He might be insane. (2015)

With a costume informed by Spider-Man, or more particularly "Spider-Man with guns and swords," Deadpool is "a smart-ass mercenary" (Lussier 2016) with "Wolverine's genetically endowed healing factor through artificial means" (Marvel Directory, n.d.). Or more particularly he is "the guy [Weapon X] experimented on before Wolverine" (Lussier 2016). For this good fortune of limitless regeneration, and apparent immortality, the character of Wade Wilson pays a heavy price: substantial harm to his skin, which leaves his face seemingly irreparably disfigured. Wade is rejected from the Weapon X project, and as part of his self-realized rebirth, he becomes Deadpool.[2]

There are a number of iterations of the Deadpool character. We are first introduced to him in the pages of *The New Mutants #98* (1991), after which he appears in *X-Force, The Avengers,* and *Daredevil,* among others. Gerry Duggan, writer of recent iterations, notes that Deadpool has had many parents: "Gail Simone, Rick Remender, Joe Kelly, Mark Waid, Jimmy Palmiotti, Dan Way, and so many more creators left Deadpool better than when they found him" (quoted in Lussier 2016). Yet, as Willaert (2013) notes, "while Rob Liefeld and Fabian Nicieza are credited with creating Deadpool, it was Joe Kelly who reinvented him into a popular character."

Joe Kelly and Ed McGuinness's Deadpool series began in 1997, and in it we are offered a number of the less salubrious features that we quickly came to expect from the character. This includes some of the more unpalatable details about his living situation. For instance that "he'd been keeping an old blind woman he called Blind Al as a prisoner in his home for years" (Willaert 2013), albeit as part of their mutually abusive relationship, where the doors are not always locked. Even so, the high levels of abuse are striking. As Willaert (2013) describes, it "messed with your head."

Hamilton (2016) notes it was around this time that Deadpool "morphed into an action comedy parody of the cosmic drama, antihero-heavy comics of the time." Williams (2015) also suggests that around this time "Deadpool became less a villain and more an antihero. Essentially, he's a sociopath trying to do good with a questionable grasp on morality."

The hero/antihero distinction is worth addressing briefly here, though it is not a simple distinction to draw. In terms of common usage, the Oxford English Dictionary (OED) describes a hero as a person (typically a man, but that is a separate even if relevant argument to consider) "who is admired for their courage, outstanding achievements, or noble qualities." It is clear that Deadpool meets few, perhaps none of these qualities. Meanwhile, the antihero, typically a literary character, is defined in terms of an absence: the absence of *typical* heroic features, or as someone who "lacks conventional heroic attributes" (OED).[3]

Part of this can be understood in terms of a shift from the idol of heroic action to the celebration, or at least acceptance, of imperfect heroism, marking the move from hero to antihero. As Lamont (1962, 73) describes, people had looked to a "spiritual leader, warrior, saint, intellectual seeker after truth, the hero of society [who] was to guide humanity toward values shared by all, but best expressed in one." The modern postwar, post-idol, postmodern era, with humanity itself threatened, began however to look beyond simple binaries of saints and sinners. Here the "*unusual* man or woman, the person with greater insight and vital forces, becomes a rebel or a monster" (Lamont 1962, 73, emphasis added). In this fecund space the antihero takes the hero's place. (For discussion on the origins and psychological dimensions of these developments, see also Shafer and Raney 2012; Jonason et al. 2012.)

But does the antihero tag fit our foul-mouthed mercenary? Central to Deadpool's identity are his vigilantism, anarchism, and heroism, but also his villainy. He is *rebel* and *monster* (Lamont 1962, 73), though in more unpredictable and often shocking ways. He talks relentlessly, to other characters, and to the audience, and has the nickname "Merc with a Mouth." He both inhabits and encourages a world without certainty, without meaningful existence, and one that too often lacks clear links between reasoning and action. A world that is not, in fact, so unlike our own.

Deadpool's mercenary character has sometimes been softened, yet even then "the element of his moral ambiguity remained" (Hamilton 2016). Hamilton adds:

Many were uncomfortable with this, especially comic die hards, but writer Joe Kelly notes, "With Deadpool, we could do anything we wanted because everybody just expected the book to be cancelled every five seconds, so nobody was paying attention. And we could get away with it." This could be part of the reason that the fourth wall breaking story element was created. That's the thing about art, sometimes it's impossible to create it in an intentional manner. In a way, Deadpool was defined by the negligence that Marvel showed it. (2016)

Similarly, Willaert (2013) suggests that:

Kelly took a character who is essentially a sociopath, and threw him into a situation where he's inspired to become a hero; attempting to navigate the path of good without the benefit of a moral compass. As a result, we began to sympathize with him . . . and Kelly used this to his advantage, in order to send us on an emotional rollercoaster ride. He'd use humor to lull you into a false sense of security, so he could pull the rug out from under you with a serious moment when you least expect it. Kelly would regularly remind us what a despicable person Deadpool has been, yet we'd continue to root for the character, because we could see how hard he was trying to figure out this whole hero thing and wanted him to succeed. (2013)

Why does Deadpool act as he does? Like Meursault in *The Outsider* (Camus [1942] 1982), Deadpool *chooses*, but sometimes without purpose. Unlike the Joker (*Batman*) or *Watchmen*'s the Comedian (see Moore and Gibbons 1986) we have regular access to Deadpool's thinking. Not that it helps. Deadpool's moral code is written, rewritten, ignored, even absent.

So while Deadpool may not neatly fit alongside other more conventional antiheroes, especially those more consistent or predictable in their complexity, he does offer an interesting example of what we can call an *existential antihero* with whose actions the reader becomes entangled, "bound to the image" (Petty 2015, 157). Via Deadpool, we are confronted with limitless choice, action, responsibility. He shows us what Sartre described when he said we are condemned to be free; a burden both liberating and overwhelming. To explain this a little more, we need a clearer picture of what is meant by *existentialism*.

The Existential Deadpool

To make my case for Deadpool as an existential antihero, I focus exclusively on the version of existentialism outlined by Jean-Paul Sartre in *Being and Nothingness* (2001), first published in 1943, and *Existentialism and Humanism* (1973). The latter text is a transcript from a lecture he gave in 1945 and offers the clearest and simplest account of his approach to existentialism.[4] Alongside this I mostly focus my attention on Deadpool as presented in the miniseries *Deadpool Kills the Marvel Universe* (Bunn and Talajić 2016), the reasons for which should become evident.

First we need to start with some of Sartre's foundation claims. His ideas are meaningful within the atheistic tradition, where existence *precedes* essence—first you *exist*, which is existence without essence, and then you *become*. Except that to *become* is far too static as a term. Really what Sartre has in mind is the transitory concept of *being* or *becoming*, because what it is to be, is to be constantly in motion, movement, or flux.[5] In this we find the clearest account of the three concepts that frame Sartre's account of existentialism: freedom, choice, and responsibility. All three are tied to the idea of Deadpool as existential antihero.

The reason is simple: in each endeavor, Deadpool confronts an often-colorful range of choices open to him, even beyond what others might consider reasonable choices. This includes attacking those who might be trying to help him, for instance, or willfuly betraying those who seem to be on his side. In these ways he offers a truly authentic, which is to say *utterly his*, version of *being*. He holds the keys to his own choices, and he is, or at least should be, responsible for these choices. In fact he often does pay a heavy price for the decisions he makes, starting with the suffering experienced during a very painful transition as a result of the highly experimental treatment he opts to undergo.

Through the choices that Deadpool makes, he decides what will happen to him. In this way, his freedom is not just attainable; it is already within his grasp. As Sartre notes, the individual is "nothing else but that which he makes of himself" ([1945] 1973, 28). One never is something, in final terms, since that denies a person's potential to change; a person is never finished. As Sartre notes elsewhere, a person must be invented each day (Sartre [1947] 1988). The only thing that cannot be chosen is freedom itself—we are free whether we want to be or not. Deadpool certainly behaves as if he is fully free, though we will return to the complexity of his freedom later in this chapter.

Sartre's emphasis on freedom makes particular sense when considered in context, a context that includes his experiences living in Nazi-occupied Paris. The existential account of human freedom he presents fits a very particular need of a country seeking to liberate itself from that occupation. His contemporaries, Albert Camus, Maurice Merleau-Ponty, and Simone de Beauvoir, shared these concerns, and there is overlap with the kinds of American comics published in the wake of the end of World War II. On this, Regalado (2005, 85) suggests that "Superman, and the hundreds of superheroes that come after him, can be seen as affirming the primacy of a besieged humanity by transcending these forces of modernity." Resistance in this context includes against "the corruption and violence that often enable the development of modern societies" (85).

Where there is optimism in freedom, it makes sense that heroes are transcendent and that they survive. Or that if they die, their death should at least be meaningful. Perhaps the death is heroic, perhaps tragic, perhaps avenged. Yet Deadpool's is not a world of optimism, nor one where heroes are safe or where *meaning* is secure. The title *Deadpool Kills the Marvel Universe* rather gives away the outcome: many Marvel heroes are killed, and not always with satisfying explanations. Deadpool offers reasons for his behavior, that much is true, but these reasons are not always good ones. It is true to say that the miniseries is outside what might be considered a central Deadpool canon, so the deaths (as much else) may be largely irrelevant. This does not, however, mean that the action of killing is any less significant. Because here, as elsewhere, what is key is that *freedom* for Deadpool means that what he *might*

Figure 3.2: Deadpool floats in the cosmic void. From *Deadpool Kills the Marvel Universe #4*. Cullin Bunn and Dalibor Talajić, 2016. © Marvel Comics.

do, he often does, and the only predictable detail is that he is not particularly predictable. In this way Deadpool exhibits other existential traits, such as one who is in the constant flux of *being*.

At the time when Sartre was writing, psychoanalysis was increasingly popular in Europe. In response to claims about the ego as a driver of action and will, Sartre responds that it is not, in fact, representative of *an inner core* of being, whether that is taken to mean a source of action, emotion, or even character. Instead he says it is a construct, by which he means a product of a person's self-image. In other words an image in the eyes of oneself and of others, which is built from the bricks of past behavior and feelings, as well as of current behaviors, and even future intentions, insofar as they guide current action. Similarly, as discussed in *Being and Nothingness* ([1943] 2001), consciousness is nothing; not a substance, it is utterly empty. It exists only in its awareness of itself and the world. This, he suggests, is the basis of its freedom, but also the source of its dilemma: it is *nothing*, but it wants to be *something*. On this account, a person is a being without an essential nature, a being who can be identified, in the literal sense of that word, with neither her past, nor indeed her present self. And since consciousness is nothing, we therefore choose what we give in to, including, Sartre suggests, our emotions.

When Deadpool floats in the cosmic void in *Deadpool Kills the Marvel Universe* issue #4 (Bunn and Talajić 2016), we are offered a kaleidoscope of his multiple possible realities, each with a different existence, and each as meaningless as the rest (see figure 3.2). As the authors note in the concluding-sequence script, here you can find "any other variations of Deadpool you might want to create" (2016). In Deadpool we have the *choose your own adventure* of an existential nightmare—you can choose, but is your choice really your own, and in any event, does it really matter? As the disembodied voice in Wade's head poignantly notes, "Even the progenitors of *our* universe may be nothing more than the playthings for other entities." Whether the player is the reader, the consumer, the investors or managers, capitalism or deities is not really the point.

Once the standard moral structure disintegrates, as it does in Camus's *The Outsider*, we are left with meaningless choices that, on closer inspection, do not look all that much like choices after all. For these reasons we can see why Sartre's efforts to protect the Kantian categorical imperative, by virtue of the claim that "in fashioning myself I fashion man" (1973, 30), or that "nothing can be better for us unless it is better for all" (1973, 29), falter.[6] In fact, as Camus's Meursault shows us, social conscience too often weakens when faced with abject meaningless and futility. Deadpool the hero, the antithesis of a hero, but really the reality of a hero, in all his antirealism, shows us this in stark color. In that way Deadpool shows what Meursault had only hinted at, namely the utter emptiness of an existential space that is defined by choice and free will alone, especially where these dominate the primary intention of each protagonist.

On the one hand, Sartre dismisses any account that would diminish or deny the role of the authentic will who chooses, who is free, and who takes responsibility for all such choices and the consequences of those choices. In this respect, he urges each individual to live their authentic life. It is not, on this account, acceptable to simply follow what others are doing. Yet, on the other hand, as should already be clear, what it means to be authentic is unclear. Sartre takes as a given that the answer will become clear to the person who freely seeks it.

Yet it is the question of free will, on which authenticity hangs, that throws into sharp relief Deadpool's freedom to choose. He seems to believe that he has free will, but in the final scene of *Deadpool Kills the Marvel Universe* we are reminded that his free will is a construction by the creative team of Cullen Bunn, Dalibor Talajić, and colorist Lee Loughridge. Deadpool is therefore both active (free will is central to his character and identity) yet passive (he is but a character in a comic, after all). This seeming contradiction of will and passivity echoes, even mocks, our own existence. After all, the humans who control Deadpool are themselves vulnerable to being controlled. This seems true for all humans. How can we be authentic, my students regularly plead, if so much of who we are (language, culture, even taste) is learnt with and from other people? There is no simple answer I can provide, at least not without being in bad faith (more on which below).

Without certainty, without a concrete self to rely on, and with a bewildering array of choices and concomitant responsibilities, how can the individual choose between right and wrong? How can they know what they ought to do in a given situation? Sartre's answer is simple: choice is not easy, yet still we must and can choose. On his account we do not need either restriction or pseudo-certain guidance. He shows this in the example of a young man who must choose between leaving to fight for the Resistance, to which the young man could make substantial contribution, or to stay and care for his ailing mother, who clearly depends on him. Sartre suggests that it is not enough to say of the young man that he is free to "choose—that is to say, invent" (1973, 38). Whatever he chooses will be uncertain, and either choice will be to the detriment of the other.

In his 1929–30 *Lecture on Ethics*, Wittgenstein points to a similar problem when he suggests that a book that is truly about ethics would need to contain more than a book could ever possibly contain (Wittgenstein 1965, 7). Ethics is *supernatural*, he suggests, while language contains only limited potential to express more than facts. To capture all the complexity of the young man's choice in Sartre's example, or of Deadpool's choices in multiple examples, and to do so in ethical terms requires that we capture each complex facet. We must also include every doubt and each uncertainty, among other factors. It would be more than one book could contain.

To explain this idea further, Wittgenstein offers the analogy of the teacup which can only hold a small amount of liquid, but into which we try to pour a gallon. So it is with choices. Which road should the young man choose? Which choices should Deadpool make? Who can know for certain? Even apparently binary choices are rarely so limited. The young man has many other options besides those noted above. He could choose to do neither of the above, or to try and timeshare between the two, or some other thing entirely. What we have in Deadpool is an account of that limitless choice, one that is often taken to an absurd conclusion, whether to shocking or hilarious effect, or both.

Characters who share similar complexity with Deadpool nevertheless act with a more often predictable intentionality. The "masked avengers in *Watchmen* are nuanced beings, inescapably mired in all-too-human complexities, prejudices and their own shallow and self-serving desires" (Petty 2015, 159). They are characters for whom *something* always matters. Their moral code is often deontological or steeped in consequentialism. Rorschach for instance has a "rigidly held moral code. . . . Within his fatalistic worldview there is no moral ambiguity . . . nor any room for hope" (Petty 2015, 155). Spider-Man similarly has a moral code, even if there is superficial ambiguity. The reader in such instances is guided. There is a code to reflect on, despite such uncertainties. As already noted, Deadpool's moral code is never certain, never a given. It is sometimes ignored, and sometimes absent. The scope of possible choices is never closed. And there is no intention to ignore the absurdity that comes from the effort to find meaning and certainty where uncertainty necessarily exists.

Wittgenstein suggests that in order to explain the *right road* to travel down in practical terms we only need to point to "the road which leads to an arbitrarily predetermined end" or goal (Wittgenstein 1965, 7). Yet this is unsatisfactory as a guide to moral choices and does not address the very real uncertainty that is felt when we struggle to weigh the different goals in terms of value. The needs of one may outweigh the needs of another in one moment, only to change in the next. To pretend the choice of a moral road is always or ever obvious would be to deny the uncertainty we face in our very particular circumstances. Yet if we persist in this endeavor of certainty and aim to identify an *absolutely* right road, then, says Wittgenstein, it must be "the road which everybody on seeing it would, with logical necessity, have to go, or be ashamed for not going" (Wittgenstein 1965, 7).

It is clear that we rarely have such certainty available to us, and therefore that ethical guidance cannot in absolute terms offer a secure route to this kind of road. The flipside of this conclusion is that we therefore open the gates to all sorts of contextually or even subjectively "right" choices, with all the mess that goes with that. This is perfectly exemplified by Deadpool who often rationalizes his choices, and at the very least identifies them as his own. Deadpool acts because he believes his choices are his, authentically; he is deeply disturbed by the discovery that this is not in fact the case.

At the end of *Deadpool Kills the Marvel Universe* (Bunn and Talajić 2016), Deadpool breaks through to the *center-point of existence*. There he finds the artists and storytellers vainly focused on their own presentation, and on the seemingly trivial minutiae of text formatting (see figure 3.3). These perpetrators of the devastation caused by Deadpool's access to the truth are now presented as characters themselves. Characters in his world; characters in ours. They are at once creators of the destruction that we have seen, while yet presenting themselves as oblivious to, or indifferent to, the same. Their complicity becomes ours when Deadpool looks at us and says, "I see you out there . . . watching," with a threat to come for us too, "soon enough" (2016). In this middle ground between his world and ours, we see that the violence both matters and does not. It is at once trivial (it is, after all, only a comic), while yet being representative of a greater truth about our reality: violence that is gruesome, unpleasant, morally objectionable, and repulsive is attractive to the reader. We are simultaneously appalled and engrossed, as with the rubber necking that happens toward traffic collisions. We choose to look or not, just as we choose to engage with Deadpool's world or not.

Of the young man in Sartre's example Jopling (1992, 120) suggests: "There is no possibility of putting his choice of a way of life on a secure and rational foundation." It will necessarily contain what is sometimes crippling uncertainty and doubt. With that assessment we are faced with the rather painful conclusion that all who follow this reasoning must ultimately come to: each is alone with their decisions, and each is condemned to make them, come what may. Even choosing not to choose is itself a choice. The relationship between freedom and responsibility is like a weight upon our shoulders. We are, as Sartre states, "condemned to be free" (1973, 34). Our freedom to choose, which necessitates responsibility for our choices, results in the outcome that freedom is less what an individual wants, in some abstract sense of the term, and more about what they decide in each moment to do. And as already noted, we do not choose to be free.[7]

Sartre recognized that such freedom can be overwhelming, and describes this feeling as *vertigo*. To understand this idea we first need to see that in practice, Sartre says, it can be easier to deny our freedom than to employ it. It is a little like when a person hides behind a self that they construct

Figure 3.3: The artists drawing themselves. From *Deadpool Kills the Marvel Universe* #4. Cullin Bunn and Dalibor Talajić, 2016. © Marvel Comics.

and abstains thereafter from active choice, deferring instead to what this construct requires (whether according to their own expectations, or those of others). This happens when they fear change, for instance, such that limiting what they understand to be their range of choices can make choosing easier. Especially because freedom, with the range of possibilities it offers, can be daunting or even threatening.

One reason for this experience of vertigo is because we choose and act without really *knowing* that we choose for the good or for the bad. We may feel or think that it will be good to do something, we may even believe or experience certainty about our decision, but very little of this can amount to the kind of absolute certainty that *knowing* implies. I choose to help someone in a particular moment, and it seems the right thing to do, but how can I *really* know that in acting I have not caused some greater harm? The decision whether to give money to someone in need provides a fairly simple example of this kind of dilemma, but with enough examination the same uncertainty can be found in almost any example.

Vertigo is therefore the very real fear of what we, or rightly *you or I as individuals*, could do at any given moment. It certainly seems to capture the very real feeling that goes with a seemingly impossible choice, yet an equally real need to make a decision. The popular conception of *existential angst* has also sometimes been used to describe this phenomenon, especially as it relates to the impossibility of certainty and the absurdity that arises when we nevertheless seek such certainty. If anything could be the case, then what scope is there for meaning or truth, the argument goes. And without meaning or truth, our search for the same seems at best pointless and at worst, absurd. It is the scope for vertigo that provides an apparent cognitive dissonance in our decisions, such as for someone who has no wish to commit or experience violence yet enjoys or is attracted to the representation of such in comic form.[8] Deadpool's actions are violent, often unforgivably so, but that we choose to engage with these experiences as an enjoyable way to spend our leisure time tells us something about the scope of unbounded freedom.

There is no real way to avoid vertigo. More than this, to try and free oneself from the unpleasant feelings that arise can result in *bad faith*. For instance, a person might try to deny their *transcendence*, by which they deny their freedom, potential, and choice. They might do this in order to avoid the feeling that a decision is theirs to make, with all the responsibility that goes with that. I might say, for example, that I cannot do otherwise than to spend a sunny day inside writing this chapter. *It is not a choice*, I might tell you; *I have to do so*. In fact, it is always a choice, says Sartre. I could choose not to write the chapter. I could choose to pull out from the task, to change my career, to drop out of work altogether. I would of course need to take responsibility for the effects of that choice. In this example, the editor might be disappointed, especially after waiting so long and so patiently, and my manager might also wonder at my choices. But none of these outcomes obscures or alters the reality that such choices are always very much mine to make.

We feel this freedom most when we consider the scope we have to do something that we yet have no intention of doing. As when a person who is not suicidal stands at the edge of a cliff and ponders the likelihood of flying rather than falling if they just step off. As they stand too close to the edge and wonder. And more than this, feel the shock and even sickness that comes from realizing that there really is little to stop them from doing this should they choose to do so. Except of course for their decision not to. In that moment, where the decision not to act seems tenuous, weak, vulnerable, arbitrary, that is when we face the full force of vertigo.[9] Deadpool of course might jump, or more likely he would push someone else off the edge. In this way he represents the full force of vertigo realized, especially as the writers and illustrators live out their own existential impulses. We see this when writer Fabian Nicieza (cited in Lussier 2016) notes, "I always say I'm a happier person when I'm working on the character because he allows you to purge a lot of crap from your subconscious. . . . He is like a walking enema for foul thoughts."

Another way to be in bad faith is for a person to deny their *facticity*, or the things that we cannot (in principle) change. These may be few, but they are undeniable. My age is not in my control, nor that I was born, nor that I will die. I can choose to campaign against the need for money to survive and to campaign for a national basic income, but I cannot deny that in the current capitalistic system in which I live, I need money to survive. We choose to continue along a path, but that does not mean that all we find along the path is similarly in our control. That said, while it is true that we cannot write or even rewrite our facticity, "the capacity to determine how some of these characteristics are to be constitutive" (Jopling 1992, 134) remains very much in our control. On this account a situation is not static, nor are the options as limited as we might sometimes want to tell ourselves. Irrespective of external influences, Sartre says, an individual both needs and has the capacity to overcome barriers. We may be limited by the world, but we can always try to *do* something, even if these are ultimately just gestures, a small resistance in the face of helplessness, for example. If nothing else, Sartre suggests, we can effect change in our attitude.

We can read Deadpool's defiant gestures through this lens, regardless of whether they are ultimately futile. He shows this each time he refuses to do as he should, to behave as expected, or to toe the heroes' line. The truths about futility, meaning, resistance, freedom, and so on offered by Deadpool are welcome and desirable. They seem to offer answers to some important questions about our human existence. Yet it is not certainty that is supported by these pages of text and color. In fact, any truths found in these pages mimic the existential truths of our lived reality: seemingly meaningful existence has no meaning beyond that which we give. Wittgenstein (1965, 6) points to this when he describes the idea of facts without ethics. For instance, he says, though we can "read the description of a murder with all its details physical and psychological, the mere description of these facts will contain nothing which we could call an ethical proposition. The murder will be on exactly the same level as any other event, for instance the falling of a stone." This image is brought to life when we see in full, glorious color the many brutal murders committed by Deadpool and yet continue to turn the pages.

That a murder *might* mean more to us, or that we might want it to, is evidently not something captured in the event itself. We turn the pages of a Deadpool comic, but we might do so with the comfort that they're not real murders after all. So it is in our feeling toward the event that the meaning of a murder is captured. It is also in the wish for the event to contain this meaning. For instance, we may want to say that it is always a morally heinous act to commit murder. Yet to say this requires that we also explain why some murders are tolerated and others are sanctioned. If the rule is that murder is the *wrong road*, we ought to be compelled never to follow it. My wish for this while ignoring that people do murder other people and that this is sometimes sanctioned in law, in culture, in religion would lead me into bad faith. That I wish it is not so does not deny the facticity of its being so. Deadpool recognizes and embodies this contradiction (some lives are somehow valuable; others are not), and his actions demand that the reader also recognize it. This, I suggest, should cement his identity as an existential antihero. But I have one more argument to really seal the deal, and this is to suggest that this existential choice, freedom, and responsibility, plus associated concepts of vertigo and bad faith, become ours to carry once Deadpool breaks the fourth wall. It is here that his claim to some sort of heroism, by showing stark truths about human existence, can finally be established.

Existential Fourth Wall-Breaking

Breaking the fourth wall happens when a creative medium acknowledges, within its own presentation, that the reality it presents is not in fact real. So, in comics, this happens "[w]hen a comic strip acknowledges that it is only a comic strip" (Thoss 2011, 554). While Thoss (2011, 552) also notes a "conspicuous and significant increase in metareference" in the comic genre, Deadpool is unusual in that the breaking of his wall has now come to define his identity. In fact it is an identity tied up with the breaking of things generally: of rules, of people, of walls. While the breaking of the wall does not necessarily impact on the reality of his existential existence, it does, I suggest, offer a direct challenge to ours.

In one sense, breaking the fourth wall presents a fertile method for engaging the reader in the backdoor antics, private thoughts as well as the central or trivial beliefs and observations of characters, things that no other character may know. In this respect, it occupies a similar space to that of the theatrical aside or soliloquy favored by William Shakespeare, or the *Dear Reader* trope that is popular with novelists like Jane Austen. Breaching the performance fantasy also plays a role in pantomime. Yet, such literary devices allow us to slip through the wall for typically only a short time, inviting intimacy, colluding with and entreating an audience to join the protagonist in their world.[10] Where the fourth wall is challenged continually, the structure of the work is compromised, and the audience's passivity—their very identity as audience—is confronted.

The character Deadpool regularly and uncompromisingly directs his attention outside of his story, toward author and audience alike, and to the surprise of other characters. This part of his identity seems to have occurred somewhat circumstantially. Kelly explains that "addressing the audience came about simply because the character was 'completely insane.'... 'The fact he's so nutty and out of his mind made it appropriate to do that stuff. And honestly, I was kind of finding my voice as a writer'" (Lussier 2016). This is now crucial to his identity as Deadpool and is also central to his position as an existential antihero, one who regularly "confronts the senselessness of death, the concomitant emptiness of the future, and the conclusions that life in the present must thus have no absolute meaning or significance" (Palumbo 1983, 69, as a description of Spider-Man). Deadpool the sometime vigilante, sometime anarchist, hero and villain, breaks the fourth wall of meaningful existence particularly when he disrupts the expected relation between reason and action. Why does Deadpool act as he does, I ask again? Who knows,

Figure 3.4: Deadpool's truth in *Kills* as experienced by Professor X. From *Deadpool Kills the Marvel Universe #3*. Cullin Bunn and Dalibor Talajić, 2016. © Marvel Comics.

must remain the answer. Deadpool *chooses*, but sometimes without purpose. Maybe nothing matters, yet actions are still chosen.

In *Deadpool Kills the Marvel Universe* issue #3 (Bunn and Talajić 2016), Deadpool explains to Professor X, "So what if I break the fourth wall? It's the fourth wall that's been breaking me . . . crushing me . . . crushing each and every one of us . . . for as long as we've been in existence" (ellipses in original). Soon after, Wade gives Professor X access to his mind, and it is clear that the truth of this statement is felt by Xavier. This is shown in the subtlety of Professor X's verbal response, "Oh . . . I *never* . . . realized," (ellipses in original) as compared to the magnitude of his bodily response: this reality seems to cause *brain death*, as Wade describes it. Or as he then goes

Figure 3.5: Deadpool's truth in *Kills* as experienced by Taskmaster. From *Deadpool Kills the Marvel Universe #3*. Cullin Bunn and Dalibor Talajić, 2016. © Marvel Comics.

on to declare, "The truth will set you free, huh? Or vegetize you at least!" This idea of the power of truth is reinforced later in issue #4 when he fights Taskmaster, whose ability to mimic Deadpool's moves gives him access to Deadpool's inner voice and thereby access to the truth about existence (see figure 3.5). Taskmaster's fear quickly becomes his vulnerability and thereafter his downfall. But what is the truth that Deadpool has faced and wants others to know?

Actually it's pretty unexciting. Truth in this context includes recognition that capitalist market priorities dominate the seemingly extraordinary and metaphysical world of all superheroes. As he bluntly states to Wolverine in issue #3, "Your tendency to come back from the brink of death has nothing to do with your healing factor. Your mutant power isn't regeneration. It's popularity." And in this moment we see that the dedication of so-called heroes toward a good or an ethical end is in fact cover for the real aims and goals: to sell comics. These characters we are induced to like are likable not because they are inherently good, but because they are useful. They, like us, are but pawns in a capitalist machine, and in that machine all meaning is manufactured for the good of money acquisition.[11]

Our participation in the harm and presentation of harm is not incidental. We are complicit because the harm is for our consumption, and in that, our existential identity is engaged as consumers of harm. If we are what we do, in a simplistic account of Sartre's existentialism, then what we are (as readers of superheroes, Deadpool not excluded) is at the mercy of capitalist-driven presentations of violence, heroism, and harm. This is not to say we cannot choose otherwise, our freedom remains, after all, but for as long as we find meaning in the aims of capitalism, there too we find the nexus of our identity.

In *Deadpool Kills the Marvel Universe* (Bunn and Talajić 2016), we are targeted directly by Deadpool. As Uatu the Watcher is killed in issue #1, so our fate as watcher is also in jeopardy. "Who were you talking to?" Wade demands of Uatu (who had been talking directly to us, the readers), and when answer there comes none, he adds, "Well whoever they are—those little Peeping Toms out there in never-never land—they're gonna want to keep their eyes peeled. They're gonna want to see what's next. They're gonna want to watch this world burn." Deadpool, "the man looking in from the outside," as he describes himself in issue #4, stands in our shoes as well as his own, in his world and ours. In each he sees, and shows, the meaninglessness, even pointlessness, of existence. Our freedom to choose is tied to our willingness to recognize these existential truths, and for those unwilling to see them, he responds sometimes with scorn, sometimes pity, but more often than not, with indifference. There is no single right road, despite what some of the other heroes might think or pretend, so Deadpool turns his attention to defying the structures that perpetuate the myths of certainty, whether of moral codes, or of meaning.

Scherr (2013, 142) notes that breaking the wall in literature points "to the existence of several levels of address happening simultaneously." For Deadpool, there is his existence in the comic, his engagement with the (his) authors, and finally his direct address to us as audience. Yet Scherr (2013, 142) questions, "how can we untangle (or perhaps we cannot untangle) these layers of narration?" What Scherr (2013, 143) describes as being "fully immersed in the emotional world of the text," I suggest is a call to reciprocal recognition between the reader and the work, with all the blurring of identities that such relationships demand. The reader must respond and engage. There are choices to make, responsibility to take, and little or no guidance as to what judgment to follow. As per our engagement with Rorschach "the act of looking becomes implicative; the spectator is bound to the image (the act of looking imbuing it with meaning) and is thus no longer able to claim distance or detachment from it" (Petty 2015, 157). Via Deadpool, existential antihero, the sheer potentiality of choice, action, and responsibility becomes clear. Deadpool shows us what Sartre had stated: we are condemned to be free, and that is a burden both liberating and overwhelming.

When Deadpool breaks that wall between his world and ours, we as audience are forcibly, yet somehow willingly (we do keep reading, after all) deprived of passivity. As the character entreats the reader to respond and engage, the audience has choices to make and responsibility for their ongoing participation in such worlds. This freedom—the necessary choices and the resultant responsibility—is central to existential principles, where existence precedes essence, and the reader is in the constant process of becoming that which they *will* and choose via action. In this way, breaking the fourth wall represents an opportunity for existential reflection and engagement by the audience. This is particularly clear in those instances where Deadpool is at his most morally repugnant, while in so doing suggesting that such action is mostly irrelevant anyway. Where, on the one hand, we have the choice to step off a cliff or not, on the other we have the choice to read and view horrible things, or to take a stand against them. Just as we have the choice to look at the car crash that both repels and attracts our attention, or to show the people involved some kindness and respect by looking away.

And if by now, dear reader, you are not convinced, then at least you know that it is your decision to make, with all the responsibility that goes with that. This, like any other choice, no matter how difficult, unpleasant, or overwhelming, is decidedly, uncompromisingly, and necessarily yours to make. And the worst part about all this is that these choices may be just as repugnant and yet as meaningless as those made by Deadpool. For all these reasons and more, he stands as the existential antihero for all who must choose and all who must live with the choices that they make.

Notes

I will try to keep this acknowledgment footnote brief, but it is not easy when the two people in question have provided so much. Also, since I have avoided Deadpool-style meandering soliloquys elsewhere in the chapter, I am hoping I might be permitted to get away with a stream of consciousness here. First to thank Dr. Thomas Giddens, and not because I have to (he is not the sort to need empty praise). Instead I thank him most sincerely because he has been truly helpful, supportive, and thoughtful throughout. He is an exceptionally reasonable editor and without him there would not be this chapter. Despite all of which assistance, any failings are fully my own. Second to Dr. Stephen Rainey, my fellow philosopher in the interdisciplinary wonderland. For the usual support, understanding, and proofreading, but also much more. When I did not want or know how to prepare my comics bio-panel for the introduction, he took my ideas and made them real. You may think the sketch is basic at best, but without his help you would be looking at the scribblings of an incompetent three-year-old who does not even want to draw anything, thank you very much. He also helped to formulate note one (below). In short, a huge and important influence, even if (once again) he can take no blame for the failures which must, dear reader, remain ever and unequivocably of my own fault. I also want to thank the contributors at the "Comics and Critique" symposium where this paper was presented, so this is that. Finally to the reviewers, who said helpful things, thanks very much.

1. In terms of its critical studies identity, this chapter offers an analysis of some philosophical theories of being, particularly in relation to the social and political dimensions of those theories. The chapter explores how these analyses illuminate the character of Deadpool, and in this way it offers an exploration of Deadpool's comics medium itself. This is especially in relation to the breaking of the fourth wall and how this aspect of Deadpool in particular represents a reflexive moment in both the comic book story and the relationships among comics media, character mediation, and audience.

2. Readers familiar with Deadpool's history will know the controversy surrounding the Deathstroke (DC) / Deadpool (Marvel) overlap. I do not discuss this here, except to acknowledge it. Indeed the similarity in name makes the overlap pretty obvious.

3. It is worth noting that heroes in ancient Greek mythology are more akin to modern day antiheroes than this definition suggests.

4. Existentialism is a broad philosophy with a rich history and lots of central protagonists. This includes philosophers like Kierkegaard, Nietzsche, and Heidegger, all with more or less connection to theistic and/or political accounts of the term. I have limited my focus to Sartre. For more on Heidegger and Nietzsche in relation to comics, see Thomson (2005).

5. In this he has borrowed liberally from Heidegger's *dasein*.

6. Sartre's account of authenticity is sometimes understood as a kind of radical individualism (see for instance Soloman 1988, who describes Sartre as the ultimate individualist). This is rather reductive, however, and ignores Sartre's account of the individual as responsible both for one's own development and for humankind generally. Every action is, in the Kantian deontological sense, an example for the rest of humanity. His comment that "in fashioning myself I fashion man" (1973, 30), represents his attempt to show why existentialism and humanism are intimately connected (note also that the title of the text is *Existentialism Is a Humanism* in some translations).

7. It is worth noting that Sartre's ideas seem to evolve from these more extreme claims in his early work to a rather softer approach offered in the later philosophy. It seems that he began to recognize the external and (at times) uncontrollable limitations and constraints to a person's freedom, or for their potential to choose. This includes, for instance, "class background and historical milieu" (Jopling 1992, 128). Perhaps for these reasons we see in his later philosophy a focus on the "practical freedom to change our situation" (Jopling 1992, 128) as opposed to psychological freedom. We nevertheless remain responsible for our actions. Simone de Beauvoir offers some important criticism of Sartre's rather stark accounts

of existential choice and freedom, not least by addressing the very limited choices available to some as compared to that which is available to others. More particularly, she points to the variance in both scope and quality of available choices for different kinds of people in different kinds of circumstances. See *The Second Sex* ([1949] 2010) for more commentary on Sartre's sometimes naïve account of freedom, among other analysis.

8. It is worth a nod to Aristotle's *Poetics* here, particularly on the topic of catharsis.

9. I have used this example to explain Sartre's concept of vertigo many, many times over the years. In that time, very few people (vanishingly few) have expressed surprise at the idea. Typically the response includes relief at hearing their own experience expressed, and knowing they are not alone in these thoughts. This seemingly common, but worrying or even shameful mental experience neatly describes the existential anxiety caused by limitless potential. It is a feeling akin to that described by popular reference to *The Imp of the Perverse*. This phenomenon, named after the character in a short story by Edgar Allan Poe, enables the author to explore just these kinds of apparently self-destructive impulses, though it is important to note that vertigo has no inherent or predetermined moral right or wrong attached to or implied by it, nor is it inherently self-destructive. The sense of finding freedom overwhelming is what remains central.

10. There are of course many similar and related techniques, including where the nature of reality is challenged by characters, with the opportunity to enter another realm or level (depending on the working metaphor). Yet stories and films in this genre (such as *The Matrix*, *Being John Malkovich*, and *Inception*) do not challenge the fourth wall, and thus are not considered here. Meanwhile, novels such as *If on a Winter's Night a Traveler* by Italo Calvino, and *Six Characters in Search of an Author* by Luigi Pirandello do break walls, though more typically from author to audience. There is not, however, the sense in which the character's very development or identity relies on such actions, so these offer little by way of comparison to Deadpool as a fourth wall-breaker.

11. For further reading on this, see Brienza and Johnston (2016). And on the wider contextual factors of comics production and how they can be understood to affect the comics produced, see notably the chapter by Maggie Gray in the present volume. And on the evils of capitalism in an ecological context, the chapter by Thomas Giddens.

References

Brienza, Casey, and Paddy Johnston. 2016. *Cultures of Comics Work*. London: Palgrave Macmillan.

Bunn, Cullen, and Dalibor Talajić. 2016. *Deadpool Kills the Marvel Universe*. New York: Marvel.

Camus, Albert. (1942) 1982. *The Outsider*. Translated by Joseph Laredo. London: Penguin.

de Beauvoir, Simone. (1949) 2010. *The Second Sex*. Translated by Constance Borde and Sheila Malovany-Chevallier. New York: Vintage Books.

Hamilton, Stephen. 2016. "History of Deadpool." *Geeks*. Accessed July 6, 2018. https://geeks.media/history-of-deadpool.

Jopling, David A. 1992. "Sartre's Moral Psychology." In *The Cambridge Companion to Sartre*, edited by Christina Howells, 103–39. Cambridge: Cambridge University Press.

Jonason, Peter K., Gregory D. Webster, David P. Schmitt, Norman P. Li, and Laura Crysel. 2012. "The Antihero in Popular Culture: Life History Theory and the Dark Triad Personality Traits." *Review of General Psychology* 16 (2): 192–99.

Lamont, Rosette C. 1962. "The Hero in Spite of Himself." *Yale French Studies* 29: 73–81.

Lussier, Germain. 2016. "The Unlikely Origins of Deadpool, The X-Men Character Who Conquered All Media." *Gizmodo*, August 2, 2016. https://io9.gizmodo.com/the-unlikely -origins-of-deadpool-the-x-men-character-w-1757814457.

Marvel Directory. n.d. "Deadpool." Accessed July 6, 2018. http://www.marveldirectory.com/ individuals/d/deadpool.htm.

Moore, Alan, and Dave Gibbons. 1986. *Watchmen*. New York: DC Comics.

The New Mutants #98. 1991. New York: Marvel Comics.

Palumbo, Donald. 1983. "The Marvel Comics Group's Spider-Man Is an Existentialist Super-Hero: Or 'Life Has No Meaning without My Latest Marvels!'" *Journal of Popular Culture* 17 (2): 67–82.

Petty, James. 2015. "Violent Lives, Ending Violently? Justice, Ideology and Spectatorship in *Watchmen*." In *Graphic Justice: Intersections of Comics and Law*, edited by Thomas Giddens, 147–63. London: Routledge.

Regalado, Aldo. 2005. "Modernity, Race, and the American Superhero." In *Comics as Philosophy*, edited by Jeff McLaughlin, 84–99. Jackson: University Press of Mississippi.

Sartre, Jean-Paul. (1943) 2001. *Being and Nothingness*. Translated by Hazel E. Barnes. London: Routledge.

Sartre, Jean-Paul. (1947) 1988. *What Is Literature? and Other Essays*. Translated by Bernard Frechtman. Cambridge, MA: Harvard University Press.

Sartre, Jean-Paul. (1948) 1973. *Existentialism and Humanism*. Translation by Philip Mairet. London: Methuen.

Scherr, Rebecca. 2013. "Teaching 'The Auto-graphic Novel': Autobiographical Comics and the Ethics of Readership." In *Graphic Novels and Comics in the Classroom*, edited by Rob Weiner and Carrye Syma, 134–44. Jefferson: McFarland.

Schilpp, Paul A., ed. 1997. *The Philosophy of Jean Paul Sartre*. La Salle: Open Court.

Shafer, Daniel M., and Arthur A. Raney. 2012. "Exploring How We Enjoy Antihero Narratives." *Journal of Communication* 62 (6): 1028–46.

Simone, Gail. 2003. *Agent X: Deadpool Walkin' Part 3. Vol 1 #15*. New York: Marvel.

Soloman, Robert C. 1988. *Continental Philosophy since 1750: The Rise and Fall of the Self*. Oxford: Oxford University Press.

Thomson, Iain. 2005. "Deconstructing the Hero." In *Comics as Philosophy*, edited by Jeff McLaughlin, 100–29. Jackson: University Press of Mississippi.

Thoss, Jeff. 2011. "'This Strip Doesn't Have a Fourth Wall': Webcomics and the Metareferential Turn." *International Ford Madox Ford Studies* 10: 551–68.

Willaert, Kate. 2013. "You Don't Know Merc: A History of Deadpool." *A Critical Hit,* July 8, 2013. http://www.acriticalhit.com/you-dont-know-merc-a-history-of-deadpool/.

Williams, Owen. 2015. "Deadpool: A Complete History." *Empire*, August 24, 2015. https:// www.empireonline.com/movies/features/deadpool-complete-history/.

Wittgenstein, Ludwig. 1965. "I: A Lecture on Ethics." *Philosophical Review* 74 (1): 3–12.

4

Theological "Seeing" of Law

Daredevil, Christian Iconography, and Legal Aesthetics

TIMOTHY D. PETERS

Introduction

My argument in this chapter is that comics involve a form of critical *seeing*—and, in particular, a critical seeing of law. I analyze not just what it is that we *see* when we read or view comics, but a way of "seeing" both law and the world "with" comics and in a theological context. The etymology of "comics," as Thomas Giddens has argued, intertwines law and comics in this mode of critical seeing: the Greek *komos* invoked both a space of play and merriment but also a mediation between the ordering of *nomos* and the chaos it supposedly subdues (Giddens 2018, xiv–xv). The playfulness of the comics image, its ability to catch and direct the eye, combined with the substantive themes of law and justice regularly deployed in the multiplicity of comics narratives (Phillips and Strobl 2013), become important for an understanding of an aesthetics of the legal and of the legal imaginary—an imaginary made up of images that are fed by these (amongst other) visual forms (Douzinas and Nead 1999; MacNeil 2007; Sherwin 2011; Goodrich 2014). Operating at the intersection of critical comics studies and cultural legal studies, this chapter unpacks this form of critical legal visuality through a reading of the superhero character Daredevil and his comics. While Daredevil provides an obvious reference point for a legal reading (as both a superhero fighting for justice beyond the law *and* his alter-ego Matt Murdock's role as lawyer), it is the focus on the themes of sight, the visual, and blindness that draws my attention here. Daredevil/Murdock's blindness invokes the idea of justice being blind and the depictions of Lady Justice or Justitia as blindfolded. However, the significance of the image of the blindfold is that it is a projection of blindness—a taking up of a nonlooking—that is presented in visual form: we are enjoined to *see* both Justitia's blindfold and Daredevil's mask which projects this blindness. This chapter begins to elaborate an analysis of comics as a form of critical seeing, by drawing on the work of Maurice Merleau-Ponty and not only his phenomenological account of sight, perception, and vision but the way in which he approaches cultural and artistic visual texts as ones which encourage us to "see with" them. In the context of Daredevil, it is the very focus on the embodied nature of Daredevil's experience and perception that draws out this mode of experiential seeing.

I then bring together the theological jurisprudence of Daredevil and theological readings of Merleau-Ponty through an analysis of two particular narrative arcs. In Kevin Smith's *Guardian Devil* Daredevil is positioned in an explicitly theological context—with virgin births, Christian redeemers, antichrists, and demons—encouraging him to exercise a theological seeing by faith. The theological aspects of this narrative are then revealed to be a series of illusions, special effects, and drug-induced sensations leaving a mundane vision of reality denuded of any spiritual content. By contrast, Frank Miller and David Mazzucchelli's *Born Again* takes a different approach to such theological content by a deployment of the comics form which draws explicitly on Catholic iconography. The formal aspects of the comics involve a theological "seeing" of reality and invite an affirmation of the real as actual: a "seeing" of the transcendent within the immanent, and the invisible within the visible. This can be contrasted with the approach to the law in the comics that sees it bound to a certain manipulability and plasticity which, in its very questioning of sight, opens it up to *further* deception. My argument is that the process of "seeing with" the comics form invokes both a greater sense of encountering and experiencing the world as real, as actual, and with which we should engage but also, following Giddens, a possibility of re-forming our approach to law itself.

The Blind Lawyer, the Vigilante Superhero, and Lady Justice

Given his appearance on both the big (Johnson 2003) and "small" (Goddard 2015) screen in recent years, the origins of Daredevil are fairly well known. First debuting with his own title in April 1964 (Lee, Everett, and Rosen 1964), Daredevil is the superhero alter-ego of Matt Murdock, attorney-at-law. Matt was encouraged to study rather than play with other kids by his father, boxer "Battlin' Jack" Murdock, so that he could make something of himself and become a doctor or lawyer. One day Matt is hit by radioactive waste from a truck while pushing a blind man out of the way. The accident caused both Matt's blindness *and* a "superpower" enhancement to all his other senses, including a radar sense which enabled him to agilely move about and develop heightened gymnastic and fighting abilities. After Matt's father is murdered for not throwing a fight, Matt seeks revenge and eventually becomes the superhero Daredevil—but at the same time desires to "follow the rules," studies prodigiously, and becomes a lawyer. Daredevil therefore embodies the oscillation between "pre-modern law" focused on crime-control and "modern law" focused on due process, which makes up what Jason Bainbridge (2007, 471–76) calls superhero comics' "postmodern interrogation of law." Daredevil also embodies the superhero critique of the law (Peters 2018) by remedying the law's failures and symbolic blindness "to the truth of a 'clearly guilty' criminal" and providing "justice via alternative methods" (Sharp 2012, 358, 361; Young 2016, esp. 58–64). As Anthony Spanakos (2014) notes, Daredevil's critique of the failures of the law even extends to taking up the position of sovereign himself in order to restore a sense of order to the City (see Bendis and Maleev 2010, in particular the "Hardcore" [issues #46–50] and "The King of Hell's Kitchen" [issues #56–60] narrative arcs).

The situating of Daredevil as a figure of both law and "blind justice," while regularly referred to throughout earlier iterations (Young 2016, 22, 62–64), was rendered explicit on the cover of issue #3 of the 2014 Matt Waid run on Daredevil (Waid et al. 2014, #3; see figure 4.1). The focus of the cover is a statue of Justitia, blindfolded with sword and scales. The two basins of the scales form the eyes of a silhouette of Daredevil in the sky behind, invoking the idea of Daredevil hovering behind Lady Justice herself. The connection is further emphasized within the narrative by a reporter who refers to Daredevil being "as blind as the justice he represents" (Waid et al. 2014, #3). This emphasis on the trope of blindness is important. The blindfolds on depictions and sculptures of Justitia around the world are generally seen to invoke "a positive emblem of impartiality and equality before the law" (Jay 1999, 20; see also Curtis and Resnik 1987; Resnik and Curtis 2011; Goodrich 2014; Manderson 2015). Such impartiality is supposedly found in the recourse to procedure, to the law which blinds itself from the particularities of the individual before it, treating like case as like (Jay 1999, 26). Yet, it is the focus on procedure or due process of the law that the superhero figure himself challenges, wanting to deliver a "clear-seeing" justice not bound by the technicalities of the law (Sharp 2012; see also Peters 2018). The superhero therefore would seem to be the *opposite* of the blind justice of the law. While Matt Murdock the lawyer invokes the blindfold of the law's procedure, Daredevil the blind

Figure 4.1: From *Daredevil Vol. 1: Devil at Bay.* Mark Waid, Peter Krause, Javier Rodriguez, and Chris Samnee, 2014, #3. © 2014 Marvel Characters, Inc.

superhero is more "seeing" in delivering justice. Murdock/Daredevil's two personas therefore represent the tensions of modernity's subsumption of the particularity of justice to the generality of law (Jay 1999; see also Bainbridge 2007; Sharp 2012).

The blindfold, however, is a relatively recent appearance in the history of depictions of Justice (see Jay 1999; Curtis and Resnik 1987; Resnik and Curtis 2011; Goodrich 2014). As Jay and others have pointed out, earlier figures of Justitia, whether Roman or medieval, showed images of justice as unveiled, making judgments on the basis of visual evidence and clear-sightedness (Jay 1999, 19). It is only at the end of the fifteenth century that "a blindfold began to be placed over the goddess's eyes, producing what has rightly been called 'the most enigmatic of the attributes of Justice'" (Jay 1999, 20, quoting Jacob; see also Goodrich 2014, chapter 5). What is more, the first depictions of the blindfold were not presented in seriousness but involved a fool covering Justice from behind—invoking, at least to a degree, the sense of merriment, foolishness, and *komos*, referred to in Giddens's (2018) work noted above. "Initially . . . the blindfold implies that Justice has been robbed of her ability to get things straight, wield her sword effectively, to see what is balanced on her scales" (Jay 1999, 20). While these early images were satirical and the blindfold depicted in a negative fashion, it was not long before the blindfold became viewed positively, supposedly indicating impartiality and equality (Jay 1999; Goodrich 2014; Manderson 2015). Yet, as Robert Cover pointed out, the concrete significance of the image is not that it represents blindness but rather that the putting on of a blindfold involves a willingness to impose "a makeshift screen between reality and decision" (Curtis and Resnik 1987, 1728, quoting Cover). This is a deliberate turning away from sight because of the risk of being influenced by it—an act of self-restraint which the legal rules of procedure seek to reaffirm: "[p]rocedure is the blindfold of Justice" (Curtis and Resnik 1987, 1728, quoting Cover).

The historic symbol of the blindfold therefore has a degree of interpretive ambiguity. At one level it is a symbol of error, as the "Figure of Error" in Cesare Ripa's *Iconologia* portrays: "a blindfolded man, groping his way along while tapping the path ahead with a stick" (Goodrich 2014, xxiv). Peter Goodrich describes one of the images in Barthelemy Aneau's *Jurisprudentia* in this context which depicts Justitia as fully sighted "and declaiming from the book of the laws to the muddled, blindfolded assembly of lawyers" (Goodrich 2014, 147). This image suggests "that lawyers do not see very much and are indeed impeded in their efforts by their inability" but it also indicates their "confusion, limitation and, quite simply, lack of vision" (Goodrich 2014, 149).

At the same time, Aneau presents another interpretation—that of restoring justice to its principle position and the requiring of lawyers to undergo severe and lengthy training to understand the law and justice. The blindfold therefore marks ascetism, "deprivation, self-abnegation, and purification" with the aim of preparing the "lawyer-interpreter for a better world and its higher law" (Goodrich 2014, 160). This involves a refusing of the deceptiveness of sight, but at the same time the inability to see with one's physical eyes requires a looking elsewhere, "to use the inner eye, the eye of the spirit, and to search for law *non extima sed intima*" (Goodrich 2014, 161)—inwardly, not outwardly. The symbol of the blindfold reflects not only error but a turn to another form of sight and represents, as Goodrich notes, a spiritual journey from blindness to sight beyond the senses (Goodrich 2014, xxv). Such would appear to be an important warning in today's oversaturated and hypervisual culture of what Richard Sherwin (2011) has termed the "neo-baroque" in which representations proliferate, churning through fictional and factional genres seamlessly, producing a never-ending combination of visual texts for consumption (see Crawley and Peters 2018).

There is a final ambiguity in the figure of the blindfold, however, one which is explicitly deployed by Daredevil. If the blindfold is both a symbol of error and a self-imposed limitation with the aim of being able to "see" more clearly, what do we make of the doubling of such symbolism in relation to someone who is physically blind? Matt's blindness involves his own inability to see through his eyes; it is a physical incapacity (though made up for by his enhanced senses). At the same time, he puts on a mask which covers the eyes signifying, emphasizing, and projecting this blindness. As Daredevil, he requires others to *see* that he is blind, and his inability to see literalizes the sense in which the lawyer must go beyond that which is seen with the eyes. Daredevil's blindness results in his seeing not with the material or physical eye, but with an inner eye, not necessarily an "eye of the spirit" (though at times that is referred to as well), but with his radar sense, and an eye that enables a *greater* seeing than the physical eyes of those around him. In a similar sense, the image of the blindfold as a figure of Error becomes paradoxical: while Ripa's *Iconologia* portrays Error as an image of blindness, a warning about the deceptiveness of the image, "the injunction not to look is transmitted through the medium of an image" (Goodrich 2014, xxvi). The putting on of the blindfold by both Justitia and Daredevil involves a refusal of the deceptiveness of sight and a turning away to something else—but the *image* of the blindfold is one that requires us to *see* it.

A Phenomenology of Comics: Daredevil, Sight, and Embodied Perception

The figure of the blindfold is also symbolic of a greater question about the nature of sight and perception—one that has particular significance in the context of comics studies. For, what is it that we "see" when we look at comics? Ian Hague (2014) has recently argued for the need to go beyond the traditional understanding of comics as an exclusively *visual* medium. He focuses, rather, on our experience of reading a comic as a material one that involves a process of seeing, hearing, feeling, and experiencing the form itself. Hague, therefore, critiques the focus of comics scholarship which operates in accordance with an "ideal perspective"—that what we "see" is supposedly the comic itself "as a clean, flat manifestation of images that are consistent from one copy to the next" and which can be discussed as such (Hague 2014, 34). The problem with this is that, as a result, we ignore the differences of the material experience (Hague 2014, 34–38). Hague provides a sophisticated working through not just of the visuality of comics (both text and images as well as other material aspects—the texture of the paper, the nature of color, the function of eye-motion) but also of our other sensory experiences: the sound of the comic being opened, pages being turned, the feel and smell of the paper. In this focus on the materiality of the comic, he understands the experience of the comic as a "performance" which involves multiple components and an interactivity with the reader/viewer (Hague 2014, 36).

Hague's "multisensorial" approach to comics aims both to move away from the analysis of components that "*simulate* sensation through processes such as synaesthesia" as well as to go beyond seeing comics as a mono-sensory medium (Hague 2014, 27). Drawing on Will Eisner's notion of a "contract" between the producer and receiver of a comic, Hague turns to the "physicality of the comic" as "the site at which the relationships between producer and receiver are negotiated" (Hague 2014, 28). Scott McCloud's (1993) seminal work, *Understanding Comics*, comes under fire a number of times, in particular because of the way McCloud describes comics as mono-sensory. However, what seems to be skimmed across by Hague in his critical approach is the way in which McCloud argues that comics *do* involve the other senses, not just in terms of synaesthesia but through the concept of "closure" and the readerly involvement required through the blank spaces *between* images. There would therefore seem to be some overlap between Hague's focus on the comics as an interactive performance and McCloud's participatory approach which sees the creator and reader "join in a silent dance of the seen and the unseen.

The visible and the invisible" (McCloud 1993, 92). McCloud's language here resonates with the work of Maurice Merleau-Ponty, whose phenomenology of embodied perception and account of cultural works challenge aspects of Hague's focus on materiality.[1] For the comics experience always encompasses *both* the materiality of the comics *as well as* a recognition of that which is depicted in them. Simon Grennan (2017), following Richard Wollheim, has recently analyzed this in the context of a phenomenology of the experience of narrative drawing, arguing that when we read or observe narrative images we engage in a process of "seeing in"—a twofold experience of *both* the materiality of the image *and* that which it depicts (on "seeing in" see Wollheim 2003; see also Alloa 2011). The success of the image often depends on how successful this process of "seeing in" of what is depicted is realized. This reflects and encompasses a particular sense of the embodied experience of the world and our perception of it, as well as the nature of the depictive image. Merleau-Ponty's phenomenology, which Grennan also draws on, emphasizes that what we experience in perception *is not* the individual sense-data that is then reconstructed within the mind, but rather we perceive the object itself (Merleau-Ponty [1945] 2005): "we perceive not just sensations, but things, persons, and indeed, a world" (Edgar 2016, 15). The significance of artistic and cultural works, then, is not so much in their materiality as an object, or in the way in which they represent something that is absent, but how they present a way of seeing itself (Merleau-Ponty [1961] 2007).

As Emmanuel Alloa notes, Merleau-Ponty's focus on the experience of artistic and cultural texts goes beyond the notion of the "twofoldness" of "seeing in" to think their manifoldness (Alloa 2011, 7–8). In his discussion of painting in the essay "Eye and Mind," Merleau-Ponty uses an example which McCloud (1993) also incorporates into his history of comics—the animal paintings at Lascaux. He notes that the animals painted:

> are not there in the same way as are the fissures and limestone formations. Nor are they elsewhere. . . . I would be hard-pressed to say where the picture is that I am gazing at. For I do not gaze at it as one gazes at a thing, I do not fix it in its place. My gaze wanders within it as in the halos of Being. Rather than seeing it, I see according to, or with it. (Merleau-Ponty [1961] 2007, 355, final emphasis added)

When we look at the comics page, while there is ink, color, shading, and lines, as well as the very textures of the paper itself, it is the *images* that we see and they "are not there in the same way" as the page itself. These images are not representations—"a tracing, a copy, a second thing" or "extras that I borrow from the real world in order to aim across them at prosaic things in their absence." Rather they involve "the inside of the outside and the outside of the inside, which the duplicity of sensing [*le sentir*] makes possible and without which we would never understand the quasi-presence and imminent visibility which makes up the whole problem of the imaginary" (Merleau-Ponty [1961] 2007, 356). For Merleau-Ponty this turns on the way in which the function of perception is one that is embodied and does not involve a Cartesian separation of the mind from the body, but rather a process of seeing the world itself: "Since things and my body are made of the same stuff, it is necessary that my body's vision be made somehow in the things, or yet that their manifest visibility doubles itself in my body with a secret visibility" (Merleau-Ponty [1961] 2007, 355). The comics form can therefore be understood not in a representational sense, nor in terms of the individual components that make it up (even if, as Hague demonstrates, an understanding of its materiality is important), but rather in the way in which it enables us to "see with" it and in doing so to also see *beyond* what is simply depicted, for it enables a seeing of the invisible in the visible.

Such an approach becomes particularly important in considering Daredevil because of the way in which the visual form is used to depict Daredevil's blindness as well as his *other* senses. This has been of significance since issue #1 of the first series (Lee, Everett, and Rosen 1964), which explains the enhancement of each of Daredevil's other senses (hearing, smell, touch, and taste) with images depicting the relevant organs (ears, nose, fingers, and mouth). Daredevil then describes his "radar sense" as "a strange tingling sensation when I approach any solid obstacle, warning me which way to turn" (Lee, Everett, and Rosen 1964). This allusion to the organs of the other senses, as a visual representation of Daredevil's enhanced senses is reiterated in later versions of his origin story. Daredevil's superpowers, therefore, involve an extension of his engagement with the world beyond the ordinary forms of habituation and enworldedness that we experience, and there were early attempts to render this experience in visual form. In the comics this takes on a particular iconographic form with Daredevil's radar sense represented by concentric circles radiating out from him and his ability to hear heartbeats represented by the superimposition of EKG-like waveforms onto the page (Young 2016, 29–30). In the 2003 film, these iconographic forms are dramatically reoriented in a way that attempts to present Daredevil's "seeing" of the world through his radar sense via the deployment of blue sound waves in the blackness of blindness. Both Petra Kuppers (2006) and

Larrie Dudenhoeffer (2017, 39–50) have analyzed this filmic portrayal by drawing on Merleau-Ponty's example of the blind man's stick which "has ceased to be an object for him, and is no longer perceived for itself; its point has become an area of sensitivity, extending the scope and active radius of touch, and providing a parallel to sight" (Merleau-Ponty [1945] 2005, 165, quoted by Kuppers 2006, 92). For Kuppers, the visual rendering displays how "the materiality of the world becomes accessible" and "everything is connected—everything exists in the same stratum, not in the separation of vision but in the connectedness of touch" (Kuppers 2006, 93). However, this form of "seeing" is still an iconography—not presenting the actual experience of the world for Daredevil, but its *representation* through these images. It is not an experience of Daredevil's experience of the world but a visual representation of it that we see.

In contrast to this filmic interpretation of what Daredevil "sees," which remains caught in the visual, I turn to the way in which a "seeing with" the comics form can provide a greater way of engaging the other senses. In Frank Miller and David Mazzucchelli's *Born Again*, Murdock, having escaped a murder attempt by the Kingpin and beaten, feverish, and sleeping in the streets, remembers the accident which caused both his blindness and heightened senses (Miller and Mazzucchelli 1986). While not an uncommon retelling of the story there is something unique in the way in which Miller and Mazzucchelli present this form of remembering as an experience for the reader—an experience which captures Murdock's present doubled against his historical memories, along with the experience of blindness. Over the five pages covering this period a vertical thin left panel depicts Matt lying hurt and asleep. On the right are long horizontal panels depicting his remembering, which starts with the young Matt pushing an elderly gentleman out of the way of an oncoming truck and being hit by radioactive waste. As he remembers the recovery period in the hospital, the reader is provided with an ocular representation of blindness. Matt's thoughts are depicted over multiple "blank," or rather black, frames (see figure 4.2)—a blackness representing the experience of blindness which the young Matt woke up to.[2]

At one level this would appear to simply be a process of telling the story through words in a literary form, because the reader "sees" nothing in these "blank" panels except the words. However, Matt's internal monologue, accompanied by the black panels presents both the experience of blindness but also Matt's ability then to "see" through his other senses. This "seeing" of blindness heightens the understanding that we do not experience the senses independently of each other, but, as Merleau-Ponty ([1945] 2005)

Figure 4.2: From *Daredevil: Born Again*. Frank Miller and David Mazzuchelli, 1986, #229. © 2018 Marvel Characters, Inc.

emphasized, as intertwined in the body enabling a perception of the world, a seeing which is not (just) via the eyes. This is not simply in the sense of comics as a form of visual synaesthesia but the way in which our senses themselves *always* involve an intertwined synaesthesia. Sight evokes and operates with other sensations; hearing and taste will conjure up particular images—and this is an ordinary part of all sensation (Landes 2013, 225;

Merleau-Ponty [1945] 2005). As such, this goes beyond simply the process of "seeing in" (the seeing of what is depicted) because it involves the process of "seeing" blindness—engaging the eye in seeing something which is *not* depicted (Alloa 2011). This process is developed across the panels over the five-page sequence. Initially the reader enters into the mode of experiencing Matt's senses in contrast to sight. This begins with descriptions of the sensory experience overlaid against the black panels: the touch of the sheets which are like sandpaper, the overpowering chemical smells of hospital disinfectant, the screaming of the door hinges as someone enters the room, the smell of people "like bathtubs full of sweat—smelling like eaten food—like Italian sauces and half-digested eggs" (Miller and Mazzucchelli 1986). It then shifts to oversized colored words representing the discussions which sound like shouts to Matt's ears. As the reader has gotten used to the contrast between the sense-evoking words and the blackness of the panels, the fact that Matt can "see" through these other senses is depicted by the silhouettes of the nun kissing his forehead, the gold cross hanging down which he feels. This trajectory of the panels takes the reader from initially seeing with the eyes, to a nonseeing because of blindness, then to a seeing without the eyes. For the reader, this progression is thrown into relief when the pages turn back to the regularized, color-filled panels, but in doing so it depicts a trajectory of the forms of seeing. This encompasses both an internal vision—experiencing what Matt is experiencing—at the same time as the depiction of Matt as this other body, battered, bruised, and exhausted.

This sequence presents Matt's embodied experience—emphasized explicitly by the overheightened sensations which he perceives first in terms of his own body: he describes his blood as burning, spurting "from a heart that's pounding so loudly it's trying to burst from my chest—my blood—it gushes through high power hoses and slams against the base of my skull" (Miller and Mazzucchelli 1986). The heightened reflection on what is an ordinary occurrence, estranged by Matt's description of it, returns the reader to a sense of their own body—a reflection on the sensation of blood pumping through our veins which, in ordinary circumstances, we do not feel or even think about. This emphasizes a sense of the embodied nature of our perception, which starts first with the perception of our own bodily functions. At the same time, this reflection from the portrayal of Matt's experience and perception to the reader's reflection on their own body goes to the significance of our experience of the world—a shared vision and experience of the body as the "ground that human beings share with each other and with the material world" (Edgar 2016, 4). This involves not only the way in which our experience of the world involves a reversibility of the self—as a seer I can also be seen and I am both object and subject at the same time—but also a reversibility in relation to the other: "[t]he handshake too is reversible; I can feel myself touched as well and at the same time as touching" (Merleau-Ponty 1968, 142). This encompasses a form of intersubjectivity or intercorporeality—a "shared belonging to the reversible flesh of the world" (Landes 2013, 115; Merleau-Ponty 1968)—that the reader is engaged in (see Grennan 2017).

(Theological) Seeing Is (Not) Believing: Image and Illusion in Kevin Smith's *Guardian Devil*

While my analysis above points to the way in which the presentation of Daredevil's other modes of seeing can involve an invitation to "see with" the comics form and to emphasize both embodied perception but also a recognition of our intercorporeal and intersubjective being-in-the-world, the reference to an alternative or "inner sight" also has a different allusion—one which aligns with a later development of the Daredevil mythos: his Catholicism (Morris 2005). As Paul Young notes, one of Miller's enduring additions to Daredevil was to give him religion and to make him a devout Catholic—something made explicit in *Born Again* (Young 2016, 58). Kevin Smith's *Guardian Devil* (Smith, Quesada, and Palmiotti 1998)—the narrative arc which kicked off a new era of Daredevil as part of the Marvel Knights imprint—takes this Catholic dimension even further focusing, in particular, on Murdock's "seeing otherwise" as a form of theological sight. *Guardian Devil* involves a villain trying to drive Daredevil crazy through a deliberate theological parody. Murdock receives a visit from a young mother claiming that she gave birth to a baby without having "known" a man. She says that an angel appeared to her and revealed that Matt/Daredevil would look after the baby and keep it safe because the baby is the returned redeemer. Matt subsequently receives a visit from an older gentleman claiming the opposite: the baby is the antichrist and must be destroyed. The narrative leads through a range of bizarre experiences, including visitations from the demon Baal, the use of "angel shrieks" to incapacitate Daredevil, and his mistrust of his good friend Natasha Romanov (the Black Widow) and his ex-girlfriend Karen Paige who are attempting to care for the baby. The theological tale starts to unravel when Daredevil goes to "Sorcerer Supreme" Doctor Strange who summons and questions Mephisto (Marvel's version of the Devil) about the potential return of the Christian redeemer. Mephisto laughs as the question shows ignorance of the Christian writings—the second coming of Christ will *not* be like the first so the idea that *this* virgin birth is a return of Christ is erroneous. These supernatural tropes are eventually revealed as a range of sophisticated illusions and deceptions (aided by hallucinogenic drugs) by a second-rate villain (Mysterio) diagnosed with terminal cancer who wants to generate a crisis of faith in Daredevil and make a name for himself before he dies.

Mysterio's deceptions here play explicitly on Daredevil's faith—invoking his supposed ability to spiritually "see" without his eyes. While there are a range of puns on the dichotomy of Matt's ability to see despite his blindness, this is positioned as an explicitly theological capability when Mysterio (disguised as the old man) warns Daredevil that the child is the antichrist and harbinger of destruction. In trying to convince him of the significance of the spiritual intervention, he refers to what Daredevil has "seen" over his lifetime and asks that "you call upon your lack of sight to get beyond what may seem obvious." He describes the unseen world as being "beyond human comprehension" and that it "offers no answers, and resists the categorization that humanity demands" (Smith, Quesada, and Palmiotti 1998). While this would appear to involve an affirmation of a theological and spiritual beyond that sits behind the deceptive appearances of reality, Mysterio's denouement toward the end of the narrative arc presents the opposite: the deceptiveness of such a faith and its openness to manipulation. Describing himself as "of the Church of Smoke and Mirrors" he says that he leaves praying "to the unenlightened" like Daredevil (Smith, Quesada, and Palmiotti 1998). It is therefore the desire and expectation of a theological sight or seeing that is manipulated and caught in illusion. The "turning away" from sight which the blindfold represents, does not necessarily render us immune to being deceived.

This supposedly modernist presentation (that theology is an illusion, and faith simply a manipulation that can be revealed in all its falsity) itself has a particular theological heritage—one which can be traced back not only to questions and concerns with perception and the image, but to changes in the very understanding of the nature of God. As Phillip Blond (1999, 2003) and others have noted, the rise of medieval nominalism involved a denial of universals and, in particular, the denial of universals to vision. This involved a shift away from the participatory ontology of St. Thomas Aquinas, to a voluntarist theology established by Henry of Ghent, Duns Scotus, and William of Ockham "which drained the universal forms and structures from the world of nature" (Blond 2003, 44; on the inheritance of this shift see Milbank 2013). The result was that "the world became viewed as an arbitrary epiphenomenon of God's (possibly malign) will" essentially making "the real world a myth" (Blond 2003, 45). As Blond goes on to note, the "consequence of this erasure of form or universality from visibility has dictated *virtually all* subsequent accounts of sensibility and intuition" (Blond 2003, 45). Sense experience becomes "something that true knowledge has to overcome, ignore, abstract from or add to in order to reach anything like a rational account of what it is that is seen" (Blond 2003, 45). As a result, we have come to question our perception of the world, and in particular sight, because of the risk of being deceived. What follows, therefore, is a need to turn away from sight or perception to other forms of knowledge—a point which can be traced through the origins of modernity and, in particular, Descartes's subjectivity, which focuses on a methodological doubt that would question any form of bodily experience or perception (Merleau-Ponty [1945] 2005, xvii–xviii, 429–75; see also Jay 1993). Such would seem to be of significance in today's age of the image which titillates and stimulates emotion, questioning divisions between reality and illusion (Sherwin 2011)—and which has often been linked to the denigration of comics itself.[3]

In *Guardian Devil*, Mysterio reproduces modernity's critique of theology in terms of superstition, illusion, and deception, in turn seeking to unmask or disenchant the world and stand clear-sighted on empirical or logical knowledge. The depiction of the theological narrative as deliberate deception and illusion by a second-rate character (the Wizard of Oz as a bumbling fool behind the curtain) indicates that faith in the supernatural is simply a belief in magical tricks or deception. However, the way in which Matt discovers these illusions involves a specific affirmation of sense perception itself—one which calls into question this approach to illusion as deception. Once the drugs are removed from his system, Daredevil is able to penetrate the illusions, determining that the "angel's shriek" is a recording on repeat, hearing the hum of the battery pack operating Baal's suit and feeling the synthetic cloth of Karen Paige's "flesh" in his "vision" of her in hell. It is Daredevil's enhanced sensory perception which enables him to "see through" the deceptions: specifically identifying their artificiality. Following Merleau-Ponty, this does not then call into question but rather affirms the world:

> For in so far as we talk about illusion, it is because we have identified illusions, and done so solely in light of some perception which at the same time gave assurance of its own truth. It follows that doubt, or the fear of being mistaken, testifies as soon as it arises to our power of unmasking error, and that it could never finally tear us away from truth. (Merleau-Ponty [1945] 2005, xviii)

At 5:26 p.m, the savior was left in the devil's care.

Figure 4.3: From *Daredevil: Guardian Devil*. Kevin Smith, Joe Quesada, and Jimmy Palmiotti, 1998, #1. © 2012 Marvel Characters, Inc.

What is most significant, however, is the way in which the dichotomy of illusion and deception is reproduced in *Guardian Devil* at the level of form.
One feature of the layouts and design by Smith and Joe Quesada involves a
tension between the surface and sequence (to use Hatfield's terminology)
(Hatfield 2005, 48–58; Hague 2014, 46–47). Many of the pages deploy a full-
page background image which presents part of the broader setting of the
scene, with specific panels superimposed on top of the background featuring
the narrative action. For example, at one time Daredevil attacks muggers in
the street and the background image shows aspects of the alley, whereas the
narrative and story occurs in the individual frames superimposed on top
(Smith, Quesada, and Palmiotti 1998). This tension between background
and narrative (between surface and sequence) is altered whenever there is
reference to the supernatural or spiritual occurring during the narrative. At
those points, the background image upon which the narrative panels are
superimposed, is not of the scene but rather of gothic images and figures of
angels and demons (see figure 4.3). These background images are grayed out
and feature stronger shading and etching, providing a heightened contrast
with the vivid colors and realistic lines of the narrative images. These images
present a sense of the spiritual *behind* the experiences and scenes occurring
in the diegetic world. While this provides an effective way of demonstrating
the supernatural narrative, at each of these points it is Mysterio's illusions
that are being presented—and there is therefore no literal demonic or angelic
activity occurring. That is, the background images, which evoke a sense of the
spiritual impinging upon Matt's life and experiences, portray a theological
conception of the transcendent or spiritual as separate from the world, but in
actual fact are a process of deceiving the reader. In this sense, while Mysterio
is defeated by Daredevil, the use of the comics form reproduces and affirms
his critique. *Guardian Devil* presents a form of "seeing with" comics that is
played upon to both deceive the reader and to present a world disenchanted
and denuded of theology.

Seeing the World *with* Comics: The Theological Iconography of Frank Miller and David Mazzucchelli's *Born Again*

Whereas the theological narrative of *Guardian Devil* presents a critique of
a theological form of seeing as always at risk of being caught in deception,
Miller and Mazzucchelli's *Born Again* emphasizes a different theological
seeing in the comics form. This involves not so much a "seeing in" of the

theological references (the spiritual depicted as behind the physical), but rather a form of "seeing" the transcendent in the immanent and therefore affirming a depth to the world which encompasses both our experience of the world *and* our recognition that the world is so much more than our experience of it. This approach aligns with a number of theological readings of Merleau-Ponty's work that emphasize the incarnational and participatory ontology rather than a nominalist one—a focus on our sense of participation in creation (Blond 1999, 2003; Milbank 2001a, 2001b, 2013; Edgar 2016). *Born Again* was published and set earlier than Smith's *Guardian Devil*, but draws explicitly on the Christian narrative in depicting a supposed death and resurrection for Daredevil/Murdock. At a narrative level this involves a stripping of everything from Murdock—his job, his license to practice law, his home, his savings. His girlfriend of the time ends up with his best friend and ex-partner, Foggy, and his now drug-dependent past girlfriend Karen Paige betrays him, selling his secret identity in order to get a "fix" in Mexico. Here we can see the similarities of narrative structure between *Born Again* and *Guardian Devil*, but in *Born Again* Matt discovers that it is the Kingpin pulling the strings and confronts him early on—only to be beaten, framed for murder, put in a stolen cab, and driven into the river. The narrative focus then switches from following Matt to following the Kingpin, who presumes Murdock to be dead and awaits the official report. But when the cab is eventually found weeks later, there is no body—Matt has survived in a form of resurrection. Such a reading is explicitly invoked with the titles not only of the narrative arc, but also specific issues: "Apocalypse," "Purgatory," "Born Again," "Saved." However, in contrast to *Guardian Devil*, the theological themes in the narrative remain relatively muted—there is no virgin birth, actual death, crucifixion, resurrection, or second coming. Where the theological allusions appear most significantly is in the artistic design and deployment of the comics form, which draws explicitly on famous Christian imagery and Catholic iconography—and it is this use of the *form* that invites a reading of the events in Murdock's life in a particular way.

This iconographic approach can be mostly clearly seen in the issues "Pariah" and "Born Again." At the conclusion of "Pariah," after having been hit by a car and stabbed by a low-level thug, Murdock is found by his mother, Sister Maggie. When she finds him, there is a full-page panel which depicts Matt's disheveled body in Maggie's lap and invokes the Pietà—Mary holding the body of the crucified Christ after being taken down from the cross (most famously portrayed in Michelangelo's 1499 sculpture *Pietà*). The next issue in the narrative is "Born Again" and one of the title-images of that issue further invokes the Christological reading. The cover image is of Matt in a mission underneath a church in Hell's Kitchen, laying on a white bed with bandages around his chest. There is a crucifix on the wall above him and nuns tending patients around him. While this is a simple depiction of his recovery, the white bed is framed by the white walls and two windows which together make the shape of a cross (see figure 4.4). The allusions here, which reference certain Catholic iconography that depict Mary holding the crucified Jesus on the cross, are intentional by Miller and Mazzucchelli (and are supplemented by Sister Maggie's words "He's alive . . . Praise God! . . . He's *alive!*" [ellipses in original]), but its execution is a framing device which has no diegetic significance. These theological themes are then further emphasized in the trade paperback collection of *Born Again*, whose cover image is of Daredevil holding a scared Karen Paige, swinging through the air in front of a stained glass window. The stained glass window depicts a dove above, with Sister Maggie at the top and various aspects of the narrative around the sides. At the bottom of the image is a demonic version of the Kingpin devouring human bodies.

What is relevant here is the contrast between the overt theological narrative of *Guardian Devil* (which explicitly refers to aspects of *Born Again*) and the more direct theological assertions of *Born Again* at the level of form. Whereas *Guardian Devil* presents an overt theological narrative with redeemers, virgin births, and supernatural interventions, these are all revealed in the end to be smoke and mirrors, deception and illusion—a deception which the comics form itself is complicit in, by including the background images of angels and demons. In contrast, in *Born Again* all we are presented with is the narrative which, by itself, does not necessitate such a theological reading. It is the form that involves theological imagery and invites us not to see *beyond* to an unseen spirituality but rather to *see the world* itself in a theological way. The reader is encouraged to engage in a form of "seeing with" comics, but at the same time to *read* the text in a particular way, in accordance with a very *particular* story—one which itself involves a restoring of depth to reality. For, in the context of the Christian theology that Miller and Mazzucchelli invoke, the work of Christ involves a restoring of true visibility to the world and making "what was previously invisible—visible" (Blond 1999, 234; and see: John 1:18; Romans 1:20; Colossians 1:15–16).

The Catholic iconography of *Born Again* involves a particular way of deploying the comics form which reflects (whether intentional or not) this aspect of Catholic theology—the sense of the world as both something created but also something which we participate in. As Blond has noted, "[t]his

Figure 4.4: From *Daredevil: Born Again*. Frank Miller and David Mazzuchelli, 1986, #230. © 2018 Marvel Characters, Inc.

promise of a world participating in ideality is not abstract but actual; the incarnate God is not an abstract promise concerning some other realm, but rather the bringing into reality of our own fallen world" (Blond 1999, 235). Unlike the depiction of the spiritual in *Guardian Devil*, invoking a way of seeing the world *through* theological imagery involves not a disappearing into another realm but a return to the world itself—and, in particular, in terms of our embodied and enworlded experience of it. This means not focusing on "a nominal world, behind all appearances" but on a perception of the "phenomenal reality that we all see" (Blond 1999, 235). This, in part, is the function of art. It provides "an account of, and a meditation upon, our relationship to what we are given" (Blond 1999, 220). But it also presents a very different metaphysics of comics and perception, which emphasizes both the necessarily incomplete nature of comics as well as the readerly involvement in their meaning-making. This is McCloud's participatory analysis of comics, which are reliant on the reader to "fill in the gaps" through closure (McCloud 1993; see also Hatfield 2005, 41–45), but also encompasses Hague's description of the comics "performance" which functions through the materiality of the comic itself (Hague 2014). Comics go beyond the visual both by engaging the other senses in the space *between* the panels, where the eye is *not* directed to a visual but also by encouraging the eye to "see with" the comics form that which is *not* depicted. This is significant not only because of the body's translatable and intertwined nature of perception (Merleau-Ponty [1945] 2005, 240–82), but the way in which the comics form also enables a return to the world and our experience of it—a "seeing with" the comics form that, in our embodied experience, also involves a participation in this process of seeing which always takes us *beyond* the image itself.

In the context of *Born Again* this theological seeing of the world also returns to concerns about the engagement of the law. The entire narrative is about a breaking down of the dual identities of Murdock/Daredevil—which involves, first of all, Matt losing his license to practice law because of criminal charges of bribery, perjury, and misconduct manufactured by the Kingpin. While Daredevil as the superhero invokes a justice *beyond* the law, the *Daredevil* narratives are unique in the way they weave a fine line between an extralegal justice and a following of law's form (Young 2016, 57–61). However, the law in *Born Again* is presented as something that is able to be manipulated by the corrupt—which returns us to the original figure of blind justice as a satirical critique, rather than a positive emblem. For, even at the conclusion of the narrative arc, when the Kingpin is revealed to the public as having been involved not only in the undoing of Daredevil but also a massive military attack on Hell's Kitchen, he is still presented as being able to manipulate the law: "few of the charges stick" and "those that do are skillfully cast into years of litigation" (Miller and Mazzucchelli 1986). What's more, throughout the narrative, in contrast to Daredevil as the figure of "blind justice," the Kingpin is presented as all-seeing, knowing all that is going on in the background and controlling the various movements in the attempt to destroy Daredevil—and, in particular, manipulating the law to do so. This is driven home explicitly in one of the final panels where the Kingpin is reflecting on what he *did* achieve in relation to Matt Murdock: "The Law . . . at least I took *that* from him" (Miller and Mazzucchelli 1986). In contrast to Daredevil as the figure of the blindness of the law, this panel focuses exclusively on the Kingpin's eyes which are open, staring intently at the reader. The Kingpin represents a particular modern vision of the law itself—not as an enterprise that is essentially bound to life, justice, or community, but as an abstracted technology that can be controlled, manipulated, and deployed for particular ends. The fact that the Kingpin is presented with eyes wide open while at the same time as reflecting on his ability to have "taken" the law away links to a particular view of those who "have" the law as those who are explicitly authorized to "see" it (licensed to practice it, authorized to judge in its name), but who at the same time are required to restrict their ability to see anything else.

Conclusion: Toward Comics as a Participatory Legal Aesthetics

Both Daredevil's mask and Justitia's blindfold are representations of particular restrictions on our modes of seeing the world, but at the same time a projection of a *refusal* to look out of the risk of being deceived, the need to remain separate and for judgments to occur at a distance. In contrast, our embodied perception and experience of the world involves a radical reaffirmation of and participation *in* the world—not as virtual or abstract but as real and actual. Comics as a medium may be uniquely positioned for such an approach for it engages us in a performative and participatory way of *seeing*. That is, comics have the potential to draw us as a reader *into* our participatory role not only in the world but in the law itself. Giddens turns to comics as a means of multimodal knowing which can provide a way of analyzing and critiquing law's tendency toward focusing on a particular form of rationality which blinds itself from its unconscious other, from humanity, from the visual and aesthetic, and provides a means via which the law can be re-formed (Giddens 2018). My argument here is similar, except my view of the world is not as a chaos that requires mediation, whether by *nomos* or *komos*, but rather an understanding of a more foundational *nomos*, which we participate in—not only in the sense of artifice, but in the sense of our cocreation of the world. Comics provides a form of seeing that requires our participation in its (in)completion. Such is a theological position because "there are no totalised phenomena for theology, no attempted copies or representations of other images, and no fulfilled completed phenomena. These are only actualised and temporal manifestations of creation become ever-more real as a result of participating in the fully realised actuality of the Father and the Son" (Blond 1999, 235).

Comics therefore asks more of us than a passive "watching," or a distanced viewing, and it challenges the view of the world that is out there separate from us (Edgar 2016). Such a representational understanding of the world sees the mind as something separate from our body—an "ego looking through our body at what it sees" (Milbank 2001b, 490). Yet this is not the case because "our body itself" is that "which sees and touches," because our body is "both object and subject, and must be object if it is to be subject" and the basis of sensation is *not* through an "unendangered removal from things" but rather an "endangered being amongst things" (Milbank 2001b, 490). Such an approach becomes significant in the context of the law and its attempts at "blind justice"—the blindfold that not only *blinds* the wearer but also *projects* this blindness promotes a distance from the world. We need rather to understand more fully our participation and complicity in the nature and structure of the law itself. This means *not* looking to a systematized reduction of the law as something always externally imposed upon us—caught in the spectacle of violence that we love to watch—but rather to the fact that we form part of the law, and therefore need to take responsibility for it ourselves. Such does not leave us simply in a concern over either the image or sensory perception as a deception of appearances behind which we need to look to find the world, but rather points to an affirmation and *seeing* of the world and of each other in our embodied and bodily forms. This is not to retain a detheologized view of the world but to take us beyond the deficient theologies of modernity (including the concern about the split of mind and body, which renders us always concerned about the inability of an interiority to express itself and engage with the other) by turning to the sense of embodiment and the world which grounds our being together and involves a *seeing* of the other. The very image of the blindfold is one that, in projecting a limitation, presumes the possibility of an all-seeing view—that without the blindfold we would see all. The significance of the comics form is that it can provide a way of seeing the world in our very embodied position as one that renders our partial yet encroaching view of the world. It is not through the taking on or projecting of a blindness that we are able to escape illusion, but rather in the explicit sense of *opening* our eyes and seeing the invisible in the visible.

Notes

I would like to thank Dr. Thomas Giddens for the invitation to be part of this project and all the participants in the "Comics and Critique" Symposium, Centre for Law and Culture, St Mary's University, Twickenham, for such fruitful engagement. Thanks also to the anonymous reviewers for their generous and insightful comments, and to Chantelle Peters for her drawing of my bio panel! All errors remain my own.

1. McCloud's language of "the visible and the invisible," implicitly (if not intentionally) invokes Merleau-Ponty's (1968) incomplete final work published posthumously as *The Visible and the Invisible*.

2. This is still a "representation" as the physical experience of blindness does not necessarily involve a seeing of "blackness," but as a representational device it invokes the experience of nonseeing.

3. On which point, see the chapter by Christopher Pizzino in the present collection.

References

Alloa, Emmanuel. 2011. "Seeing-as, Seeing-in, Seeing-with." In *Image and Imaging in Philosophy, Science, and the Arts. Volume I. Proceedings of the 33rd International Wittgenstein Symposium*, edited by E. Nemeth, R. Heinrich, W. Pichler, and D. Wagner, 179–90. Frankfurt: Ontos.

Bainbridge, Jason. 2007. "'This Is *the Authority*. This Planet Is under Our Protection'—An Exegesis of Superheroes' Interrogations of Law." *Law, Culture, and the Humanities* 3: 455–76.

Bendis, Brian Michael, and Alex Maleev. 2010. *Daredevil by Bendis and Maleev: Ultimate Collection*. Vol. 2. New York: Marvel.

Blond, Phillip. 1999. "Perception: From Modern Painting to the Vision in Christ." In *Radical Orthodoxy: A New Theology*, edited by John Milbank, Catherine Pickstock, and Graham Ward, 220–42. London: Routledge.

Blond, Phillip. 2003. "Prolegomena to an Ethics of the Eye." *Studies in Christian Ethics* 16 (1): 44–60.

Crawley, Karen, and Timothy D. Peters. 2018. "Introduction: 'Representational Legality.'" In *Envisioning Legality: Law, Culture and Representation*, edited by Timothy D. Peters and Karen Crawley, 1–17. Abingdon, UK: Routledge.

Curtis, Dennis E., and Judith Resnik. 1987. "Images of Justice." *Yale Law Journal* 96 (8): 1727–72.

Douzinas, Costas, and Lynda Nead, eds. 1999. *Law and the Image: The Authority of Art and the Aesthetics of Law.* Chicago: University of Chicago Press.

Dudenhoeffer, Larrie. 2017. *Anatomy of the Superhero Film.* Cham, Switzerland: Palgrave Macmillan.

Edgar, Orion. 2016. *Things Seen and Unseen: The Logic of Incarnation in Merleau-Ponty's Metaphysics of Flesh.* Eugene, OR: Cascade Books.

Giddens, Thomas. 2018. *On Comics and Legal Aesthetics: Multimodality and the Haunted Mask of Knowing.* Abingdon, UK: Routledge.

Goddard, Drew, creator and producer. 2015. *Daredevil.* Netflix.

Goodrich, Peter. 2014. *Legal Emblems and the Art of Law: Obiter Depicta as the Vision of Governance.* New York: Cambridge University Press.

Grennan, Simon. 2017. *A Theory of Narrative Drawing.* New York: Palgrave Macmillan.

Hague, Ian. 2014. *Comics and the Senses: A Multisensory Approach to Comics and Graphic Novels.* London: Routledge.

Hatfield, Charles. 2005. *Alternative Comics: An Emerging Literature.* Jackson: University Press of Mississippi.

Jay, Martin. 1993. *Downcast Eyes: The Denigration of Vision in Twentieth-Century French Thought.* Berkeley: University of California Press.

Jay, Martin. 1999. "Must Justice Be Blind? The Challenges of Images to the Law." In *Law and the Image: The Authority of Art and the Aesthetics of Law,* edited by Costas Douzinas and Lynda Nead, 19–35. Chicago: University of Chicago Press.

Johnson, Mark Steven, dir. 2003. *Daredevil.* Twentieth Century Fox.

Kuppers, Petra. 2006. "Blindness and Affect: Daredevil's Site/Sight." *Quarterly Review of Film and Video* 23: 89–96.

Landes, Donald A. 2013. *The Merleau-Ponty Dictionary.* London: Bloomsbury.

Lee, Stan, Bill Everett, and Sam Rosen. (1964) 2016. "Daredevil #1: The Origin of Daredevil." In *Daredevil Epic Collection: The Man without Fear,* edited by Cory Sedlmeier. New York: Marvel.

MacNeil, William P. 2007. *Lex Populi: The Jurisprudence of Popular Culture.* Stanford, CA: Stanford University Press.

Manderson, Desmond. 2015. "The Metastases of Myth: Legal Images as Transitional Phenomena." *Law and Critique* 26: 207–23.

McCloud, Scott. 1993. *Understanding Comics: The Invisible Art.* New York: HarperPerennial.

Merleau-Ponty, Maurice. 1968. *The Visible and the Invisible.* Edited by Claude Lefort. Translated by Alphonso Lingis. Evanston, IL: Northwestern University Press.

Merleau-Ponty, Maurice. (1945) 2005. *Phenomenology of Perception.* Translated by Colin Smith. London: Routledge.

Merleau-Ponty, Maurice. (1961) 2007. "Eye and Mind." In *The Merleau-Ponty Reader,* edited by Ted Toadvine and Leonard Lawlor, 351–78. Evanston, IL: Northwestern University Press.

Milbank, John. 2001a. "The Soul of Reciprocity Part One: Reciprocity Refused." *Modern Theology* 17 (3): 335–91.

Milbank, John. 2001b. "The Soul of Reciprocity Part Two: Reciprocity Granted." *Modern Theology* 17 (4): 485–507.

Milbank, John. 2013. *Beyond Secular Order: The Representation of Being and the Representation of the People*. Hoboken, NJ: Wiley-Blackwell.

Miller, Frank, and David Mazzucchelli. 1986. *Daredevil: Born Again*. New York: Marvel.

Morris, Tom. 2005. "God, the Devil, and Matt Murdock." In *Superheroes and Philosophy: Truth, Justice, and the Socratic Way*, edited by Tom Morris and Matt Morris, 45–61. Chicago: Open Court.

Peters, Timothy D. 2018. "'Seeing' Justice Done: Envisioning Legality in Christopher Nolan's *The Dark Knight Trilogy*." In *Envisioning Legality: Law, Culture and Representation*, edited by Timothy D. Peters and Karen Crawley, 68–95. Abingdon, UK: Routledge.

Phillips, Nickie D., and Staci Strobl. 2013. *Comic Book Crime: Truth, Justice, and the American Way*. New York: New York University Press.

Resnik, Judith, and Dennis E. Curtis. 2011. *Representing Justice: Invention, Controversy and Rights in City-States and Democratic Courtrooms*. New Haven, CT: Yale University Press.

Sharp, Cassandra. 2012. "'Riddle Me This . . . ?' Would the World Need Superheroes If the Law Could Actually Deliver 'Justice'?" *Law Text Culture* 16: 353–78.

Sherwin, Richard. 2011. *Visualizing Law in the Age of the Digital Baroque: Arabesques and Entanglements*. London: Routledge.

Smith, Kevin, Joe Quesada, and Jimmy Palmiotti. 1998. *Daredevil: Guardian Devil*. New York: Marvel.

Spanakos, Anthony Peter. 2014. "Hell's Kitchen's Prolonged Crisis and Would-Be Sovereigns: Daredevil, Hobbes, and Schmitt." *Political Science and Politics* 47 (1): 94–97.

Waid, Mark, Peter Krause, Javier Rodriguez, and Chris Samnee. 2014. *Daredevil Vol. 1: Devil at Bay*. New York: Marvel.

Wollheim, Richard. 2003. "In Defense of Seeing-In." In *Looking into Pictures: An Interdisciplinary Approach to Pictorial Space*, edited by Heiko Hecht, Robert Schwartz, and Margaret Atherton, 3–15. Cambridge, MA: MIT Press.

Young, Paul. 2016. *Frank Miller's Daredevil and the Ends of Heroism*. New Brunswick, NJ: Rutgers University Press.

COMICS INTERLUDE #2

Let's Get Critical!

BY LYDIA WYSOCKI

5

The Freedom of the Press

Comics, Labor, and Value in the Birmingham Arts Lab

MAGGIE GRAY

"The freedom of the press belongs to those who control the press."
—SEE RED WOMEN'S WORKSHOP C. 1976

Introduction

There is a tendency in comics studies, and the formalist and structuralist approaches that dominate it, to treat comics as discrete "texts" abstracted from the social contexts of their production and processes of their material facture. Thus questions of labor and value, the relationship between the way making comics is organized and the forms of value ascribed to and inscribed in them, have been largely overlooked.

However, countervailing strands of scholarship concerned with the sociology and political economy of comics as cultural work, attending to the labor of numerous agents involved in their production; the social, technological, economic, and institutional forces that shape it; and the way that labor is subjectively experienced and culturally evaluated, have become increasingly prominent. From early sporadic interventions (McAllister 1990; Norcliffe and Rendace 2003; Rogers 2006), this approach has become more concrete, with dedicated edited volumes (Brienza and Johnston 2016) and research projects accumulating and interpreting primary data (Woo 2015).

Such scholarship sits within growing critical attention to cultural work accompanying the consolidation of the "creative industries" as a focus of economic activity and public policy. Building from leading research in this area (e.g., Banks 2007; Hesmondalgh and Baker 2011; McRobbie 2014), it also draws on established theoretical frameworks including institutional theories of art, notably Howard Becker's concept of an "art world" (see Beaty 2012), and approaches in cultural sociology, such as Richard A. Peterson's "production of culture perspective" (Brienza 2010), and Pierre Bourdieu's "fields" of (cultural) activity (1993). This chapter engages with this approach and asserts the exigency of questions of labor and value to a "critical comics studies," by analyzing a particular site of comics work, the Birmingham Arts Lab Press (ALP) (1969–1982) and its Ar:Zak imprint, exploring its distinctive organization of cultural labor and the kinds of creative production thereby enabled.

Many of the challenges encountered in this area of study concern what Benjamin Woo calls the "exceptional character" of creative labor and cultural goods (2013). The comics world, like wider fields of art, design, and media, is bisected by contradictions between the evaluation of cultural work as both wage labor and creative practice, and the symbolic objects produced as both commodities and artworks. Key to these tensions is *autonomy*, a concept in this context with strong roots in the Marxist distinction between unalienated and alienated labor, closely related to the commodity fetish—autonomy as the freedom to actively determine and take pleasure in work, and to recognize that labor and the social use values thereby created in its products. This stands in contrast to the extraction of surplus value from labor subjugated and reified in capitalist relations of exploitation, and the determination of the value of what is produced by exchange—a value from which its creators are alienated, appearing as an objective character of things rather than deriving from social relations between people (Marx [1867] 1976, 164–65). As noted in comics scholarship, the concept is itself an arena of cultural antagonism, whereby the "relative autonomy" experienced by creative workers in postindustrial economies serves as an ideological gloss for both the intensifying precarization of cultural labor within work's general neoliberal restructuring (Woo 2015), and the siloing of cultural capital through social exclusion from creative practice (Johnston 2016).

This chapter draws on historical research into the ALP and Ar:Zak, the aspirations and experiences of those involved, to interrogate the levels of autonomy realized. Locating it concretely within broader sociopolitical contexts, it scopes the degree to which the ALP's distinctive cooperative formation was determined by its foundation in the Arts Lab movement and broader countercultural efforts to socialize the means of cultural production, as well as its connections to the ensuing community arts and alternative press movements. Further, it frames this reconfiguration of creative practice in relation to wider political aims to create alternative participatory democratic institutions contesting capitalist social organization and hegemonic power. In doing so, it echoes Nicole Cohen's argument for "a Marxist political economy of cultural work . . . concerned with the dynamics of the labor-capital relation" and the "contradictions that structure this relationship" (2017, 39), agreeing that cultural work under capitalism is different but not exceptional, remaining a site of struggle between antagonistic interests. It therefore turns to Marx's theory of alienation, exploitation, and the commodity.

In advocating a Marxist conception of cultural labor, this chapter argues what is often overlooked in this vein of comics studies is the relationship between struggles over the organization of labor and the antagonistic forms of value articulated in the work produced. There can be a tendency in efforts to counteract formalist auteurism by spotlighting the collective labor enabling comics' creation, to elide the degree to which "the formal properties of the comics art object," its "textual and material surfaces," embody struggles over labor and value (Brienza and Johnston 2016, 2, 7). Where attention has been paid to the impact of production contexts on the comics made, it has tended to focus on content and the ideologies thereby articulated, rather than material and visual form. This chapter therefore equally draws on Marxist aesthetic theory to examine how struggles over labor and value enacted in this site of production are registered in the very form of the comics produced.

The Arts Lab Movement

The Arts Lab movement has received relatively little attention in critical accounts of the UK counterculture, and similarly, both the alternative press movement in which the ALP was situated and the British underground/alternative comics scene of which Ar:Zak was part have a marginal presence in academic study. It is therefore necessary to reconstruct these nested contexts to identify their specific configuration of creative labor and the impact of wider structural tensions.

Arts Labs, a network of countercultural arts cooperatives that sprouted across the UK in the late 1960s, have been described as one of the most important cultural innovations of that era (Everitt 1999, 20). As detailed elsewhere (Gray 2017, 35–40), the movement began with the setting up of the first Arts Laboratory in London's Covent Garden—an abandoned warehouse transformed into a multipurpose arts space, doubling as a hippie crash-pad. The aim was to produce a site for creative production and consumption that would be self-determining and cooperatively managed, accessible and antihierchical, experimental and interdisciplinary. There was a strong emphasis on autonomy in and across different artforms, enabling artists to play with various materials and media and transgress disciplinary borders by sharing knowledge and resources within a collaborative community. The lab thus screened experimental cinema, exhibited mixed-media visual arts, and staged radical theater, but also explored hybrid forms blending drama, mime, and dance; film, installation, and live art.

This was driven by the idea that artists should be enabled to freely create and disseminate work outside the restrictions of both traditional institutions and the commercial market. The lab was seen as a way to "change art . . . and transform relations of production" (Brett 1981), by rendering creative practice collectively and democratically available, and situating the value of art in the social experience of its making and consumption, rather than cultural objects bought and sold. Contesting the established arrangement and evaluation of cultural production meant challenging distinctions between artists and audiences, often through forms of spontaneity, provisionality, and interactivity. Fringe theater companies regularly appearing at the lab, like The People Show, were keenly interested in improvisation and audience involvement, and several of the artworks exhibited were similarly participative, such as Roelof Louw's *Soul City*, a pyramid of oranges dematerializing as viewers took them.

The lab was thus deeply embedded in countercultural values of play, indeterminacy, ambiguity, collectivism, and autonomy. It echoed the hippie underground's attitudes to art and politics more broadly, whereby, drawing on Herbert Marcuse's ideas, the aesthetic was seen to stand in critical alterity to the unfreedom of capitalist society (Stephens 1998, 98). It accordingly sat within a wider network of "anti-institutions" similarly run on a participatory democratic basis (Gray 2017, 38–39) and a sensibility that rejected the separation of art from day-to-day experience through both its rarefication in remote cultural institutions and the reification of creativity in commercial popular culture. In the late sixties underground there was a growing emphasis on "cultural democracy" which intensified in the 1970s, connected to "the idea of breaking down art into everyday life" explored by Joseph Beuys, Henri Lefebvre, and Paolo Freire (Hope 2008, 26).

However, the creative autonomy of these spaces was subject to both internal and external pressures. As with many hippie anti-institutions, the Arts Lab's loose unstructured organization led to frequent internal conflicts. There were "tensions over its use as both an accessible community resource and a laboratory for artistic experimentation," and the way that collective decision-making was overruled (Gray 2017, 39), with a splinter group breaking away to form a New London Arts Lab in 1968. The original lab, threatened with eviction, closed in October 1969, while the new lab's building was demolished in 1971. However, during this period the number of labs nationally had rapidly expanded, the longest running being Birmingham's.

The Birmingham Arts Lab

The Birmingham Lab was founded in 1968 by a group of artists then working at the city council–funded Midlands Arts Centre. Frustrated by its "autocratic" administration (Williams 1968) and "too-sensible agenda" (Wakefield 2015) that obstructed more avant-garde activity, they decided to organize their own collectively managed, independent space where artists could work in a "creatively uninhibited environment" serving as a community social and cultural center (Birmingham Arts Laboratory Fund 1968). In January 1969 they procured an old youth center on Tower Street in the working-class district of Newtown. A former gym became a cinema and theater, with cast-off cinema seating installed and a projection box crafted from materials stolen from local building sites (Wakefield 2015). Later, expansion into lower floors provided a studio for rehearsals, performances and exhibitions, and spaces rented to local artists. Like the original lab, it doubled as an "artistic commune" with people sleeping in the storerooms, water tank, and even the spaces between floors (*The Birmingham Arts Lab* 1998).

Programming was diverse and ambitious, featuring fringe theater, international art house film, experimental music, poetry readings, and alternative comedy, alongside compound work fusing dance, film, spoken word, installation, light, and sound. Participation and accessibility were paramount, seen in off-site events and festivals, collaborations with local arts organizations and community groups, and, above all, in the open workshops in everything from interactive environmental performance to painting. Notably, several key figures involved in Ar:Zak and the ALP were drawn into the lab via these workshops. Suzy Varty joined the dance workshop, while Hunt Emerson participated in Jolyon Laycock's sound workshop and activities like 1972's *Anti-Symphony*, involving clanging bits of metal miked up to amps and speakers. While these were among the "most peculiar events" of his life, "daft nonsense . . . obscure for the sake of it" (Emerson 2018), what this kind of collaborative, interactive practice highlighted was the ability for cultural consumers to become producers, and the workshops were figured as a way to make the means of artistic production and presentation available to those typically excluded. Thus the theater workshop was committed to staging plays by local writers, and the film workshop was a crucible for the Birmingham Film Co-op, providing resources, training, and funding for local filmmakers and community organizations.

Like its predecessors, the Birmingham Lab therefore aimed to be a center of autonomous avant-garde cultural production as a result of being a self-managed, not-for-profit cooperative. It aimed to create an inclusive "community in the Arts" in which anyone could get involved, making "the often expensive equipment required by the experimental artist" publically available (Birmingham Arts Laboratory 1970). This was seen to have a social benefit for local communities and a wider political value as part of efforts toward participatory democracy. For key member Peter Stark, communal involvement in artistic work enabled people to "release their own personal creativity" and thereby develop "an awareness of . . . the possibilities for greater control of their own life"—fostering a broader political autonomy (in *The Birmingham Arts Lab* 1998). This included significant feminist activity, with a Women's Art Group (WAG) staging exhibitions and mail art events, and the lab was also affiliated to the West Indian Narrative, a group evolving a distinct Afro-Caribbean aesthetic. It was thus embedded in broader social movements and the larger community arts movement of the 1970s, which developed underground ambitions to contest cultural hegemony by putting the means of symbolic production in the hands of wider groups of people (Grosvenor and Macnab 2015, 131).

Although initially self-funded, with constant financial problems, the Birmingham Lab owed much of its longevity to funding from public bodies. Stark sat on the New Activities Committee of the Arts Council of Great Britain (ACGB), as well as its successor, the Experimental Projects Committee. Through dogged effort, the lab managed to obtain money for specific initiatives, general funding to cover running costs, and capital grants for equipment, from both the ACGB and the regional association West Midlands Arts (WMA). However, in return its organization gradually became more formalized, registering as a charity, with full-time administrators appointed in 1973, and a managing board established in 1976. In 1977 it moved to a larger premises on Gosta Green within the Aston University campus, financed by c. £100,000 of funding from WMA and the British Film Institute ("Back to Birmingham" 1977). The renovated site had a newly equipped cinema space and expanded music workshop, but a proposed performance area never materialized, and focus became concentrated on film. In 1982 it was finally merged with the university's Centre for the Arts into the Triangle Arts Centre.

The Arts Lab Press

Many participants retrospectively bemoaned the move as diluting the lab's commitment to autonomous, antihierachical self-management, reproducing the institutional constraints that had spurred its creation, and quashing the liberating atmosphere of creative mayhem embodied in the ramshackle Tower Street space. However, one area that seemed to maintain its "chaotic, wild, noisy and shambolic" character was the ALP, installed in a crumbling old shop next to a pub (Emerson 2018).

While several other labs had printing workshops screen-printing posters and duplicating schedules, the Birmingham Lab was distinctive in founding its own press with substantial reprographic capabilities. In 1969 a silkscreen operation producing lab publicity was set up, selling its services to the students' union and local music promoters to cover costs, followed by loan of a small offset duplicator for printing programs. Downstairs expansion in 1972 saw a dedicated silkscreen space used by Ernie Hudson, Bob Linney, and Ken Meharg to create eye-popping posters for lab events. Former showers were converted into a dark room, with a large photographic enlarger laid on its back and used in reverse as a camera. This supported the photography workshop but also enabled halftone screening, color separation, and printing plate production. Alongside a second-hand A4 offset printer—a "rattling old Multilith . . . held together by faith and elastic bands" (Emerson 2018)—an independent press could therefore be established, able to produce a range of high-quality print matter, cheaply, quickly, and in considerable runs.

Its primary function was to print the lab's quarterly programs, leaflets, and posters, alongside workshop materials like poetry zines and music scores—in many ways holding its existence as a multidisciplinary arts space together. But it furthermore operated as a community printshop, supplementing the lab's income by offering resources and services to local bands, community organizations, and activist groups. As Emerson put it, "We printed and helped produce many different community magazines, newsletters, etc. with a more sympathetic approach than a normal commercial printer" (2018). This situated it within a larger network of community printshops and printing co-ops that had sprung up in the 1970s with the rise of urban community activism and supporting a range of social movements and protest groups (Baines 2016, 83–96). Overlapping with the community arts movement, community printshops aimed to challenge the commercial industry by making reproductive technologies more democratically accessible through collectivized control and diffusing technical knowledge. They were also closely tied to the alternative press movement, similarly aimed at demystifying and socializing communications media and enabling grassroots cultural expression—as Jonathan Zeitlyn argued in a DIY print manual, "when people learn to print they realise . . . the printer can also be the writer; there is no magic about the printed word" (1980, 58). The ALP was listed in directories of community presses and had close links to the alternative press movement, printing local paper *Street Press*, cofounded by Midlands Alternative Press Syndicate's initiator John Keetley, who worked as the lab's design and publicity coordinator from 1972 to 1973.

Ar:Zak

In 1974 Hunt Emerson, then working as a printer at Birmingham Polytechnic, took over Hudson's paid position operating the lab's A4 litho, which he began to use to run off copies of his own comics. The following year he replaced Keetley overseeing design, layout, and darkroom duties, and Martin Reading came in to run the press, later joined in 1976 by printer Dave Hatton and a larger A3 Rotaprint offset machine. Together with writer and actor Paul Fisher, Emerson and Reading set up the comics imprint, Ar:Zak, under the ALP's remit. They brought in a group of comics artists, many from the counterculture, underground comix, and the alternative press, including Suzy Varty, who'd helped establish the Newcastle Arts Lab before moving to Birmingham and cofounding *Street Press* with Keetley, and Chris Welch, previously involved with underground papers *Oz* and *IT* and their comix offshoots *COzmic Comics* and *Nasty Tales*.

Ar:Zak's first comic was a pilot copy of the anthology *Streetcomix*, included as a supplement in poetry zine *Street Poems* in 1976. Its success led to five further issues showcasing a diverse range of work from Ar:Zak members (Emerson, Varty, Welch, Steve Berridge, and Pokkettz [aka Graham Higgins]); underground cartoonists like Mike Weller and J. C. Moody; alternative press illustrators like Steve Bell and Clifford Harper; and creators from the wider alternative comics scene like Bryan Talbot and Angus McKie. They also produced *Moon Comix*, edited by David Noon, and several one-off titles, including the UK's first (nearly) all-women anthology, *Heroïne*, put together by Varty, the ALP's only female member.[1] Varty was involved in WAG's lab activity and the women's liberation movement more broadly, and had links with Trina Robbins and US women's comix, with *Heroïne* including work by both WAG members and Robbins. Ar:Zak also put out a series of cheap "microcomiks" by Varty, Weller, Pokkettz, Bonk (aka Alecks Waszynko), Damien

Ledwich, and Mike Matthews, and sold their services to others to print their own anthologies, including Matthews's *Napalm Kiss*.

Ar:Zak thus was part of a wider "movement of independent comics publishers" (Emerson 2018) with roots in the underground press. Their aim was to devise and publish as many comics as they could, without restrictions as to subject, theme, genre, or graphic style (Emerson 2018; Varty 2018), enabling the dissemination of work "in a less commercial vein than that usually associated with the comics medium" (*Streetcomix #2* 1976, 3). As well as providing resources and media for cartoonists to print and circulate their work, Ar:Zak also organized two "Konventions of Alternative Komiks" gathering the alternative comics scene together, the first held at Tower Street in 1976. These provided a space to discuss issues of shared concern, including distribution, finance, and sexism, as well as hosting talks, exhibitions, workshops, and collaborative jams. Ar:Zak printed special convention programs, *KAK Komix*, and *KAK '77*, and follow-up reports and jam outcomes were printed in *Streetcomix*, which also reviewed other alternative, indie, and fanzine publications.

Alternative Organization

Ar:Zak can therefore be seen as embedded in and sustaining an alternative comics movement committed to creating comics free from the constraints of the commercial field with respect to content and form, artistic development and innovation, access to resources and sociality. As an imprint it sat in stark contrast to the commercial publishers of the time and the production of popular media more broadly in terms of structural factors and organizational practices shaping the work produced.

Mainstream British comics publishing, concentrated in the hands of a few companies like IPC and DC Thomson, was highly rationalized. Strict production schedules were maintained, and costs and prices kept low, through a quasi-Fordist division of labor between scriptwriters, illustrators, letterers, designers, etc., and a separation between freelancers employed on a work-for-hire basis paid by the page, and salaried in-house editorial, administrative, managerial, and technical staff. Legal ownership of work was transferred to the publisher and creator anonymity was often strictly enforced, primarily to mitigate pay demands. At DC Thomson trade union membership was forbidden (Sabin 1993, 33). Content and visual style needed to be commercially viable, and were therefore governed by formulaic conventions and conservative standards, tied to what was deemed marketable to and appropriate for an assumed juvenile audience. This was underpinned by law in the form of the 1955 Children and Young Persons (Harmful Publications) Act, which, although rarely enforced, included similar restrictions to the United States Comics Code, and bolstered by the need to attract and maintain advertising revenues, as well as mechanisms of distribution, with major wholesalers like WH Smith refusing to carry "magazines which didn't project careful marketing or social respectability" (Norch n.d.).

Ar:Zak operated in a very different organizational context. It had a much less pronounced specialization of labor, with contributors able to get involved in its organization and have input across production stages, within an informal, nonhierarchical structure. Artists were credited and retained copyright, as well as being paid for their work. They had more creative control, with fewer gatekeeping restrictions or editorial limitations, and more flexible deadlines, allowing for a diversity of content and styles, and formal experimentation. This was connected to an intended adult readership, also allowing for the exploration of political and contentious topics, including issues of gender, sexuality, class, ecology, and racism. Being less profit driven meant Ar:Zak could also challenge readers, most notably with *Heroïne*, intended "as a forum for women artists to exercise *their* imaginations, rather than those of a male audience" (*Streetcomix #6* 1978, 33). This open, heterodox approach was enabled by distribution through underground publisher and wholesaler Hassle Free Press and PDC, a distribution cooperative set up to support the alternative press movement. Ar:Zak titles were therefore sold through an alternative network of comic shops, science fiction bookstores, and radical bookshops, as well as being available directly via mail order. In turn, these shops provided revenue by advertising in Ar:Zak publications, along with alternative papers like *Undercurrents* and *The Leveller*. Ar:Zak and the ALP's situation within the overlapping networks of the alternative comics and alternative press movements was further underscored by the fact the lab ran a magazine stall stocking local and alternative publications, expanding to its own bookshop.

Cooperation vs. Alienation

Ar:Zak's publishing practice, as part of these wider alternative cultural fields, was therefore constructed in critical opposition to established conditions of comics work. This was enabled by the ALP's specific organizational framework, shaped by the communalist principles of the wider lab, itself situated within broader efforts toward participatory democratic cultural production. In Raymond Williams's terms, the press can be seen to have instituted an alternative form of communications through applying a cooperative rather than instrumental rationality, based on collective ownership, self-management, communal use, and autonomy (Fuchs 2017, 745–47). The degree of creative autonomy Ar:Zak offered to its contributors and users thus hinged on the degree of autonomy those working at the press had over their labor and its outcomes. As Emerson put it, "the Arts Lab was a very congenial place to work. . . . We ran ourselves . . . and we had control of this resource" (2018). As such, it can be read as part of efforts to move away from alienated forms of mass cultural work toward less alienated forms of artistic practice.

From a Marxist perspective, within capitalist commodity production alienation is experienced as four broad relations: workers are alienated from each other (separated yet interchangeable); from what is produced (in which their input is abstracted and disguised); from their productive activity (which is subjugated, homogenized, and reified); and from human species-being (the way we creatively transform the world to meet our needs) (Ollman 1976, 131–52). At the ALP work was not organized along a disassociated and hierarchized division of labor—like the lab at large it was "run by the people who work creatively in it" (Birmingham Arts Laboratory 1970). Within Ar:Zak cartoonists did layout and paste-up, writers and artists were editors, editors made printing plates, printers were administrators, and, as in the lab generally, administration itself was "kept to a minimum and done by the people who it affects" (Birmingham Arts Laboratory). As part of a self-governing artists' community that jointly determined their own labor and worked across roles and disciplines, they were therefore less alienated from each other. This emphasis on work as a social practice was inscribed in the comics produced, as seen in figure 5.1, the inside cover of *Streetcomix #6*, which used a full page to present the Ar:Zak collective of drawists and boogiers, wordists and noise makers, printers and bikers.

With this collaborative determination of the whole process of production, rather than routinized, fragmented, reified activity subject to external direction, they were less alienated from the work produced. The difference between this and mainstream production contexts was represented in "The Dottytone Saga" by Mike Weller (see figure 5.2). An underground cartoonist, whose work is refused by a professional art agency, blags his way into a job as a ghost assistant, inking the work of a comics "star" whose strips have been licensed on a ridiculous array of merchandising. His own work in

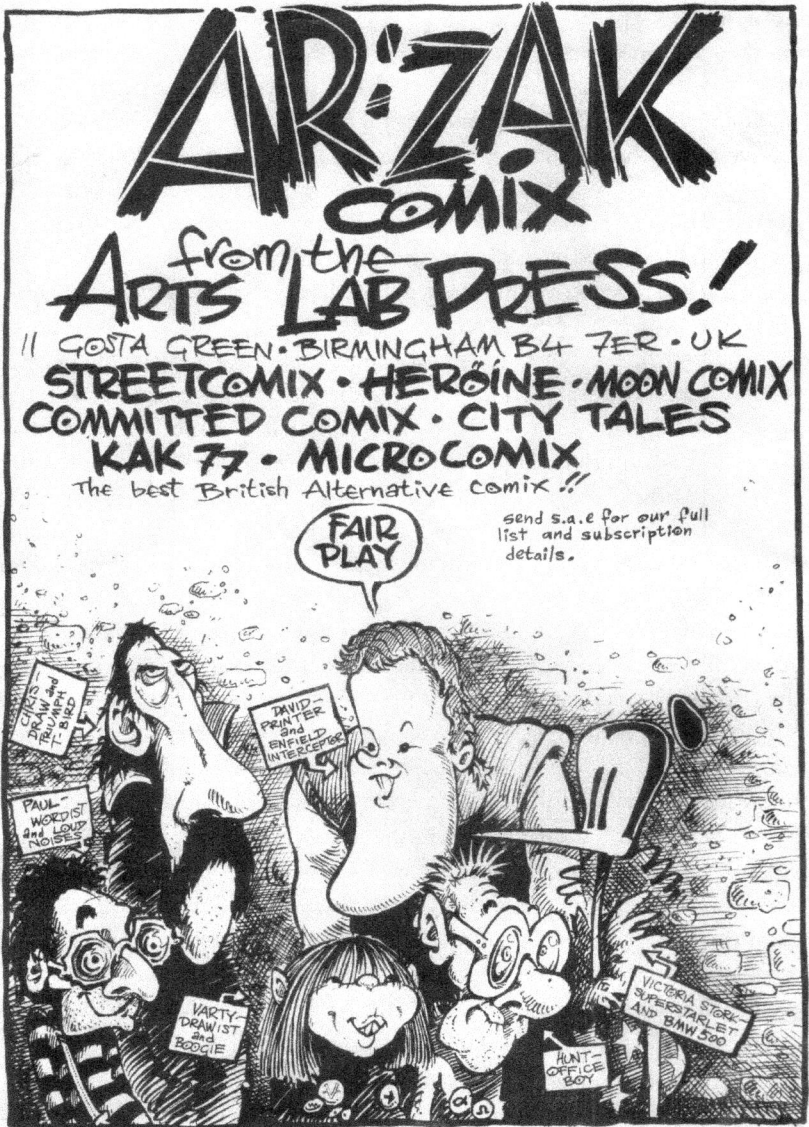

Figure 5.1: Ar:Zak comix from the Arts Lab Press. *Streetcomix #6*, 1978, 2. Birmingham: Ar:Zak. © Hunt Emerson.

Figure 5.2: From "The Dottytone Saga." *Streetcomix #5*, 1978, 9. Birmingham: Ar:Zak. © Mike Weller.

making these commodities remains invisible and abstracted, until his pen leaks all over the cartoonist's "dottytone" artwork and cannot be removed. By contrast, Weller's' own idiosyncratic underground drawing and application of patterned screentone is prominent and attributed, the concrete labor that has gone into producing the strip reflexively highlighted—including not only the cartoonist's labor, but that of the wider Ar:Zak team of designers and printers.

Because this work was cooperatively controlled and organized more for the intrinsic value of the process (the development of artistic aptitudes and affective pleasures of creative expression) rather than instrumentally objectified and subjected to the maximization of surplus value, participants were less alienated from their activity. For Emerson, his time at the lab "was the most fun I've ever had at work" (in Walker 2014), and the playfulness and adventurousness of Ar:Zak's approach to cultural production was seen in their experimental attitude to both the visual style of the work published and its material form, the way it was printed. All told, this meant involvement in cultural production at Ar:Zak and the ALP was closer to a form of labor aligned to human needs for creative praxis, subjective affirmation, and the development of "free mental and physical energy," through differentiated and fulfilling activity (Marx [1844] 1959).

Crucially this was work which did not feel like work, as Varty put it "work with . . . the press was never 'work' for me, it was just what I did" (2018). Emerson "valued the freedom and the creativity" which made it "better than working a real job" (2018). However, like many of those involved in Arts Labs, access to this autonomous creative practice in part depended on gaining an income by other means. Both Emerson and Varty took on commercial freelance illustration and design projects while working at the lab, potentially facilitated by the skills and experience gained. Such commissions became Emerson's "night job" and he ultimately left the paid position at the press in 1979 to freelance professionally full-time. Varty, who also worked at a feminist playgroup, took over, but left herself to take on more freelancing, "mainly because of being a single parent" (2018). The hidden subsidizing of its activities by low wages, and even voluntary wage cuts to "help the lab get through tough patches" (Emerson 2018), was identified in the lab's 1972–73 application to the ACGB as the main way it was keeping afloat (Burt 1973), a situation not unique in the Arts Lab and community arts movements.

Thus the ALP remained situated within the wider structural antagonism of labor and capital and generalized relations of exploitation, even while it contested them. Emerson and Varty's experience of work at the lab as "not work—as fun or leisure" (Woo 2015, 62), in some ways relates to the romanticized ideology of the bohemian working for love mobilized alongside increasing casualization in the creative industries since the 1970s. In the post-Fordist shift to globalized flexible accumulation, "relative autonomy" over the creative process experienced by freelancers is exchanged for the extraction of surplus value through increasing unpaid labor time, offloading financial risks and costs to workers, and intensifying competition between them resulting in downward pressure on wages. This is combined with aggressive copyright strategies and intensified exploitation of intellectual property through transmedia syndication and licensing (Cohen 2017, 51–54). Subjective autonomy and high levels of affective engagement in creative labor thus become a mechanism for self-exploitation, mystifying the "sacrificial labor" of the artist (Ross 2003, 142) and masking expropriative economic dynamics and antagonistic social relations.

Art into Everyday Life—Ar:Zak as a Comics Workshop

However, Ar:Zak was distinct from this piecework model of exploitation central to the commercial comics industry, in terms of not only the levels of creative autonomy facilitated, but the ascription of copyright to contributors and commitment to the distribution of surplus values. Moreover, while retaining copyright can be related to forms of authorial proprietorship that occlude social production—distinguishing imaginative art from technical craft—Ar:Zak's countercultural attitudes to technology and its aims of realizing social ownership of the mechanical means of cultural production undermined the use of bourgeois ideologies of artistic autonomy to identify only the concrete labor of content-providers as auteurs, masking their imbrication in relations of exploitation.

Offset lithography, prevalent in commercial printing at the time, required substantial capital investment, and the industry was therefore monopolized by a few large companies. This contributed to the restrictions facing alternative media—seen in the fact hippie papers often had to switch printers as a result of police harassment or refusals to handle contentious material. For comics artists, going to a commercial printer meant making "large, unmanageable, expensive print runs" (Emerson 2018), which equally impinged production of experimental or controversial work, or self-published projects altogether. For many, the only way to get comics printed independently was to appropriate "day job" office facilities to make very limited runs, with

Emerson, for example, "sneaking poor ghostly photocopies" of his underground-inspired *Large Cow Comix* while working at a prison, until he was discovered and reprimanded (2018).

Having access to "the means of production" as both Emerson (2013) and Varty (2018) term it, was thus crucially important in enabling the publication of comics outside restrictive publishing standards. With an open call for contributions, *Streetcomix* was "inundated with submissions, some of them very good, none of them commercial" (Emerson 2018), and able to encourage work from artists who would struggle to find a place in the commercial industry either because their visual style was too unorthodox, their subject matter taboo, or just because they lacked technical accomplishment.

Thus, having access to the capability to independently print work meant Ar:Zak could make the means of cultural production more democratically accessible—intimately connected to the ALP's wider affiliation to the community arts movement. Emerson has argued it was this approach to comics publication, and the working methods developed at Ar:Zak, that made them "well placed as a community press" (2018). In many ways the press was a print workshop, enabling people not only to print their own publications outside commercial restrictions, but to participate in printing as a design practice itself. This was crucial in that it extended autonomy not only in terms of the "idea creation" stages of cultural production but stages of reproduction. This stood in stark contrast to commercial practices in which the "relative autonomy" apportioned to workers involved in areas of ideation and expression that resist abstraction are counterbalanced by "tightening control over the reproduction, distribution, and circulation of cultural commodities" (Cohen 2017, 45), subjecting in-house technical and administrative workers to rationalization.

The organization of work at Ar:Zak and the ALP meant conventional hierarchies of mental and manual labor, imaginative conception, and mechanical execution, entrenched as part of the immanent drive to increase surplus value, were contested. Cartoonists like Emerson and Varty were able to also work as designers and print technicians, and printing itself was reconfigured as an artistic activity concretely visible in the work produced. The same transdisciplinary, experimental approach found in wider lab activities was taken to printing. According to Emerson, the "printing press was part of the creative process" and the group pushed their machinery to its limits, doing things not supposed possible:

People would push the boundaries because they had the opportunity to do so. . . . We were printing from photographic negative on to metal plates, and we used to work on the negatives, scratching out and painting. . . . We'd be getting effects in the drawings, collaging things with feathers and bits of rubbish, . . . playing around and experimenting. (Emerson 2013)

An example of this was "Ice Age" (figure 5.3). The artwork for this apocalyptic tale of ecological devastation included cut up scraps of type strewn across pages combining scratchy cartooning with collages of such experimental dark room material, including images of a feather and a piece of cheesecloth.

This centrality of the printing press to the degree of affective engagement in creative labor enabled at Ar:Zak was equally demonstrated in Fisher's *Streetcomix* editorials, written under the pseudonym Mr Hepf. In issue #3 he becomes tangibly entwined with the machinery:

Mr Hepf rises from his multilith multiberth, pulling his inky oily fingers through his blond:brown hair . . . he inks his roller, takes his first sticky bite into his cold:kipper muesli sandwich and plugs in . . . his life spans so many print runs and will encompass many more . . . Such is Mr Hepf. Groaning bodily over centre spreads . . . Making plates to eat his dinners . . . He rises with the machine and sinks when it pauses. (Streetcomix #3 1977, 40)

Ownership of the press was therefore an essential part of the autonomy enjoyed at Ar:Zak, "a rare and exciting opportunity" that meant they could "design and publish comics exactly as we wanted" (Emerson 2018).

Transcending the division between "artistic" and "technical" labor was a key part of the Arts Lab ethos, distributing expertise as a way of both improving art (through collaborative, interdisciplinary experimentation) and democratizing culture and media. Many of the other workshops shared this outlook—in film "much of the enjoyment . . . lay in the raw mechanics" (Wakefield 2015). Ambitions for the 3D design workshop hinged on "bridging the gap between industrially available technology and the arts," challenging the ways new media technologies were being applied in contemporary art "superficially and with little or no understanding" (Birmingham Arts Laboratory 1970).

Integrating creative expression and technical know-how was an essential aspect of the workshop model central to the wider community arts and alternative press movements and ambitions for cultural democracy. By actively transferring knowledge and skills within communities it was hoped to "break down the barriers between professionals and audiences and [question] the

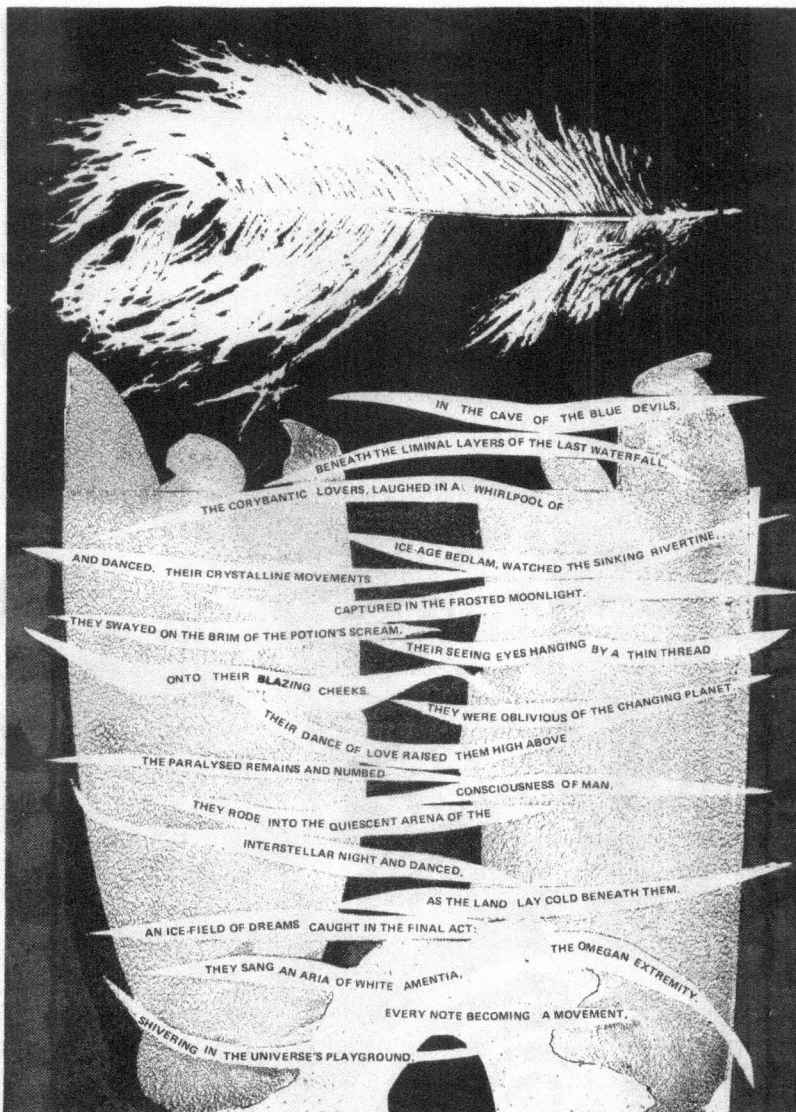

Figure 5.3. From "Ice Age." *Streetcomix #4*, 1977, 15. Birmingham: Ar:Zak. © Nick Blake and Robin Sendak.

autonomy of the artist," so art could escape its rarefication and "become an integral part of everyday life," thereby transforming social reality (Grosvenor and Macnab 2015, 117). At the heart of the workshop ideal was the conviction creative practice could be taught and learned, "an implicit demystification of any kind of activity that has been seen historically as the preserve of an elite or a clique whose 'talent' or gifts are accepted as intuitive, natural and thus unassailable" (Long, Baig-Clifford, and Shannon 2013, 382).

Ar:Zak itself can therefore be seen as a comics workshop, similarly aimed at using social ownership of the means of production to make skills of fabrication and channels of communication more democratically available, enabling consumers to become producers. This echoed Walter Benjamin's argument for a functional transformation of the apparatus of cultural production, by renouncing the positioning of art as an exceptional activity and "promoting the socialization of the intellectual means of production" ([1934] 2008, 93) then being rediscovered by the poster workshops and community printshops of the wider alternative press movement (Baines 2016, 76). It equally reflected the aims of the Arts Lab movement itself toward less alienated forms of both cultural production and consumption, through more reciprocal interactions between artist and audience and a more active and socialized aesthetic experience (Mészáros 1972, 205–10).

Beyond Industrial Heteronomy *and* the Autonomy of Art

Yet by pointing toward the supersession of art as a separate sphere and the extension of creative autonomy into everyday life, including implicitly all forms of work, the cooperative workshop model had a larger political aspect. Ambitions toward cultural democracy were seen as deeply embedded in broader insistence on implementing participatory democracy in all areas of life and its imaginative, affective transformation. This differentiates the autonomy of the ALP from the bourgeois ideology of artistic autonomy. Ar:Zak therefore does not fit neatly into Rogers's (2006) conception of a continuum between "industrial" and "artisanal" modes of comics production,[2] or the related distinction between heteronomous and autonomous fields, drawn from Bourdieu, applied by Beaty and others.

Ar:Zak contested industrial commercial practices in its transformation of established conditions of alienated labor, moving closer to the creative freedom of "artisanal" production. However, this was not by aligning comics production with an autonomous principle favoring the individual artistic genius and singular artwork founded on a romantic model of authorship—as seen in later alternative scenes fetishizing the handmade and recondite, and shoring up the status of the comics auteur and auratic work (see Beaty 2007). Ar:Zak instead combined artistic experimentation with an alternative cooperative mode of production aiming to challenge cultural hegemony exercised through economies of scale. As Emerson characterized it, their work was "a kind of step between commercial printing and self-publishing" (2013) using social ownership of industrial reproductive technologies to publish titles in higher print runs. Ar:Zak by no means competed at the level of mainstream comics publishing (or even other alternative comics like Talbot's *Brainstorm*) in terms of numbers of copies, printing 3,000–4,000 (occasionally up to 9,000) copies of their titles, distributing approximately 1,500 and selling between 500 and 1,000 (Emerson 2018; Walker 2014)— about 1/25 the scale of mainstream runs, and 1/3 of nationally distributed undergrounds. However, they were still operating at a higher capacity than self-publishing and fanzine levels, where individuals struggled to produce more than a few hundred copies.

The emphasis thus was not on producing work for a narrow audience with high levels of cultural capital by claiming comics as commensurate to high art, but enabling those excluded from making print culture and media to do so through collective pooling of resources. Within the context of the wider lab, this was part of aims to integrate artistic practice into the everyday lives of a wider community, offering young people in particular "the opportunity to extend their awareness through their own creativity," as producers as well as consumers of popular culture (Birmingham Arts Laboratory 1970).

Ar:Zak's purpose as a comics workshop was therefore not to realign comics publishing as a gentrified autonomous art practice, but like other community workshops to "seize control of the means of production" in order to reconfigure the organization of cultural labor on a democratic participatory basis (Long, Baig-Clifford, and Shannon 2013, 382). This included contesting the forms of value attributed to the work produced. Just as the cooperative logic of the workshop model suggested a mode of production beyond oppositions of a heteronomous culture industry and autonomous bourgeois art world, it similarly aimed to "intervene in and challenge habitual modes of representation" (382), equally experimenting with distinctions between mass cultural commodities and esoteric artworks to explore the possibilities for a popular art.

Artwork vs Commodity: The Art-Capital Contradiction

As Cadrette argues, the underground had "sought to develop comix as a uniquely expressive form of artistic practice, rather than just a means of generating profit" (2016, 104), constructing alternative criteria of evaluation. Positing comics as an artform rather than mass cultural commodity ascribed to them an antithetical kind of value, derived from the situation of artistic labor outside the rationality of socially necessary labor time (Spaulding and Denby 2015). The labor of making "art" arguably cannot be reified, homogenized, and thereby rendered exchangeable, and its value is therefore measured differently, in effect on the terms of its own uselessness. Detaching comics from commercial forms of production in which they are subsumed into capital affiliated them with this distinctive, intrinsic aesthetic value resulting from art's self-mediating autonomy, as opposed to the heteronomously determined exchange value of the commodity.

Distancing themselves from underground comix to a degree, and influenced by sophisticated European adult titles like *Métal Hurlant*, Ar:Zak was certainly interested in approaching comics as an art form, combining aims to print on as big a scale as they could with a commitment to high-quality reproduction, with some interior color pages as well as covers, on superior paper stock. This was explicitly positioned in opposition to the commercial "full colour, glossy cover, hiding the guts printed badly on newsprint approach" (*Streetcomix #4* 1977, 49). For this they met criticism from within the alternative comics scene, facing the response at KAK "you can stick your artistic integrity up your arse" (49).

This artistic approach to printing was echoed by the experimental approach of the strips reproduced, which challenged established conventions by playing with decorative layouts, Op-Art patterns, wordless strips, collage, washes, cut-out shapes, incongruous typefaces, underprinting type, and overprinting colors. *Streetcomix* included contributions pushing accepted boundaries of the comics form, such as Pokkettz's Heath Robinson–like diagrams and Jerzy Szostek's annotated photomontage, echoing the lab's interdisciplinary approach—equally seen in noncomics material: articles by comedian John Dowie, etchings by Siobhan Coppinger, photography by Derek Bishton.

Thus Ar:Zak positioned their work in opposition to the standardization, pseudo-individuation, mythic repetition, and false harmony identified by Theodor Adorno and Max Horkheimer as characteristic of the culture industry's fetishized commodities (2002, 94–135), instead championing the nonsubsumable autonomous value of comics as art.[3] This included resisting tendencies to politically instrumentalize comics that put them at odds with elements of the alternative press, arguing "our medium is capable for being a vehicle for radical aware ideas without becoming propaganda" (*Streetcomix #6* 1978, 33).

However, this did not mean that their titles were situated as highbrow or abstruse. Many contributors, like their underground precursors, appropriated the visual styles and iconography of cartoon animation and early newspaper strips—Emerson owing as much to George Herriman's "Krazy Kat" as Moebius's "Arzach" (after which the imprint was named). This stylistic alignment with comics' mass cultural roots was matched by narratives focused on blue-collar characters and everyday urban life (including alienated work), maintaining a fair dose of underground bad taste, sex, and violence.

Similarly, despite commitment to quality printing, Ar:Zak titles were not presented as treasurable objects of aesthetic contemplation distinct from comics' disreputable status as disposable ephemera. They included pull-out inserts and pin-up back covers encouraging physical disassembly, as well as drawing styles and printing methods emphasizing material facture—scratchy lines and dense hatching, large areas of screentone, stenciled type and erratic hand lettering, frayed edges, and wonky margins. Along with frequent metafictional references to the acts of making comics, including submitting to Ar:Zak and printing at the press, this reflexive DIY aesthetic demystified creative production in a way commensurate with the workshop model. As Emerson put it, "despite it being very 'arty' the Lab was never a precious, aesthetic place. We all worked very hard and at great pace and . . . learned to make design decisions on the hoof" (2018), prioritizing improvisation, experimentation, and making do with available resources over the accomplishment or transcendental value of the final outcome. This worked against the autonomy of "pure art" that (like the commodity) concealed the work's determination by the social context of its production, instead foregrounding the collaborative technical processes of its making.

This meant that while Ar:Zak repudiated the instrumental alienation of creative labor for the extraction of surplus value and the colonization of everyday life by the commodity form, it equally contested the bourgeois heroic myth of artistic autonomy and art as a mystified metaphysical practice that excluded those lacking social privilege (see Johnston 2016), opening comics production to groups historically marginalized from and within it, most notably women. Straddling the contradictory status of the comics made as both artworks and commodities, this offered the possibility of comics as a "fusion of popular art and avant-garde" (Buhle 2009: 37), an experiment in their functional transformation into a contentious democratic cultural form (both communally useful and critically useless) undertaken in a laboratory of artistic practice.

Conclusion

The contradictions of this reconfiguration of comics work and the value of the comics produced should be evident. The ALP used the alterity of creative labor to challenge alienating capitalist relations of production but remained within structural antagonisms of exploitation and a profit-driven market economy, its cooperative community workshop model navigating between and against industrial and artisanal modes. The comics made disputed the commodification of the creative activity that produced them by articulating the alternative autonomous value of comics as art, while challenging the separation of art from subjugated everyday life through a DIY aesthetic. These paradoxes were deeply connected to the contradictions of the Arts Lab itself, as a cooperative that struggled to make a surplus to share, where creative autonomy was predicated on low wages and voluntary work, and which ultimately relied on state subsidy that undermined its cooperative rationality and, through strategies of "repressive tolerance," co-opted its aims toward cultural democracy in depoliticized, paternalistic policies as a kind of outsourced social work (Hope 2008, 34–36).[4]

Ultimately Ar:Zak could not survive, criticized within alternative scenes as not "political enough" but failing to compete with mainstream publishers, they "struggled to find an audience" and gave away more comics than they ever sold (Emerson 2018). However, while this demonstrates the limitations of attempts to institute small-scale cooperative organization within general capitalist social relations, the example of Ar:Zak, ALP, the Birmingham Lab, and Arts Lab movement pointed toward alternative modes of collectively organizing cultural production situated in critical difference to both alienating industrial practices and bourgeois ideologies of art. Despite reproducing "the defects of the existing system," they stood "within the old form" as an "example of the emergence of a new form" (Marx [1894] 1981, 571) experimenting with broader possibilities for the democratic organization of work beyond capitalist commodity production. Situated within wider counter-cultural and radical social movements, these struggles over the autonomy of creative labor and the autonomous value of art were therefore embedded in broader political struggles for the socialization of the means of cultural production, the communalization of channels of creative expression and participatory democratic social organization. Made in this context, as the outcome of these antagonistic social processes and interactions, the comics produced bore its imprint—as José María Durán puts it, "the social fabric unfolds in the form given" to art (2016, 228), struggles over labor and value being woven into the textual and material surfaces of comics.

Notes

1. This distinguished the ALP from explicitly feminist (including women-only) poster workshops and printshops that saw "'mastering' traditional male-identified technology" as part of "dismantling limiting constructions of gender" (Baines 2015, 183). Varty recalls: "It didn't seem strange to me to be the token woman at Ar:Zak. I was working alongside people I knew and we shared common beliefs," and was "actively encouraged" to produce *Heroïne* (2018).

2. N.B. Rogers's "artisanal" equates more to atelier/studio practice than craft workshop production.

3. Although for Adorno the autonomous artwork is radically entwined with the fetishized commodity—free from use value as irreducible abstraction, it effectively becomes pure exchange value, immanently contradicting the commodity form by embodying it too absolutely, thereby revealing "everything cannot be reduced to exchange-value" (Martin 2007, 23).

4. This co-optation of the community arts movement itself fed into 1990s neoliberal policies celebrating "social inclusion" through art which disguised the intensifying "marginalization of women, ethnic minorities and working class from participation in cultural labour markets" (Oakley 2013, 57).

References

Adorno, Theodor and Max Horkheimer. 2002. *Dialectic of Enlightenment: Philosophical Fragments*. Edited by Gunzelin Schmid Noerr. Translated by Edmund Jephcott. Stanford, CA: Stanford University Press.

"Back to Birmingham." 1977. *Observer*, September 11, 1977.

Baines, Jess. 2015. "Nurturing Dissent? Community Printshops in 1970s London." In *Civic Engagement and Social Media*, edited by Julie Uldam and Anne Vestergaard, 174–93. London: Palgrave Macmillan.

Baines, Jess. 2016. *Democratising Print? The Field and Practices of Radical and Community Printshops in Britain 1968–98*. PhD diss., London School of Economics.

Banks, Mark. 2007. *The Politics of Cultural Work*. New York: Palgrave Macmillan.

Beaty, Bart. 2007. *Unpopular Culture: Transforming the European Comic Book in the 1990s*. Toronto: University of Toronto Press.

Beaty, Bart. 2012. *Comics versus Art*. Toronto: University of Toronto Press.

Benjamin, Walter. (1934) 2008. "The Author as Producer." *The Work of Art in the Age of its Technological Reproducibility and Other Writings on Media*. Edited by Michael W. Jennings, Brigid Doherty, and Thomas Y. Levin. Translated by Edmund Jephcott, Rodney Livingstone, Howard Eiland, 79–95. Cambridge, MA: Belknap Press of Harvard University Press.

Birmingham Arts Laboratory. 1970. *Application to The Arts Council of Great Britain for the year 1970–1971, January*. ACGB archive, New Activities—Birmingham Arts Lab files, ACGB/112/279/41. V&A Archive of Art and Design, London.

Birmingham Arts Laboratory Fund. 1968. *Leaflet: These People Are after Your Money*. ACGB archive, New Activities Committee files, ACGB/112/279/43. V&A Archive of Art and Design, London.

The Birmingham Arts Lab: The Phantom of Liberty. 1998. Birmingham: Birmingham Museum and Art Gallery.

Bourdieu, Pierre. 1993. *The Field of Cultural Production: Essays on Art and Literature*. Cambridge, UK: Polity Press.

Brett, Guy. 1981. "The Art of the Matter." *City Limits*. November–December, 1981.

Brienza, Casey. 2010. "Producing Comics Culture: A Sociological Approach to the Study of Comics." *Journal of Graphic Novels and Comics* 1 (2): 105–19.

Brienza, Casey and Paddy Johnston, eds. 2016. *Cultures of Comics Work*. London: Palgrave Macmillan.

Buhle, Paul. 2009. "The Undergrounds." In *Underground Classics: The Transformation of Comics into Comix*, edited by James Danky and Dennis Kitchen, 35–45. New York: Abrams Comic Art.

Burt, Sue. 1973. *Letter to Nick Barter, Secretary to the Experimental Projects Committee, 2 July*. ACGB archive, Experimental Projects Committee files, ACGB/43/42/10. V&A Archive of Art and Design, London.

Cadrette, Ryan. 2016. "From Turtles to Topatoco: A Brief History of Comic Book Production in the Pioneer Valley." In *Cultures of Comics Work*, edited by Casey Brienza and Paddy Johnston, 97–112. London: Palgrave Macmillan.

Cohen, Nicole S. 2017. "Cultural Work as a Site of Struggle: Freelancers and Exploitation." In *Marx and the Political Economy of Media*, edited by Christian Fuchs and Vincent Mosco, 36–64. Chicago: Haymarket Books.

Durán, José María. 2016. "Artistic Labor and the Production of Value: An Attempt at a Marxist Interpretation." *Rethinking Marxism* 28 (2): 220–37.

Emerson, Hunt. 2013. "Back to the Lab: Hunt Emerson. Flatpack Festival: Projects." Accessed January 14, 2015. http://www.flatpackfestival.org.uk/2013/03/back-to-the-lab-hunt-emerson/.

Emerson, Hunt. 2018. Personal communication with the author, March 24.

Everitt, Anthony. 1999. "Ted Little." *Guardian*. August 12, 1999.

Fuchs, Christian. 2017. "Raymond Williams' Communicative Materialism." *European Journal of Cultural Studies* 20 (6): 744–62.

Gray, Maggie. 2017. *Alan Moore, Out from the Underground: Cartooning, Performance, and Dissent*. London: Palgrave Macmillan.

Grosvenor, Ian and Natasha Macnab. 2015. "Photography as an Agent of Transformation: Education, Community and Documentary Photography in Post-War Britain." *Paedagogica Historica* 51 (1–2): 117–35.

Hesmondhalgh, David and Sarah Baker. 2011. *Creative Labour: Media Work in Three Cultural Industries*. London: Routledge.

Hope, Sophie. 2008. "The Economics of Socially Engaged Art." Accessed December 18, 2017. http://welcomebb.sophiehope.org.uk/Sophie_ActionResearch/contextual%20analysis.pdf.

Johnston, Paddy. 2016. "Under the Radar: John Porcellino's *King Kat* Comics and Self-Publishing as Cultural Work." In *Cultures of Comics Work*, edited by Casey Brienza and Paddy Johnston, 145–60. London: Palgrave Macmillan.

Long, Paul, Yasmeen Baig-Clifford, and Roger Shannon. 2013. "'What We're Trying to Do Is Make Popular Politics': The Birmingham Film and Video Workshop." *Historical Journal of Film, Radio and Television* 33 (3): 377–95.

Martin, Stewart. 2007. "The Absolute Artwork Meets the Absolute Commodity." *Radical Philosophy* 146: 15–25.

Marx, Karl. (1844) 1959. *Economic and Philosophic Manuscripts*. Translated by Martin Milligan. Marxist Internet Archive. Accessed February 10, 2018. http://www.marxists.org/archive/marx/works/1844/manuscripts/preface.htm.

Marx, Karl. (1867) 1976. *Capital: A Critique of Political Economy*. Vol. 1. Translated by Ben Fowkes. Harmondsworth: Penguin.

Marx, Karl. (1894) 1981. *Capital: A Critique of Political Economy*. Vol. 3. Translated by David Fernbach. London: Penguin.

McAllister, Matthew P. 1990. "Cultural Argument and Organizational Constraint in the Comic Book Industry." *Journal of Communication* 40 (1): 55–71.

McRobbie, Angela. 2014. *Be Creative: Making a Living in the New Culture Industries*. Cambridge, UK: Polity Press.

Mészáros, István. 1972. *Marx's Theory of Alienation*. 3rd ed. London: Merlin Press.

Norch. n.d. "Freewheel Bookshop." Accessed March 26, 2018. http://norch.co.uk/freewheel/4593846736.

Norcliffe, Glen and Olivero Rendace. 2003. "New Geographies of Comic Book Production in North America: The New Artisan, Distancing, and the Periodic Social Economy." *Economic Geography* 79 (3): 241–63.

Oakley, Kate. 2013. "Absolute Workers: Representation and Participation in the Cultural Industries." In *Theorizing Cultural Work: Labour, Continuity and Change in the Cultural and Creative Industries*, edited by Mark Banks, Rosalind Gill, and Stephanie Taylor, 56–67. London: Routledge.

Ollman, Bertell. 1976. *Alienation: Marx's Conception of Man in Capitalist Society*. 2nd ed. Cambridge: Cambridge University Press.

Rogers, Mark C. 2006. "Understanding Production: The Stylistic Impact of Artisanal and Industrial Methods." *International Journal of Comic Art* 8 (1): 509–17.

Ross, Andrew. 2003. *No-Collar: The Humane Workplace and Its Hidden Costs*. Philadelphia: Temple University Press.

Sabin, Roger. 1993. *Adult Comics: An Introduction*. London: Routledge.

See Red Women's Workshop (c. 1976). *The Freedom of the Press Belongs to Those Who Control the Press*. Poster. Reproduced in Jess Baines. 2012. "Experiments in Democratic Participation: Feminist Printshop Collectives." *Cultural Policy, Criticism and Management Research* 6: n.p. https://culturalpolicyjournal.wordpress.com/past-issues/issue-no-6/feminist-printshop-collectives/.

Spaulding, Daniel and Nicole Demby. 2015. "Art, Value, and the Freedom Fetish." *Mute*, May 28, 2015. http://www.metamute.org/editorial/articles/art-value-and-freedom-fetish-0.

Streetcomix #2. 1976. Birmingham: Ar:Zak.

Streetcomix #3. 1977. Birmingham: Ar:Zak.

Streetcomix #4. 1977. Birmingham: Ar:Zak.

Streetcomix #6. 1978. Birmingham: Ar:Zak.

Stephens, Julie. 1998. *Anti-Disciplinary Protest: Sixties Radicalism and Postmodernism*. Cambridge: Cambridge University Press.

"Ted Little." 1999. *Independent*, September 6, 1999.

Varty, Suzy. 2018. Personal communication with the author, March 1.

Wakefield, Thirza. 2015. "Beau Brum: Remembering the Birmingham Arts Lab." *Sight and Sound*, August 7, 2015. http://www.bfi.org.uk/news-opinion/sight-sound-magazine/features/beau-brum-remembering-birmingham-s-arts-lab.

Walker, James. 2014. "Hunt Emerson and the Birmingham Arts Lab." Accessed February 10, 2018. http://dawnoftheunread.wordpress.com/2014/09/08/hunt-emerson-and-the-birmingham-arts-lab/.

Williams, Mark. 1968. *Letter to Treasurer, Arts Council of Great Britain, 8 October*. ACBG archive, New Activities Committee files, ACGB/112/279/43. V&A Archive of Art and Design, London.

Woo, Benjamin. 2013. "Why Is It So Hard to Think about Comics as Labour?" *Comics Forum*. Accessed December 18, 2017. http://comicsforum.org/2013/12/09/why-is-it-so-hard-to-think-about-comics-as-labour-by-benjamin-woo/.

Woo, Benjamin. 2015. "Erasing the Lines between Leisure and Labor: Creative Work in the Comics World." *Performing Labor in the Media Industries* 35 (2): 57–64.

Zeitlyn, Jonathan.1980. *Print: How You Can Do It Yourself*. 3rd ed. London: Inter-Action.

6

Hate, Marginalization, and Tramp-Bashing

A Raceclass and Critical Realist Approach to Researching British National Identity through Comics

LYDIA WYSOCKI

Not everyone reads the same comics. The world would be a strangely totalitarian place if we did. But even when we do read the same comics, it is far from certain that different readers read the same meaning from those comics. In this chapter I use three examples of "British comics" taken from a larger empirical project about the connection between comics and discourses of "Britishness," and align these with a Critical Realist framework. This advances and uses specific social science theoretical and analytical tools for understanding comics as material culture. As such, in the later part of this chapter I will make explicit a wider conceptual framework based in sociocultural theory, using this to show how the study of comics can approach larger questions of representation and identity formation.

This chapter is not an introduction to Critical Realism, but an initial step in using Critical Realism for the study of social forces as they are made evident in comics as cultural products. It relies on a familiarity with empirical approaches to research, locating Critical Realism as part of Marxist methods in social science. Critical Realism is a notoriously unwieldy framework when presented in the abstract: I will summarize it briefly here and hasten to show it more thoroughly through examples. In seeking to understand the depth and complexity of the social world, Critical Realism is a rejection of earlier positivist stances (Archer 1998, 199). Initially led by Bhaskar (1979; 1975), essential readings in the field (Archer et al. 1998) outline key concepts especially that of stratification (Bhaskar 1998). This is taken further with great clarity by Sayer (1992):

We do not understand a book (any more than we come to understand a foreign language) by observing and analysing the shape of words or their frequency of occurrence, but by interpreting their meaning. (Sayer 1992, 35)

It is this multilayeredness that I will emphasize in this innovation of using a Critical Realist approach for the critical study of comics. I am taking a mixed methods perspective on Sayer's focus on meaning, though note that the strengths of Critical Realism have been demonstrated in both heavily quantitative (Elder-Vass 2010) and predominately qualitative work (Jones 2016).

The understanding of a stratified social world offered by Critical Realism can support the critical study of comics in considering what is inherent in a specific comic and what is dependent upon specific readers' readings of that same comic. Whereas a phenomenological approach holds that actors' interpretations matter most, for Critical Realists the social world does hold truths though identifying and analyzing them is a complex undertaking. Bhaskar's articulation of three "overlapping domains of reality" (Bhaskar 1975, 56) is not a linear way to dig deeper in the hope of hitting truth, but a way to approach this complexity of the social world. Those three strata of the *real*, *actual*, and *empirical* (Bhaskar 1975) address how that which is not immediately obvious is no less present: not every phenomenon is observable, but the potential and effects of forces and powers can be determined. Such meticulous approaches to complexity enable Critical Realism to be used as an underlaborer to Marxism, which as Banfield (2016) reminds us was Bhaskar's original intent. My focus here is on using precision tools for analysis, to work toward understanding and then changing the world for the better (Banfield 2016).

I will list three examples of comics as allied to Sayer's (2000) definition of each of Bhaskar's three domains, before moving on to each example in turn. The *real* addresses the structures and powers of objects, here through the example of claims to contested readings of a MAC cartoon (McMurtry 2015) in the *Daily Mail* newspaper that contributes to the normalization of hate. Going deeper, the *actual* explores what happens when powers are activated, here in the example of the extent to which a sample of comics in *Beano* annuals include diverse representation. Deeper still, the *empirical* moves to the domain of experience, here exemplified through the small-press comics *The Manly Boys Annual* and *Comely Girls Annual* (Tillotson and Brookes 2014). These examples are taken from my ongoing larger study of readers' readings of British comics 2010–2017, chosen from a longer list refined from reviews, best-of lists, and questionnaire data on what readers read (see Wysocki 2018).

Example 1. Real: The Normalization of Hate

On 17 November 2015 the *Daily Mail* published a cartoon by Stanley "MAC" McMurtry "apparently comparing refugees to rats" (D. Brown 2015). MAC's depiction of people and rats crossing a European border prompted readers' comparisons with a 1939 cartoon from Nazi Germany that showed rats forced out of Germany then running toward a door labeled "democratic countries." That same morning, Twitter user "@cuphook108" tweeted both images, writing:

> One is a Nazi cartoon laughing at Jews denied entry to democratic countries. The other is the Daily Mail today. (@cuphook108, quoted in D. Brown 2015)

That tweet was shared over sixteen thousand times and reported in multiple (inter)national newspapers (including D. Brown 2015; HER 2015; Levenson 2015), alongside similar comparisons made by other social media users.[1]

Within its original publication context MAC's comic is particularly eye-catching as a hand-drawn, albeit digitally produced, image filling approximately a third of a 38cm by 30cm page of typeset text and smaller images. The uses of visual and verbal language in comics, and indeed the distribution of those comics, play out in ways particular to the comics medium. The process of spreading that language uses particularly accessible formats, here in mass market print and digital newspapers and through sharing on social media. Indeed, this is not an example of extreme views by a cartoonist at the periphery of the comics industry: in 2003 McMurtry received an MBE for services to the newspaper industry (British Cartoon Archive 2016), went on to win the Cartoonist of the Year 2016 Award at the Society of Editors' Press Awards (Press Awards 2016), and retired from the *Daily Mail* in December 2018 after a fifty-year career (Kay 2018). The work of critical comics studies involves understanding where the power of comics comes from and how it operates.

Among the twenty-five reader comments on Buchanan's (2015) article in the *Independent* reporting on the outcry caused by this cartoon are readings that the rats *are* Muslims, and that rats are *amongst* Muslims:

Both instances are depicting a minority and persecuted group as rodents and sub-humans. (Username: Doveylr)

One depicts the Jews as all rats, [sic] the other depicts rats (terrorists) amongst normal muslims [sic], a clear difference. (Username: Epiphany)

It could be that this *real*, tangible, object—the comic as published—does contain potential for both readings, in which case polysemy is at work. Though consistent with Bakhtin's ([1965] 1968) concepts of polyphony (multiple discourses) and polyvocalism (multiple voices) in a given text, polysemy's focus on multiplicity of meaning goes deeper.[2] It builds on Vološinov's ([1929] 1973) writing on the multiple meanings inherent in a given word or sign, taken further still by Kristeva (Kristeva 1986; Dentith 1995). Polysemy considers that the meaning of a given utterance is itself unstable. It is not a case of reading around multiple otherwise stable meanings or becoming attuned to multiple voices expressed within a single text,[3] but an acknowledgment that each sign is inherently unstable.

To reject this focus on polysemy would lead to a belief that there is a single correct reading. Indeed, in speaking to the *Independent*'s journalist the *Daily Mail*'s spokesperson had no time for claims of polysemy. Without specifying which was the "correct" reading, they claimed readers had deliberately twisted the cartoon:

We are not going to dignify these absurd comments which willfully misrepresent this cartoon apart from to say that we have not received a single complaint from any reader. (Daily Mail spokesperson, quoted in Buchanan 2015)

While it is easy to reject the *Mail*'s own statement as a refusal to engage with complexity, it can be trickier to unravel the *Guardian*'s attempt at a more nuanced report. An appeal to polysemy is seen in the equivocation of Bland's (2015) article in the *Guardian*, in which reporting that "not everyone agrees" and "[c]artoonists have often come in for this kind of criticism" soon progressed to handwringing:

Your view of the validity of these claims is likely to depend on your view of whether such images rise to the level of trope—a persistent visual association that a casual viewer will have somewhere in the back of his [sic] mind—or are just part of the cartoonist's general

armoury that happens to have been deployed in a particular context.
(Bland 2015)

The argument that multiple readings are possible here functions as an attempt to downplay accusations of hateful depictions of Muslims and Jews. It evades the need to expose, name, and dismantle the inequitable structures that underpin representations, which as Apple (2011) tells us are among the tasks of a critical scholar. Bland's appeal is directed to an audience sufficiently well read to distinguish between animalization as a deliberate historical reference and animalization as a generic cartooning technique. Yet Bland falls into what Billig (2005) has critiqued as the recycling of stereotypes, a process of "validating prejudiced images" (Billig 2005, 165) whether or not the speaker believes the stereotypes that they employ. As such the attempted differentiation between deliberate stereotyping and generic cartooning crumbles. Even without reproducing McMurtry's cartoon writing about it still contributes to drawing attention to a cartoon that can be easily found online, adding to the haze of multiple possible readings without making visible a framework for why likening loosely defined groups of people to rodents is dehumanizing. Polysemy is here used as a weak response that evades critical engagement with a hateful text, rather than a nuanced and powerful way to explore how different readers read the same comic.

This emphasis on audience goes further still. The particular instance of opprobrium I have discussed here was @cuphook108's tweet published on Twitter, then republished in the *Independent* (D. Brown 2015). The neat visual comparison with the horror of Nazi propaganda also plays out in looking down at the ignorance of *Daily Mail* readers for consuming such overt hatred, again also found in reader comments on Buchanan's (2015) article:

Are we meant to be surprised? The Daily Mail and its readership were astoundingly sympathetic to the ideologies of fascism and social Darwinism at the turn of the century, right up until the war itself. The intent of the paper and the nature of the readers hasn't changed since. (Username: Featherstone1)

Look at the ignorance of using, let alone falling for, the same propaganda as in Nazi times! We more discerning readers do not fall for such base tricks. This is a classed distancing from racism as something done by lower-status publications and readers, not by readers of the higher-status *Independent*. Even in considering McMurtry's cartoon inciting race-based hatred of immigrants, class is not far away.

A Critical Realist focus on the *real* shows that it is not enough to hold a distasteful example at arm's length and reject it as ignorance. Identifying the exercise of power, and the operation of social forces of race and class, requires interrogation of what is presented as normal, as much as the periodic public shaming of specific newspaper cartoons and other comics for the aberrant use of overt hatred in their words and/or pictures. Interrogating a surface-level object—the dehumanized depiction in McMurtry's cartoon—and reactions to that depiction start to glimpse the layers left to uncover even in an apparently clear-cut instance of the mainstreaming of hate speech through a newspaper editorial cartoon. Having scratched the surface, I turn next to *actual* examples of representation in comics that can appear equitable but still hide marginalization in plain sight.

Example 2. Actual: Sidelining Progress

My Content Analysis approach in this section is based on methods from Nancy Larrick's 1965 study "The All-White World of Children's Books" (Larrick 1965). Larrick identified a sample of children's books and counted how many—how few—included Black characters, before going on to interrogate those representations in more detail. I am revisiting her method as a useful middle step though note that this binary classification of ethnicities, used as a proxy for the more complex social construct of race, should not be taken as an end point nor should it be used as a method for real humans. It is useful here for taking stock of the state of this sample of British comics.

"Ball Boy" is a recurring comic about a children's football team. It is a recurring single- or multipage strip in the *Beano* comics anthology. My sample is the *Beano* annual for each year 2010–2017, not a full run of "Ball Boy" but a sample curated by *Beano*'s editors. I counted every appearance in the comic of all characters on each page of each year's annual, as a basic categorization by race and gender. These were coded into one of five groups: White Male, White Female, BAME Male, BAME Female, or any other nonhuman character. From my Content Analysis of all comics in this sample of annuals "Ball Boy" stood out as having the highest proportion of Black and Minority Ethnic (BAME) characters. Many other series within *Beano* annuals had none at all: of 383 chapters within these eight annuals, only 111 chapters included any appearances by a BAME character. The latest available UK census data on ethnicity gives a national population average of 86% White, 14% BAME (Office of National Statistics 2011). In this sample 73% of "Ball Boy" characters are White and 27% are BAME, comfortably exceeding the

Table 6.1: Mean average utterances per appearance: "Ball Boy" in Beano annuals 2010-2017.	
Category	Utterances per appearance
All human characters	0.41
White characters only	0.44
BAME characters only	0.32

14% national average of BAME Britons. Given that a recent study of children's books published in 2017 found only 4% of that sample included any BAME characters (Centre for Literacy in Primary Education 2017), it is refreshing to see an ethnically diverse team; all the more so because this sample of "Ball Boy" strips are about the continued mediocre performance of the team, not overtly about wider social issues–based storylines.

This optimism is however short lived. A Content Analysis approach to counting how many times each character speaks shows that BAME characters speak less often than do White characters. I refer to these speech acts as utterances, following Vygotsky and Bakhtin (Emerson 1983), regardless of how many words or symbols comprise each utterance: it is the act of speaking that is a key way to determine that a character is participating in the action of a comic. I counted all utterances as denoted by a speech or thought bubble, as both voiced and unvoiced speech are habitually made visible in the comics medium. Dividing the number of utterances by the number of appearances calculates a mean average number of utterances per appearance (Table 6.1).

Whereas the mean average number of utterances per appearances for White characters is slightly above the average for all human characters, the mean average number of utterances per appearance for BAME characters is below that same benchmark. Combing through the data year by year there is little to buck this trend. Only in 2014's sample were BAME characters more talkative than their White teammates. In 2010's annual speaking parts for BAME characters were so rare that it was more likely that an utterance was by a talking animal (102 utterances) than by a BAME character (9 utterances), let alone a White character (698 utterances).

Comparing utterances to appearances on the page is countable evidence that BAME characters are marginalized in comparison to White characters. BAME characters are more likely to have a nonspeaking role, as a sign that their participation in the story is sidelined. Their potential power of speech or thought is not activated, as determined at this *actual* level by comparison with the expectation that utterances be equally shared among characters. At this *actual* level, Content Analysis can show where to look before Critical Discourse Analysis (Halliday 1978) begins to identify what is really going on. In considering the stratified nature of reality a Critical Realist approach to comics shows that there is more than immediately meets the eye.

As such, comics could represent fertile ground for the analytical tool of microaggressions (Sue 2010). As everyday slights, often invisible to the perpetrator, the cumulative effect of microaggressions in speech and action harms the recipient. Microaggressions can be difficult to pinpoint in everyday life. Yosso et al. (2009) and Solórzano et al. (2000) listed examples that could all too easily be dismissed as one's own oversensitivity were it not for their samples of Black and Latinx students' lived experience of what it is like to be marginalized. Microaggressions are ephemeral in nature, but the richness of interactions represented in comics form gives a tangible, countable record of interactions. Indeed, microaggressions can include nonverbal interactions; my focus on utterances here forms part of a researcher's choice of suitable methods in a given context and would necessarily be different for wordless comics. Unlike video recordings of natural interactions, used in therapeutic settings as Video Interaction Guidance (Kennedy, Landor, and Todd 2011) to help people better understand how to interact with others, representations of microaggressions in comics are already mediated by the comics creative team. I use the term "creative team" here not to remove the artist-writer's agency, but to acknowledge the shared responsibility with editors, publishers, colorists, letterers, distributors, and myriad other subdivisions of labor in making comics.[4]

Work on race blindness (Frankenberg 1997; Pearce 2005) and "happy talk" about race and diversity (Bell and Hartmann 2007) shows how the very discourses that should advance equity and multiculturalism (Modood 2013) are turned back on themselves (Hikido and Murray 2016). Scharrer and Ramasubramanian (2015) saw students identify and critique stereotypes, only to go on and use them in making their own films. When students then defended this as satire, Scharrer and Ramasubramanian identified this as the embeddedness of their prejudice; moreover, if these student filmmakers believed they were right to use stereotypes to show discrimination, there remained no guarantee that audiences would interpret the effect (or motives) in a favorable light. The inclusive intent of writing and drawing BAME characters in a comic can here belie a reflex of what roles they are given to play. At an extreme level there could be no need for comics creators to produce deliberately discriminatory work, as McMurtry did, if in attempting to be inclusive this implicit bias spills onto the page. Here the microaggressions recorded in comics show that damage can also be caused by attempts to help. Inadequate attention to fair representation obscures the issues at stake and in so doing perpetuates the potential for harm and denies the possibility of social change.

Staying with the *Beano*, comparable slippage can be seen with regard to social class in "The Bash Street Kids," a recurring multipage comic about a teacher and his class. The building, class, and staff of Bash Street School has changed little since the strip began in 1954 (Albion British Comics Database Wiki 2017). Their rival school is Posh Street, with specific comparisons made that compare Bash Street and Posh Street kids. In 2016's annual, Bash Street's teacher worries that the class kids are not ready to play against Posh Street not through a lack of skill, but through dirt (figure 6.1). The association of uncleanliness and low social status returns later in the same story when Posh Street's minibus splashes the Bash Street kids with mud. This reductive representation of social class is not an isolated example. It is also seen in the Bash Street Kids' tower block home, unmodernized school building, and struggling teacher. Difference is often played for laughs and even in a comic that revels in tangents and non sequiturs, few references to class are central to the plot of the story. Though there may be an assumption that readers are on the Bash Street Kids' side, this nevertheless builds up to a cumulative message that poor people are dirty and unsuccessful, posh people are clean and successful, and that this disparity is funny.

I have here written separately about race and about class, but this is incorrect. These are not separate: both examples are about race and both are about class. The footballers in "Ball Boy" vary in ethnicity, but the team always has neat matching football shirts and goalposts with nets on them. Until 2015's annual a flatcap and sheepskin coat contributed to a caricature of a working-class football manager, then in 2016 the character was changed to a more dynamic sweatsuit-wearing manager with floppy hair. Equally it was not until 2015 that the Bash Street Kids had meaningful, sustained engagement with a BAME person in the form of their new headteacher, Mr De Testa. Until then their world was an all-White bubble with social class the only aspect of their identity that mattered. This is not to downplay the importance of class-only or race-only based analysis, but to note that understanding this as raceclass (Leonardo 2012) reveals the intertwinedness of both these harmful social constructs. The timescale of these design changes within my 2010–2017 sample positions them as part of *Beano*'s "digital makeover" in which "[s]ome veteran characters have been tweaked to make them more inclusive" (Clarke 2018). There is a tension between celebrating the *Beano* creative team's work

Figure 6.1: Extract from "The Bash Street Kids," *The Beano Annual 2016*, 28. © DC Tomson.

in acknowledging and acting upon the need for more equitable representation, and remembering that underlying tensions of representation require ongoing critique and reflection not mere surface-level adjustment.

Example 3. Empirical: Village Greens and Superdiverse Cities

> Can you send me a title? An image for the website post would be good too. Any comics of people playing cricket? (very British!). (Thom Giddens, email to author, April 28, 2017)

In writing this chapter about contested ideas of Britishness and how these are written into and read out of different comics, I hesitated over editor Thom's request for an image. Intentionally or not, had his request defaulted to the same pastoral scene as John Major's comments in the House of Lords (Cruse 2008)?

> John Major, the former Prime Minister, evoked a pastiche of various images: " . . . long shadows on county cricket grounds, warm beer, invincible green suburbs, dog lovers and—as George Orwell said—old maids bicycling to Holy Communion through the morning mist." (Cruse 2008, 3, ellipsis in original)

Even alongside an abstract I was reluctant to highlight a single comic in isolation. Delaying writing, I looked for something—anything!—in my idiosyncratic collection of comics that was made and published in the United Kingdom and featured people playing cricket. The closest I found was the cover of *The Manly Boys Annual* by Steve Tillotson and Gareth Brookes (2014): two boys in cricket whites hold cricket bats aloft as a tramp cowers at their feet; a third boy in cricket whites looks on, cheering (see figure 6.2).

This tramp-bashing parody of old annuals (e.g., figure 6.3), and more recent nostalgia-fueled retro style annuals, may well not have been what Thom meant. There are no cricket-specific comics in the rest of this compendium of comics and other words and pictures, though *Comely Girls Annual*, sold as a double pack with *Manly Boys*, does feature one of my favorite comics of all time: "St William's Plays Up" (figure 6.4). Girls play hockey on a vicarage green, wearing sport skirts and knee socks, and they refer to a recent village fete. This pastoral idyll bears almost no resemblance to my own schooling. But every utterance in the comic is primarily an insult, typically

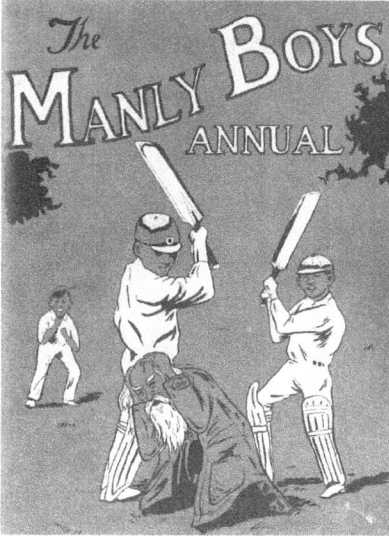

Figure 6.2: Cover of *The Manly Boys Annual*. Steve Tillotson and Gareth Brookes, 2014. © Steve Tillotson and Gareth Brookes.
Figure 6.3: Cover of *The Boy's Own Annual*, vol. 62, 1939–40; unknown artist. © Lutterworth Press.

crude name-calling about sexual behavior: their verbal violence matches the physical violence of the gameplay. This is far more familiar from my own schooldays at a comprehensive school in a "super-diverse" (Suzanne Hall 2017) British city, despite my never having played hockey on a village green.

These personal reflections show my multifaceted reasons for finding, reading, enjoying, and remembering a specific comic. They indicate an *empirical* level of experience deeper than the *real* and *actual* strata already discussed. But it is not enough to only present my reading of a comic. How do other people read this same comic? Is the setting and content familiar or unfamiliar to them, is the language unremarkable or shocking, and what do they consider acceptable behavior at a village fete? Is their reading of this comic in line with the creators' intended meaning, or have they—have I— read it wrong? I note two points to advocate for more research into readers' readings of comics.

First, have other people read this comic? *Manly Boys* was initially self-published in 2009 with a print run of 400 copies, then in 2014 revised and reissued in a second printing (as a double pack with new comic *Comely Girls Annual*) of 500 copies by Avery Hill Publishing, a micropublisher based in London.[5] Extracts, but not the full comic, can be found online. A total print run of 900 copies is not insignificant, but even allowing that circulation

Figure 6.4: First two panels of "St William's Plays Up." Steve Tillotson and Gareth Brookes, 2014. © Steve Tillotson and Gareth Brookes.

(readership) may be higher, it suggests a modest number of readers as part of small press or micropublishing within an international comics industry where print and online readership can reach far higher numbers. UK comics publishing is a diversified industry. Some of the most comprehensive data for this period is in John Freeman's (2017) spreadsheet of Audit Bureau of Circulation data, giving insights into comics sold in newsagents with reported sales at most in the tens of thousands. Yet there is no single measure of circulation that encompasses serialized and standalone comics-form works, specialist comics distributors and retailers, general bookshops and newsagents, online retail, and events and marketplaces, all whether direct from publishers and creators or via distributors.

Second, do other people read it not at face value? Skewering pastoral tradition, lampooning the same sense of twentieth-century British history upheld by other comics collectors, mocking the upper-middle-class version of girlhood often celebrated in the girls' comics that Gibson's (2015) readers recalled with warm affection in oral histories of their girlhood reading. There is something here that requires meticulous, precise engagement with readers to address this *empirical* level of social reality, in addition to the *real* and *actual* levels already discussed. Opportunities for this engagement with readers' readings have been explored in other multimodal media but have been largely absent in the study of comics. Kehily's (1999) work on magazines aimed at teenage girls focused on group readings that negotiate a collective moral understanding of the text. The 1990s moral panic among adults at teen magazines' frank discussion of sex and sexual health did not match what Kehily found in how groups of teens discuss their own standpoints when reading the same magazines. Indeed, teens' sophisticated strategies were in stark contrast to adult outrage at face value readings, contributing to a discussion of how adults police cultural products intended for teen and child readers (Saguisag 2017). Barker's (1984) account of the British horror comics scare came close to this duality in noting that the Comics Campaign Council's (CCC) objections to imported horror comics comprised:

> not the comments of analysis, but of outrage. It is not an adequate defence that there was no discipline of media studies or the like at the time, since no one even considered the need for a discipline. They rejected the need for disciplined comment at all. When looking at the comics, caution could be thrown to the winds of a commonsense ideology, for the dangers were "obvious." (Barker 1984, 39)

In discussing prevalent types of horror comic stories Barker presented his own readings of horror comics as a universalizing address to his readers but still acknowledged that children might not respond as the comics "intend or propose" (Barker 1984, 133). As discussed earlier in this chapter, the concept of polysemy allows that the intent or proposition of a specific comic remains unstable even to adult readers. In *The Orphan*, the most prominent comic discussed by Barker from among the CCC's (and as Barker notes, Fredric Wertham's) many objections, it was the implied violence and deceit a child perpetrated against her parents that prompted adults' concern. But without empirical research it is far from certain that child readers interpreted this as gravely as did adults, particularly as the implied menace is not revealed until the comic's final panel. What contemporary child readers made of *The Orphan* may never be known, especially as the tantalizing potential that this could be one of the comics featured in Wertham's (1954) case notes of comics-reading children has been dashed by Tilley's (2012) discovery that Wertham falsified his research findings. It does however indicate that the potential for mismatch between intent and outcome goes far beyond clever panel layouts or optical illusions as a bit of fun by skilled artists and writers. There is a complexity to reading comics that critical scholars are as yet only beginning to explore.

Toward a Critical Theoretical Framework

Taking a Critical Realist approach in setting out three examples of comics at three layers of analysis has demonstrated the use of analytical tools that address the embeddedness of issues of representation in reading comics. For me this analysis must be part of a theoretical framework that foregrounds a socially connected exploration of meaning, always with the awareness that language is not a neutral carrier of meaning. As such I now turn to discuss the wider theoretical framework underpinning my use of Critical Realism as a specific approach in the social science study of comics, and to problematize the specific context of British comics.

Approaching comics as cultural products emphasizes a need to acknowledge multiple possible readings of comics texts without denying a classical Marxist argument that some properties are inherent in that text (Bhaskar 1979). Just as a heavy bag is heavy, not only perceived to be heavy, discriminatory content and language are discriminatory, not only perceived to be discriminatory. Stuart Hall and colleagues at the Centre for Contemporary Cultural Studies challenged older notions of media texts as "'transparent' bearers of meaning" (Stuart Hall 1997, 117) to show that a given culture's practices and values become embedded in its products:

> It is by our use of things, and what we say, think and feel about them—how we represent them—that we *give them a meaning*. (Stuart Hall 1997, 3, emphasis in original)

A sociocultural understanding of learning (Vygotsky 1978; Wertsch 1981) shows that it is through language that we construct and understand our social world. Even when reading alone, reading only has meaning because of the social construction of meaning supported by language. To identify this transfer of meaning from creator to comic to reader one must consider at what level to research it. A focus on sign/signifier/signified classification (Saussure [1916] 1983) can support formalist approaches to the comics medium, with uses in identifying and learning to replicate or experiment with specific techniques. The limits of a semiotic-based grammarian approach are seen in Forcevilles's (2011) study of emanata at the level of phoneme/grapheme: his focus on *Tintin* does indeed showcase a range of mark-making phenomena in making comics, but fails to engage with the tropes and ethics of Hergé's portrayal of indigenous characters as childlike drunkards. This wider critical engagement is essential for the critical study of comics as it highlights the gap between marks on a page and readers' interpretations of those marks.

Stuart Hall's explanation of the process of encoding/decoding meaning (1980) can offer a bridge between sociocultural theory of learning and a focus on cultural products. Hall showed the potential for either match or mismatch in the reader's reading (process of decoding) of what the writer wrote (process of encoding). When writers and readers have sufficiently similar frames of reference this transfer of meaning can be seamless, but when writers and readers have different frames of reference there is potential for miscommunication. In comics this (mis)communication is at stake in words, pictures, and words and pictures together (multimodally), all of which are open to match or mismatch of intended and received meanings. This liminal space could indicate scope to advance sociocultural theory to more explicitly include not only images but the interdependence of words and pictures as exemplified in the comics medium.

In delimiting a field of study, "British comics" is a term often used yet rarely interrogated. Its appearances include as a subset of a larger field in Sabin's *Adult Comics* (1993) which differentiated the history of British comics from the wider history of comics in Britain. Gravett and Stanbury's *Great British Comics* (2006) discussed a range of examples without attempting a comprehensive survey, and Chapman's (2011) *British Comics: A Cultural History* tacitly limited itself to floppy serialized comic books without due attention to the breadth of the medium or range of the industry. Hoggart's (1957) view of British servicemen reading American comics as "the passive visual taking-on of mass bad art geared to a very low mental age" (201) has been repeatedly cited by comics scholars as a way to move beyond his narrow and negative view—not least by the editors of the first UK academic journal of comics studies (Huxley and Ormrod 2010, 1). It would however be insufficient to define British comics, or indeed any other national or regional categorization, as "not American." A meaningful discussion of British comics requires an acknowledgment that what counts as a comic, and what counts as British, is contested.

Comics is a medium and an industry, as well as the name given to a particular subset of serialized story papers. Other subsets of that same medium include webcomics, newspaper cartoons, strip comics, graphic novels, and yet more forms. Too narrow a focus fails to engage at the level of a medium. The push for comics' legitimation as part of a literary canon (Magnussen and Christiansen 2000; Miodrag 2013) can help attract attention to exceptional creative works. The corollary to this pursuit of exclusivity is the risk of splintering off some comics, and some voices, as intrinsically more worthwhile than others. Attempts at canonization have already seen the graphic novel upheld as an emphatically middle-class version of comics, to the extent of reviews that strain to refer to the text as anything other than comics (Cooke 2015), and indeed the absurd neologism of "mini graphic novels" (Rockman 2015). The question of what is a comic highlights the risk that new or different work is pushed aside for not sitting comfortably with traditions of style, genre, or format, or has its uniqueness ground down in order to better fit existing categories as a marketable product.

Defining Britishness is something Britain has struggled with since its construction as a nineteenth-century political union of Great Britain (island home to the countries of Scotland, England, and Wales) with Ireland (now island home to the sovereign states of Northern Ireland and the Republic of Ireland). This United Kingdom of Great Britain and Northern Ireland was built on industry and migration at home and in its empire, and now as a postcolonial state still struggles with how to teach this as history (Cole 2004; Colley 1992) and how to live it (Gillborn 2005; Gilroy 1991). The dominant late twentieth-century project of multiculturalism as a pluralistic way of being British (Modood 2013; Parekh 2000) has since met claims that state multiculturalism has failed (Cameron 2011), and that what Britain needs is to "be far more muscular in promoting British values" (Cameron 2014). At the time of writing, that muscular approach to unity is legislated not as a comprehensive national vision, but as four Fundamental British Values stipulated as part of the Prevent strand of the CONTEST antiterror strategy:

> democracy, the rule of law, individual liberty, and mutual respect and tolerance of those with different faiths and beliefs. (Department for Education 2014)

Prevent is aimed at countering a threat that includes both specific real international terrorist threats and risks of radicalization, and more nebulous constructions of fear and difference. Current policy enforcement has been critiqued as disproportionately targeting BAME—particularly Muslim—Britons (Lander 2016; Bolloten and Richardson 2015). A further critique of Prevent is that it contains little if anything uniquely British, as distinct from the values underpinning universal human rights. While the House of Lords briefing note on Britishness (Cruse 2008) gave an indication of the breadth of this debate, the aforementioned quote by former Prime Minister John Major also showed that in debates of national significance romanticized vignettes of cricket and Christianity are never far away. The "Life in the UK" citizenship test has been critiqued for a similar lapse into pub quiz point-scoring rather than practical skills and knowledge needed by citizens (Brooks 2016). In this context the proliferation of clickbait articles and quizzes promising to reveal "How British are you?" (Thomas 2014) is perhaps not unexpected. The fluctuations of defining British national identity show that national identity is not only something for new nations to strive for with the fervor of Ignatieff's (1993) hot nationalism, but a prolonged project of determining and enacting what it is to be British in everyday life as a manifestation of Billig's (1995) banal nationalism. It is in this politicized context that a focus on representation in British comics is so sorely needed.

Comics scholarship in the United States has already included a critical focus on race and class. Whaley's (2015) *Black Women in Sequence* restores attention to comics creators and characters important to their fans but denied a place in the mainstream comics industry; Jeffrey Brown's (2000) *Black Superheroes, Milestone Comics, and Their Fans* shows the power of a niche yet significant creator-owned publishing company; and Stein's (2012) interview with cartoonist Keith Knight touches on the everydayness of race in comics. Yet in UK comics studies this remains an under-researched field. Strengths are seen in practice-based research projects including McNicol's (2018) work with Bangladeshi migrant women, and through nonacademic work including the *Critical Chips* zine (Akhtar 2017) and the Full Colour Mentoring Project (BHP Comics 2018). There is ample precedent in UK cultural studies for a more explicitly critical turn. Stuart Hall and colleagues' *Policing the Crisis* (1978) was unequivocal in naming the social forces of race and class at work in contemporary media at a time when the field of cultural studies on Britain was still in its infancy. These forces are evident in the published form of a text: they may be different for comics in a tabloid newspaper with multimillion readership in print and/or online, a children's comics annual, or a small-press comic with a finite print run, but are evident in each example. The effects of these social forces go beyond the published form of a text to the language in which that text is created, and the values embedded in that language.

Comics are not made or read in a vacuum. They use visual and verbal language that can only be understood as part of our social world. Through a sociocultural understanding of language the possibility of multiple readings of a given comic becomes clearer, and comics that initially appear to give balanced depictions might on closer inspection belie deeper inequities. A Critical Realist understanding of the social world as stratified identifies levels at which the critical study of comics is possible. As these examples have shown, as critical scholars we must ask whose version(s) of British national identity are evident in which specific comics, and indeed which readers' readings of those comics are prioritized. These tasks are well within the scope of critical approaches to comics studies.

Notes

1. Attentive readers might notice that neither the MAC cartoon nor the Nazi cartoon to which @cuphook108's tweet compared it are reproduced in this chapter, though they can be found online. There are ethical and legal reasons for this omission. For example, there is a case for documenting examples of racist caricature as part of promoting social justice, particularly when such materials become ephemeral (for which see Pilgrim 2015). There is also a case for not adding to the distribution of discriminatory cultural products. I have an ethical objection to including a full reproduction of either MAC's cartoon or the Nazi cartoon to which it was compared, as to do so would lavish more attention on hateful depictions than I can justify for this critique within a subsection of a chapter. At the time of writing the tweet is visible within Dave Brown's (2015) article in the *Independent*; I will gladly email a PDF to any interested readers (lydia.wysocki@ncl.ac.uk).

2. I thank one of the peer reviewers for querying my use of the term *polysemy* with regard to Bakhtin, and trust that my clarification with this chapter shows how it goes further than either polyphony or polyvocalism. As Dentith (1995) notes, Russian linguist Vyacheslav Ivanov has reattributed books by Vološinov and Medvedev as by Bakhtin writing under another name, or a theorist very close to Bakhtin's circle; Emerson (1983) takes a similar stance. This may initially appear a piece of Soviet theorist trivia, as if Bakhtin's translated works were not already the subject of multiple interpretations. But consistent with the politicized context of Bakhtin's work and his difficulties in publishing his early radical ideas, it is not inconceivable that he sought alternative ways forward through a pseudonym or a colleague.

3. For an extended Bakhtin-inspired discussion of multiple voicedness in comics as heteroglossia, see the chapter by Paul Fisher Davies in the present volume.

4. *Beano's* practices in crediting comics creators are inconsistent, both within the weekly comics and in *Beano* annuals. Earlier "Ball Boy" strips in this period are credited to, or in the style of, Dave Eastbury, and later strips appear to be by Chris McGhie (McGhie 2018). "The Bash Street Kids" strips in this period seem to be attributed to David Sutherland (ComicsUK 2017), though again with some uncertainty.

5. I am grateful to Steve Tillotson and Gareth Brookes for sharing information on the print run of their comics.

References

Akhtar, Zainab. 2017. *Critical Chips 2*. Leeds: Comics and Cola.
Albion British Comics Database Wiki. 2017. "Bash Street Kids." Accessed August 13, 2018. http://britishcomics.wikia.com/wiki/Bash_Street_Kids.

Apple, Michael W. 2011. "The Tasks of the Critical Scholar/Activist in Education: The Contribution of José Gimeno Sacristán." *Revista de Educación* 356: 235–50.

Archer, Margaret. 1998. "Introduction: Realism in the Social Sciences." In *Critical Realism: Essential Readings*, edited by Margaret Archer, Roy Bhaskar, Andrew Collier, Tony Lawson, and Alan Norrie, 189–205. London: Routledge.

Archer, Margaret, Roy Bhaskar, Andrew Collier, Tony Lawson, and Alan Norrie, eds. *Critical Realism: Essential Readings*. London: Routledge.

Bakhtin, Mikhail. (1935) 1981. "Discourse in the Novel." In *The Dialogic Imagination*, 259–422. Translated by Caryl Emerson and Michael Holquist. Austin: University of Texas Press.

Bakhtin, Mikhail. (1965) 1968. *Rabelais and His World*. Translated by Helene Iswolsky. Cambridge, MA: MIT Press.

Banfield, Grant. 2016. *Critical Realism for Marxist Sociology of Education*. London: Routledge.

Barker, Martin. 1984. *A Haunt of Fears: The Strange History of the British Horror Comics Campaign*. London: Pluto Press.

Bell, Joyce M., and Douglas Hartmann. 2007. "Diversity in Everyday Discourse: The Cultural Ambiguities and Consequences of 'Happy Talk.'" *American Sociological Review* 72 (6): 895–914.

Bhaskar, Roy. 1975. *A Realist Theory of Science*. Leeds: Leeds Books.

Bhaskar, Roy. 1979. *The Possibility of Naturalism: A Philosophical Critique of the Contemporary Human Sciences*. Brighton: Harvester Press.

Bhaskar, Roy. 1998. "General Introduction." In *Critical Realism: Essential Readings*, edited by Margaret Archer, Roy Bhaskar, Andrew Collier, Tony Lawson, and Alan Norrie. London: Routledge.

BHP Comics. 2018. "Full Colour Mentoring Project." Accessed August 13, 2018. https://bhpcomics.squarespace.com/fullcolourproject/.

Billig, Michael. 1995. *Banal Nationalism*. London: SAGE.

Billig, Michael. 2005. *Laughter and Ridicule: Towards a Social Critique of Humour*. London: SAGE.

Bland, Archie. 2015. "Rats: The History of an Incendiary Cartoon Trope." *Guardian*, November 18, 2015. https://www.theguardian.com/artanddesign/shortcuts/2015/nov/18/rats-the-history-of-an-incendiary-cartoon-trope.

Bolloten, Bill, and Robin Richardson. 2015. "The Great British Values Disaster—Education, Security and Vitriolic Hate." *Institute of Race Relations*, February 12, 2015. Accessed September 15, 2017. http://www.irr.org.uk/news/the-great-british-values-disaster-education-security-and-vitriolic-hate/.

Boy's Own Annual, The, volume 62. 1939–40. Unknown artist/writer.

British Cartoon Archive. 2016. "Cartoonist Biographies: Stan McMurtry [Mac]." Accessed August 13, 2018. https://www.cartoons.ac.uk/cartoonist-biographies/m-n/StanMcMurtry_Mac.html.

Brooks, Thom. 2016. *Becoming British: UK Citizenship Examined*. London: Biteback Publishing.

Brown, Dave. 2015. "Offended by the Daily Mail's Cartoon of Refugees and Rats? Fine—But You Don't Have a Right to Censor It." *Independent*, November 17, 2015. http://www.independent.co.uk/voices/offended-by-the-daily-mails-cartoon-of-refugees-and-rats-fine-but-you-don-t-have-a-right-to-censor-a6738356.html.

Brown, Jeffrey A. 2000. *Black Superheroes, Milestone Comics, and Their Fans*. Jackson: University Press of Mississippi.

Buchanan, Rose Troup. 2015. "Daily Mail Criticised by Social Media Users for Cartoon on Refugees." *Independent*, November 17, 2015. https://www.independent.co.uk/news/media/daily-mail-criticised-by-social-media-users-for-cartoon-on-refugees-a6737976.html.

Cameron, David. 2011. "PM's Speech at Munich Security Conference." Delivered February 5, 2011. Accessed August 13, 2018. http://webarchive.nationalarchives.gov.uk/20130102224134/http://www.number10.gov.uk/news/pms-speech-at-munich-security-conference/.

Cameron, David. 2014. "British Values Aren't Optional, They're Vital." *MailOnline*, June 15, 2014. http://www.dailymail.co.uk/debate/article-2658171/DAVID-CAMERON-British-values-arent-optional-theyre-vital-Thats-I-promote-EVERY-school-As-row-rages-Trojan-Horse-takeover-classrooms-Prime-Minister-delivers-uncompromising-pledge.html.

Chapman, James. 2011. *British Comics: A Cultural History*. London: Reaktion Books.

Clarke, Steve. 2018. "*Beano*, Revived and Rebranded for Today's Kids." *Variety*, April 7, 2018. https://variety.com/2018/tv/features/rebranded-beano-dennis-the-menace-emma-scott-interview-1202742519/.

Centre for Literacy in Primary Education. 2017. "Reflecting Realities: Survey of Ethnic Representation within UK Children's Literature 2017." Accessed August 13, 2018. https://clpe.org.uk/library-and-resources/research/reflecting-realities-survey-ethnic-representation-within-uk-children.

Cole, Mike. 2004. "'Brutal and Stinking' and 'Difficult to Handle': The Historical and Contemporary Manifestations of Racialisation, Institutional Racism, and Schooling in Britain." *Race Ethnicity and Education* 7 (1): 35–56.

Colley, Linda. 1992. "Britishness and Otherness: An Argument." *Journal of British Studies* 31 (4): 309–29.

ComicsUK. 2017. "Leo Baxendale." Accessed August 14, 2018. http://comicsuk.co.uk/forum/viewtopic.php?f=127&t=7276&hilit=bash&start=15.

Cooke, Rachel. 2015. "The Best Graphic Books of 2015." *Guardian*, December 7, 2015. https://www.theguardian.com/books/2015/dec/07/best-graphic-books-2015-adrian-tomine-rachael-ball-jillian-tamaki-andy-hixon.

Cruse, Ian. 2008. "House of Lords Library Note for Debate on 19th June: Britishness." Accessed September 15, 2017. http://researchbriefings.parliament.uk/ResearchBriefing/Summary/LLN-2008-015.

Dentith, Simon. 1995. *Bakhtinian Thought: An Introductory Reader*. London: Routledge.

Department for Education. 2014. "Promoting Fundamental British Values as Part of SMSC in Schools: Departmental Advice for Maintained Schools." Accessed August 13, 2018. https://www.gov.uk/government/uploads/system/uploads/attachment_data/file/380595/SMSC_Guidance_Maintained_Schools.pdf.

Elder-Vass, Dave. 2010. *The Causal Power of Social Structures: Emergence, Structure and Agency*. Cambridge: Cambridge University Press.

Emerson, Caryl. 1983. "The Outer Word and Inner Speech: Bakhtin, Vygotsky, and the Internalization of Language." *Critical Inquiry* 10 (2): 245–64.

Forceville, Charles. 2011. "Pictorial Runes in *Tintin and the Picaros*." *Journal of Pragmatics* 43 (3): 875–90.

Frankenberg, Ruth. 1993. *White Women, Race Matters: The Social Construction of Whiteness.* Minneapolis: University of Minnesota Press.

Freeman, John. 2017. "The British Comic Industry Q&A." *Down the Tubes.* Accessed August 13, 2018. http://downthetubes.net/?page_id=7110.

Gibson, Mel. 2015. *Remembered Reading: Memory, Comics and Post-War Constructions of British Girlhood.* Leuven, Belgium: Leuven University Press.

Gillborn, David. 2005. "Education Policy as an Act of White Supremacy: Whiteness, Critical Race Theory and Education Reform." *Journal of Education Policy* 20 (4): 485–505.

Gilroy, Paul. 1991. *There Ain't No Black in the Union Jack: The Cultural Politics of Race and Nation.* Chicago: University of Chicago Press.

Gravett, Paul, and Peter Stanbury. 2006. *Great British Comics: Celebrating a Century of Ripping Yarns and Wizard Wheezes.* London: Aurum Press.

Hall, Stuart. 1980. "Encoding/Decoding." In *The Cultural Studies Reader,* edited by Simon During, 507–517. London: Routledge.

Hall, Stuart, ed. 1997. *Representation: Cultural Representations and Signifying Practices.* Milton Keynes: Open University Press.

Hall, Stuart, C. Critcher, T. Jefferson, J. Clarke, and B. Roberts. 1978. *Policing the Crisis: Mugging, the State, and Law and Order.* London: Macmillan.

Hall, Suzanne M. 2017. "Mooring 'Super-diversity' to a Brutal Migration Milieu." *Ethnic and Racial Studies* 20 (9): 1562–73.

Halliday, M. A. K. 1978. *Language as Social Semiotics: The Social Interpretation of Language and Meaning.* London: Edward Arnold.

HER. 2015. "The Daily Mail Have Published a Cartoon Depicting Refugees as Rats and Terrorists." *Her.ie,* November 18, 2015. https://www.her.ie/life/the-daily-mail-have-published-a-cartoon-depicting-refugees-as-rats-and-terrorists-265391.

Hikido, Annie, and Susan B. Murray. 2016. "Whitened Rainbows: How White College Students Protect Whiteness through Diversity Discourses." *Race Ethnicity and Education* 19 (2): 389–411.

Hoggart, Richard. 1957. *The Uses of Literacy.* Harmondsworth, UK: Chatto and Windus.

Huxley, David, and Joan Ormrod. 2010. "Editorial." *Journal of Graphic Novels and Comics* 1 (1): 1–4.

Ignatieff, Michael. 1994. *Blood and Belonging: Journeys into the New Nationalism.* London: Vintage.

Jones, Hanneke. 2016. "Discussing Poverty with Student Teachers: The Realities of Dialogue." *Journal of Education for Teaching* 42: 468–82.

Kay, Richard. 2018. "Mac's Last Laugh! After 50 Years, Britain's Best Cartoonist Draws His Brilliant Career to a Close." *Mail Online,* December 20, 2018. https://www.dailymail.co.uk/news/article-6518201/Macs-laugh-50-years-Mail-cartoonist-draws-brilliant-career-close.html.

Kehily, Mary Jane. 1999. "More Sugar? Teenage Magazines, Gender Displays and Sexual Learning." *European Journal of Cultural Studies* 2 (1): 65–69.

Kennedy, Hilary, Miriam Landor, and Liz Todd, eds. 2011. *Video Interaction Guidance: A Relationship-Based Intervention to Promote Attunement, Empathy and Wellbeing.* London: Jessica Kingsley.

Kristeva, Julia. 1986. *The Kristeva Reader*, edited by Toril Moi. Oxford: Basil Blackwell.

Lander, Vini. 2016. "Introduction to Fundamental British Values." *Journal of Education for Teaching* 42 (3): 274–79.

Larrick, Nancy. 1965. "The All-White World of Children's Books." *Saturday Review of Literature*. Accessed December 22, 2017. http://www.longwood.edu/staff/miskecjm/384larrick.pdf.

Leonardo, Zeus. 2012. "The Race for Class: Reflections on a Critical Raceclass Theory of Education." *Educational Studies* 48 (5): 437–49.

Levenson, Claire. 2015. Après les attentats de Paris, un dessin du Daily Mail associe rats et réfugiés. *Slate FR*, November 17, 2015. http://www.slate.fr/story/110157/dessin-daily-mail-rats-et-refugies.

Magnussen, Anne, and Hans-Christian Christiansen, eds. 2000. *Comics and Culture: Analytical and Theoretical Approaches to Comics*. Copenhagen: Museum Tusculanum Press.

McGhie, Chris. 2018. "How to Draw Ball Boy!" Video [01:32]. Accessed August 14, 2018. https://www.beano.com/posts/how-to-draw-ball-boy.

McMurtry, Stanley. 2015. "MAC ON . . . Europe's Open Borders." *Daily Mail*, November 17, 2015. http://www.dailymail.co.uk/news/article-3321431/MAC-Europe-s-open-borders.html.

McNicol, Sarah. 2018. "Telling Migrant Women's Life Stories as Comics." *Journal of Graphic Novels and Comics* 9 (4): 279–292.

Miodrag, Hannah 2013. *Comics and Language: Reimagining Critical Discourse on the Form*. Jackson: University Press of Mississippi.

Modood, Tariq. 2013. *Multiculturalism*. 2nd ed. Hoboken, NJ: Wiley.

Office for National Statistics. 2011. "Ethnicity and National Identity in England and Wales: 2011." Accessed August 26, 2018. https://www.ons.gov.uk/peoplepopulation andcommunity/culturalidentity/ethnicity/articles/ethnicityandnationalidentityin englandandwales/2012-12-11.

Parekh, Bhikhu. 2000. *Report of the Commission on the Future of Multi-Ethnic Britain*. London: Runnymede Trust. http://www.runnymedetrust.org/publications/29/74.html.

Pearce, Sarah. 2005. *You Wouldn't Understand: White Teachers in Multi-ethnic Classrooms*. Stoke on Trent: Trentham Books.

Pilgrim, David. 2014. *Understanding Jim Crow: Using Racist Memorabilia to Teach Tolerance and Promote Social Justice*. Oakland: Ferris State University and PM Press.

Press Awards. 2016. "Winners for 2016." Accessed March 2, 2018. http://www.pressawards.org.uk/page-view.php?pagename=winners-2016.

Rockman, Zoom. 2015. *IKEA BABY—Mini Graphic Novel*. Self-published.

Sabin, Roger. 1993. *Adult Comics: An Introduction*. London: Routledge.

Saguisag, Lara. 2017. "*RAW* and *Little Lit*: Resisting and Redefining Children's Comics." In *Picturing Childhood: Youth in Transnational Comics*, edited by Mark Heimermann and Brittany Tullis, 128–47. Austin: University of Texas Press.

Saussure, Ferdinand de. (1916) 1983. *Course in General Linguistics*. Translated by Roy Harris. LaSalle, IL: Open Court.

Sayer, Andrew. 1992. *Method in Social Science*. 2nd ed. London: Routledge.

Sayer, Andrew. 2000. *Realism and Social Science*. London: SAGE

Scharrer, Erica, and Srividya Ramasubramanian. 2015. "Intervening in the Media's Influence on Stereotypes of Race and Ethnicity: The Role of Media Literacy Education." *Journal of Social Issues* 71 (1): 171–85.

Solórzano, Daniel, Miguel Ceja, and Tara Yosso. 2000. "Critical Race Theory, Racial Microaggressions, and Campus Racial Climate: The Experiences of African American College Students." *Journal of Negro Education* 69 (1/2): 60–73.

Stein, Daniel. 2012. "'I Was Writing about Racism Long before I Was Making Fun of Presidents': An Interview with Cartoonist Keith Knight." *Studies in Comics* 2 (2): 243–56.

Sue, Derald Wing, ed. 2010. *Microaggressions and Marginality: Manifestation, Dynamics, and Impact.* Hoboken, NJ: Wiley.

Thomas, David. 2014. "How British Are You?" *Telegraph*, June 15, 2014. Accessed August 13, 2018. https://www.telegraph.co.uk/education/10899837/Quiz-How-British-are-you.html.

Tilley, Carol L. 2012. "Seducing the Innocent: Fredric Wertham and the Falsifications that Helped Condemn Comics." *Information and Culture: A Journal of History* 47 (4): 383–413.

Tillotson, Steve, and Gareth Brookes. 2014. *Manly Boys & Comely Girls Double Pack!* London: Avery Hill.

Vološinov, V. N. (1929) 1973. *Marxism and the Philosophy of Language.* Translated by Ladislav Matejka and I.R. Titunik. London: Seminar Press.

Vygotsky, L. S. 1978. *Mind in Society: The Development of Higher Psychological Processes.* Cambridge, MA: Harvard University Press.

Wertham, Fredric. 1954. *Seduction of the Innocent.* New York: Rinehart.

Wertsch, James V., ed. 1981. *The Concept of Activity in Soviet Psychology.* Armonk: ME Sharpe.

Whaley, Deborah Elizabeth. 2015. *Black Women in Sequence: Re-inking Comics, Graphic Novels, and Anime.* Seattle: University of Washington Press.

Yosso, Tara J., William A. Smith, Miguel Ceja, and Daniel G. Solórzano. 2009. "Critical Race Theory, Racial Microaggressions, and Campus Racial Climate for Latina/o Undergraduates." *Harvard Educational Review* 79 (4): 659–89.

Wysocki, Lydia. 2018. "Linking Research and Practice: Qualitative Social Science Data Collection at a UK Comics Convention." *Journal of Graphic Novels and Comics*, October 6, 2018. https://doi.org/10.1080/21504857.2018.1524393.

7

Comics and Heteroglossia

PAUL FISHER DAVIES

What happens if we look at comics through the lens of *dialogue*? In what ways could we understand the practice of comics-making and comics-reading as engagement in dialogue? This chapter explores some of the ways in which comics may reveal their dialogic structure, predominantly in the textual form they take, but also in the emerging development of the form and in the methods of their production. Other chapters explore these latter approaches in more detail,[1] but I argue here for the form of the text itself absorbing some of the dialogic nature of social intercourse in which comics production is embedded, and the nesting of dialogue within comics, as well as comics within dialogue, as a continuum between the text and its contexts. I use a model from linguistics to shape this exploration, but that model will deliberately and explicitly be one that takes language to be a socially mediated exchange (and not a fixed and externally coded semiotic structure). This will mean positing that comics-making may be fruitfully treated as a form of utterance, and that it is in the nature of the comics text that the multiplicity of utterances enacted in writing and drawing in the text may be considered constitutive of comics' character.

Comics distinctively represent a range of "voices" in their texts—from the prominent voices of characters as represented in the prototypical word balloons, whether speech or thought, through the narrating voices found in caption boxes not anchored to a depicted participant, and the "voice" implicit in the marks made on the page, their style, their perspective, the point of view of the visual creator. Some comics theorists have aimed to piece apart these voices and name them, using the tools of narratology: Groensteen (2010) has brought to recent prominence the separation of *narrator* or *recitant* who speaks from *monstrator* who shows, and recent attention has begun to be paid to Philippe Marion's (1993) further focus on the *graphiator* who makes marks. The questions in narrative, "who speaks?" and "who writes?"

may be answered in the plural. This is not just to say that comics are frequently collaborative endeavors (though they are), nor just to say that even a single creator takes on a variety of roles in the creation of a comics text (she does)—artist, writer, penciller, inker, letterer, and more. It is to say that the text is fundamentally polyvocal in its multiplicity of voices, fundamentally dialogic in its sequence of visual and verbal utterances and nested exchanges between speakers, producers of meaning both represented and implicit. This polyphony of diverse voices has been called *heteroglossia*, and I explore a range of possible meanings of that term below, before concluding what it may mean for comics as a form. I consider its application to comics not only as texts, but briefly on our way there, also as collaborations and developing oeuvres of creators, and as a historically unfolding text type: at each level developing as a form of dialogue.

What Is Heteroglossia?

The notion of heteroglossia explored in this chapter will be one drawn in its core formulation from the work of Martin and White (2005) on the resources of interpersonal *appraisal* found in a text. Interpersonal resources of a text include those which incorporate into that text the evaluative judgments and emotional attributes a creator attaches to the content of what is created. They also include the interactive features of a text, those which engage the reader or interlocutor in dialogue, or incorporate the reported or anticipated responses of an imagined interlocutor into the text, regardless of whether actual interaction may be entered into. This feature of a text nests it into the social sphere, necessarily; our relationships with others, and our human responses to the content of what we create, condition and form those texts. I turn to a particular variety of linguistics in order to think about comics as such a socially embedded text and use a tradition of linguistics that emerges from sociology, anthropology, and pragmatics in order to articulate my approach to comics' heteroglossic nature.

The word *heteroglossia* comes historically from the work of Mikhail Bakhtin, coined in "Discourse in the Novel" (Bakhtin [1935] 1982a); it will be useful to explore, in the dialogic spirit, some definitions offered by commentators on his work, which will begin to raise some of the issues at stake in applying the notion to comics.

Absent a clean definition of the term from Bakhtin, the first account I cite is from Pam Morris's collection *The Bakhtin Reader* (1997), which brings together a range of selections from Bakhtin's thought framed with editorial material.[2]

> For Bakhtin, discourse always articulates a particular view of the world. According to Bakhtin, earliest society is characterised by "monoglossia," or a stable, unified language. "Polyglossia" refers to the simultaneity of two or more national languages in the same society, a phenomenon in which developed, as Bakhtin points out, in ancient Rome and during the Renaissance. "Heteroglossia" (the Russian *raznorechie* literally means different-speech-ness), refers to the conflict between "centripetal" and "centrifugal," "official" and "unofficial" discourses within the same national language. "Heteroglossia" is also present, however, at the micro-linguistic scale; every utterance contains within it the trace of other utterances, both in the past and in the future. The discursive site in which the conflict between different voices is at its most concentrated is the modern novel. One way of representing heteroglossia in the novel is by hybrid construction, which contains within it the trace of two or more discourses, either those of the narrator and character(s), or of different characters ("quasi-direct discourse"). "Heteroglossia" should not be confused with "polyphony." The latter term is used by Bakhtin primarily to describe Dostoyevsky's "multivoiced" novels, whereby authors' and heroes' discourses interact on equal terms. "Heteroglossia," on the other hand, foregrounds the clash of antagonistic forces. (248–49)

So "heteroglossia" here further implies a hierarchy of discourses, arranged not equally in parallel, but languages in subordination to others, and is distinguished both from "polyglossia" and "polyphony," though I am interested in all these related concepts. The "traces of other utterances" reflect the ways in which comics necessarily quote and reuse tropes found in other comics; and the hierarchy of voices finds its inscription in the nested structure of comics, as I explore later.

The second definition is somewhat more encompassing, from the glossary to Holquist and Emerson's translation of *The Dialogic Imagination* (Bakhtin 1982b):

> [Heteroglossia is the] base condition governing the operation of meaning in any utterance. It is that which insures the primacy of context over text. At any given time, and any given place, there will be a set

of conditions—social, historical, meteorological, physiological—that will insure that a word uttered in that place and at that time will have a meaning different than it would have under any other conditions; all utterances are heteroglot in that they are functions of a matrix of forces practically impossible to recoup, and therefore impossible to resolve. Heteroglossia is as close a conceptualisation as is possible of that locus where centripetal and centrifugal forces collide; as such, it is that which a systematic linguistics must always suppress. (428)

Here the claim for heteroglossia is broader and takes as its focus the dependence of utterances upon context, including but not limited to the context of other utterances framing and preceding it. It is thereby a characterization of language, and in particular of language as it is conducted in context. Holquist's definition ends with an echo of Bakhtin's critique of "systematic linguistics" as an approach to accounting for meaning exchange, and it is worth exploring where this attitude comes from. Vološinov in *Marxism and the Philosophy of Language* (Vološinov [1929] 1997) rejects linguistics with the claim that it is a *monoglot* approach to language, on the basis that it is taken to isolate a complete and inert system of language separate from its dynamic contexts (35–36). The linguist whom Vološinov has in mind, of course, is Saussure, and his abstraction of *langue* as separate from the utterances of *parole* (Saussure [1916] 2013). This form of linguistics Vološinov places in opposition to an analysis of language which takes into account context and contains human evaluations (36). The operation of intonation and its effect on meaning is invoked to illustrate this. "Linguistics" as a discipline, then, is taken here to mean that which disregards context and acknowledges only certain elements of linguistic behavior as salient to a fixed system.

But it is exactly the context-bound nature of utterance, as exemplified in the simultaneous valency of multiple functions of language including such elements as intonation contours, and the ability of the framework to account for the language of evaluation, that is central to M. A. K. Halliday's systemic-functional model of language (Halliday and Matthiessen 2014). Halliday's approach stresses the social nature of language—it is a "social semiotic," to adopt the title of one of Halliday's key essays (Halliday 1978). It is founded on the work of Halliday's teacher, J. R. Firth, who himself built on anthropologist Bronisław Malinowski's idea that the "context of situation," the social context in which language is used, is an inseparable component of the meaning of any utterance (see Halliday and Hasan 1985 for an accessible discussion of this line of influence). The idea of heteroglossia as it has been outlined above is inherent to this approach, because it takes as its fundamental unit the contextualized utterance, and takes as a tenet the importance of building a model of language from the bottom up based on corpora of actual usage. It takes the language system as a socially negotiated and developing network of choices available to speakers undertaking a multiplicity of individual acts of meaning-making. A substantial tradition of critical linguistics has emerged from Halliday's approach (Hodge and Kress 1988; O'Toole 2010; Fairclough 2010; Painter, Martin, and Unsworth 2013), including the use of Halliday's categories to construct a methodology for critical discourse analysis, and many approaches to multimodal applications of linguistics—those which take into account the visual as well as the verbal resources of meaning making (see Kress and van Leeuwen 2006 for perhaps the most prominent and influential enactment of this strategy).

   This openness to application to a range of semiotic systems, in particular the framework's separation of meaning-making *functions* from the *realizations* of those functions in particular semiotic systems, makes Halliday's linguistic approach an approach well suited to helping make sense of comics. Comics, as we will see, is a nested, contextualized medium; the utterances of speakers are framed in the depictions of worlds, and vice versa. The move of treating a drawing in a comic as a visual utterance, in dialogue with other utterances that constitute a work, and in dialogue with other participants in the "speech act" represented by the work—coauthors, readers, other images in the same work, in other works by the same author, and in the wider works of comics in the same genre and others—can offer a fruitful framework for thinking about the comics text as inseparable from the social context of its production. It can also help by recruiting developments made in linguistics which offer frameworks for describing this dialogue of utterances. A descriptive framework for comics which is compatible with these descriptions of social interactions mediated by language helps account for the involvement of language alongside and amongst drawing in the comics text, and extends beyond the innovations of Kress and van Leeuwen and O'Toole in adapting Halliday to visual works.

   I am not quite arguing here either for or against the idea of a language of comics. This has been used as a metaphor in characterizing comics conventions broadly, much as the metaphor of hybridity has been similarly employed. The crucial separating out of realizations of meaning-making functions in particular grammars that lies at the heart of Halliday's approach also defends this approach to comics from the danger of positing minimal units of comics (see Miodrag 2013 for a discussion). Phonemes, morphemes, words in a syntax, and such realizations of meaning are features of particular grammars, rather than of the meaning-making endeavor that motivates the use of grammars. Language most certainly appears in comics often, and such languages that are found there are amenable to discussion using linguistic methods, as explored in Frank Bramlett's (2012) collection of essays on linguistics and the study of comics, which also seeks to take such a study beyond the looseness of metaphor. But we meet problems if attempting to map the realizations of linguistic functions in lexicogrammars to comics directly, as in the work of Cohn (2013) for instance; we cannot expect the comics forms to map neatly to, say, phrase structure grammars based on English. But we can expect comics' images, at some appropriate level of abstraction, to be doing the same sort of work that language does—if comics images are to be "read" as telling stories and unfolding texts at all. The work comics image-making does is collaborative with, and integrated with, the work of the language the comic incorporates (if any). So a framework which can describe the parameters of such a collaboration, accounting for the function of images in compatible ways with the function of wordings, will prove a valuable framework for conceptualizing how comics work.

Amongst those who have adopted Halliday's framework to describe language behavior, J. R. Martin and P. R. R. White, in their text focusing on interpersonal evaluations in language, *The Language of Evaluation: Appraisal in English* (2005), draw on Bakhtin's dialogism to present one of the means of engaging with others and weighing up viewpoints. They adopt the term *heteroglossia* for this, set in opposition to a *monoglossia* which speaks from a singular authorial position and does not account for the views and statements of others. Alongside the resources of emphasis, force, and focus in the selection and intonation of words, and the resources of evaluative adjectives emphasizing judgments on persons and appreciations of things, they note the engagement of many spoken and written texts with the views of others, by means of citing, countering, anticipating, and incorporating the views of others:

> We can categorise utterances accordingly to this two-way distinction, classifying them as "monoglossic" when they make no reference to other voices and viewpoints and as "heteroglossic" when they do invoke or allow for dialogistic alternatives. (99–100)

Such heteroglossia in a text may further be classified as *dialogically contractive*, which is to say when other voices and viewpoints are appropriated to support the thrust of one's main argument, bringing those voices metaphorically together, or *dialogically expansive*, where the field of possible points of view is opened up and alternatives are entertained seriously. The corpus of texts Martin and White are interested in includes primarily argumentative texts and media texts. However, dialogue and heteroglossia in Martin and White's terms, the incorporation of multiple voices in a text, are not limited to these genres; and it is not just the genre of argument or propositions which may be brought into collision by these means. The ways in which any authors and speakers recruit others' voices in order to bolster arguments and persuade an audience, in whatever genre, form the concern of this framework for analysis.

Heteroglossia further implies the coexistence of disparate languages, dialects, or (to use a more modern notion) sociolects, within a single text—for example, a novel, to take the instance of most immediate concern to Bakhtin. This conception of heteroglossia as it appears in fiction emerges alongside Bakhtin's argument that the heteroglossic novel thereby reflects a fundamental dialogism in *existence*: that there is a necessary multiplicity to human experience, and a reciprocity of one individual's perspective to another, where each is "other" to the other, and each perceives the other's contexts (Bakhtin 1982b).

Dialogue, in the sense of this broader notion from Bakhtin, may be mapped to a Hallidayan understanding of the acts of creating meaning: using the resources of language to assemble a meaning that is reliant more or less on its contexts, of person, purpose, time, place, genre, and so on. There are parallels between Bakhtin's and Halliday's conceptions of language, bound by the attitude to all language as utterance first and foremost. It is through this utterance, the operation of language upon the other, that we find the locus of power relationships between interlocutors.

Seeking Heteroglossia and Dialogism in Comics Texts: Three Levels

To turn to the comics text as a potential site of this dialogism and heteroglossia, there are a range of levels at which we may seek mappings. I approach the question through a set of distinctions used by Halliday to conceptualize the development and unfolding of language as a live, meaning-making system in constant development. Again, Halliday's fundamental thinking about language as a system is in contrast to the idea of a fixed, synchronic *langue* after

Saussure which may be understood as a static cross-section of the language system in operation at a given point in time. This notion is a target of criticism not only for Bakhtin, shedding doubt on the enterprise and value of linguistics in general, but may be leveled at the use of linguistics as a model for understanding comics. A linguistics adequate to the task of describing a developing medium, for which the "rules" are as yet undetermined and creators are regularly improvising under the influence of an emerging canon and of other media, should be flexible and interested in acts of meaning-making as potentially singular and *sui generis*, rather than the implementation of a set code. Halliday's linguistics presents just such a model.

There are three nested levels at which we may view the dynamic unfolding of meaning-making systems, the smallest scale being the most significant for the present study. Halliday proposes that all texts, whether spoken or written, unfold over time as they are generated by speaker and listener, reader and writer: this is the *logogenesis* of the text, and I split this into three further perspectives in the section exploring this scale of the genesis of the text below. A second scale on which language unfolds is *ontogenesis*: for Halliday, this is the emergence of language in the development of the individual, reflecting Halliday's interest in children's language acquisition, the path of a young human being "learning to mean." The third scale, over which language as a system is constantly developing, growing, splitting, and adapting, is *phylogenesis*—and this choice of terms reflects a parallel with the growth and evolution of organisms in nature (see Halliday and Matthiessen 2006; Martin and White 2005). I consider each of these levels of analysis in descending order and pay most attention in this chapter to logogenesis, the level of the text.

Phylogenesis

On a phylogenetic level, that of the development of comics as a genre (or medium, or art-form if you prefer) over considerable stretches of time, dialogue exists between the oeuvres of creators and the genres in and against which they operate. This large-scale dialogue is very much what Bakhtin had in mind as part of his initial conception of dialogism (1982b). What we learn from Bakhtin here, alongside his criticism of fixed, monolithic linguistics, is that any description of comics poetics should not just be synchronic, but must acknowledge diachronic change and development, through dialogic interactions between creators and modes, patterns of influence that continue to form and develop the potentialities of comics discourse. Innovation in comics creation must operate over/against the systems of comics that have normalized and set the ground assumptions of the form, and likewise, any rules we may identify in comics must be open in principle to challenge and change.[3] The effects of operation of such maxims depend on dialogue with the assumptions they outline—breaches and floutings can only be read as such against a background of norms.

Likewise, satirical modes such as those employed by Dave Sim in *Cerebus* (1991) depend on a recognition of the traditions they satirize; and then, the texts become available for antithesis or synthesis themselves, whether satirizing, countering, or adopting and extending. Chris Ware adopts the register, visual and verbal, of early comics texts including Krazy Kat and Mickey Mouse in his *Quimby* stories (Ware 2003); the formal sophistication and play that he develops in these become a backbone of his densely layered, nested stories in *Jimmy Corrigan* (Ware 2001); and these forms are adopted by such creators as Kevin Huizinga (e.g., Huizenga 2006) in their turn. Patterns of influence then stratify the development of comics as a "phylum": creators and whole genres respond to each other; tease, satirize, and deny each other; synthesize and carry forward the forms and resources that have been used to make meanings in comics. It would be the task of another discussion to attempt to outline these networks of historical dialogue more fully.

Ontogenesis

At a closer level, the comics text unfolds as a dialogue between creators: writer and artist prototypically, perhaps even when these roles are within one and the same individual. This then supports the sort of dialogue between visual and verbal modes alluded to above, its work distributed between different contributors to the creation of the text. They need a shared language in which to converse: Halliday's framework offers a way to describe this. But also, as those creators themselves develop, their relationship may mature, they may come to an understanding or shift in power. Where there is a single creator, the writing may escalate in sophistication or scope; or the drawing may develop in its resources, whether materials, metaphors, precision, or convention, for example. This can be seen in the increasing sophistication of the work of Sim in *Cerebus* (1991), beginning as a knockabout pastiche, and developing through densely plotted satire, to become more-or-less *roman à clef* encodings of situations alive in the comics world at the time of writing. Sim also acquires a collaborative partner in background artist Gerhard, whose detailed environments lend a lamination of richness to *Cerebus*'s world-building.

David Petersen's artwork in *Mouse Guard* (2007) rapidly develops in its skill, depth, and detail across its several volumes, its worked surface changing the density of visual description offered in each enclosure, and thereby changing the pace at which the reader's eye dwells on each image. It is interesting also how *Mouse Guard* becomes a collaborative work, and develops as nested stories in the *Legends of the Guard* collections (Petersen and Bastian 2011; Petersen and Willingham 2014; Petersen and Morrissey 2015). The development of the artist—parallel to what Halliday calls "ontogenesis" in language acquisition, the process of learning to mean as the individual grows in resources and sophistication—is a model of artistic growth conducted through dialogue: interaction with the self, a will to improve upon past work created by one's former incarnation; interaction with collaborative partners, whether writers, artists, background artists, or those with less clearly delineated roles—Dupuy and Berberian's ongoing collaboration (e.g., Berberian and Dupuy 2004; 2012) comes to mind; or interaction with audiences and readers: Sim maintained a lively dialogue with readers of *Cerebus*, Petersen draws and inks live in broadcasts on YouTube, and writers and artists have long collaborated in person or through mediation of scripting and editorial commentary on the work they create. Dialogue over time and among the selves that create comics is essential to comics' nature.

In Halliday's characterization, children's language acquisition is a matter of "learning how to mean" (Halliday 2004). The ontogenesis of language in the individual is a case of taking more and more control over a wider yet more specific set of resources for creating this meaning. The child begins by recruiting the resources of its body in dialogue, for pragmatic purposes enacted in a social context. Starting with this beginning proto-language, children gradually approach the adult system they find around them socially; converging on this system helps them in their goal of making meanings. In analogous ways, the neophyte comics creator adopts forms found in the comics previously created, available to be read in the world; the comics creator does not generate forms *ab ovo*, but by adapting, responding to, and innovating around the comics the creator has read and has created. This leads to the next level of consideration of the emergence of comics as a form of social semiotic in Halliday's sense: the unfolding of a sequences of realizations of meaning-making, each choice adopted and adapted from the socially determined network of possibilities the creator encounters in the discourse of the medium.

Logogenesis

The unfolding of a text will be the primary level at which I seek here to identify heteroglossia and dialogism in comics discourse. Comics unfold at a number of nested levels: in the progression of images and texts, not just from panel-to-panel, for panels are themselves highly complex clusters of images and texts; but from image-to-image within each panel enclosure, from balloon-to-balloon, and from word-to-word within enclosures. Comics have often been seen as linearly unfolding "tracks" of images in parallel with "tracks" of words (e.g., McCloud 1993), but actually, these two modes hand over from one to the other; they exist nested, quoted, inside each other, and they mutually cooperate to construct *clusters* of meaning which interact at different narrative levels as well as in linear sequence: that is to say, "vertically," as well as "horizontally." I will call the sequential interplay between panel enclosures *paratactic dialogism*, treating the panels as sequences of utterances in exchange with one another, bearing implications and engaged in dyads of call-and-response akin to the patterning of conversation—and amenable to some of the tools for analysis of conversation that have emerged from pragmatic linguistics in the past. I will call the nested enclosure of clusters—especially word/thought balloons appearing within panels, and then shifting to take up different diegetic levels of narrative and further enclosing nested narratives—*hypotactic dialogism*, by parallel to hypotaxis in language, by which method a writer or speaker may incorporate reported speech and thought. This nested structuring of comics has been under-appreciated in contrast to the notion of *sequential* art commonly focused on in the literature (since, for instance, Eisner 2008). Finally at the level of logogenesis, the dialogue between the modes themselves should be considered, which is to say that verbal and visual meanings collaborate, depend upon one another, and interact—whether hypotactically or paratactically. I will call this *transmodal dialogism*, and consider the problem of reference, or "phoricity" between and across the modes used in comics. A fuller account of each follows in the next several sections.

Paratactic Dialogism

We can read the sequentiality of comics as akin to the to-and-fro of discourse, with panels adopting the role of turn-taking exchanges. Conversations between participants in dialogue together operate on a set of assumptions, held by each participant, by dint of which the conversation can proceed economically—and by means of which participants can imply (implicate) more than is explicitly said. This concept was outlined by philosopher of language H. P. Grice (1975) as what he called the "cooperative principle" of conversational implicature. It will be useful to outline this set of social principles as a way of approaching the social compact entered into by a reader in engagement with a creator of comics.

Grice proposed that conversation partners assume that both are engaged in a cooperative endeavor, seeking to conduct their exchanges with optimal parsimony, clarity, supportiveness, and focus on the topic at hand. The fact that this is evidently not borne out in actual conversations is a strength of the theory: since both participants expect each other to greet each turn in the conversation with the same principle(s) in mind, these expectations can be exploited—flouted—in order to generate implicated meanings which are not explicitly stated in the wording of the conversation. Grice proposed four "maxims of conversation" that constitute the particular expectations comprising the cooperative principle: that turns will be no longer or shorter than necessary (the maxim of quantity); that they will be truthful and based in sufficient evidence (the maxim of quality); that they will be relevant to the agreed topic at hand (the maxim of relation); and they will be pitched in an appropriate and understandable register (the maxim of manner). Deliberate deviation from each of these may produce effects of irony, innuendo, subtle critique, the wielding of power, hinting, and other well-known behaviors of conversational exchange.

I have proposed that a parallel set of maxims is sustained in the parsing of comics texts (Davies 2013; 2015). Despite the separated nature of the participants in comics texts, reader(s) and creator(s) divided both in time and space, the structure is still a sequence of "utterances," as an exchange of correspondence might be, and we bring shared assumptions to the dialogue of clusters and panels. It is the operation of mutually shared assumptions, and the way in which implicatures may be built upon these, that I carry over here from Grice.

Since the reader is generally a receptive participant, making sense of panels and clusters rather than creating additional panels and clusters, the underlying principle here is one of cohesion, a *principle of synecdoche*: that the array of images on the page add up to some larger meaning which a reader may piece together.[4] Imagetexts in comics, the drawings, clusters, and panels that comprise the comic, are not to be understood as isolated works, but as contributory elements of a larger whole. To read an array of images as such is to read it as comics: this reading practice is a fundamental first step in becoming a competent consumer of the text (see Davies 2013). It embeds dialogic structure, the extended interplay of contributions to a whole text, in the nature of comics themselves.

The maxims of comics are not the same as those of conversation, but comparable in their style and effect, and also emerge from Kantian categories, as did Grice's. I propose four maxims of comics, with the same caveat offered by Grice, that these may be amenable to expansion and revision. First, a maxim of identity: that images that look sufficiently similar are taken to be identical—three images of Charlie Brown do not denote three Charlie Browns, nor three separate attempts to render alternative Charlie Browns, but mutually construct one Charlie Brown. A second and third maxim form two related continuities: that the images comprising a comics sequence occur at different but contiguous points in time, especially where they render the same individual; but not at different points in space. Space is understood to stay the same from image to image, and time to move forward. It is important of course to add here the rejoinder: *unless we show otherwise*. Comics frequently need to change time and space, but to do so they must indicate this through some means: a change of background, or a wording that marks a leap in time or simultaneity ("meanwhile . . ." or "yesterday . . ."), or an indication in image or text that draws attention to a new establishment of place. If the text does not so indicate, the reader will assume continuities of time and space. As well as these maxims of the continuity of time and space, a reader sustains a final maxim of causality: that elements appearing in comics are not unmotivated, but are caused by other elements, either in the same panel, elsewhere on a page, or elsewhere in the extended comics text. This maxim is most straightforwardly followed in the observance when a consecutive panel follows logically or causally from the previous one, representing a transformation, motion, response, or other such entailment from what has come before—and *response* most certainly invokes a framework of dialogue. But it is frequently honored in the breach: an apparently unmotivated or impossible image prompts the reader to look to other panels, over the page or later in linear sequence, to motivate for example a shocked look (what shocks the character?) or a sudden transformation of a character, as in *manga* tradition, into a pig or ass (impossible in the context, it cannot be literal—so must be motivated by a metaphorical reading). This parallels the operation of conversation: apparent non sequiturs create implicatures, not by "alchemy" (see McCloud 1993 for this mystical metaphor) but according to a tacit set of reading practices shared by creator and reader as cooperative participants in the dialogue of meaning exchange represented by the comics text. This interplay reflects the *interpersonal* function of comics in the interactive sense emphasized in Halliday's system.

Hypotactic Dialogism

But dialogism, in the core sense here of heteroglossic inclusion into a text of the discourse of others, is not merely a matter of taking turns with others in the making of meanings or constructing a paratactic sequence of utterances. The heteroglossic, as well as the polyvocal (if a distinction is to be sustained), is a matter of absorbing the views of others into one's own discourse: of acknowledging, citing, quoting, representing dialogues, framing others' views, and so on (Martin and White 2005). Beyond the intertextual reuse of other texts, modeling one's text after others' or alluding by repetitions, this heteroglossia engages explicitly with others' views, assigning them to the other speaker or thinker, projected by reporting verbs, quotation marks, and similar means.

This projection of discourses, heteroglossic and polyvocal, is enacted in the nested visual structures of comics. Within the frames of "panel" borders appear similar frames, the "balloon" borders—whether outlined in line, or marked by a change of tone or color, or implicit in a change of mode. In my view these abstract enclosures function so similarly as to be treatable as one and the same: they enclose a cluster or set of clusters of text and/ or image; they modalize the material enclosed as thought, speech, diegesis, dream, and so on; they project the ideation of character or of creator. On this view, the panel is an utterance: the frame is always already a speech balloon. Characters speak in their context, and these contexts may shift metaleptically (to use a concept from Genette 1983) so that different voices take over the telling of the graphic narrative. This includes the projection of the creator's visual discourse in the primary "speech balloon," the abstract enclosures of the panel. Although this enclosure does not carry a tail or trail assigning the content to a represented character, the possibility of changing levels of discourse between panels and balloons strongly suggests that the panel is itself a projected *text world* attributable to an implied author or narrator (see below for a fuller discussion of this notion of text worlds). The notion of a *monstrator*, a viewing and depicting figure behind the creation of the panel (Groensteen 2010), is compatible with this view; it of course chimes with the notion of an implied author (Booth 1983) in narratological discourses which is applicable to the verbal *narrator* whose voice may appear in captions, inscribed within panels outside of word balloons, or simply coexisting with drawings on a page that does not use panelization. The distinction of *graphiator* (Marion 1993) from monstrator—that individual (or team) who marks the page, in addition to that which views the scene—is also useful, and shows that even the creator is polyvocal, made of multitudes, seeing, speaking, and marking in ways which may or may not add up to a singular coherent viewpoint, the perspectives of which, literal or metaphorical, may shift from image to image, enclosure to enclosure, and cluster to cluster.

Just as the nestedness of discourses may enrich the novel, so the graphic narrative is always by its nature dialogic and polyvocal. Framing stories and characters present substories and the characters within them; layered worlds, histories, and attitudes may dwell not only in the abstract enclosures of thought and world balloons, but also in backgrounds, inscribed on pages and walls, and we may change narrative level in order to explore these. In a classic text such as Art Spiegelman's *Maus* (2003), the world of represented author figure Artie frames the reported history of Vladek which constitutes the bulk of the tale; but also the narrative early in book two shifts up a narrative level to view Spiegelman's experience, transformed as pastiche, in writing the graphic novel and dealing with public response to it. In this second volume, Spiegelman also represents other nested narratives from a distinct viewpoint, a past voice of the author, in the inclusion of previously created pages from "Prisoner on Hell Planet," representing elements of the same story recounted in *Maus* but from the perspective of the younger author as an earlier creator. A useful framework for thinking about these different narrative levels, in addition to Genette's classification of metalepsis, is Paul Werth's text world theory (Werth 1999; Gavins 2007). This takes as its starting point the *discourse-world* shared by interlocutors (in the case of comics, this is the world in which I buy a comics text and hold in my hands a page bearing text and images inscribed by a creator), within which may be represented text worlds, in which references to "here" and "now," "I" and "you" no longer match the material participants of meaning exchange, creator and reader, but those participants in the meaning exchange embedded within the physical text. Within a story so told, there may of course appear "sub-worlds," in which the represented characters tell a story about other times, other lives, other places, creating text worlds within text worlds. This nesting may run to many laminations (to adopt the terminology of Goffman 1986, in his discussion of iterative social framing), and this is constitutive of the rich patina of graphic narrative. Luckily, we as readers are skilled users of language, which features recursive nested structures as a fundamental, frequently encountered, and familiar feature, and we are highly adept at tracking these worlds. This further allows a creator (or team) to stretch and play with the possibilities of disrupting this structure, subverting the sorts of expectations readers may have about the separability and basis of these text worlds, as, for instance, in the work of Ibn al Rabin (2013; Molotiu 2009).

Transmodal Dialogism

This flexibility, this transferability and cooperation between modes in comics discourse, the written and the drawn, the verbal and the visual, leads to a further notion of a dialogue: the particular interaction between word and image in collaboratively constructing the graphic narrative text. This is most prototypically seen in the relationship between enclosed dialogue, typically realized in verbal language, and enclosing context, typically visual. However, while word and image may coexist within the same cluster, verbal discourses, typically a narrating voice appearing in captions or in the margins of an image, may also provide verbal context for an enclosed image. That collaboration between the modes depends on specific patterns of cohesion between word and image (in addition to that obtaining between word and word, and between image and image). Cohesion in written and spoken text is a part of the *textual* metafunction of language in M. A. K. Halliday's system (Halliday 2005; Halliday and Matthiessen 2014), and has been explored in detail by Halliday and Ruqaiya Hasan in *Cohesion in English* (1976). Some work has recently begun in exploring such patterns in multimodal and comics texts (see Saraceni 2000; Stainbrook 2016; Saraceni 2016).

Halliday and Hasan (1976) detail the patterns of repetition and reference that bind any given text together, so that a text's parts depend on each other, mutually reference each other, and can rely on readerly assumptions so as to allow a text sequence to be more parsimonious than otherwise. Repetition of lexical items shows that a text remains on topic, as does the maintenance of a semantic field or words with related meanings. We can save on repetition by use of deictic pointer words such as "this," "that"; pronouns "it," "she," "he," and so on; and by substitutions of placeholder words such as "one" or "do." The ultimate substitution is substitution by zero, or *ellipsis*, the omission of features that can be understood to carry over from context. (So a question, "are you going out tonight," may be followed by "I am," without the need to append "going out tonight.") These patterns contribute to the construction of a more or less unitary and cohesive text, whether monologue or dialogue, and the location of the referent on which a cohesive feature depends can also characterize the text. Successive elements of the text build on the contributions of earlier elements. Textually cohesive reference depends on material elsewhere within the given text: it is *endophoric* reference. In a linear written or spoken text, this may further be clarified as the typical *anaphoric* reference, where the referent is to be found earlier in the text, or the more marked *cataphoric* reference, where an item cannot be understood (fully) until its referent is encountered later in the text (e.g., "About suffering *they* were never wrong, *the old masters*"). *Exophoric* reference is reference outside the text—and it is thereby not normally a cohesive feature, not binding the text by dependencies within itself, but asserting the text as bound to its context by depending on elements outside itself. But it is here that graphic narrative presents a difficulty: for in comics a verbal reference may refer outside its verbal environment to a visual context—that is nonetheless part of the overall graphic narrative text. Phoricity is thereby complicated, and the framework innovated by Halliday and Hasan is not designed to cope with the structure of comics.

The notion of phoricity in comics was set aside by Stainbrook in his recent consideration of comics cohesion (2016), since it presents these problems; but I think it can be recuperated and will be a valuable tool for characterizing with specificity the nature of the dialogue between text and image in graphic narrative. To anaphoric and cataphoric, endophoric and exophoric, I propose one can add *intraphoric* reference and *interphoric* reference. The latter coinage, interphoric reference, returns to the earlier examined characterization of dialogism in parataxis—sequences of enclosures connect and co-refer, speaking to each other. The referent of a word in one enclosure may be found in an adjacent one, or even one on a different page; and this makes concrete the sort of interconnectedness suggested by Thierry Groensteen's "braiding" and "arthrology" (Groensteen 2007). Dependencies are still within the text itself, but across enclosures arrayed at the same level. The other coinage, intraphoric reference, describes hypotactic relations: a deictic term in a word-balloon or thought-balloon enclosure may have as its referent something depicted in the same enclosing panel; commonly, another word in another balloon, or an individual or item in the balloon's context, but existing within the text world of the character uttering or thinking the text. The most basic instance of this is every time a character refers to "I." These categories classify the particular kinds of textual properties that tie together paratactic and hypotactic dialogism in comics texts, respectively.

In this way, comics texts are a network of connecting, interrelating elements, across modes, across and within enclosures, across narrative levels even, presenting multiple viewpoints, voices, perspectives, and registers in words and images. This is more than just repetition of motifs, but can be described in terms of specific relationships between modes, and between hierarchically arranged structures of nesting, in which visual or verbal utterances may be incorporated by others, and raised into focus or subordinated into the background. The logogenesis of the graphic narrative text is a matter of the unfolding of these connections, sequences, dependencies, and referents, and a significant pleasure of the comics text is in experiencing the rich texture of these layers of related meaning.

Conclusion

This third, and closest, level of the unfolding of a system of meaning-making completes the tripartite view of dialogism in comics I have set out to out-line in order to identify heteroglossia in the comics text. I have dwelt on the level of logogenesis most, since this has been my focus of interest as a social semiotician. But the Hallidayan approach I use in thinking about how comics mean, and how creators mean with comics, is explicitly intended to connect that meaning at the level of the text to personal and social histories, permitting an account of comics in which the social and material contexts of production are integral to, and not separate from, the meanings the com-ics text shares with us.

This lens of dialogue has led us through the metaphorical dialogue of genres and traditions across large scales of time, through the possibility of dialogue between individuals in the construction of the text, and between selves across the productive lifetime of a creator, down into the structure of comics texts themselves. Looking at comics as dialogic has given us a way to consider the social assumptions shared by readers and creators in the exchange of meanings from image to image, and the ways in which these can be exploited. Beyond that implicitly paratactic structure, the familiar concep-tion of comics as sequences of images, the idea of heteroglossia, particularly as in the conception offered by Martin and White of the incorporation and embedding of multiple voices and views within a text as a form of social engagement, has led us to explore the opportunities comics afford for the complex involvement of those voices into the text. Far from being simple and obvious picture-stories, comics can and do integrate the densely nested possibilities found in the *functional* structure of language, the rich network of dependencies, social assumptions, and world-tracking we sustain in our social lives, into their richly laminated, heteroglossic text.

Notes

1. See, notably, Maggie Gray's chapter in the present volume.

2. It is worth noting that the idea of heteroglossia as a multiplicity of voices is immediately salient: here I quote Morris quoting Bakhtin, and in the "Bakhtin" reader is included a range

of material published under the names Vološinov and Medvedev, which later scholarship has claimed was authored in large part by Bakhtin himself; an assertion around which there is a range of further commentary (see, for example, Morson and Emerson 1990; Hirschkop and Shepherd 2002). Morris finds herself appending multiple names when attributing quotations: Medvedev/Bakhtin, Vološinov/Bakhtin. For simplicity, where I cite these texts from Morris (1997) I have chosen to use a single name (i.e., "Vološinov [1929] 1997").

3. The maxims of comics I describe below, though they take the form of their articulation from Kantian categories as a starting point, can only emerge from socially and historically established norms of meaning-making behavior—creators' and readers'—just as the maxims of conversation develop from norms of interaction among interlocutors. As Grice (1975) observes of his own set of maxims of conversation, they may be open to expansion or adaptation.

4. Here in "synecdoche" I am reaching for a term that suggests more than metonymy, suggesting the constitution of comics by interrelated fragments, but not quite holography, which would imply that the whole is contained in each part. The parallel is to Grice's cooperative principle, that each element bears in mind its contribution as regards the overall function of the mutually constructed text, and is understood in relation to that purpose.

References

Bakhtin, Mikhail M. (1935) 1982a. "Discourse in the Novel." In *The Dialogic Imagination: Four Essays*, edited by Michael Holquist, 259–422. Translated by Caryl Emerson. Austin: University of Texas Press.

Bakhtin, Mikhail M. 1982b. *The Dialogic Imagination: Four Essays*, edited by Michael Holquist. Translated by Caryl Emerson. Austin: University of Texas Press.

Berberian, Charles, and Phillippe Dupuy. 2004. *Get a Life*. Montréal: Drawn and Quarterly.

Berberian, Charles, and Phillippe Dupuy. 2012. *Monsieur Jean*. Los Angeles: Humanoids.

Booth, Wayne C. 1983. *The Rhetoric of Fiction*. Rev. ed. Chicago: University of Chicago Press.

Bramlett, Frank, ed. 2012. *Linguistics and the Study of Comics*. London: Palgrave Macmillan.

Cohn, Neil. 2013. *The Visual Language of Comics: Introduction to the Structure and Cognition of Sequential Images*. London: Bloomsbury Academic.

Davies, Paul Fisher. 2013. "'Animating' the Narrative in Abstract Comics." *Studies in Comics* 4 (2): 251–76.

Davies, Paul Fisher. 2015. "On the Comics-Nature of the Codex Seraphinianus." *Studies in Comics* 6 (1): 121–32.

Eisner, Will. 2008. *Comics and Sequential Art: Principles and Practices from the Legendary Cartoonist*. New York: Norton and Company.

Fairclough, Norman. 2010. *Critical Discourse Analysis: The Critical Study of Language*. 2nd ed. London: Longman.

Gavins, Joanna. 2007. *Text World Theory: An Introduction*. Edinburgh: Edinburgh University Press.

Genette, Gérard. 1983. *Narrative Discourse: An Essay in Method*. Reprint ed. Translated by Jane E. Lewin. Ithaca, NY: Cornell University Press.

Goffman, Erving. 1986. *Frame Analysis: An Essay on the Organization of Experience*. New ed. Boston: Northeastern University Press.

Grice, H. P. 1975. "Logic and Conversation." In *Syntax and Semantics*, Vol. 3, *Speech Acts*, edited by Peter Cole and Jerry Morgan, 41–58. New York: Academic Press.

Groensteen, Thierry. 2007. *The System of Comics*. Translated by Bart Beaty and Nick Nguyen. Jackson: University Press of Mississippi.

Groensteen, Thierry. 2010. "The Monstrator, the Recitant and the Shadow of the Narrator." *European Comic Art* 3 (1): 1.

Halliday, M. A. K. 1978. *Language as Social Semiotic: The Social Interpretation of Language and Meaning*. Baltimore: University Park Press.

Halliday, M. A. K. 2004. *The Language of Early Childhood*. Vol 4. Edited by Jonathan Webster. London: Continuum.

Halliday, M. A. K. 2005. *On Grammar*. Vol. 1. London: Continuum.

Halliday, M. A. K., and Ruqaiya Hasan. 1976. *Cohesion in English*. London: Longman.

Halliday, M. A. K., and Ruqaiya Hasan. 1985. *Language, Context, and Text: Aspects of Language in a Social-Semiotic Perspective*. Victoria: Deakin University Press.

Halliday, M. A. K., and Christian Matthiessen. 2006. *Construing Experience through Meaning: A Language-Based Approach to Cognition*. Study ed. London: Continuum.

Halliday, M. A. K., and Christian Matthiessen. 2014. *Halliday's Introduction to Functional Grammar*. Abingdon: Routledge.

Hirschkop, Ken, and David Shepherd, eds. 2002. *Bakhtin and Cultural Theory*. 2nd ed. Manchester: Manchester University Press.

Hodge, Bob, and Gunther R. Kress. 1988. *Social Semiotics*. Ithaca, NY: Cornell University Press.

Huizenga, Kevin. 2006. *Curses*. Montréal: Drawn and Quarterly.

Ibn al Rabin. 2013. *Lentement aplati par la consternation*. Geneva: Atrabile.

Kress, Gunther, and Theo van Leeuwen. 2006. *Reading Images: The Grammar of Visual Design*. 2nd ed. London: Routledge.

Marion, Philippe. 1993. *Traces en cases: Travail graphique, figuration narrative et participation du lecteur: Essai sur la bande dessinée*. Louvain-la-Neuve: Academia.

Martin, J. R, and P. R. R White. 2005. *The Language of Evaluation: Appraisal in English*. New York: Palgrave Macmillan.

McCloud, Scott. 1993. *Understanding Comics: The Invisible Art*. New York: HarperPerennial.

Miodrag, Hannah. 2013. *Comics and Language: Reimagining Critical Discourse on the Form*. Jackson: University Press of Mississippi.

Molotiu, Andrei, ed. 2009. *Abstract Comics: The Anthology*. Seattle: Fantagraphics.

Morris, Pam, ed. 1997. *The Bakhtin Reader: Selected Writings of Bakhtin, Medvedev, Voloshinov*. London: Bloomsbury Academic.

Morson, Gary Saul, and Caryl Emerson. 1990. *Mikhail Bakhtin: Creation of a Prosaics*. Stanford, CA: Stanford University Press.

O'Toole, Michael. 2010. *The Language of Displayed Art*. 2nd ed. London: Routledge.

Painter, Clare, J. R. Martin, and Len Unsworth. 2013. *Reading Visual Narratives: Image Analysis of Children's Picture Books*. Sheffield: Equinox Pub.

Petersen, David. 2007. *Mouse Guard: Autumn 1152*. London: Titan Books.

Petersen, David, and Jeremy Bastian. 2011. *Mouse Guard: Legends of the Guard*. Vol. 1. London: Titan Books.

Petersen, David, and Paul Morrissey. 2015. *Mouse Guard: Legends of the Guard*. Vol. 3. Los Angeles: Archaia.

Petersen, David, and Bill Willingham. 2014. *Mouse Guard: Legends of the Guard*. Vol. 2. London: Titan Books.

Saraceni, Mario. 2000. "Language beyond Language: Comics as Verbo-Visual Texts." PhD diss., University of Nottingham.

Saraceni, Mario. 2016. "Relatedness: Aspects of Textual Connectivity in Comics." In *The Visual Narrative Reader*, edited by Neil Cohn, 115–27. London: Bloomsbury Academic.

Saussure, Ferdinand de. (1916) 2013. *Course in General Linguistics*. Reprint ed. London: Bloomsbury Academic.

Sim, Dave. 1991. *Cerebus*. Kitchener, ON: New Holland Publishers.

Spiegelman, Art. 2003. *The Complete Maus: Graphic Novel*. London: Penguin.

Stainbrook, Eric. 2016. "A Little Cohesion between Friends; Or, We're Just Exploring Our Textuality: Reconciling Cohesion in Written Language and Visual Language." In *The Visual Narrative Reader*, edited by Neil Cohn, 129–54. London: Bloomsbury Academic.

Vološinov, Valentin. (1929) 1997. "Marxism and the Philosophy of Language." In *The Bakhtin Reader: Selected Writings of Bakhtin, Medvedev, Voloshinov*, edited by Pam Morris, 26–37. London: Bloomsbury Academic.

Ware, Chris. 2001. *Jimmy Corrigan: The Smartest Kid on Earth*. London: Jonathan Cape.

Ware, Chris. 2003. *Quimby the Mouse*. Seattle: Fantagraphics.

Werth, Paul. 1999. *Text Worlds: Representing Conceptual Space in Discourse*. London: Longman.

8

Women's Cartoons and Comics in the Twenty-First Century

How the Humor in Simone Lia's Fluffy Challenges Gendered Assumptions around Parenting

NICOLA STREETEN

My original intention for this chapter was to demonstrate a hidden, but insidious economic precarity in the practice of contemporary graphic novelists in Britain that contradicts an assumed "success." I planned to show how this is gendered and how neoliberal ideologies reinforce this position. But I got sidetracked down a theoretical rabbit hole with no simple solutions becoming apparent. The challenge of writing anything that moved beyond a prolonged complaint seemed insurmountable. At the same time I was keen to position my contribution within a critical comics studies framework. It is the gender focus of my starting point, rather than the neoliberal aspect, that promised this. With a masculine history of comics in the West, the developing discipline of comics as an academic field should be vigilant, in my view, in considering the lesser documented histories which include those reflecting the voices and positions of women.

Two obvious thoughts would not go away. First, it is at the point of having children that new parents must often alter their working hours to adapt to this change. This is not specific to making comics and neither is it gendered. Second, continuing my generalization, the problem is not having children *per se*, but the dominantly gendered social assumptions around responsibilities and roles associated with childcare and parenting. It is here that gender becomes part of the discussion. A solution has preoccupied feminist theory and activity in Britain since 1970 with one of the original four demands of the Women's Liberation Movement being the provision of free twenty-four-hour childcare[1]—a demand that continues unmet more than five decades later. But my interest here is not in presenting a solution, nor is my aim to identify how the comics industry can adapt to become transformative in addressing childcare and work. Rather, my intention is to examine how the comics form is being used with humor by women to comment on care and masculinity. I analyze *Fluffy*, by British cartoonist Simone Lia (2007) to illustrate this.

The point I make is within a celebratory framework: that the rise in visibility of women's comics in Britain affords possibilities for platforming feminist messages in a way that is accessible, enjoyable, and humorous. A combination of humor with the comics form invites the reader to question both personal and collective assumptions that may exist around parenting. In doing so, this offers the potential to influence wider social change. My choice of *Fluffy* is based on the subtlety of Lia's provocation, presented through hilarious and surreal incongruity. Though *Fluffy* is not intentionally a feminist work, Lia uses humor to critically address questions of parenting and equality within the domestic or childrearing sphere as well as within heterosexual relationships.

To contextualize my analysis I start with a reflection on recent historical developments in comics in Britain as a backdrop to the publication of *Fluffy*. I argue that the confident entrance of cartoons and comics by women into the mainstream in British culture was made possible in a wider context by cultural structures built specifically by feminist activity from the 1970s on—for example, the continuing feminist presence and influence within publishing and the introduction of women's studies to academia.[2] However, specifically within the field of comics there were two notable influences. First, the popularity of the graphic novel, or long-form comic book, which introduced the form to a new audience unfamiliar with comics and outside the traditional mainstream fan-based comics readership. Second, the rise of the hand-drawn in the digital age and a comics community that grew up around this activity which has been increasingly characterized by a distinctly feminist voice. While both elements began earlier than the 2000s, the impact became more established during the 2000s, interweaving with each other to impact a popular if small section of the comics industry in Britain. Lia's practice and the publication of *Fluffy* interacted with the popularity of the graphic novel and the rise of the hand-drawn and a burgeoning community. As emphasized, Lia does not acknowledge her practice as feminist, but I argue it reflects the issues nevertheless, perhaps as a result of feminism becoming immersed in a changing infrastructure.

The Graphic Novel

The financial and critical successes of graphic novels include Art Spiegel-man's *Maus* (2003), Alison Bechdel's *Fun Home* (2006), Marjane Satrapi's *Persepolis* (2007), and Chris Ware's *Jimmy Corrigan* (2001) and have been written about within comics studies (Beaty 2009; Chute 2010; Hatfield 2005; Sabin 1996). I do not wish to duplicate this other than to note the relevant significant consequences. One has been the wide exposure and introduction of the comics form to a nontraditional comics reading public, which has included women. Another outcome has been an association between comics and serious subjects (Beaty 2009, 231–32). Here, a recognition of the commercial potential of autobiographical comics is the nongendered reason for the increase in published graphic memoirs by women. The insistence of "truth" through the autobiographical voice, applied to the comics form, introduced it as a platform for women's personal stories. Since the phrase "The personal is political" from Carol Hanisch's 1969 essay of the same title (Hanisch 1970), "the field of autobiography has become a central preoccupation and testing-ground for feminism" (Cosslet, Lury, and Summerfield 1992, 2). The association with literature in the use of *novel*, though arguably problematic in that it imposes a classed elitism to the cartoon form, has allowed women's works to enter a mainstream market. In other words, it is not the comics industry that has supported the resulting increased visibility of women cartoonists, but the literary industry. During the 2000s, autobiographical graphic novels were increasingly used to address issues around identity. Simone Lia's *Fluffy* benefited indirectly from this growing popularity. Her narrative is fictional, indeed fantastical; *Fluffy* is the story of a baby rabbit that insists that a single man, Michael Pulcino, is its father, or "daddy." Yet the presentation suggests the autobiographical through the firm immersion of the dialogue and events within the everyday and the domestic.

When the volumes of *Fluffy* were collected together for publication, it was as a graphic novel, a book. The word *comic* or *zine* had been replaced, injecting respectability and widening the audience. The presentation in book form represented a different symbolic space within contemporary culture. The 1980s feminist cartoon book format was usually around 21.2 x 14 cm (5.5" x 8.5"), a digest paperback following the comics digest tradition of published collections of newspaper cartoons.[3] This physical format signified humor. The production of the graphic novel followed the conventional taller size of the novel, approximately 15.2 x 22.9 cm. The association with the book signified, as Miriam Rivett writes, "fixity, permanence and a consequent gravity" (quoted in Sabin 1999, 31) and drew in middle-class audiences. The conventions in terms of size, typeface, design, and layout impacted the reception of the works, setting up an "interpretive framework" (31). The measurements of *Fluffy* are 16.2 x 17.1 cm positioning it simultaneously as both and not quite either the novel and the humorous cartoon book. This also allows *Fluffy* to claim allegiance to its small-press provenance and an initial appearance as self-published volumes. But even in their original printed volumes the works evaded singular categorization, because the professional or tutored aesthetic differed from the ephemeral quality of the photocopied zines of the 1980s and 1990s that continued to influence small-press activity. Lia's production included close attention to paper stock, use of color, type, and printing. Distribution of zines or small press may in earlier decades have relied on feminist or radical bookshops. Not only had such shops by now largely disappeared from the landscape, but comic book shops and general bookshops were widening their stock beyond the superhero mainstream comic to include small-press publications and alternative graphic novels and memoirs. Lia was able to sell her early volumes through these outlets. While her approach was professional, Lia's alliance with the grassroots ethos of the low-tech, hand-drawn works and accompanying community played an important part in her career. Such activity did not contradict technological developments, as it may be tempting to assume, but was complementary.

The Hand-Drawn in the Digital Age

The growth of the internet and technological developments that made communication global affected the production, distribution, and consumption of cartoons and comics in the twenty-first century. The internet enabled rapid information exchange and created a platform that nurtured virtual communities and reinforced physical ones. In the 2000s, cartooning activity in the British comics community was taking place online; however, at the same time there was a growth in the production of handmade, low-tech printed zines and comics. Alongside this, groups of people continued to create physical meeting spaces. The appearance of comics studies in academia was an important part of the wider community building around comics in Britain during this decade. These changes supported the potential for a more viable economic position for cartoonists and women entering the field. I will interpret this situation with reference to historical activity to illustrate the distinctly feminist tone I alluded to earlier.

The resurgence of the handmade and small-press activity within the digital age shares grassroots characteristics of second and third wave feminist activity and socialist political activism. One example of this was the first Ladyfest festival which took place in Olympia, Washington, USA, in 2000, with over two thousand people attending. The first British Ladyfest took place in 2001 in Glasgow and continued at different locations around the UK as well as globally until 2012 (Ladyfest 2005). Legacies of the 1990s Riot Grrrl movement, Ladyfest festivals were celebrations of DIY feminist activism, including a range of art forms. Zines were an aspect of the festivals, described by feminist scholars Red Chidgey, Rosa Reitsame, and Elke Zobl as examples of the "visual ephemera of the transnational contemporary 'third wave' feminist moment" (Chidgey, Reitsame, and Zobl 2009, 5), emerging directly from and representing grassroots feminist networks.

In 2003 Ladyfest Bristol and Manchester curated the first British art exhibition of women comics-makers, entitled The Cave of Comic Queens. It included established small-press comics artists such as Lorna Miller, Lee Kennedy, Jeremy Dennis, and Carol Swain. The Ladyfest Manchester festival program (2003) stated:

> Comics are just so overlooked, as an art form, as a narrative form; and because they are completely male-dominated. Walk into any comic bookshop and look on the shelves and in the racks, how many women artists can you find? You'd never guess the wealth of talent there is in this country alone. (quoted in Blasé 2007)

Chidgey, Reitsame, and Zobl argued that this activity offered insight into the conditions of production for feminist activity of the 2000s. The defining features of collaboration and often anonymously produced works seem to echo the approach of second wave feminist activity.

In many cases there was a mixture of styles and topics, and an interest in the community and social aspects in the mode of production were emphasized. For example, in 2001, Selina Lock, a comics writer, along with partner Jay Eales, had been active in running Caption Comics Festival. They cofounded the small publishing press Factor Fiction, and in 2008 Lock edited the first in a series of anthologies, The Girly Comic Book 1, "with no other guiding principle than having every strip feature a female lead" (Bruton 2009). The decision not to restrict the comic to work by women was because most submissions were from men. She therefore aimed to produce a "girl-centered, girl-positive comic written and illustrated by anyone" (Lock

2008). With a wide variety of topics and styles, the series included works by established cartoonists from the small press, such as Lee Kennedy, Jeremy Dennis, and Jenny Linn-Cole. At the same time, the anthologies introduced works by many younger artists such as Kate Brown, Asia Alfasi, Karen Rubins, Karrie Fransman, and Laura Howell (who was the first female artist to have worked on the *Beano*). The series ran until 2011.

In the digital age, examples of British women's comics anthologies utilized the internet and social media in the call for works and publicity, but the emphasis was on the hand-drawn and the final collections were in physical printed form.[4] In the same way, the comics community relied on the digital to communicate information, but at the same time there was an increase in the importance of physical meetings.

From Comics Collective to Comics Community

The emerging comics anthologies were sold at comics festivals and initiatives across Britain. I interpret this as a manifestation of the feminist collective continually transforming, responding to and shaped by the economic, political, and social climate. One noteworthy example has been Thought Bubble, set up in 2007 in Leeds as a nonprofit organization by cartoonist Lisa Wood (also going by the name Tula Lotay), after she completed her university education and was working at Leeds comics shop Travelling Man (Chapman 2015). It has become the biggest festival of its kind in Britain, offering a welcoming community atmosphere. Wood's aim was to provide "an annual celebration of sequential art in all its forms, including everything from superhero comics to independent and small-press artists and writers" (Thought Bubble 2016). Examples of community activity revolved around the sale of handmade zines and small-press publications and also had a social element, such as musical events and panel discussions.

The affiliation of comics studies academic conferences with the festivals[5] is relevant because it is through this strand of activity that I met Sarah Lightman, with whom I cofounded Laydeez do Comics (LDC) in 2009, "like a combination between a book club and a series of TED talks" (Davis 2013). A women-led, but not women-only forum to test new works and ideas, we have hosted monthly events for emerging artists to present alongside more established practitioners. Advertised online to a public audience as free events, these quickly established LDC as a hub of the small British comics community. This grassroots activity has been based on goodwill and always stressed the importance of social interaction. Yet it has relied on the internet and social media to promote globally and has been documented and archived online through regular blogposts. The social activity has been an essential element of both my own and Lightman's academic research and our approach to academia; as Lightman has noted, "creating in real life what you may be studying" (Lightman 2010). My brief overview of aspects of the landscape in Britain in the 2000s in relation to small-press comics is by way of positioning Simone Lia's activity which I now turn to.

Simone Lia

During the 2000s a younger generation of women cartoonists were emerging from higher education in Britain, often at postgraduate level, where there was an acceptability and increase in the use of the comics form, by illustration students in particular. The increase in university-educated practitioners was in itself no different to the cartoonists who were visible in the previous decades. What had changed in Britain by this decade was that the opportunity for a university education was widening, allowing more people—more women—to benefit. What had previously been an opportunity only available for white, middle-class students was now beginning to change. While the fees and removal of grants limited the appeal to nonprivileged families, I argue a result of this was more university courses being introduced that facilitated a greater visibility for women's work. Once trained, these female creators made use of practices, traditions, and networks within the grassroots alternative press.

The work of British-born Maltese illustrator Simone Lia is an example. In 2000, having completed her BA (Hons) in illustration at the University of Brighton in 1995 as a first-generation university student, Lia studied for an MA in illustration at the Royal College of Art, London. Intending to further develop her career in children's book illustration, she was introduced to the possibilities of the comics form by fellow student Tom Gauld. They collaborated on a comic called *First*, an assemblage of both their works, photocopying and distributing it themselves. This won them an award sponsored by Deutsche Bank that enabled them to professionally print a thousand copies of their follow-up publication, *Second* (Barton 2007). Lia and Gauld set up Cabanon Press in 2000 to self-publish their works, and between 2003 and 2005 Lia produced *Fluffy* in four volumes; in the tradition of the small or alternative press it was "a story of unanswerable questions, love, despair, adventure and happiness" (Lia 2007, 1). The subject matter she was dealing with was not directly or intentionally feminist in nature, but my analysis will show that in the means of production, style, and the subject matter, the work addressed feminist issues.

According to the *Down the Tubes* website there were only 110 comics shops in Britain in 2016 (Freeman 2016). Of those, 18 stocked small-press, self-published publications as well as nonsuperhero graphic novels (Stringer 2016). The comics shops in Britain largely sold mainstream comics until the 1980s, when new styles of works appeared. By 2003, when Lia and Gauld were self-publishing, there were a number of comics shops in London where they could sell them. They had also sent copies to book publishers. When they were approached by the editor of Bloomsbury to publish *First* and *Second* together as *Both*, it was as a result of a purchase or "discovery" at the comics shop rather than from receiving a copy at the office (Lia 2012). Lia had also been publishing *Fluffy* in volumes and when Jonathan Cape approached her to publish *Fluffy*, it was a result of word of mouth rather than from seeing the copies she had sent in—which had actually been added to the slush pile! The discovery of her work from a zine-style handmade grassroots provenance was a key part of the process. It added authenticity to the work.

Although Lia drew on grassroots modes of production and distribution, it is her professional training that marks the change in this sector of the comics industry in Britain. She began by self-publishing, but her entrance into the industry was as a highly trained illustrator from a leading art school. As mentioned earlier, her application of the DIY ethos was within a framework of high production quality, critical design practice, and commercialization.

The critical acclaim and popularity *Fluffy* received following publication provided a positive endorsement of women cartoonists in Britain. I also argue that its popularity relied on a tragicomic characteristic (see, for example, figure 8.1) and that the use of the aesthetic of cute combined with the storyline reinforces this, such as the pestering and persistence of a child that is captured for comic effect by the baby rabbit as shown in figures 8.2 and 8.3.

The work is drawn in a simple, very dark blue line and digitally shaded with a blue-toned gray. The work appears black and gray. This is an example of the distancing from the ordinary. The printing used one color, costing the same as black, but requiring knowledge of the process to achieve a small subtle difference that gives the final product a designed aesthetic.

The style and storyline incorporate cute and whimsy. The baby-cute of the rabbit is what Hannah Arendt calls the "modern enchantment with 'small things' . . . the art of being happy . . . between dog and cat and flowerpot"

Figure 8.1: Page from *Fluffy*, 2003, 18.
© Simone Lia.

Figure 8.2: Page from *Fluffy*, 2003, 19.
© Simone Lia.

Figure 8.4: Page from *Fluffy*, 2003, 32.
© Simone Lia.

(Arendt cited in Ngai 2012, 3). In reviewing *Fluffy*, journalist Carrie O'Grady referred to the Japanese term *kawaii*, meaning "infinitely precious just for managing to exist so bravely and perkily despite being so small and vulnerable in a cruel world . . . [a] leftfield brand of alterno-cuteness" (O'Grady 2007). She identified in *Fluffy's* character a nod to the cute of iconic Japanese cartoon characters such as Hello Kitty and the Pokémon character Pikachu, noting their popularity as part of 1980s rave culture. Yet Lia does not rely on the large eyes and small mouth trope of the Japanese characters. Instead, her reference is to the *ligne claire* tradition of dots for eyes, as used by Hergé for Tintin and his cute companion dog Snowy.

I propose the "alterno-cuteness," or "vulnerable yet brave," quality is what feminist academic Sianne Ngai is addressing in her theorizing of cute in *Our Aesthetic Categories: Zany, Cute, Interesting* (2012). Ngai refers to "cute" as an aesthetic category to understand and describe modern aesthetic experiences. She argues that the "hypercommodified, information-saturated, performance-driven conditions of late capitalism" (Ngai 2012, 1) have changed our everyday aesthetic experiences.

The cute aesthetic represents an ambivalent emotion; a longing for closeness expressed in a commodification. The aesthetic evokes something like a cuddle to death response, simultaneously a positive reaction with a negative aggression—or a smile with tears (Ngai 2012). This emotional paradox or aggressive cuteness of the drawn rabbit in *Fluffy* serves to visually mirror elements of such contradictory emotion in the storyline, that is, the conflicting emotions Pulcino feels toward the rabbit. One example of this is Michael Pulcino's "unhealthy relationship with Fluffy's nursery school teacher" (Lia 2007, 95). Over four pages, the panels show the mounting tension as the woman teacher constantly phones and emails Pulcino. Meanwhile Fluffy visibly adds to the strain in his life, with one panel showing Fluffy swinging from a lightbulb (figure 8.4). Visually this conveys Pulcino's love-hate of both his relationship with the teacher and with the rabbit. Throughout the narrative Pulcino's contradictory emotions toward the teacher are conveyed. He does not want to continue the relationship, yet does not finish it. This is shown in other aspects of his everyday life. His relationship to his work demonstrates a similar ambivalence. He continues only because he cannot think of any other way to earn a living (95). His emotional and consumer relationships illustrate Ngai's claim of being controlled by a cycle of production, circulation, and consumption.

Fluffy is very funny—it is a tragicomedy. Ngai does not address the humor of cute and whether laughter is an aesthetic response. Yet in this case the

Figure 8.4: Page from *Fluffy*, 2003, 33. © Simone Lia.

cuteness of the drawing appears to intensify the incongruity and the humor derived from it. The reader laughs at Pulcino's situation of high tension, anxiety, and contradictions. When his sister later refers to the teacher as a "freaky bunny boiler," it elicits a shocked response from Pulcino: "don't say things like that" (Lia 2007, 112).

The reference is to a scene in Adrian Lyne's 1987 psychological thriller *Fatal Attraction*. The film hinges around a single woman, Alex, who has an affair with married man Dan and becomes pregnant by him. Alex is presented as a career woman who becomes obsessive and deranged in her want for a husband and child. When spurned by Dan, she boils the pet rabbit belonging to Dan's child and finally kills herself. As Suzanne Leonard describes:

> Alex's life of financial independence and sexual freedom is cast not as a feminist dream, but rather as a nightmare of regret and worry, a representation which betrays the threat that non-normative women pose to patriarchal structures. (Leonard 2009, 63)

Alex is presented as a "cautionary figure;" the implication is that it is her professional success that turned her into a psychotic killer. Leonard quotes feminist popular culture scholars Susan Bromley and Pamela Hewitt who describe the message of the film as "women who opt for the career track are to be viewed not merely as unfeminine, but also as destructive who must be themselves destroyed" (cited in Leonard 2009, 62). In *Misogynies*, Joan

Smith quotes Michael Douglas, the actor who played the (cheating) husband as saying:

> Any man would be a fool who didn't agree with equal rights and equal pay, but some women, now, juggling with career, lover, children, wifehood, have spread themselves too thin and are very unhappy. It's time they looked at themselves and stopped attacking men. (Douglas cited in Smith 1989, 25, emphases in original)

In this way, Douglas blurs his identity. His role is as actor, created to elicit empathy from the audience, yet he steps outside the screen to make a judgment about women. In his role beyond the film, he is still evoking the empathy from an audience; the boundary is blurred between his role as actor and his role as victimized man.

While the "bunny boiler" reference elicits humor in *Fluffy*, in the incongruity of the rabbit, what is notable is the use of the term twenty years after the film's release and that it continues to be used with a very clear cultural meaning, even by those who have not seen the film. Michael Pulcino's sister, Rosetta, who makes the comment, has been introduced to the reader as unhappily married: "After the wedding Rosetta realised . . . she didn't really love Fabrizio" (Lia 2007, 96). In making the comment she is alluding to the idea that through her very status as married she is unthreatening. Leonard quotes critic Laurie Stone who wrote about the film in *Ms.*: "good women stay home . . . while single working women are damaged, barely even human, and want to destroy the family they also secretly covet" (cited in Leonard 2009, 66).

The comic amusement from this reference in *Fluffy* is in the continual haziness of a fanciful double incongruity. Firstly, the speaking rabbit introduces the fantastical notion of animals as human. Although anthropomorphic animals are a common trope of children's picture books, *Fluffy* confounds this. While it may provide appeal for a child, Lia's work eschews the traditional bright colors of children's picture books, or Pikachu, and displays a sophistication in its humor that is clearly directed at adults. The rabbit signifies a human toddler and Lia draws on the funny things that children say and their innocence, such as "I've forgotten how to breathe" and "This ice cream is nice because of the ketchup" (Lia 2007, 102). The reader is asked to withhold reality, to distance themselves from the mundane realities of childcare in enjoying the premise. Fluffy goes to nursery and the teacher becomes a character in the narrative, reinforcing the nonsensical premise. Yet at moments Lia demands the reader switch back to recognizing Fluffy as a rabbit, triggering laugher from the absurdity, as with the "bunny boiler" comment. French philosopher Henri Bergson wrote that "We laugh every time a person gives us the impression of being a thing" (Bergson 1911, 56). The success of the comic effect, he said, lies in "its power of suggestion, i.e., in making it acceptable" (61). It is this impression, or switching between the reality and fantasy, that Lia achieves and which renders the comedy of the narrative.

But there is a bitter aftertaste in our laughter at the "bunny boiler" reference. The backdrop of "raunch culture"[6] genders the choice of rabbit, lending it the playboy bunny-girl signification of sexual submission. As Levy puts it, a "tawdry, tarty cartoonlike version of female sexuality has become so ubiquitous, it no longer seems particular," noting that Hugh Hefner, founder of *Playboy*, is being "embraced by young women in a curious way in a post-feminist world" (Levy 2005, 5). In *Fatal Attraction* the spurned woman is portrayed as a deviant, a predatory woman stalker whose psychotic behavior reinforces the traditional heteronormative gender roles through emphasizing the "healthy" behavior of the wronged wife. While Lia plays with the incongruity of the rabbit/toddler identity of Fluffy, she is also playing with gender incongruities. The implication in *Fatal Attraction* is of a causal link between female independence and a successful professional career, and an inability to achieve "normality" through marriage. In *Fluffy*, this idea is ridiculed through visualizing Pulcino's inability to change the discontents in his everyday life. The gender norms present in *Fatal Attraction* are gently challenged in *Fluffy*. A single man is in the position of main carer of a young child, challenging stereotypes of the woman as child carer . . . except it is not a child, it is a rabbit. The absurdity invites us to question the assumptions made around men as carers of children. I propose that if the character of Michael Pulcino were a married man or a woman, the humor would be dissipated.

Conclusion

I briefly introduced the background within comics activity in Britain that was taking shape when Simone Lia produced *Fluffy* and then presented my analysis of *Fluffy* as a "success." I claim it as a success because of the very subtle way humor is applied with the comics form to contribute to a debate that is not funny. By provoking thought through laughter, Lia presents a story with a feminist message at its core in a way that is not obvious and not intentional on her part.

Fluffy is a work that is critically acclaimed and Simone Lia is considered one of the most successful contemporary graphic novelists and cartoonists in Britain as a consequence. But what I have not addressed is whether *Fluffy* can be considered a "success" financially. It is this question I steered away from but which needs acknowledgment as part of my conclusion. While such probing must surely surround all artistic endeavor, what differentiates the economic precarity within small-press or graphic novel activity from other "creative industries" such as graphic design or fine art is that the infrastructure to support the activity is not yet established in Britain. For example, the gallery structure of fine art does not exist for comics and graphic novels; the publishing structure that supported creative writing is not sufficient to support comics; and comics does not yet exist as an academic subject that is established enough to provide related jobs, as in other creative professions. Nevertheless, to finish on a hopeful note, publication of new works by women cartoonists continues, including those addressing feminist issues, whether subtly or evidently and the infrastructure is constantly developing to find ways to support activity that may not in itself be sufficient to survive.

Notes

1. The four basic demands identified by feminism in 1970 were equal pay, equal education and job opportunities, free contraception and abortion on demand, and free twenty-four-hour nurseries (British Library 2015).

2. By 1988 eleven feminist publishing companies had set up in Britain (Cochrane 2013). Four of these included women's cartoon books in their title lists. These were distributed to a total of around sixty feminist and radical bookshops which opened during the 1980s and 1990s, supported by the newly growing network of independent distributors. In 1980 the University of Kent, Canterbury, introduced the first named program, a master's degree in women's studies (Downing 2013).

3. Such as collections of Reg Smythe's *Andy Capp* cartoons, or Carl Giles's cartoon collections.

4. For example, in 2003 cartoonist Jeremy Dennis (Day) cofounded the *Whores of Mensa* comics anthology with cartoonists Sasha Mardou, Lucy Sweet, and later Ellen Lindner. In 2011 Ellen Lindner took over editorship of the anthology under the new name of *The Strumpet*. In 2009 Glasgow-based cartoonist Gill Hatcher founded Team Girl Comic, a collective of Scotland-based cartoonists that met to talk about comics and to produce two comics anthologies a year.

5. For example, Comics Forum has run annually in conjunction with Thought Bubble since 2009 and the Transitions conference has run annually since 2009 and is affiliated with Comica Festival, London.

6. North American feminist Ariel Levy states in *Female Chauvinist Pigs: Women and the Rise of Raunch Culture* (2005) that "If you were to put the last five or so years in a time capsule,

womanwise, it would look like a period of explosive sexual exhibitionism, opportunism, and role redefinition" (Levy 2005, 118). She refers to the popularity of American TV shows such as *Sex in the City*, the burlesque revival, the introduction of beauty procedures such as Brazilian bikini waxes, the 700 percent increase in breast augmentations in the United States since 1992, the introduction of "Cardio Striptease" classes at gyms in New York, Los Angeles, Miami, San Francisco, and Chicago, and the increase of vaginoplasty or vaginal rejuvenation, cosmetic surgery to alter the labia and vulva to make the vagina "attractive" (Levy 2005, 20–23). Popular culture, she asserts, reinforced this behavior as "empowering and cool" for women (118).

References

Barton, Laura. 2007. "Rabbiting On." *Guardian*, February 14, 2007. https://www.theguardian. com/books/2007/feb/14/fiction.laurabarton.

Beaty, Bart. 2009. "Autobiography as Authenticity." In *A Comics Studies Reader*, edited by Jeet Heer and Kent Worcester, 226–35. Jackson: University Press of Mississippi.

Bechdel, Alison. 2006. *Fun Home: A Family Tragicomic*. London: Jonathan Cape.

Bergson, Henri. 1911. *Laughter: An Essay on the Meaning of the Comic*. New York: Macmillan.

Blasé, Cazz. 2011. "A Shocking Shade of Pink." *The F Word*, August 13, 2011. http://www .thefword.org.uk/features/2011/08/shocking_pink.

British Library. n.d. "Shrew." Accessed July 21, 2014. http://www.bl.uk/learning/histcitizen/21cc/ counterculture/liberation/shrew/shrew.html.

Bruton, Richard. 2009. "The Girly Comic Book Volume 1—Not Your Usual Anthology." *Forbidden Planet*, April 22, 2009. Accessed June 19, 2016. http://www.forbiddenplanet .co.uk/blog/2009/the-girly-comic-book-volume-1-not-your-usual-anthology/.

Chapman, Daniel. 2015. "'Thought Bubble Is a Reflection of What I Love'—Lisa Wood Comic Book Artist." *The City Talking: Leeds*, #17. http://www.thecitytalking.com/ 2014118thought-bubble-is-a-reflection-of-what-i-love-lisa-wood-comic-book-artist/.

Chidgey, Red, Rosa Reitsame, and Elke Zobl. 2009. "Ladyfest: Material Histories of Everyday Feminist Art Production." *N. Paradoxa* 24: 5–12.

Chute, Hillary L. 2010. *Graphic Women: Life Narrative and Contemporary Comics*. New York: Columbia University Press.

Cochrane, Kira. 2013. "Has Virago Changed the Publishing World's Attitudes Towards Women?" *Guardian*, March 14, 2013. http://www.theguardian.com/books/2013/mar/14/ virago-changed-publishers-attitudes-women.

Cosslett, Tess, Celia Lury, and Penny Summerfield, eds. 2000. *Feminism and Autobiography: Texts, Theories, Methods*. London: Routledge.

Davis, Julie. 2013. "Laydeez do Comics." *Art Animal: A Women's Art Magazine*, February 13, 2013. http://www.artanimalmag.com/feature-laydeez-do-comics/.

Downing, Lisa. 2013. "Identity Crisis for Women's Studies." *Times Higher Education*. Accessed March 30, 2015. http://www.timeshighereducation.co.uk/features/identity-crisis-for -womens-studies/2004832.article.

Freeman, John. 2016. "The British Comic Industry Q&A." *Down the Tubes*. Accessed February 1, 2017. http://downthetubes.net/?page_id=7110.

Hanisch, Carol. 1970. "The Personal Is Political." In *Notes from the Second Year: Women's Liberation: Major Writings of the Radical Feminists*, edited by Shulamith Firestone and Anne Koedt, 76–77. New York: Shulamith Firestone and Anne Koedt.

Hatfield, Charles. 2005. *Alternative Comics: An Emerging Literature*. Jackson: University Press of Mississippi.

Ladyfest. 2005. Accessed May 8, 2016. http://ladyfest.org.

Leonard, Suzanne. 2009. *Fatal Attraction*. Oxford: Wiley-Blackwell.

Levy, Ariel. 2005. *Female Chauvinist Pigs: Women and the Rise of Raunch Culture*. New York: Free Press.

Lia, Simone. 2003. *Fluffy*. London: Cabanon.

Lia, Simone. 2007. *Fluffy*. London: Jonathan Cape.

Lia, Simone. 2012. Talk at Laydeez do Comics, December 15, 2012, The Rag Factory, London.

Lightman, Sarah. 2010. "Cartoon County Interview #3: Sarah Lightman of Laydeez do Comics." *Mindless Ones*, October 10, 2010. Accessed June 18, 2016. https://mindlessones.com/2010/10/20/cartoon-county-interview-3-sarah-lightman-of-laydeez-do-comics/.

Lock, Selina, ed. 2008. *The Girly Comic Book 1*. Oxford: Factor Fiction.

Ngai, Sianne. 2012. *Our Aesthetic Categories: Zany, Cute, Interesting*. Cambridge, MA: Harvard University Press.

O'Grady, Carrie. 2007. "All Ears." *Guardian*, February 10, 2007. https://www.theguardian.com/books/2007/feb/10/featuresreviews.guardianrreview18.

Sabin, Roger. 1996. *Comics, Comix and Graphic Novels: A History of Comic Art*. London: Phaidon.

Sabin, Roger, ed. 1999. *Punk Rock: So What? The Cultural Legacy of Punk*. London: Routledge.

Satrapi, Marjane. 2007. *The Complete Persepolis*. London: Random House.

Smith, Joan. 1989. *Misogynies*. London: Faber and Faber.

Spiegelman, Art. 2003. *The Complete Maus*. London: New York: Penguin.

Stringer, Lew. 2016. "Comic Shops Helping the Small Press (More Updates!)." *Blimey!* March 15, 2016. Accessed: 26 February 2017. http://lewstringer.blogspot.co.uk/2016/03/comic-shops-helping-small-press-more.html.

Thought Bubble. 2016. Information. Accessed June 19, 2016. http://thoughtbubblefestival.com/information/.

Ware, Chris. 2001. *Jimmy Corrigan: The Smartest Kid on Earth*. London: Jonathan Cape.

9

Politicization of Life and Auto-Thanatopolitics in *V for Vendetta*

VLADISLAV MAKSIMOV

The iconic Guy Fawkes mask has become a staple symbol of resistance to authority; from hacktivist groups (Stoehrel and Lindgren 2014) to the Occupy movement (Lush and Dobnik 2011), the mask continues to surface in mass protests. *The Economist* (C.C. 2014) described the mask as "the face of post-modern protest" (n.p.). Nevertheless, as with any societal symbol, the mask and the character it refers to occupy a contested space and carries real regulatory consequences, and the state is neither neutral nor indifferent to such manifestations. It becomes quite clear that the state does not desire to see such manifestations once legislation prohibiting the wearing of the mask is passed, as it did in the United Arab Emirates (Barakat 2012).

What is so special about V's story and so uniting about the mask? Why does it lend itself so well to representing postmodern societal tensions?[1] What is it about the plot or our antihero that makes V a great candidate to represent such diverse fights as Anonymous's vendetta against scientology (Bilton 2011), the Occupy movement's struggle against inequality, or the protest of Hungarian teachers against the over-centralization of the education system (BBC 2016)? In other words, what is it about the story of the downfall of a postapocalyptic fascist regime in Britain that excites the imagination of thousands of protesters around the world?

To begin to answer these questions we must consider the relationship between liberation and will, sovereign and subject, and bodies in struggle against oppression in Alan Moore and David Lloyd's *V for Vendetta*.[2] In the context of emerging literature within critical comics studies exploring the limits of sovereignty (see Curtis 2016, 153–78), V's tale presents an opportunity to delve into the boundaries of sovereignty, its birth, violence, and death. These complex relationships are reflected in the illustrious phrase of

V directed at Evey as she emerges from his torture chamber: "I offered you a choice between the death of your principles and the death of your body" (Moore and Lloyd 2008, 171), and Evey chose the latter. This dichotomous choice is what seems to be the inescapable price to pay for freedom. But what is the relationship between the principle and the body? What are these principles that we must be willing to die for?

As we begin an investigation into the semiotics and the political of V's formula, we must examine closely the constitutive parts of the equation. After all, *V for Vendetta* is a story of principles and principals, the ruled and what is left beyond the reach of power. Principle, that is the truth, the cornerstone of the system, the underlying axiom migrated to English, through Old French, from the Latin *principium* ("source") coming from *princip* ("first, chief") (Stevenson 2015b). The word has always been different in English from the noun principal, the leader, the senior, the head, yet the latter finds its origins in latin *principalis* ("first, original"), itself formed from *princip* (Stevenson 2015a). In other words, in choosing between our body, or more specifically its death, and our principles, we are asked to find the originary meaning, the primal guiding point, the root of the cognates, without which the center cannot hold. In case we make the right choice, the cell door opens, the bars fall away, and we are promised to be facing freedom, the multiplication of which forms V's vision of anarchy.

A closer take through the looking glass, however, begins to outline the tensions of these concepts, an apparently oxymoronic relationship between the choice of the *princip*, that which is no longer divisible and is the key to the cage of the body, beyond which lies anarchy and the promised freedom itself—the Greek *an-* ("without") and *árkhōs* ("leader"), from *árkhein* ("to rule"), from *árkhō*, in Homer meaning both "to begin" and "to command" (Benmakhlouf et al. 2017; Hoad 2003). The symmetry of the *princip* and *árkhō* lays bare the complex relationship of choosing what is "first" inside, the origin beyond the body and yet inside it, which will bring about the rejection thereof from what surrounds the body. The interwoven discourse of outside and inside, the excluded and included, the power and the rule are at the heart of the dynamics of rise and fall in *V for Vendetta*. In order to reconcile them, we must disentangle this seemingly contradictory relationship between the body and that which is excluded from it, its birth, life, death, and rebirth.

I first demonstrate that the bodies and their localities are interwoven in a complex mesh of biological, political, and mechanical relationships, which problematize the boundaries of sovereign power. Next, we trace the birth of Norsefire's regime, its relationship to bare life, and the many iterations of the camp in the novel to find that, in the zone of indistinction where bare life and the sovereign come closest to one another in an inextricable bond, by the inability to complete a thanatopolitical act bare life can absorb the potentiality of sovereign violence. Bare life cannot be liberated in the proper sense, because its appearance is tied to the politicization of animal life through sovereign power. Yet as violence reaches its apogee, bare life comes closest to the source of its creation. I conclude by arguing that as the camp encompasses all aspects of life the dynamics between sovereign power and bare life turn not *dis*uniting or *emancipatory*, but rather "transformative," "transfigurative" and, ultimately, autodestructive.

Body (Bio)politic

The body can be viewed as a vessel: that which is inside constitutes parts of it, while it is defined by not belonging to that which is outside. The appearance of the body, both physical and metaphysical, permeates the entire novel; the bodies are sexualized, violated, survive, regenerate, and die. Of particular interest is the relationship between the *body politic* constitutive of Norsefire's regime, its logistics, and that of V's home, the Shadow Gallery.

The state's logistical makeup takes the literal names of organs with the Finger representing police power, the Mouth producing propaganda, the Eye and the Ear as the surveillance apparatus, the Nose as the investigative unit, all constituting the ruling mechanism: the Head. The regime has not only exerted its biopower on its citizens, it symmetrically copies their bodies, producing a carefully crafted maze of oppression. Subversively, the internal organization and construction of the Shadow Gallery, which V admits to having built himself (Moore and Lloyd 2008, 18) symmetrically transposes the macro-level construction of the regime. While Norsefire rules England through the Head encompassing the five senses, the Shadow Gallery exposes what is lacking, the nonmaterialistic qualities that make up the human experience, the mind (Moore and Lloyd 2008, 219). The Gallery's mouth gives voice to films and preserves culture, its ears are attuned to the creativity of the music room furbished with a piano, its enclosed garden full of roses fills the air with pleasant scent, while the hands can create in the laboratory that is informed by science. Yet this relationship is peculiar and complex.

The interconnections between the outside and inside, the state and the Shadow Gallery are mediated by the disquieting duplication of function as well as the biological connections between the two. The seed of creation in science can be used here, as outside, for the manufacturing of explosives. The linkages transgress the realm of utilization and metaphor. The Shadow Gallery does not have eyes, but houses the optic nerve, which is connected to the Eyes of the regime. Thus, the sinuses of the Gallery are not only linked between themselves but with the Head; as in an organism, "everything is connected" (Moore and Lloyd 2008, 218). Just as the mind is part of the head through forming an indivisible bond, so V is part of the regime. Their relationship may be antagonistic, as the repulsion of two poles, but the infrastructure links them together into an inseparable whole.

Fate, the supercomputer embodying the bureaucratic regime, overarching but normally only accessible to the leader, houses the records of the totalitarian state. It is the single point of failure, the point where V can enter into the most precious caverns of the regime. The machine is the accumulation of senses, the processor and simultaneously the very manifestation of sovereign power. Once the access to it is lost, the human entity representing the regime, Leader Adam Susan, dies as well. The keeping of dates, persons, numbers, the ability to track and be remembered defines the mechanical soul of the regime. It is the human subjects that operate the machine; it is devoid of humanity but it has a personality. Fate has a Voice, the propaganda broadcast; you are able to speak to it, as the Leader does on numerous occasions. Still, it is its coldness, steadiness, and predictability that attracts Adam Susan. In sum, while the body of the regime may seem organic from without, the inner workings of it are nonhuman.

The history of the unity between the biological and the mechanical is highlighted by the novel. In the narrative of Norsefire's rise to power, we find out that "all the fascist groups . . . got together with some of the big corporations that had survived" (Moore and Loyd 2008, 28). Presumably, the technological prowess came from the corporations, thus forging the unity between the human body and the body constituted. The artificial person, the Head, is a clear allusion to the state as conceived by Western juridico-political thought, pointing to parallels drawn between the body of the nation and the body of a corporation (Frederic 1901). *V for Vendetta*, in some ways, thus offers the extreme version of corporate totalitarianism, where the fictitious body of the corporation is inextricably merged with the body of the subjects forming the fictitious body of the state.

At this point, it is important to highlight that medieval Christian thought saw a parallel between the *pars principans* of the body, the soul that rules the *corpus*, and the rulers acting for the political body: "these *principes* were instituted, not for their own sake but for the sake of the people" (Chroust

1947, 449; see also Kantorowicz 1997). The body politic of V's postapocalyptic England, in this light, is then mutilated beyond recognition. The war first leads to disintegration of the state, only to be reunited in a grotesque image of itself. What this process underscores, however, is that sovereign power in Norsefire's England must be understood as a cyclical constitution. The symmetry between the *princip* that Evey finds within herself, and the *princip* at the heart of the regime is a mirrored inversion, where the machine constitutes the center for the state, the most hidden and human part holds the center for Evey. Another symmetry is that between the body of the regime and the body of the Shadow Gallery form the two poles of the same plain. Connected through the transmission mechanism of Fate, it is what allows the virus of V to spread.

In order to see the way in which bodies and their discontents permeate the narrative, we must consider the relationship between the old symbols of power in the dystopian England and the body politic. Westminster only attracts prostitutes at night (Moore and Lloyd 2008, 13), while law is repeatedly accused of being unfaithful. In part, these are clearly symbols of corruption and venality yet they evoke a deeper malaise of the system. Moral decay is resonant with the image of a prostitute, whose commodity is their own body. The commodification of bodies is complicated by their numerous relationships.[3] Leader Susan treats Fate as his one and only love; V's original love is Justice, whom he accuses to be the mistress of Susan. V's new love is for Anarchy, and in revenge, he enters into an affair with Fate. These metaphorical cycles of fraud and deceit have real consequences for both the Leader and V; like the Shadow Gallery and the body politic of the regime they are connected. These connections are brought to the forefront by the acknowledgment that destruction has physical consequence: V's destruction causes physical pain, it does "the unthinkable," it "hurt us" (Moore and Lloyd 2008, 16). The *pluralis maiestatis* once again sheds light unto the intimate connection between the body of the state and the body of the leader, but also invokes the doctrine of the king's two bodies, the metaphysical and biological; the two are collapsed into one between Fate and the Leader.[4] Thus, while old symbols such as Westminster and the Old Bailey can fall without causing much concern, their demise highlights that these acts constitute a threat.

Homo Sacer

Having outlined the relationship between the bodies of the state and V's home, their two respective leaders, and their complex relationships, we see that symmetries abound. The Head is connected to the Shadow Gallery both physically through the "nervous system," and by proving the inversion functions of the Mind. Susan is connected to V through these localities, as well as their loves and passions. How can we then understand the relationship between the body politic itself and those who are excluded from it? Those who exist beyond its reach?

Agamben's influential contribution through the concept of bare life provides some clues. Agamben places the inclusion of bare life, the politicized *zoē*, as the fundamental activity of sovereign power, the production of the *homo sacer*, the man who can be killed without committing homicide (Agamben 1998).[5] If it is "not simply *homo*, but rather *corpus* that is the new subject of politics" (Agamben 1998, 124), we must consider that the bodies figuring at the forefront of the battle between Norsefire and V are nothing more than bare life. The relation between V and the subjects of the regime is symmetrically identical to that between Norsefire and its subjects, who have been stripped of their *bios*, whose life can be taken, but not sacrificed in the sense that their killing is no longer considered homicide. This is clear in the arbitrary killing of Fingermen, the automatic extermination of anyone opposed to the regime without trial or jury. This relationship corresponds directly, though mirrored symmetrically, to the violence exerted by V. The most shocking aspect of V's killing of Fingermen is their status to him as bare life: V kills them "ruthlessly, efficiently, and with a minimum of fuss . . . [they] were two human beings and he slaughtered them like cattle" (Moore and Lloyd 2008, 24).[6] It is precisely in the acknowledgment of the human quality once present but now stripped where the bodies caught in the killing between V and Norsefire acquire their status of *homines sacri*. However, in order to further disentangle the means by which both the regime and V come to regard the subjects caught within postapocalyptic England so evidently as bare life and bare life only, we must consider the process of its creation.

> And the root of modern democracy's secret biopolitical calling lies here: he who will appear later as the bearer of rights and, according to a curious oxymoron the new sovereign subject . . . can only be constituted as such through the repetition of the sovereign exception and the isolation of corpus, bare life, in himself. (Agamben 1998, 124)

In other words, sovereignty, as it is shattered into all the sovereign subjects, bears with it the necessary production of bare life. From this perspective, as the nuclear holocaust obliterates modern democracy in England, subjects are left with nothing but bare life. Following the nuclear holocaust, the creation of the regime through the merging of the fascist band Norsefire with corporations produces the bearer of sovereign power within its subjects but fails to produce rights, as the state of exception becomes total.

> The totalitarianism of our century has its ground in this dynamic identity of life and politics, without which it remains incomprehensible. . . . When life and politics—originally divided, and linked together by means of the no-man's-land of the state of exception that is inhabited by bare life—begin to become one, all life becomes sacred and all politics becomes the exception. (148)

Thus, while the similarities between the Third Reich and Norsefire's Christofascist regime abound, the novel takes this modern political development to its logical extreme, where the illusion of right is completely shattered and the state of exception encompasses all life.[7] That is to say the citizens living in V's England cannot be properly called as such, as they have no right but to life; they are subjects in the proper sense of the word. This is the context in which V, or more precisely the body which becomes V, is born; like all, he is *homo sacer*, bare life that can be killed but not sacrificed. Law applies to him in no longer applying, withdrawing completely when he is taken into a camp. The regime attempts to kill him. For what is an injection expected to cause death in the camp if not an execution? Yet, the poison combined with the letters of Valerie causes a transformation. It modifies him and the result of this transfiguration is what must be explored.

The birth of V problematizes the ability of any subject to kill bare life without committing homicide. In other words, the inability to kill bare life is the centerpiece of the novel. This scandalous process of transformation begins with the combination of the chemical and biological; the poison injected into V grows through his gardening practices and blooms into his fiery birth. It is precisely the inability to die that transforms a body into V, giving birth to a resistant agent to the sovereign's thanatopolitics. The poison is not able to kill the body, and through not dying bare life absorbs the potentiality of sovereign violence, becoming its embodiment. Through this transformative process he enters the sphere of the sovereign, where one may kill but not offer sacrifice. This then allows him to exert sovereign violence, that which neither posits law nor preserves it, that which is neither homicidal nor sacrificial, rendering the point between the outside and inside indistinguishable. V is merged with the very essence of the regime at the source of sovereign power, taking on the inhuman function of sovereignty in subsuming the bare life of its subjects within it. The fact that V was previously stripped of all but bare life is what makes this transformation possible, his *bios* completely destroyed. By entering the Larkhill camp as a space of total exception, V not simply becomes the ultimate empty shell, left with nothing but bare life, but also approaches the point of indistinction, the shadow zone where sovereign power lies. This, in turn, is why the sovereign violence intended to kill him in its inability to do so replicates and metastasizes itself within him, simultaneously tying him to the sovereign and rejecting him completely. V at this point becomes one with sovereign power, while being the inverted image of it.

If V is then the symmetrical inversion and reentrance of transformed excepted life into the political, we must reconsider the relationship between the regime and V's own creation, the Shadow Gallery, in light of synergies between the rule and its exception.

The Camp Within and Without

> The camp is the space that is opened when the state of exception begins to become the rule. (Agamben 1998, 168–69)

The images of the camp reverberate throughout the work both in the reflections of the past, the narrative of the present, and, eventually, in the foreshadowing of the future. From the very beginning in the first frames we are confronted with the imagery of the camp with CCTV cameras reading "for your protection" as workers pour out from the nondescript building surrounded with barbwire, while the megaphone reminds us that these structures exist for "your own health and safety," underlining the absurdity of biopower (see figure 9.1). The first pages echo the separation; the reader faces the "quarantine" and "detention," the expulsion of bare life within the polis (Moore and Lloyd 2008, 9).

What we see in the postapocalyptic Christofascist Britain then is the reflection of Agamben's reading of the Hobbsian state of nature becoming a real epoch (Agamben 1998, 105–6), when a principle internal to the political body that can be seen only when considering the body *as if dissolved* is truly unveiled, in that the *nomos* having been dissolved in its reconstitution lay

Figure 9.1: Workers pour out from a building surrounded with barbwire. Alan Moore and David Lloyd, 2008, 5. © DC Comics.

bare the state of exception placed within it. Similar to the universal state of exception that lies at the heart of the modern political state, the camp in *V for Vendetta* is no longer hidden behind the law; it encompasses everything, in which the inhabitants are all *homines sacri*. If the camp is the paradigm of the modern biopolitical state, the point of indistinction between law and fact, order and nature, the universal camp shows its form throughout the novel. Thus, if we are to believe Agamben that the camp is the fundamental biopolitical paradigm of the West, the story of V is at least partially fascinating because it suggests the existence of self-destructive consequences of thanatopolitics. The camp, as the zone of indistinction, can produce unintended and uncontrollable consequences precisely because here we get closest to the source of sovereign power; if the biological body can survive an attempt at its extermination in the zone of indistinction between law and fact, that very act can only be interpreted as political, and thus automatically conjoined with the political body. What is then the relationship between the Shadow Gallery, the place where sovereign power does not seem to be able to exercise its violent tendencies, and the city?

The Shadow Gallery is not simply a nonlocation, an ephemeral place. It exists simultaneously within the state and yet exists outside its reach.

The relationship between Norsefire's England and the Shadow Gallery at first sight seems as that of abandonment, both literal and juridical. As we later find out, however, it can be physically accessed through the deserted and dilapidated Victoria station, which nevertheless bears the designation of "this station is closed" (230), shut down and forgotten by the state, outside its reach.[8] As discussed above, they are nevertheless interconnected both logistically and metaphysically. What is a shadow if not the zone of indistinction between light and darkness? The object lives off the shadow as much as the shadow's existence depends on the object, as the rule lives off its exception. If the shadow then is the state of exception, it is clear that it is located within the boundaries of the city, as modern sovereign power subsumes bare life through included exclusion within itself, so V creates a zone of exception within the universal camp of Norsefire's city. What is important to see is that this exception is created within the context of a zone where law and fact coincide. The double exception resolves the question why the sovereign cannot exercise its violence. If the Shadow Gallery is connected to the regime with an unbreakable bond, that is to say it is the universal camp's derivation, what it excepts is precisely the sovereign itself. Thus, the mechanism of the sovereign ban is symmetrically inverted within its walls; whereas the sovereign violence manifests to the logical extreme without, within it bears no power.

This inversion echoes through V's description of the Shadow Gallery and his actions within its boundaries. He takes Lewis Prothero, his prison guard from the time of his birth, into the Shadow Gallery's reproduction of the Larkhill Resettlement Camp, re-creating the camp within a camp, underscoring the inverse symmetry with the outside world's camp. We see that as the mirror images exchange places the experiences are once again inverted. Normally, one can find relief from the universal camp of Norsefire inside the Shadow Gallery, but as V places another mirror within the state of exception, the place that once seemed as out of reach for the sovereign becomes a torture chamber. The Droste effect interrogates the relationship between the sovereign and the state of exception, with V embodying its physical presence within what has already been derived, the Shadow Gallery. The *mise en abyme*, the relationship of potentially infinite exceptions, unexpectedly and subversively showcases V's own status as the extension of sovereign power within these increasingly shrinking spaces of inversion.

Accordingly, what at first sight appears to be a complement actually simultaneously inverts and subverts the City, increasingly descending into the abyss. V, in his grand tour of the Shadow Gallery, says to Evey as they reach greater depths: "Naturally, this room's the pinnacle of an inverted hill, which one descends to reach the peak, but, once arrived, can see for miles" (Moore and Lloyd 2008, 220). On the one hand, this line corresponds to the ability to surveille the citizens through the CCTVs of the Eye, but it also showcases the interlinkages between the physico-spatial and the politico-juridical. As Evey and V descend through spaces representing knowledge, belief, and romance in order to see through the Eye, so one descends into greater depths of the structures of power and the sovereign violence through their multiplication. When Evey says that she wants to "turn the page *upside down* and read the answers" what she does not realize is that it is precisely what V wants her to do.

The Unmaking of a Statistic: Rebirth

To resolve the apparent paradox of liberation from *árkhōs* by choosing the *princip*, we must now examine the dynamic between V and his protégé, Evey.

When discussing the death of the sovereign in premodern states, Agamben reads the axioms *le mort saisit le vif* and *le roi ne meurt jamais* in the context of dynamics between bare life and sovereignty: "at the moment of the sovereign's death, it is sacred life grounding sovereign authority that invests the person of the sovereign's successor" (Agamben 1998, 101). In order however to experience what V has, Evey will have to go through her own arch. When V first meets Evey, she is a "statistic" and a "victim," standing in sharp contrast to V's stature in the Larkhill Resettlement Camp, where Norsefire refused to keep any records.[9] At the time of V's first appearance, Evey, as a *homo sacer*, already reduced to bare life, was going to experience the full extent of the sovereign's thanatopolitics, her violation and killing imminent. V then does not simply save her, but takes her outside the regime's universal camp, or more precisely, to greater depths of it. He does not extract her from the power of the regime completely, rather placing her into the inverse camp, that which is outside the reach of the sovereign and yet is exposed to it through the presence of V in the most direct manner (Moore and Lloyd 2008, 29, 86). As discussed above, V is inextricably involved in the regime's sovereign life, taking on characteristics of it and carrying them inside him. We must see then the encounter between Evey and V in the context of a confrontation of sovereignty and bare life. It is during her first stay in V's abode that Evey is given the choice to go transform the bare life produced by the sovereign into something else, because in the Shadow Gallery there

Figure 9.2: Evey and V make a deal in front of *The Martyrdom of Saint Sebastian* (1475) by Antonio and Piero del Pollaiuolo. Alan Moore and David Lloyd, 2008, 43. © DC Comics.

are "no deals unless you want them" (Moore and Lloyd 2008, 43). As we shall see later, it is precisely the option to choose that sets her apart from V.

The setting in which Evey is given this choice merits some consideration (see figure 9.2). When Evey makes the deal with V, they are standing in front of *The Martyrdom of Saint Sebastian* (1475), a painting by the brothers Antonio and Piero del Pollaiuolo. The choice of this particular character of Christian mythology is not coincidental. St. Sebastian spent his life covertly aiding Christians and converting nonbelievers. When captured and sentenced to death by arrows he survived and returned to preach publicly. The parallels between V's capture, sentencing, and survival are evident. The patron saint of those desiring martyrdom and noble death, St. Sebastian gives a background to the conversation between Evey and V, in which she is given the choice to step beyond her current status of a statistic, and eventually become something more than bare life. Her life will have to be used in subversion of sovereign power, bare life that cannot and yet must be sacrificed.

From this perspective, Evey confusing V for her father is not accidental; he is her patriarch in that once she agrees to the deal he will control her transfiguration, her rebirth that first necessitates death. In order to set her free from the prison that is happiness (Moore and Lloyd 2008, 169), he takes her out of the land of "do-as-you-please," out of the Shadow Gallery, to expose her to love and a sense of belonging; she must have what she has been taught to seek during her life because she cannot accomplish her transfiguration until she acquires something that she thinks can be lost. He lets her illusion come into full fruition before accomplishing her transformation. Once Evey experiences both happiness and loss, the killing of her lover, she is ready to be given the choice between freedom and bare life, the *princip* and *árkhōs*.

Once inside the reproduced version of the camp set up in the Shadow Gallery, Evey does not mind the rat with whom she shares her cell "because she is no better" (Moore and Lloyd 2008, 154). Being "no better" than a rat is here a virtue, it makes possible the seeing of the bars and outlines the choice we must make between the *princip* and *árkhōs*. When she makes her choice and abandons herself to the ceasing of bare life she is "transfixed" and "transfigured."[10]

Though Evey's transformation is complete, it is clear that she is different from V, at the very least because V sees her as the creator counterpart to his essence as a destroyer. The actions of V after his fiery rebirth and escape from Larkhill help us understand this dynamic. He sets on a course of destruction of anyone who may have identified him before from his rebirth and merging with sovereign power. In this way he leaves society behind, becoming the idea, a pure political being without any natural life. His actions become the only definition of his being which juxtaposes him to the thanatopolitics of Norsefire, set on exterminating on the bases of race, sexuality, and ethnic belonging. This irony is thus not coincidental; the regime does not only incidentally create its downfall, V's implication in sovereign power is a direct consequence of thanatopolitics. Once perceived uniformity is achieved and all illusions of rights which are only necessary in preservation of identity fall away, sovereign violence reaches its peak and the camp becomes truly universal. What remains inside is bare life that can be killed. Thus, V's shedding of bare life is the direct consequence of uniformization and survival of sovereign violence. This differentiates him from Evey's birth, where only a choice was made but no survival was necessary.

Agamben's discussion of the placement of sovereignty at the moment of birth, and thus the making of animal life, also automatically the bearer of sovereignty (Agamben 1998, 128–29), has implications for the rebirth of Evey and V. V, as a bearer of sovereign power, is born inside and because of the sovereign power, he is inextricably implicated in the regime. Evey, on the other hand, undergoes her rebirth outside the sovereign's reach and is hence given the chance to be born truly free. Her birth takes place outside the nation, outside the regime, and she is not implicated in it. Her birth is special because it escapes and transcends both *ius soli* and *ius sanguinis*. She is not born within confined territory; she is both in the ephemeral, the Shadow Gallery, and she is born to no one but her own choice. While she is as connected to V as V is to the regime, with his death the last connection is broken and she is only left with her *princip*, and in this, she is "the first."

The differences between V and Evey thus become clear: Evey can become the creator after V's death, bearing constitutive power in true freedom; her rebirth happens subject to choice and outside the reach of sovereignty. V, on

Figure 9.3: V's blood appearing on one side of the stairs. Alan Moore and David Lloyd, 2008, 248. © DC Comics.

the other hand, is tied to the sovereign in his rebirth by an unbreakable bond of sovereign violence and must die with him. This bond is also reflected in the imagery during the birth of both the regime and V. The mustard yellow color scheme used to depict the chaos following nuclear holocaust and chemical weapons that gave birth to Norsefire's regime corresponds to the colors of the mustard gas explosion used by V to destroy the Larkhill concentration camp. This stands in sharp contrast to what surrounds Evey during her birth: the lifegiving power of water as it falls from the sky, the rain in which Evey stands bare following the rejection of *árkhōs*. V seems to be cognizant of this connection as he stages the death of the leader to coincide with his own. Finch shoots V as Rosemary shoots the leader, the two aspects of the sovereign meeting their end at the same time. V's cancer reaches its peak as the biopolitical body of the regime meets its autodestructive end.

The complex dialectic between V and Evey has its apex when V returns mortally wounded. As Evey attempts to understand his last words, she follows the blood stains V left throughout the Shadow Gallery, descending deeper into his mind through physically going down to the train tracks, following his bloodline. As she reaches the deepest levels, the bloodpath separates, appearing on one side of the stairs but not the other. Evey takes the unmarked side. Here, once again the difference between her and V is underscored visually, while V is inseparable from the sovereign violence that preceded him and the violence that gave him birth, Evey is able to take an unstained path (see figure 9.3). Once she reaches the tracks, she looks at the map of the London Underground full of interlinkages and connections, both realizing that V's last will is to erase Downing Street as a symbol of executive authority, but also seeing her own shadow, showcasing her connection and yet separation from V. It is after this realization that Evey begins to make a full circle around the Shadow Gallery, first following the blood path, then, when it ends at the train that is designated to be both the funeral place of V and the weapon that erases the last symbol of old sovereign power, truly assuming her new identity. Just as finding the Victoria station served as the completion of V's identity, so Evey's circular walk around the Shadow Gallery, resembling walking meditation, brings to fruition her character as a liberated being. Her certainty that she is "going to walk up these stairs and through that door and you will be alive" is not misplaced: V, the idea and not the man is waiting for her upstairs, culminating in Evey donning the mask (Moore and Lloyd 2008, 248).

Thus a function of rebirth in V is the stripping away of the originary fiction of man as citizen and thus a sovereign subject. The transformative and transfigurative acts of choosing the first, the chief, sheds the citizen as the illusory casket that has been abused and violated, giving birth to a purely political being, one that has abandoned itself to death. The difference between Evey and V is such that Evey comes into this world due to V's ability to create the condition within which the choice is hers, a choice he himself has never had. While his birth is not accidental, as it is a direct consequence of the ultimate degree of sovereign violence where biopolitics turns into thanatopolitics, he remains tied to the sovereign as his rebirth inextricably implicates him in the regime. In this sense, Evey can be truly free because of the autodestruction brought about by V's birth, and as she had a choice in stepping onto this path, she has a choice to decide whether to follow him after his inevitable death. That choice, however, presupposes his own death, since as long as V *is*, Evey is not left to her choice to either be or not be.[11] V's death actualizes the (im)potentiality within Evey, with his absence she is with foundation and without beginning.

Auto-thanatopolitics and the (Rebirth) of Sovereignty

What is at stake then in *V for Vendetta* is a scandalous notion that the choosing of the *princip*, the first, the chief or the *principal*, is precisely what liberates the bare life that accepts its abandonment to death. As others have noted, Agamben leaves open the question of the potentials of bare life in opposition to the sovereign, for instance in the form of "emancipatory movements," (Ziarek 2012) partially due to the fact that nothing is left in bare life that allows it "to oppose the demands of sovereign power" (Agamben 1998, 187). We might see this conclusion, however, in light of the determination that "the ban . . . ties together the two poles of the sovereign exception: bare life and power, *homo sacer* and the sovereign" (Agamben 1998, 110). It occurs exactly in the zone of indistinction where, oxymoronically, bare life and the sovereign come closest to one another in an inextricable bond. Emancipation, differentiation, or separation is not possible precisely because of the sovereign's implication in the production of bare life. Bare life cannot oppose the demands of sovereign power because it can only exist within its reach. However, the derivation of that statement is not necessarily true, which is what the story of *V* is tasked to demonstrate. The more extreme and evident the presence of the camp becomes, the more universal its reach, the closer the two conjoined poles of the same dimension approach each other, eventually the possibility of endowing bare life with sovereign power emerges. Bare life cannot separate itself from sovereign power by definition, because its appearance is tied to politicization of animal life through sovereign power. It hopelessly lives off it like a shadow lives off the object. However, a shadow melts into its creator at midday. As sovereign power and violence reach their apex, bare life comes closest to the source of its creation. In other words, the dynamics between the poles may not be repulsive, *dis*uniting, or *emancipatory*, but rather "transformative," "transfigurative" and ultimately, autodestructive.

If the principle of self-preservation is "the innermost center of the political system" (Agamben 1998, 36), and if sacred life has been shattered into every individual body (Agamben 1998, 124), then the point at which bare life ceases to be politically relevant and biopolitics turns into thanatopolitics is the point at which a failure to kill can be autodestructive, as the impotentiality inverts sovereign power since here both bare life and sovereign power rest in the zone of indistinction, which is the zone of indifference between law and act. If every act and word of sovereign power, and most importantly its manifestation, is indistinguishable from law in the universal camp, then failure to execute the act and thus the law necessarily is magnified as it brings into question the prerogative of the sovereign ban in that bare life becomes sacrificial because of its extrication from sovereign violence. It is sacrificed by the sovereign itself, creating a paradoxical state in which the attempt of the act both equates to law and yet excepts the subject of the act from itself. As this impossibility cannot hold, sovereign power collapses within itself, creating both the law by proclaiming the act and the exception to it, which directly coincides with the act. The law and exception become indistinguishable. The act of the failure to exterminate becomes law and continues to live as part of the system, not as inclusion by exclusion, but as exception by inclusion.

The initial tension between choosing the *princip* as the means to liberation from the *árkhōs* thus disappears, since the two are not contradictory and exclusive, but rather exclusive by inclusion. Similarly, the survival of V excludes him from sovereign power by including him in the sovereign ban. When V explains to Evey that the choice of *princip* over her bare life is liberating, we should then read liberation not as emancipation, but as "seeing of the bars" and learning of "how to breath," not an extractive but a transmutative process. *V for Vendetta* subverts the sovereign ban into itself, considering the inversion of the biopolitical paradigm, where the camp is not the cornerstone of the modern state and is inextricably incorporated into its biopolitics, included by its exclusion, but the way the sovereign that has been shattered into the bodies of subjects can manifest itself inside the camps by letting itself not be. Both V and Evey take the option to not be, and by this choice transcend the animal component of bare life, leaving behind only the act of politicization. This act is not separative, but incorporative, and bears autodestructive consequences for sovereign power. None of these transformations are incidental, but rather a direct consequence of sovereign violence that has resulted in the production of bare life.

Not all thanatopolitical acts will lead to the creation of a V-like character, just as not all mutations produce a cancerous cell in the body. In fact, none of the thanatopolitical acts may. What V's story is tasked to demonstrate is that as the universal camp encompasses all aspects of life, and as bare life and sovereignty meet in the zone of indistinction, the principles on which the constituted order rests become less stable. Bare life cannot oppose sovereign power; it is at the very center of its logic. However, when the boundaries of within and without disappear, and the exception becomes the rule, the center will not hold.

Notes

I would like to thank Peter Goodrich, Thomas Giddens, and the reviewers for their help, comments, and suggestions. A special thank you to Kamilla Nabiyeva for her endless patience, interest, and support. Any errors are exclusively my own.

1. This chapter attempts to answer broader questions of *V*'s appeal. For analysis of protests featuring the Guy Fawkes mask, see Gerbaudo (2017). Call (2008) argues that the mask has become a "free floating signifier," a symbol that is "so freighted with multiple meanings that in the end it collapses under its own weight, and it escapes meaning altogether" (160).

2. The analysis that follows is based on the graphic novel and does not account for the adaption directed by James McTeigue (2005). For an analysis that problematizes the model of comic-to-film adaptation, see Reynolds (2009). See also, on the inversion performed by the film, Peter Goodrich's chapter in the present volume.

3. It is possible to interpret prostitution as an empowering process through which oppressed and dispossessed classes are able to regain agency over their bodies. In this particular instance, however, prostitutes are forced to commodify and attempt to transact their bodies, their most intimate property, by the regime in order to survive, as we can see from Evey's attempt to become a prostitute. There is little empowerment to be gained from a forced choice, and even the liberating potential from regaining control over our bodies is squashed by the regime when the Fingermen attempt to rape Evey. Thus, she is not even able to use her body on her own terms.

4. This notion is of course bolstered by customary farewell between Norsefire officials: England Prevails.

5. The importance of the difference between bare life and natural life cannot be overstated. "Through its division and its capture in the apparatus of the exception, life assumes the form of bare life" (Agamben 2016, 263). That is to say bare life is what is politicized and thus included by sovereign power by its exclusion.

6. The likening by V of the regime's subjects to employers of a corporation in his television address is particularly interesting from this perspective. Once again, we are confronted with the idea of the *corpus* but in a radically different light, where the past acts of individuals are aggregated and reprojected into the present, endowing every subject with individual responsibility for the entire history of humanity. The source of this responsibility then does not lie in the relationship between sovereign power and its subjects, but the reiterative process of aggregated acts. The implications of this for individual deeds are not innocuous. The historical aggregation acts as the justification for V to see every subject of the regime as equatable to the sovereign himself; there is no difference between being subject and being sovereign. The choices that led to the dynamics of modern power are collectively assigned and cannot be disaggregated. In this way V distorts and subverts the king's two bodies by the same process the modern subject is created, by shattering sovereignty.

7. Following the death of the Leader the remnants of the regime declare a "state of emergency," but clearly this is nothing but the unmasking of the fact that the state of exception was underlying the rule of Norsefire all along, since this declaration brings no change. Right before the death of the Leader, the universality of the exception is reaffirmed once more in the

preparations of the Leader's speech. The barricades are nothing but "cattlebarriers," a sham; the state of emergency (i.e., exception) was there all along (Moore and Lloyd 2008, 226).

8. Finch is able to enter in his pursuit of V because he has, through consuming LSD, synthetically entered the mind of the terrorist, temporarily becoming him and seeing the world through his eyes. This leaves a deep mark on the detective, to the point where he realizes that V has purposefully allowed himself to be shot, he chooses not to inform the regime, indicating his rejection of sovereign power.

9. The fact that Norsefire did not keep records in the camps is particularly interesting in light of the vehemence with which it kept records and files on its subjects after its power was consolidated. The absence of files does not simply erase history, it suggests its absence altogether. As elaborated by Vismann (2008), records are the materiality of law, the needs of the former shaping the latter. Files mediate law itself. Sovereign violence was in part able to reach its peak in the camp because there was nothing to give it material form, every act baring pure power over bare life, dissipating with the absence of records, with act and law indistinguishable. V's survival, nevertheless, becomes a living record of the sovereign's thanatopolitics. Records also later reemerge not simply as evidence, but as actors driving the plot forward when Dr. Delia Surridge's diary recreates history and seals the regime's fate.

10. This transformation is profoundly different from that of Rosemary Almond, who lost her abusive husband and continues to be abused by sovereign power, in her last act killing the Leader. There is an askew connection between Rosemary and Evey, their relationship that of a distorted reflection in a house of mirrors. Rose, like Evey, has experienced attachment, is punished for her inability to liberate herself from servitude, from her status as a subject of sovereign power. Once her illusions are stripped away about her status as bare life, working as an adult entertainer in a cabaret where she is often raped and violated, Rose, like Evey, has nothing to lose. Yet, unlike Evey, she never sees the bars of her prison and never learns how to breathe, never able to move beyond the anger of what has been taken away from her.

11. *Archē* carries the sense of both origin and principle. The relation of V's death and Evey's choice can then be understood in terms of being and praxis in that Evey is liberated from "being" and becomes unfounded. V by choosing to die deposes himself without abdication from life (because V, the noncorporeal idea, continues to *be*), leaving the choice of becoming to Evey, who in this choice is faced with the conflict between being (without V) and acting (abdicating the potentiality to not be and taking the act of being V). This parallels Agamben's analysis of the fracture between being and praxis, and "what is at stake between these two is the idea of freedom" (Agamben 2011, 59).

References

Agamben, Giorgio. 1998. *Homo Sacer: Sovereign Power and Bare Life*. Translated by Daniel Heller-Roazen. Stanford, CA: Stanford University Press.

Agamben, Giorgio. 2011. *The Kingdom and the Glory: For a Theological Genealogy of Economy and Government*. Translated by Lorenzo Chiesa (with Matteo Mandarini). Stanford, CA: Stanford University Press.

Agamben, Giorgio. 2016. *The Use of Bodies*. Translated by Adam Kotsko. Stanford, CA: Stanford University Press.

Barakat, Noorhan. 2012. "Vendetta Masks in UAE Colours Draw Warning." *Gulf News*, November 17, 2012. https://web.archive.org/web/20121120002154/https://gulfnews.com/news/gulf/uae/general/vendetta-masks-in-uae-colours-draw-warning-1.1105928.

BBC. 2016. "Hungary Teachers: Huge Protest against Government Reforms." *BBC*, March 15, 2016. https://www.bbc.com/news/world-europe-35817593.

Benmakhlouf, Ali, Fabien Capeillères, Barbara Cassin, and Jérôme Dokic. 2017. "Principle." In *Dictionary of Untranslatables: A Philosophical Lexicon*, edited by Barbara Cassin, 851–55. Princeton, NJ: Princeton University Press.

Bilton, Nick. 2011. "Masked Protesters Aid Time Warner's Bottom Line." *New York Times*, August 28, 2011. https://www.nytimes.com/2011/08/29/technology/masked-anonymous-protesters-aid-time-warners-profits.html.

C.C. 2014. "How Guy Fawkes Became the Face of Post-Modern Protest." *Economist*, November 4, 2014. https://www.economist.com/blogs/economist-explains/2014/11/economist-explains-3.

Call, Lewis. 2008. "A Is for Anarchy, V Is for Vendetta: Images of Guy Fawkes and the Creation of Postmodern Anarchism." *Anarchist Studies* 16 (2): 105–54.

Chroust, Anton-Hermann. 1947. "The Corporate Idea and the Body Politic in the Middle Ages." *Review of Politics* 9 (4): 423–52.

Curtis, Neil. 2016. *Sovereignty and Superheroes*. Manchester: Manchester University Press.

Frederic, Maitland. 1901. "The Crown as Corporation." *Law Quarterly Review* 17: 131–46.

Gerbaudo, Paolo. 2017. *The Mask and the Flag: Populism, Citizenism and Global Protest*. Oxford: Oxford University Press.

Hoad, T. F. 2003. "Anarchy." In *The Concise Oxford Dictionary of English Etymology*, edited by T. F. Hoad. Oxford: Oxford University Press.

Kantorowicz, Ernst Hartwig. 1997. *The King's Two Bodies: A Study in Mediaeval Political Theology*. Edited by American Council of Learned Societies. Princeton, NJ: Princeton University Press.

Lush, Tamara, and Verena Dobnik. 2011. "Occupy Wall Street: Vendetta Masks Become Symbol of the Movement." *Huffington Post*, April 11, 2011. https://www.huffingtonpost.com/2011/11/04/occupy-wall-street-vendetta-mask_n_1076038.html.

McTeigue, James, dir. 2005. *V for Vendetta*. Warner Brothers.

Moore, Alan, and David Lloyd. 2008. *V for Vendetta*. New York: Vertigo.

Reynolds, James. 2009. "Kill Me Sentiment: *V for Vendetta* and Comic-to-Film Adaptation." *Journal of Adaptation in Film and Performance* 2 (2): 121–36.

Stevenson, Angus. 2015a. "Principal." In *Oxford Dictionary of English*. Oxford: Oxford University Press.

Stevenson, Angus. 2015b. "Principle." In *Oxford Dictionary of English*. Oxford: Oxford University Press.

Stoehrel, Rodrigo Ferrada, and Simon Lindgren. 2014. "For the Lulz: Anonymous, Aesthetics, and Affect." *TripleC* 12 (1): 238–64.

Vismann, Cornelia. 2008. *Files: Law and Media Technology*. Translated by Geoffrey Winthrop-Young. Redwood City, CA: Stanford University Press.

Ziarek, Ewa Plonowska. 2012. "Bare Life." In *Impasses of the Post-Global: Theory in the Era of Climate Change*, Vol. 2, edited by Henry Sussman, 194–211. London: Open Humanities Press.

COMICS INTERLUDE #3

The Nested Text

BY PAUL FISHER DAVIES

THE SOCIAL CONTEXT

THE NESTED TEXT • PFD 2018

PERSONS AND THE TEXT

THE PERITEXT

The FRONT COVER

by P.F. DAVIES

The BLURB

The HANDWRITTEN BOILERPLATE

TITLE PAGE

@ 2018

The DEDICATION

for
boo.

THE NESTED TEXT

THE AUTHORIAL VOICE | THE REPRESENTED SELF | THE STORY OF THE PAST
THE DREAM | THE PICTURE IN THE BALLOON | BREAKING THE FRAME
THE SYMBOLS OF THOUGHT | THE MODAL SHIFT... | THE INSET

The FOREWORD

ED FAMOUS

I'VE

The CONTENTS PAGE

CONTENTS

1.   2.   3.

The LEAD-IN

The ANNOTATIONS

3

THE NESTED TEXT

by PAUL FISHER DAVIES • 2018

10

"Destructive Interim Formation"

THOMAS GIDDENS

Figure 10.1: From *100 Months*, 2010. © John Hicklenton.

In his final days, renowned comics artist John Hicklenton brought forth a "fuck you" to the world and his terminal illness (Bruton 2010). A graceful evisceration of the commodification of life and the exploitation of the planet, it is a work that has become Hicklenton's unfettered legacy: *100 Months* (2010), a piece of "darkly illustrated scripture" (Publishers Weekly 2012) whose title reperforms the 2008 ecological warning of planetary demise (see Simms 2008) toward which capitalism has thrown us. And while the specific timeline for ecological disaster may be debatable, *100 Months* seizes by the neck the over-consumption of Earth's resources under the pursuit of capital, partaking in a growing tradition of climate narratives (see Milner et al. 2015) by performing a devastating critique of a humanity that has driven such a destructive and loveless path; it rends the world and razes the arrogant occupation of the Earth by a thoughtless race of bipeds, emptying the planet of human presence, undoing its desecration. This is a critique that is enacted in the poetic movement of annihilation by the leading entity in *100 Months*: a being spawned by Satan. THIS IS A TALE / OF MY MOST BRUTAL OF DAUGHTERS. SHE HAS GROWN UTTERLY BEYOND MY CONTROL / SO RUTHLESS / EVEN I HAVE COME / TO FEAR HER. SO I DISOWN HER / AND UNLEASH HER UNTO YOU.[1] Her many denominations are indicative of her ecological apocalypse (100 Months, The End of All Things), but she is principally identified as Mara and appears ostensibly as a human woman, but with dimensions and viscera skewed into elegant and monstrous proportions through which she enacts a biopolitical critique of capitalism, a critique that lambastes the reduction of the living human to commodity, of life as something to be exploited for profit, of the human-made-purse, Earth-made-resource, a world where all things become valued only inasmuch as they contain or produce coin. As she intones at her outset, astride a powerful and fearsome beast that is firmly within her control: FEAR ME. ALL / WHO OBEY / THE COIN (see figure 10.1). From this ominous beginning, performative of her indubitable power and destructive force, Mara traces a crusade of violence: a movement from a solitude of darkness and pain where she has waited for 100,000 years, to the consummate butchery of the false idol that rules over the once-human world in the period of late capitalism: the Pig, the Swinegod, the Lord of the cannibalistic Longpig Paradise. This is an Earth plundered and pillaged by humans who have reduced themselves to longpig, to commodified meat, with Mara's critique deriving from her genesis inside the Earth itself. She intones: I AM THE SOUL OF THE EARTH / ANIMA MUNDI / I AM THIS EARTH. I HAVE BEEN RAPED AND TORN, POISONED / VIOLATED. YOU HAVE SUFFOCATED ME, BROKEN ME / AND DRAINED MY BLOOD / I'VE BEEN SHORN, SCORNED /ABUSED + PLUNDERED. YOU HAVE STOLEN MUCH FROM ME—/ FOR WHAT? YOUR LONGPIG PARADISE. YOUR CONCRETE STRAIGHTJACKET / YOUR GREY MAZE. YOUR RIVERS /OF IRON AND TOWERS OF GLASS. I AM ISIS, / MARA / LILITH AND HEL. YOU MAY CALL ME THE / END OF ALL THINGS. In this conflation of multiple mythic beings, Mara takes on occult connotations of sorcery, death, nature, flowing deeply into her overwhelming emanation as the heart of the planet come to wreak the destruction of all. This mythic planetary unity takes firmer grounding in its explicit relation to the carpenter, the human rendering of God who was Mara's only friend, but who was persecuted and killed by a humanity of failed compassion—an act indicative of human-ity's relation with its planetary home. MY ONLY FRIEND / ONE SO FULL OF LOVE / TORTURED, BRUTALISED / NAILED. And Christ has indeed been rebranded in some circles as an eco-messiah, bringing us the "green gospel" (see DeWeese-Boyd 2009), preaching love for all, not just the human; advocating "the extension of the love of one's neighbor and enemies . . . to the environment that provides for their flourishing" (DeWeese-Boyd 2009, n.p.). Love all thy expansive neighbors who dwell within this vast Earth community, this "communion between ecological subjects" (Burdon 2015, 8) that is emphatically more than human (see Burdon 2015, 1–14). But the Longpig adherents who value coin above all else, who subsume the Earth community into the pursuit of profit, eschewed this deific friend of the Earth, nailing him to the wood of the trees he respected as much as he did humanity, destroying him as they did the value in life and the bountiful becoming of the planet. Mara: the conflation of mystical and ecological forces, the spirit of Gaia that emerges as the ghost in the large-scale and intricately dense system of interconnecting life in the planetary biosphere; she who is the soul of the Earth, earth-goddess rendered in human form; she who now seeks vengeance, the end of all things, the logical application of all the human race has become—as longpig, as com-modity, as object—destruction itself. Humanity has lost its value, its potential has been squandered, its sacred life squeezed out with only a coin purse left in its place. FOR EVERY CUT / YOU SHALL BLEED. FOR EVERY INSULT / SHALL YOU BE HUMILIATED. THE GIFT HE GAVE / SHALL BE TAKEN FROM YOU. IN MY DESPAIR / I SHALL BE FORCED / TO UNLEASH——. I WILL LEAD THIS WORLD / INTO CHAOS——. LEAVING RUINS IN MY WAKE. The love of the eco-messiah for humans as part of the Earth community shall be taken by the planet itself, reclaimed by the Earth com-munity through Mara's sweeping performance of violence and destruction, the laying waste of civilization by the force of nature that is Mara, who un-leashes immense, planetary, all-consuming violence. A destructive perfor-mance of apocalyptic critique. Mara's appearance from the bowels of the Earth, her alliance with Christ and the mystical beyond, her monstrous otherness, place her and her violent work far outside the typical realm of violence: that of utilitarian force or punishment. THE FURY Mara and her vio-lence come from beyond—beneath, outside, under, above, without, behind—and this kind of otherworldly violence, this out-of-bounds destruction, ex-ceeds the typical logic of legal violence, of means toward ends; it steps us outside the binary order of positive and natural law, indicating something divine. Violence may be "able to found and modify legal conditions" (Ben-jamin [1927] 1978, 283), with a lawmaking or law-founding function that can render the world anew under a posited legal order, but such violence results in a tendency for the subject to be divested of all violence under the auspices of modern law, because ultimately violence "confronts the law with the threat of declaring a new law" (Benjamin [1927] 1978, 283). Retaining the monopoly on violence within the legal armature suppresses that which could undermine its primacy, indicating a second and ongoing function of violence as lawmaking: law reaffirms itself in the exercise of violence, and there is thus "something rotten" subsumed throughout the legal order that is not simply the punishment of infringements, but is the continual reestablishment of law itself (Benjamin [1927] 1978, 283). Legal violence is in a cyclical flux of foundation and formation, "its temporality is circular and dialectical" (Morgan 2007, 51). The unjustified condemning of the subject to a guilty fate follows this temporal movement of violence: guilt only exists inside the legal order, which previously did not exist and is never justified in advance (Butler 2006, 201–7): "Violence brings a system of law into being, and this law-founding violence is precisely one that operates without justification. Fate produces law, but it does so first through manifesting the anger of the gods" (Butler 2006, 207). And Mara, true to Benjamin, initially erupts as a profoundly angry god. MY NAME IS MARA. I HAVE WAITED 100,000 YEARS / IN DARKNESS AND PAIN—. . . . BUT IT IS MY TIME / TO BRING IT TO YOU MOTHER FUCKERS. FEW WILL ESCAPE MY THIRST FOR ANNIHILATION (ellipsis added). Benjamin's mythic violence—of which legal violence is an example (Benjamin [1927] 1978, 295–96)—descends from the gods as a display of their unavoidable existence as powerful: "Mythical violence in its archetypal form is a mere manifestation of the gods. Not a means to their ends . . . but first of all a manifestation of their existence" (Benjamin [1927] 1978, 294); "an outburst of anger isn't a strategy for achieving something. Its only aim is to manifest itself" (Morgan 2007, 52). "Lawmaking is power making" (Benjamin [1927] 1978, 295). But all this remains firmly within the dyadic positive/natural order of legality, outside of which we must follow Benjamin if we are to properly consider violence and its possible justifications (see Kellogg 2011, 75), to judge violence by something more meaningful than simply what it happens to achieve (Morgan 2007, 49). For neither "natural law nor positive law is capable of considering means alone since both are engaged in a project of justifying means with respect to their results" (Morgan 2007, 50). Mara, while an emanation of the gods—Satan's daughter, a deified embodiment of Gaia—seeks only destruction in her visceral rampage; she deploys violence not for its own sake, nor a violence oriented toward the creation of a new world, nor toward the display of Mara's powerful existence—but simply as violence, seeking to destroy those who have harmed, wronged, raped, abused, exploited, commodified. I HAVE SHOWN MYSELF TO THEE / AS THE DESTROYER. WHO LAYS WASTE TO THE WORLD / AND WHOSE PURPOSE / NOW IS DESTRUCTION. Mara's tirade seeks not any end: no preservation nor new making of law, nor of anything at all—she seeks destruction: the destruction of the Longpig's paradise of meaningless, soulless, commodity; her violence erupts from the Earth, tearing down the world of men. Implicit in this eradication is Benjamin's question of whether pure violence, without instrumentalization, can establish new law (see Sinnerbrink 2006, 491); whether we can overcome the cycle of legal violence that has shaped the progress of history (Morgan 2007, 51); whether a divine violence can be identified and performed legitimately; whether there is "another form of violence that is noncoercive" and that can be "waged against coercion" (Butler 2006, 201)—against law. Such violence as a principle of ethics or politics cannot be comprehended through structures of "means" and "ends," cannot be assessed by reference to its desires and impacts, so cannot be discounted as potentially legitimate, and leads us to the question of "thinking another kind of violence . . . beyond the state" (Tomba 2017, 587). A DEVASTATING SILENCE / WILL FOLLOW MY SHADOW / AS I WALK UP AND DOWN / IN THE EARTH / TO-ING AND FRO-ING WITHIN IT. BUT YOU WILL NOT HEAR ME / NOR WILL YOU BEHOLD ME / OR SMELL MY FRAGRANCE. FOR YOU SHALL HAVE RETURNED / TO THE DUST YOU CAME FROM / YOUR WORK FORGOTTEN. To steal Benjamin's own words and speak of Mara: she "strikes them without warning, without threat, and does not stop short of annihilation," releasing a "divine violence [that is] pure power over all life for the sake of the living" (Benjamin [1927] 1978, 297). And with this critique of violence, this violent critique, we arrive not at a criterion for judging violence as just, as disgraceful, but instead "at an aporia where the very possibility of human judgement is no longer secure" (Morgan 2007, 52). I AM A MURDERESS, ONE WELL USED TO VIOLENCE / AN ACT OF GOD. Mara enacts her violent critique against the destruction of life, fulfilling the destiny of the longpig logic by obliterating all humanity, a humanity that has fallen under the sway of the coin and thus become lifeless meat. She makes her brutal way to the archetypal city of Babylon, to unleash her divinity upon the profanity of the coin, to demolish those arrogant creations of a species that builds by pillaging the planet that sustains it. I STALK BABYLON'S / STINKING CITY LIGHTS. MANY TAKE / THEIR OWN LIVES. RATHER THAN FACE ME. I SINGLE OUT THE CITIES. EMPTY HEARTS COME THOU TO ME / I DELIVER YOU FROM YOUR TROUBLED PAST. THE SHADOW / OF ONE HUNDRED MONTHS / DESCENDS UPON THEM. EVERYTHING THOU HAS SET UP / SHALL BE TORN DOWN. SKYSCRAPERS LIE / IN STAGNANT WATER. BLOATED SONS OF THE COIN / FLOAT AIMLESSLY—THEIR PURPOSE DRAINED / THEIR WILLS

FORGOTTEN. This is a divine violence, not done out of some mythic display of power (see Benjamin [1927] 1978, 294–97), some bloody damage that seeks domination of the world and the humans who populate it, but out of Mara's deep-seated anguish at the loss of meaning in life as it has emerged in human form. She kills and destroys for life itself—but not mere or bare life. "There is in all life something that . . . cannot be reduced to blood" (Tomba 2017, 594). She may tear down everything that humanity has set up, she may eviscerate human bodies and butcher other beings, but Mara's violence remains "bloodless," with the bloodlessness of divine violence referring not to its physical performance, but to its character as oriented against the institution of unauthorized power and coercion, against the murdering of the soul of the living through its commodification by capital. The legal order of means and ends "powers the mythical machine" that "appears as the power of fate over the human;" but "divine violence is law destroying" (Kellogg 2011, 76): it seeks the undoing of that which perpetuates the killing of life understood in its fullest, most flourishing, and most meaningful sense. "Indeed, divine power is described as lethal without spilling blood . . . [and] acts in the name of the soul of the living" (Butler 2006, 210). This soulful life is not signaled by blood circulating in veins and arteries, by mere biomechanical operation—but by the "something" of the *anima* (see Giddens 2018, 28–61), the soul of the living. This life is not bloody, but bloodless and divine; like the violence wrought in its name. The ends of divine violence are thus "invisible," lurking "in the realm of the unknowable" (Morgan 2007, 52). Shifting the ends of violence beyond the knowable realm of blood—into the beyond, the something of the "soul of the living"—renders that violence divine. And the division between biological life and divine life, between bloody meat and bloodless living human, is one that is policed by the anthropological machine: Agamben's device that delineates between life and resources under sovereignty (see Smith 2011, 4–10). This machine represents the "ceaselessly updated decision" (Agamben 2004, 38) as to what counts as a living human and what does not; a "zone of indeterminacy" (Agamben 2004, 37), a conceptual space in which bare life is exposed to the power of the sovereign to determine the status of that life through its violent delineations. The anthropological machine is where the individual is held "suspended between a celestial and a terrestrial nature, between animal and human—and, thus, his being [is] always less and more than himself" (Agamben 2004, 29). Accordingly, the anthropological machine divides "the animal part of the person from the extra, higher human part understood variously as soul, reason, *logos* . . . [such that] the human [cannot] be understood as a biological entity, nor a set of subjective features, nor a moral content, but the fact and style of a living be-ing's capture and orientation by the apparatus [of personhood]" (Parsley 2013, 16). A person is the outcome of the operation of the anthropological machine, and as the output from this machine the apparatus of the person becomes a site where the divine and earthly—the bloodless and the biome-chanical; soul and flesh; *anima* and *sanguina*—meet. And in that meeting, anthropogenesis takes place (Agamben 2004, 79), and the person appears (Goodrich 2012). Mara's vision of the Longpig Paradise, of the triumph of late capitalism, is of a world where humans have become flesh, meat to be consumed by the market; the violent divisions of the anthropological ma-chine have become totalized; the animal in the human is separated out and preserved while the divine is eschewed and suppressed. But there is a confla-tion at work here: the joining of the hollowing out of the human with the hollowing of the Earth; the reduction of both to mere commodity as the anthropological machine no longer delineates between life and resource. Along with this hollowing there appears also to be a flattening, a rendering of the boundary between human and nature, between inside and outside, that removes any distinction between the two: everything is to be consumed. The living human is reduced not simply to the masks of juridico-political personhood, not even to "bare life," but to an inanimate object, to a resource for its own consumption, a self-commodity for self-profit, the cannibalized human, the victory of the Longpig, with Hicklenton's invocation of that col-loquialism for the consumption of human flesh thus far from incidental. This passage of human innovation—from the potential for good, to crucifixion, to urbanization, to the market, to the ravaging of the planet and the human soul beneath the paradigm of the coin—has at last awoken the ire of the Earth, unleashed as woman in the form of Mara, repeating the conflation of nature and femininity while simultaneously positioning Mara's critique as initially coming from outside the patriarchal order of capitalism. In the Longpig Paradise, there emerges no boundary as to what is natural, to what is human; divisions of in and out, subject and object, human and nature, are all ruptured and removed, leaving an abyss of commodified flatness in its place. In Agamben's terms, the violence of sovereignty "opens a zone of in-distinction between law and nature, outside and inside, violence and law," but one where the positing and conserving of law through violence is main-tained (Agamben 1998, 64). The apparatus that inspires Mara's critique—the rampant anthropological machine that no longer updates its decision, that no longer engages the oversight of a sovereign but perpetuates instead a zone where life has already been expunged—so hampers the individual that the entirety of the soul of the living is excluded from the sovereign order. The subject is cannibalized for coin, world and life are flattened to commodity as the distinction between subject and matter, living and dead, consumer and consumed, is eroded away to nothing, and a purely lateral void emerges where all boundaries or limits are pushed out to infinity: a region containing no life, meaning, or *anima*. But where the mythical violence of sovereignty sets boundaries in order to flatten them, denying access to anything beyond so that life becomes commodity, Mara's divine violence "boundlessly destroys them" (Benjamin [1927] 1978, 297), opening always to the infinite potential of otherness, to the potential rupture of the flow of history and the exploitation engendered by the discourse of means and ends (see Hirvonen 2012), by the Longpig's love of the coin. She responds with a true eschewing of boundaries, a complete denial of limits as she throws her dismembered victims into the workings of the anthropological machine and disrupts its self-serving delineations, destroying the walls that have been built to protect what is "inside" the capitalist order by denying that it has an outside. YOU SWEPT AWAY / MY NATURE FOR THIS? BEHOLD, I SHALL MAKETH / THE EARTH EMPTY / AND MAKETH IT WASTE. HER WARMTH FOR YOU IS LONG SINCE PASSED. THUS, WITH HER RAGE / I AM ENGORGED. MY BLOOD BOILS WITH HER WRATH. But Mara's flattening is not toward the commodification of life, instead seeking to open up to an otherness of planetary, cosmic living. It is a divine smashing, "not one kind of violence among others," but a breaking of the link between violence and law (Agamben 1998, 65) and a razing of the distinctions of sovereignty. And being "bloodless," in the name of the soul of the living, it is a "non-violent violence, [a] caesuratic force that does neither found any order nor base itself on any law, ideology or religion" (Hirvonen 2012, 534). And the nightmare she signals for capitalist structuring extends to all epistemic projects: she opens to a beyond that human structures cannot make present "inside" knowable forms, that remains always "outside" and accessible only without boundaries. In her divinity, in the ineffability of her ends that are located in "a higher sphere," inaccessible, and so rendering her means "pure, unrelated to an end," Mara's violent and graceful gestures suggest an epistemic as well as a supernatural beyond (Morgan 2007, 55). Benjamin talks of a "pure language" that is found in the aesthetic dimensions of poetry, of the excessive aspects of linguistic communication that are not captured in the words and cannot be translated (Morgan 2007, 53–55). And this linguistic beyond can be related to the beyond invoked in divine violence: "pure language does to meaning what pure violence does to normativity: both are manifestations of the resistance to a means-ends logic . . . divine violence destroys law's forceful application to life, pure language 'extinguishes' the capacity of language to signify, to apply to the world" (Morgan 2007, 55). Indeed, knowledge is built upon the construction of boundaries, not just in a categorical sense; the written word emerges from the striking of the text on the skin of the page (Morton 2007, 40), the drawing of form upon a limit. "The more I try to show you what lies beyond this page, the more of a page I have" (Morton 2007, 30). Pure language is the evoking of what is "more" than the page, it is the meaning of a text "beyond the content that it communicates" (Morgan 2007, 55). And accordingly the pages occupied by Mara are not margined, are not bounded in closed frames and structures. Instead, Mara's onslaught is rendered without borders, opening always to the context of its encounter, of its ecological setting, of the outside, the outwith, the not-here, the boundless beyond. She is not an example of ecomimesis—she does not seek to reflect or depict a static image of the environment—she is "eco" without the "mimesis," unbounded and thereby evocative of the environment itself and of which she is a part. The theological transcendence of her divine violence connects to the epistemic excess of the material infinity of the planetary Real. Yet the planet, like the page, also tends to be bounded. Ecological thought might stop at the edge of the biosphere, at the edge of the planetary container of all earthly life, but we can still ask: "Why stop . . . at the edge of the biosphere? And what *is* this edge," anyway? (Morton 2007, 109). In Mara's boundless appearance, as in her substantive violence, she tears down everything we have set up. But in reading this desecration of edges, we risk maintaining an edge: the fluidity between "in" and "out" can only be thought in terms of a division, an edge, between "in" and "out" (Morton 2007, 47–54). But Mara's journey does not unfold within a context of transcending boundaries, she is not signaling a merging or a fluidity between extant categories—she is the unstoppable wave of beyond that destroys, that undoes and razes, flattening all structures to the pre-epistemic otherness of which I am unable to speak—that which must not be named for to name it is to kill it. For conscious understanding "seeks what is dead, for what is living escapes it; it seeks to congeal the flowing stream in blocks of ice. . . . In order to understand anything it is necessary to kill it, to lay it out rigid in the mind. . . . My own thoughts, tumultuous and agitated in the innermost recesses of my soul, once they are torn from their roots in the heart, poured out on to this paper and there fixed in unalterable shape, are already only the corpses of thoughts" (Unamuno [1912] 1954, 90). Mara's razing is the end of this "tragic combat . . . this combat of life with reason" (Unamuno [1912] 1954, 90) just as she is the end of the battle between flesh and structure in the anthropological machine. Indeed, the conflicts are the same. But where Mara brings forth the destruction of the machine—just one of the many things of ours that she

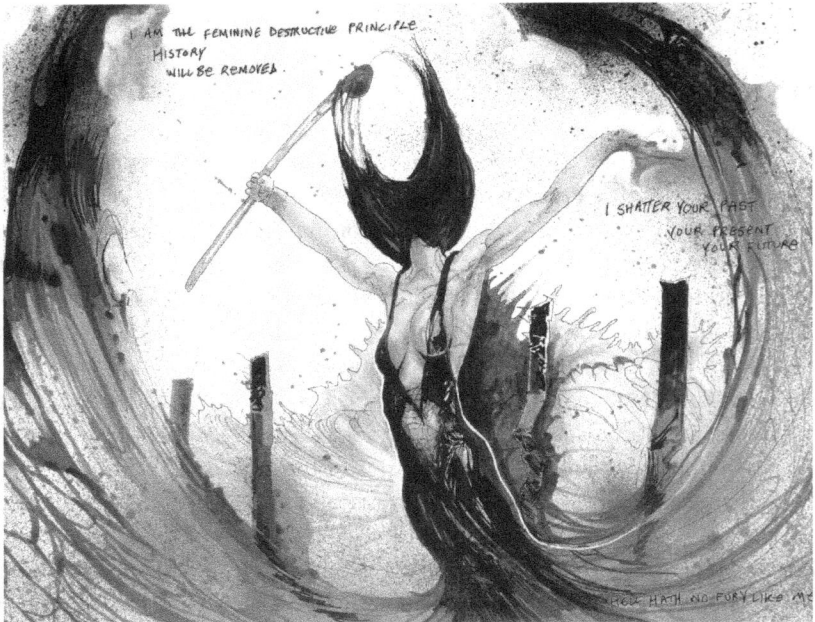

Figure 10.2: From *100 Months*, 2010. © John Hicklenton.

tears down—the Longpig Paradise is the triumphant rampage of the machine that no longer categorizes an outside. I SMELL THE FOUL STENCH / OF THE LONG-PIG. AND THE DOOMED ONES / WHO SERVE HIM. I AM THE FEMININE DESTRUCTIVE PRINCIPLE / HISTORY / WILL BE REMOVED. I SHATTER YOUR PAST / YOUR PRESENT / YOUR FUTURE. HELL HATH NO FURY LIKE ME. COASTLINES WILL CHANGE / NO NEW MAPS WILL BE MADE. The feminine destructive principle, swirling and sweeping and ripping apart as a furious force from beyond all orders, from outside the anthropocentric exploitation of the planet, from outside ecology, outside structure and formation—the living, expansive planet itself, the ghost in the intricately infinitous system of Gaia, unbounded in the cosmos, outside human knowledge—mythic, mystical, beyond, unspeakable—*anima mundi*. All this is encoded in figure 10.2, in the flowing inks and colors, the indescribable embodiment, the limitless expression, the traces of pain and human creativity, the material legacy of a dying man railing against the forces of capitalism, the violence of a sovereignty that supports it, the destruction of the planet. And so at Hicklenton's hands, at the tips of his fingers where he exscribed himself, his living body touching the writing we now touch and out of which seek to make sense (see Nancy 2008, 8–13), Mara returns us to an unstructured anarchy. NOW IN DARKNESS IS THE TRUTH REVEALED / IN THE RADIANCE OF THE ABYSS. CHAOS REIGNS. Under the unruly closure of the anthropological machine, the person becomes indistinguishable from food, from mud, from object. Becomes humus, worm, but not the living community of the planet, not the hopeful expansion of human existence into the unknowable complexity of Gaia and the universe beyond, the mortal acceptance of interconnected life (see Masciandaro 2014), nor the welcoming of an infinite kin (see Haraway 2015) or a truly boundless living—but a hollowing and removal, all life made object. Such conflation of subject and object undermines all value in human life, representing an affront to the sanctity of the living person. The apparatus of the person as a mediation between the mundane and the mystical (see Esposito 2012) dissolves, the ongoing tension between life and apparatus, the battle between flesh and structure (see Agamben 2009), ends as life is subsumed into economic commodity. Against this flattening of life to commodity, Mara brings a violent eruption from the soul of the Earth, the erasure of the chains of capitalism—of all knowing—that encircle and contain life, the *revenant* Real returning to shatter the Longpig Paradise. The planet, too, has been commodified under the Pig, reduced for economic gain; raped, pillaged, exploited. LONGPIGS! HOW I HATE THEM / AND THEIR RELENTLESS HARASSMENT OF THE EARTH. Mara is the planet's revenge, the return of sacred life from beyond the suppressive biopolitical order of commodification: the destruction of objectification: the end of all "things." From beyond. And in being beyond the patriarchal order of capital, in extravasating forth as a formation of the vast expanse of the planet to bring bloodless judgment over the biopolitical order of human civilization, she quintessentially embodies critique itself: "it is from this condition, the tear in the fabric of our epistemological web, that the practice of critique emerges" (Butler 2001). Mara's position outside all orders of humanity—as the soul of the Earth, the feminine destructive principle—signals the immensity of her critique, which "exposes the limits of that epistemological horizon itself, making the contours of the horizon appear . . . for the first time . . . in relation to its own limit" (Butler 2001). Mara, THE FACELESS PRIESTESS, comes from beyond to destroy all human endeavor. Her graceful belligerence, flowing through the pages of *100 Months*, relentlessly attacks the life-denying world of the Pig-made-God. Her attack is eviscerating, an undeniably violent and dismembering storm of pent-up wrath. She has waited 100,000 years. Her destructive path traverses the cities of the Earth, demolishing humanity and its creations, her monstrousness increasing to allow the depths of her violence to be unleashed, additional limbs emerging to carry greater weaponry with which to enact violence, her transcendence of human form indicating her progenesis from outside knowable forms. YOU MAY CALL ME / THE END OF ALL THINGS. THE DESTRUCTIVE / INTERIM / FORMATION. INVICTUS (see figure 10.3). She seeks the Pig,

Figure 10.3: From *100 Months*, 2010. © John Hicklenton.

the blasphemous god of the Longpig Paradise. She finds this "god"—and butchers it: I SHALL UNSEAM YOU FROM / THE NAVE TO THE CHOPS! SCRAGEND AND TENDERLOIN! The deification of capital, of ultimate commodification, itself reduced to nothing but meat. A BUTCHERED GOD. Mara's violence continues, destroying the Pig's offspring, slaughtering the piglets of the Swinegod, the children of the coin, the herdlike proponents of capitalism. In a moment of reverie after her brutal journey, a journey that has produced nothingness, and overwhelmed once more with the sorrow of the loss of her carpenter friend, of the community of the earth, Mara turns her head. UNH! / I HEAR THE MEWLING OF A LONGPIG NEWBORN. NO! NOT A ONE SHALL SURVIVE ME. . . . FOR THE LAW HAS / SPOKEN ITS WORD. THE LAND SHALL BE UTTERLY EMPTIED / AND UTTERLY SPOILED. THE EARTH MOURNETH / AND FADETH AWAY. THE WORLD LANGUISHETH, / AND FADETH AWAY. AND THE HAUGHTY PEOPLE / OF THE EARTH ARE HUMBLED. FOR THEY HAVE TRANSGRESSED NATURE'S LAW, ALL LAW / BROKEN AN EVERLASTING COVENANT (ellipsis added). Here are glimpses of a law-preserving violence, of an enactment of pain and suffering in the name of the law, of pure violence toward reaffirming law. But still, Mara is not seeking to preserve or create legality—but to empty the world and let it fade away, what could be seen as a deep ecocentrism that removes all that is anthropic. But in dismantling the anthropological machine such an affiliation with the *eco*centric makes little sense; Mara renders all boundless, with her "natural" law remaining inaccessible as it denies humanity any structure and meaning. But despite such statements, Mara picks up the child, the child that will undoubtedly grow to repeat the sins of its ancestors, and opens the way for something new: a promise of hope beyond the capitalist order of exploitation for coin, thus instating a future never imagined upon the embarkation of her violence. IS THIS THY MOTHER BRAT? / HER BREATH LIES FALLOW IN THE GRAVE. THOU ART THE LAST / OF THY KIND. FEAR NOT FOR I AM HERE. HUSH LITTLE ONE . . . / SHH . . . I AM A HARSH MIDWIFE——. But here it might be said that patriarchy sneaks through: Mara, the endless sweeping force of a chaotic beyond—appears to be tamed by motherhood. Her critique is ended as her supposed biological function takes over, seeming to betray, for all Hicklenton's beautiful destruction of capitalism, a degree of allegiance with the Pig. Mothers should not work, should not think or criticize the work of others, for where is the profit in childrearing? But in this we see again the rupturing of the capitalist order, for it is precisely the child that Mara chooses to raise—in her raising of violent critique as much as her adoption of humanity's ultimate orphan—that she hopes will lead to a world that does not work toward the denial of life. Her journey, her violence, is not ended—but as a divine violence is necessarily an endless moment of potential, a now "shot through with chips of Messianic time" (Benjamin [1942] 1973, 255), a trembling temporality of birth and death, of creation and destruction, with its ends forever deferred and inaccessible—a space of potential, of a messianic disruption of history that "does not mystify, neutralize or water down revolutionary politics but activates, accelerates and intensifies it" in a material struggle against instrumental violence (Hirvonen 2012, 536), that is always "about to make the continuum of history explode" (Benjamin [1942] 1973, 253). Indeed, divine violence puts time out of joint, breaking opening the present moment to an infinite potential for otherness (see Derrida 1994, 32–34). Mara's ongoing journey thus becomes one of critique as a form of violence, with its "double task, to show how knowledge and power work to constitute a more or less systematic way of ordering the world . . . but also 'to follow the breaking points which indicate its emergence'" (Butler 2001, quoting Foucault). Mara encounters the commodified world from beyond, breaking that world in her destructive performance, following those "breaking points" that ultimately take her back beyond the current biopolitical order—beyond all orders; her vengeance becomes more than just the violent enactment of hatred, but in its genesis from beyond becomes critique and shows up the violent dimensions of critique itself: that rending the processes of subjugation (see Butler 2001), dismantling the anthropological machine, is a breaking, is a violence. And critique is not just an activity, but is a way of being, an ethics, that pursues an existence not only under the subjugations of power—of neoliberalism, of commodity, of state sanctions and market forces, of Longpig edicts and human purses—but also through a self-formation, whereby "the subject is both crafted and crafting, and the line between how it is formed, and how it becomes a kind of forming, is not easily, if ever, drawn" (Butler 2001). The apparatus of late capitalism—of the reduction of human to meat, the triumph of the Longpig Paradise—shatters in its encounter with the "feminine destructive principle" that appears in the form of Mara, who exists precisely as this critical force—she is "the end of all things," the "destructive interim formation"—embodying the virtue at the heart of critique. But in birthing this critique as a woman that is conflated with nature and mystery, by appearing to be tamed in motherhood, some problematic tropes are on the verge of being repeated and enshrined in the roots of what Mara hopes to bring about, and her story risks being one of a submission to the forces of patriarchy. A femin*ist* destructive principle might have been more appropriate—signaling more solidly the rejection and movement from beyond all patriarchal orders—but the incompleteness and unfinished status of Mara's tirade, of her apocalyptic sweeping away, is a feature of her violence insofar as it remains divine. For it is symptomatic of the potentiality rendered by the messianic structure of a violence that is beyond natural and positive constructs, that is outside the question of legitimacy, outside of human ken. The moment of divine violence disrupts the historical cycle of legal violence, but does not create new structure in its place: "the presence of the messianic force in time signifies the possibility of the politics of revolt that interrupts the history of mythico-legal violence without becoming the foundation for a new political, social and legal order" (Hirvonen 2012, 541). Mara's manifestation as the supernatural earth, as a vengeful conflation of mysticism and materiality, transcends capitalist ideals and accessible epistemic form, gesturing to something else, not only in the suggestion of where she comes from or the invisibility of her ends, but also in the forever-deferred results that might stem from her pure means that have no desire in this world other than the removal of exploitative forms. And so, from out of the chaos and destruction of *100 Months* emerges not the abyss, not a nihilistic postapocalyptic wasteland, but an unstable hope; something new, inchoate, emerging, always in the future, but built on compassion rather than cannibalism, on community rather than commodity, on difference rather than sameness (see Goodrich 2003), on love rather than hunger (see Manderson 2003), and that gestures toward an openness to the infinite potential of a better world. On

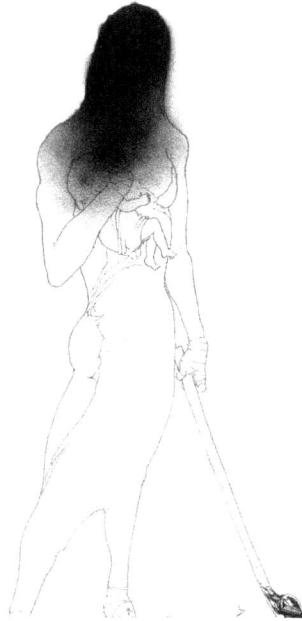

Figure 10.4: From *100 Months*, 2010. © John Hicklenton.

its face, Mara's work generates an order of existence from beyond the bio-political order of commodity through the violent disavowals and destructive rejections that are enacted as her critical force sweeps through the dominant order. But ultimately Mara's critical journey of destruction is not complete, because the violence she wrought to bring about her changes is not instru-mental: it is not a "means" to an "end," nor is it an end in itself, but is inherent in the critical pursuit inasmuch as critique seeks the disruption, destruction, replacement, expansion, challenge, or breaking of the order it is oriented against. Ultimately, *100 Months* is a reminder that critique involves violence—but a divine violence, come from beyond. Mara's appearance on the final page (see figure 10.4), as both mother and executioner, encodes much of what is at stake in her journey: the feminine force of nature, the tamed mother with a violent past, but also as a ferociously critical force whose work is not done, reminding us of the reflexivity that is needed to maintain the critical project as much as signaling the immanent potential for resistance and meaningful change. As both the remover and bringer of life, she exists both outside all human realms and as a sign of critique as a violent, unfinished form of creation: a destructive interim formation.

Notes

I wish to extend warm and meaningful thanks to the participants of the Speculative Legalities workshop—held at Griffith University, Gold Coast, on December 6, 2017—for their constructive feedback on a performance of this paper, and similarly to those in attendance at an earlier and less developed outing of the piece at the Comics and Critique symposium at St Mary's University on July 3, 2017 that formed the basis of this collection. Particular thanks also to Dan Matthews, who was generous and inquisitive enough to read and comment upon a written draft. All errors, indubitably, are my own—despite the additional constructive input of numerous peer reviewers, who also attract my thanks for their dutiful and collegial gatekeeping.

1. The printed volume of *100 Months* does not have page numbers. Where it is quoted from within the present text, the word-forms are rendered in WRITTEN-STYLE SMALL CAPS to reflect something of their appearance in the corpus of *100 Months* itself.

References

Agamben, Giorgio. 1998. *Homo Sacer: Sovereign Power and Bare Life.* Translated by Daniel Heller-Roazen. Stanford, CA: Stanford University Press.

Agamben, Giorgio. 2004. *The Open: Man and Animal.* Translated by Kevin Attell. Stanford, CA: Stanford University Press.

Agamben, Giorgio. 2009. "What Is an Apparatus?" In *What Is an Apparatus? And Other Essays*, translated by David Kishik and Stefan Pedatella, 1–24. Stanford, CA: Stanford University Press.

Benjamin, Walter. (1942) 1973. "Theses on the Philosophy of History." In *Illuminations*, edited by Hannah Arendt, translated by Harry Zohn, 245–55. London: Fontana Press.

Benjamin, Walter. (1927) 1978. "Critique of Violence." In *Reflections: Essays, Aphorisms, Autobiographical Writings*, edited by Peter Demetz, 277–300. New York: Schocken Books.

Bruton, Richard. 2010. "John Hicklenton's *100 Months*." *Forbidden Planet Blog.* Accessed July 16, 2017. http://forbiddenplanet.blog/2010/john-hicklentons-100-months-2/.

Burdon, Peter D. 2015. *Earth Jurisprudence: Private Property and the Environment.* London: Routledge.

Butler, Judith. 2001. "What Is Critique? An Essay on Foucault's Virtue." *European Institute for Progressive Cultural Studies.* Accessed May 4, 2017. http://eipcp.net/transversal/0806/butler/en/print.

Butler, Judith. 2006. "Critique, Coercion, and Sacred Life in Benjamin's 'Critique of Violence.'" In *Political Theologies: Public Religions in a Post-Secular World*, edited by Hent de Vries and Lawrence E. Sullivan, 201–19. New York: Fordham University Press.

DeWeese-Boyd, Ian. 2009. "Shojo Savior: Princess Nausicaä, Ecological Pacifism, and the Green Gospel." *Journal of Religion and Popular Culture* 21 (2): 1.

Derrida, Jacques. 1994. *Specters of Marx: the State of the Debt, the Work of Mourning, and the New International.* Translated by Peggy Kamuf. London: Routledge.

Esposito, Roberto. 2012. "The *Dispositif* of the Person." *Law, Culture and the Humanities* 8 (1): 17–30.

Giddens, Thomas. 2018. *On Comics and Legal Aesthetics: Multimodality and the Haunted Mask of Knowing*. London: Routledge.

Goodrich, Peter. 2003. "Laws of Friendship." *Law and Literature* 15 (1): 23–52.

Goodrich, Peter. 2012. "The Theatre of Emblems: On the Optical Apparatus and the Investiture of Persons." *Law, Culture and the Humanities* 8 (1): 47–67.

Haraway, Donna. 2015. "Anthropocene, Capitalocene, Plantationocene, Chthulucene: Making Kin." *Environmental Humanities* 6: 159–65.

Hicklenton, John. 2010. *100 Months*. London: Cutting Edge Press.

Hirvonen, Ari. 2012. "Marx and God with Anarchism: On Walter Benjamin's Concepts of History and Violence." *Continental Philosophy Review* 45: 519–43.

Kellogg, Catherine. 2011. "Walter Benjamin and the Ethics of Violence." *Law, Culture and the Humanities* 9 (1): 71–90.

Manderson, Desmond. 2003. "From Hunger to Love: Myths of the Source, Interpretation, and Constitution of Law in Children's Literature." *Law and Literature* 15 (1): 87–141.

Masciandaro, Nicola. 2014. "WormSign." In *Melancology: Black Metal Theory and Ecology*, edited by Scott Wilson, 81–101. Alresford: Zero Books.

Milner, Andrew, J. R. Bergmann, Rjurik Davidson, and Susan Cousin. 2015. "Ice, Fire and Flood: Science Fiction and the Anthropocene." *Thesis Eleven* 131 (1): 12–27.

Morgan, Benjamin. 2007. "Undoing Legal Violence: Walter Benjamin's and Giorgio Agamben's Aesthetics of Pure Means." *Journal of Law and Society* 34 (1): 46–64.

Morton, Timothy. 2007. *Ecology without Nature: Rethinking Environmental Aesthetics*. London: Harvard University Press.

Nancy, Jean-Luc. 2008. *Corpus*. Translated by Richard A. Rand. New York: Fordham University Press.

Parsley, Connal. 2013. "The Animal Protagonist: Representing 'the Animal' in Law and Cinema." In *Law and the Question of the Animal: A Critical Jurisprudence*, edited by Yoriko Otomo and Edward Mussawir, 10–34. Abingdon: Routledge.

Publishers Weekly. 2012. "100 Months." Accessed June 16, 2017. https://www.publishersweekly .com/978-0-9565445-2-0.

Simms, Andrew. 2008. "The Final Countdown." *Guardian*, August 1, 2001. https://www .theguardian.com/environment/2008/aug/01/climatechange.carbonemissions.

Sinnerbrink, Robert. 2006. "Deconstructive Justice and the 'Critique of Violence': On Derrida and Benjamin." *Social Semiotics* 16 (3): 485–97.

Smith, Mick. 2011. *Against Ecological Sovereignty: Ethics, Biopolitics, and Saving the Natural World*. Minneapolis: University of Minnesota Press.

Tomba, Massimiliano. 2017. "Justice and Divine Violence: Walter Benjamin and the Time of Anticipation." *Theory and Event* 20 (3): 579–98.

Unamuno, Miguel de. (1912) 1954. *Tragic Sense of Life*. Translated by J. E. Crawford Flitch. New York: Dover.

11

The Mask as Anti-Apparatus

On the Counter-Dispositif *of* V for Vendetta

PETER GOODRICH

Bereft of complexity and singular in theme, the argument that follows resolves one of the enigmas of *V for Vendetta* (Moore and Lloyd 1989). The thesis is that the graphic novel operates according to a logic of inversion, a very particular *volte-face* in which the anti-apparatus of the mask institutes a politics of impersonality. The idea as nonperson. The mutable protagonist is the utopian terrorist, the paradoxically violent anarchist as an agent of historical change. V, who in the graphic novel introduces himself with the words "I do not have a name," is a nonfigure of the not yet, proleptically a pacifist, one who destroys so as to create, who fulminates to the end of engendering a state of incompletion that alone promises novelty, the no place, the *u-topos* of anarchic self-determination.[1] V operates according to a purist politics of the unfinished, proffering the trajectory of razed spaces, a ground laid bare by its bomber, without schema or plan for a future freedom because the liberty to come, by definition, cannot be dictated by contemporary forms. V is a positive nihilist, a proponent of the transvaluation of values, and his is the hope of the hopeless, the optimism of despair, of an affirmative pessimism, and of the fecundity of freedom. In a final turn, a flourish *de résistance*, for the sake of the record, so as to clear up misunderstandings of this subcultural brilliance, the movie of the graphic novel (McTeigue 2005) operates an inversion of its own, one which upends the schema of the book so as to put into effect the very creativity and freedom in favor of which the earlier plot has argued. The comedy of the comic, the *commedia dell'arte* of the mask, the anti-apparatus of proliferated impersonality, the theatrics of belonging to the community of those who do not belong, becomes the driving figure of the film and even more so, of its afterlife, its viral and political role in resistance from Wall Street to Wollongong, Brazil to Bahrain, Harlem to Hong Kong. The film arrives as the fulfillment of the graphic lore, uniquely mobilizing comics studies as a praxis, making a movie that moves the comedy of depicting the person, the caricature of the cartoon, on to the streets.

Inaugurations

Title first. An initial alliteration. Letter then mask. So start with a parody of the performativity of the letter: a vinous virelay, a veritable virtuosity volleyed against the vapid vacancy of veridical and verbose verisimilitudes; versified vociferations, vaulting into the vagaries of the *ipsissima verba* and videographic vivisections, viewed so as to vindicate the visuals of *in veritas kino* of *V for Vendetta*. The poetics of alliteration, in other lesser words, are initially the most noticeable feature of V and a significant starting point. First letter for theme, the riddle an unfinished narrative. V is a chronogram, a symbol, a semiotic signal, a letter, and it is this enigmatic plurality of significations that allows the utopics of its heteroglossia,[2] the potential of its polysemy and elicits the first comedy and laughter of the movie because of the irony of asking an encryption, a masked man, a cypher, who he is: "Who is but the form following the function of what and what I am is a man in a mask" (McTeigue 2005). The call of the police, the paradox of the uniformed demanding singularity—the interpellation of an inappropriate singularity—triggers a renunciation of the person as mark of registration and institutional identification, and receives an augmented alliterative retort: "Voila. In view, a humble vaudevillian veteran, cast vicariously as both victim and villain by the vicissitudes of fate. This visage, no mere veneer of vanity, is a vestige of the *vox populi*, now vacant, vanished . . ." leading finally to the encryption "and you may call me V" (McTeigue 2005). The introduction is thus to a letter, an alphabetical index, which is also the sign of the mask, an impersonal form, a pluralized and interchangeable apparatus of nonidentity which image, or properly *imago*, has from classical times been the bearer of an ambivalent status as a false truth—it is not what it represents—and equally as vestige of the dead, as in the death mask of the sovereign, and here that of V's own death and rebirth as the collectivity of a letter.[3] In the graphic novel, witness to this fact, the mask visually precedes the initial entry of the protagonist V. It is pictured on a hook, a prop, an empty visage hanging limply, facing down, inert, interchangeable and about to be taken up by the gloved hand of the impressario (see figure 11.1). The moving hand hides, covers, so as to envelope

Figure 11.1: Incipit V. From *V for Vendetta*. Alan Moore and David Lloyd, 1989, 10. © DC Comics.

the face. Entry for content, first sign, glove then mask, the visual narrative is to be understood *ad apparentiam*, according to appearances, and already it sets the stage not only for the theatrics of another, communal, justice but the accompanying deconstruction of the politics of the person.

Glove then mask signal the plurality of *personae*, the replicability of masks as images, that also lie at the root of V's verbal appearance in the graphic novel, where it is a Shakespearean stanza, beginning "The multiplying villainies of nature do swarm upon him," which announces the arrival of the self-proclaimed alliterative king and bogeyman, the instigator and operator of the saga, the vengeance of *Vendetta* (Moore and Lloyd 1989, 11). The mask and masquerade, theatrics and festival, an insistent theme, is both imagistic and verbal, an integument of the face, a veiling of the visage and a covering of identity in the coding of both face and name. The anaphoric "I" is everyone who can use the first person singular. The same, it transpires, with V. Another literate fiction. The letter indexes a multiplying multitude, a collectivity, and here something more than that, a hidden assonance, a force of alliteration whereby anyone who can don the mask bears the letter and rhymes with the coding of the movement, the collectivity of *an-arkhos*: "There is more behind and inside V than any of us suspected. Not who, but what: what is she . . .

You'll learn . . ." (Pynchon 1963, 53). It is precisely this literary transference of V, letter, mask, number, gender, the *vice versa* visible, that carries the plot as a poetics, a creative and comical work that surges upon the riddle of its rhythm, the timbre of its rhyme, the method of its rune. It is this code and encoding, the rhyming sounds that play on the levels of meaning and iteration, through which the gram of the chronogram comes to signal not number but poesy, the assonance of alliteration, the isophoneme that gets repeated in the versification that runs throughout the plot and gives expression to that substitutability, that absolute impersonality that is the transfiguration of the face into the mask. That V is repeated, rhymed, strung out, incanted, and choral fits well with the underlying theme of the graphic novel which is not simply the pluralization of V, as enigma, as communal mask, and so as *vox populi* in a massive, replicated and amorphous collectivized mode, but also and attendantly the vexillation of V, meaning from early on the Roman numeral and nominal encryption is a poster and flag, a heavy signifier of a riddle, a vexillological marker of an inversion, a statement of the unsaid. It is this that becomes the rallying call to the ultimate political non*topos* and drive of the narrative, the unfinished, the creative and prolific indeterminacy of all that is without *arkhos*, free of prior law, structure, and origin, faceless behind the mask.

It is worth noting that historically the mask, a feature of theater and of the *mens emblematica* or humanist turn to imagery, necessarily figures a politics and here presents the anti-apparatus as a critique of corrupt juridical forms.[4] The mask as *imago* is the *persona*—classically father and son, *haec imago*—and generates the mode of entry into the political and juridical. The face is the *dispositif*, the apparatus of social disposition by lineage and appearance. The mask mimics the person while undoing the juristic mode of designation and destroying the individualized site of ascription and attribution. The apparatus, the dispositor of the person, may be stylized and indeed encrypted, most obviously as social presence in its legitimate forms of staged and legal appearance, in the atmospherics and theatrics of costume, court, and trial. That, however, is only a face, a guise but not yet a disguise. Against the *gravitas* of the most serious expression of the social, the visage, the close up, the mask offers *levitas*, representing the play of appearance, and here resistance to surveillance and identification, the *stasis* of political registration, the entombing of disciplinary regimes in the inexhaustible multiplicity of interchangeable (comedic) apparitions. The Renaissance satirical emblematist, the sillographer Jacob Cats perhaps puts it best in showing that there is nothing behind the mask, stating that "we know that all things are equally light" and that behind the face lies the void.[5] *Officium ludicrae*, the art and office of play is all that politics is or can aspire to be when freedom takes the reigns in recognition of the communality of invention and the necessity of dance, the shark aesthetics of *perpetuum mobile*, of constant motion.

What V as visage, as face of the sociality of being and of the *anomie* of communal freedom shows is that there is only the theater of personality, the play of politics, and that all is invention and fabrication of the real, law but a fiction amongst fictions, an image amongst images. The earlier, emblematic tradition of what we might term comical precomics, of visual legal literature or picture books understood this well. The sociality of being was defined as an entirely theatrical affair, a veritable play of masks, a devising of governance by means of the choice of a social face. The emblematist and political theorist Guillaume Perrière thus offers the plurality of masks as the signifier of good government, of "bons engins" in an inverted world of foolosophical admonition and of anti-apparatuses. If freedom is play, the recognition of the great dispositor as simply, lightly, the communality of being, the impersonality of existence and belonging, the plurality of collectivity, then the mask of V portends precisely the exposure of political pretense: "that you shall find in any place / few that do not carry a double face" (Perrière, 1540, fol. Biiii; Combe 1610, 23).

Openings: *Feux d'artifice*

Behind the mask, an emptiness, a void, the blank canvas upon which the figure and freedom of the impersonal is painted as a collective project of contributing, belonging, being in plurality. A clearing of the ground, the palimpsestic tableau has to be ready for inscription and figuration. First then, in narrative terms, the much-debated inaugural explosion, the playfully marked and spectacularly celebrated combustion, the force and fireworks. An opening inversion. In the graphic novel it is Parliament that is exothermically imploded and destroyed, brought down, as compared to the film, in which it is the Old Bailey, the central criminal court, the mask of legal sovereignty, that is blown up. In the graphic novel, it is the legislature, the two houses of government, the ultimate symbol of the political, that is removed, whereas in the movie it is the notorious courthouse, and the symbol of Justitia that suffers its symbolic end in violent demise. There is, of course, a big difference, a quantum divergence in the connotations of an overture that removes the place, the building, and so also archive of the body politic, and one which merely razes a courthouse. In one sense it is a distinction without a difference—Justitia is the sign of the totality of law, of its politics and effects, of the outside of legality that hovers over the system, and so in its idealized form it is predominantly a representation of the legislature, of lawmaking, of the poet legislator. To destroy the Old Bailey is consonant with, if not the same as, removing the Houses of Parliament and destroying the supremacy of the sovereign. Both detonations attack heavy symbols of legitimacy but the destruction, the fulmination of Parliament is a much more extreme act in that it empties the unique space of the political, and erases the very architectural structure, the monumental, permanent, and only site of the constitution, the place where the nation has always stood, and still, however precariously, stands and speaks (*parle*) its mind (*mens*) together.

To destroy is to raze, to clear the ground, to make space and while this same gesture is provided at the end of the movie, it lacks the integration and integral quality of an overture that opens the narrative with this generation of an emptying, a founding in the form of a much more patulous erasure. The ground must be cleared, meaning here that the building must go and the Guy Fawkes narrative be rewritten not as failure but as accomplishment, not destruction but creation, an opening achieved, the history of an idea. Recollect that the recusants were engaged in internecine war, they wished to displace the Protestants with Catholicism, the word with images and text, *sola scriptura* with verbiage and vestments and so remained in purpose at least internal to the monotheistic struggle for domination. It is this drama, the potential clearing of the ground, that excites the protagonist and forms the historical referent, the site of fear and possibility that V takes up. Fawkes is associated with evil and anarchy, themes that can be found in the early pictorial representations of the gunpowder plot in which a shadowy Beelzebub or *caput lupinum* is apprehended by the divine eye and a guard while skulking away from the scene of the plot. It is described as "this desperate Worke of Darknesse (*opus tenebrarum*)" and of papal devilry—*papistarum infamiam* (Herring 1641, n.p.). In most versions of the account, the divine eye relays the message *video et rideo*, I see and I laugh. (See figure 11.2.) The most apparent meaning of the couplet, first seeing and then laughing, is "I see through," or I can apprehend more, the layers of plot and meaning, *dramatis personae* and project, leading via darkness visible to arrest and apprehension by an omnivoyant celestial sovereign. The paradox of seeing in the dark, or at least of sciographic interpreting and translating of shadows, is that of revelation through the layers of obfuscation, the schismatics and sclerosis of belligerent theology and dogmatic discourse. The V of *video* references

Figure 11.2: *Video et rideo.* Francis Herring, 1641, n.p. Public domain.

insight, the history of the eye as also more esoterically the Pythagorean marriage of harmony and balance, the mystical combinatory odd number, something comical, leading thence to the genesis of laughter, the comedy of the human struggle, and in the case of V, to reappropriation through hermeneutic inversion.

The V of *video* is also potentially and comically the *versus* of opposition that turns the joke against the sovereign that sees, the *rideo* confronting and overturning the *video*, this time, and by way of a very great expanse of time. For V the *versus* is the overturning of the history of the foiled plot, its recuperation and transformation into a space of comedy, of acting, playing, laughing, dancing that metamorphoses, transports, validates, and launches. There is also a certain further humor in the inversion, the A of anarchy becoming the V as a topsy-turvy slashed A, the mark of Vendetta, of the clearing of the ground so as to unleash the alliterative multiplication and poetic proliferation of assonant V's. The isophoneme becomes numerous, plural, a mirror that repeats and institutes in infinite regress the universal singularity of its origin, the wearer of the mask. There is in other words an undoing that inverts the original narrative and transforms the gunpowder plot from regicide and treason most foul, to liberation and its accompanying narrative of persistent change. The key, the V, the pivot, lies in the continuity of change and thus the destabilizing potential of a "not yet" that is radically unforeseen, without either precedent or prefiguration, and in political terms, in the language of abolition, "unfinished."

V in essence asks the question: how do you found nothing, clear away extant structures without installing something—known in advance—in their place? For the graphic novel the principle is that of the two stages announced by Proudhon—*destruam et œdificabo*, destroy and then wait, attend, allow, and only later, come to build: "Anarchy wears two faces, both creator and destroyer. Thus Destroyers topple Empires; make a canvas of clean rubble where creators can build . . . rubble once achieved makes further ruins' means irrelevant"[6] (Moore and Lloyd 1989, 222). The theme of destruction runs throughout the work, from the opening and ironic exploding hand (of the law) that, poetically enough, kills a fingerman, through the "land of do as you please" where "*Do what Thou Wilt* shall be the whole law" and *vox populi* its expression, to the final removal of the Leader and the death of V or literal passing on of the mask.

To open, genuine dehiscence, *pupa to imago*, conception to birth and efflorescence requires a change of levels, a piercing of the real, a shedding off or abandonment of precedent, image, and law, in favor of nothing, *terra incognita*, the suspension of origin and the *an-arkon*—the no law, the shadow archive—of becoming.[7] This is nihilism in its positive Nietzschean sense of transformation. What is past is prologue. Precedent contains in its interstices the seeds of the present, and yet for V it is precisely the past, the structures that contain and trammel, program and dictate the real—the dream of the actual—which has to be changed. It is the archive, the law and the grammar that must fall for the future to open. In V's words it is music, melody, rhyme that must lead the way onto open ground and voluntary order. The arc of the argument is not always free of contradiction or inconsistency but the impetus of the narrative is constant: "anarchy must embrace the din of bombs . . . yet always must it love sweet music more." And then "how strange . . . the change . . . from ma-jor to mi-nor" (Moore and Lloyd 1989, 219). Hold on to the last figure, the minor, V minor as in *frater minor*, which recent philological excavation and scholarly archaeology has disinterred as the doctrine of divestment of property, mundane use, and abrogation of all law (Coccia 2006, 97; Agamben 2013). The minor is less than, subtracted from, regression to the *in-fans*, a return to the *imago*, beginning again, but really beginning from nothing, from the blank canvas, the rubble, the no more one, more than one, of the child. Thus the rhyme, the theatrics of the mask, the bard as harbinger again of communal change.

The theory is certainly not unknown, and there have been exponents before V of the erasure of all programs, the demise of the possible, of confusionism, of means that match and measure the ends, but the key lies in the concept of the unfinished which gains its best (though unattended) expression in the work of Thomas Mathieson. In his early book on abolition, the Norwegian radical criminologist and abolitionist insists upon the avoidance of substitution, resistance to the lure and ease of replacing the extant, and thus providing a substitutive order, the same again in different form but similar structure and limitation. There is a jump, a breach, and a rending that is necessary, an abolition that:

> takes place when we break with the established order and *at the same time* face unbuilt ground. This is to say that abolition and the very first phase of the unfinished are one and the same. The moment of freedom is that of entering unbuilt ground. Freedom is the anxiety and the pleasure involved in entering a field which is unsettled or empty. (Mathieson 1974, 25, emphasis in original)[8]

The unfinished thus not only avoids being finished but rather clings to the alternative, *alter natus*, another birth, "which is 'alternative' in so far as it is not based on the premises of the old system, but on its own premises which at one or more points contradict those of the old system" (Mathieson 1974, 13–14).

The minor, for V, is simultaneously inchoate, foreign, peregrine, strange, and yet to come. It arises, like Psaphon, from the ashes of prison, naked, reborn but unformed and in process, a survivor, a new beginning *ex nihilo* which here means born out of nihilism, living on through fire, like text, book, tome, and in the earlier tradition, the codex, emblematized in the salamander representing virtue surviving even fire. The vitality and opportunity of the unfinished is the spur and transitional point, a tone, a mood, a rhythm captured best in the iteration of V as an alliterative but singular letter at the beginning of numerous words, as start of the sentence, inaugurator of the situation, a manifold mode of appearance and simultaneously of disappearance. The penultimate chapter, exit for content, is titled "Volcano" and offers eruption and prelude to the Viking funeral, entry to Valhalla, the last bomb, one which in the words of V's inheritor, Evey, involves a literal face and life, that begins again: "But finally I lift away that maddening smile, and . . . and at last I know. I know who V must be" (Moore and Lloyd 1989, 250). V must

Figure 11.3: *Dignitas non moritur*. From *V for Vendetta*. Alan Moore and David Lloyd, 1989, 261. © DC Comics.

be Evey, and as if in a mirror darkly, the mask moves from one to another and again, difference and repetition, "I would like to introduce myself. But truth is I do not have a name. You can call me 'V'" (1989, 26; and see figure 11.3). Another mask, the same mask. Parent child, figures of reproduction and multiplication. And bear in mind also the other meanings of Eve[y] as palindrome of forbidden knowledge and equally as V in motion, V outside V, ex V, electronic V, virtual V, viral V, perhaps even eviscerated V, V's eve, the Ides of Eve, the vanishing of V. There is a sense again of *perpetuum mobile*, connotative of revolution in the sense of repeated movement, repetition as reproduction in a changed form, V's other or mystic body, the parent in the child that lives on. The message, however, the living on as more than one attends a legacy and testament to:

> freedom's necessity . . . The people stand within the ruins of society, a jail intended to outlive them all. The door is open. They can leave or fall instead to squabbling and thence to new slaveries. The choice is ever theirs, as ever it must be. I will not lead them. . . . (1989, 260)

After that, the explosion under and of Downing Street, the residence of the British Prime Minister, the synecdoche for parliamentary sovereignty, destruction finally of the emblem of the political, the personification—the *per-sonare*—of executive governance. Smoke, then darkness and an open, unlit road, headed North: "with anarchy comes an age of *ordnung*, of true order, which is to say voluntary order . . . turning, turning in the widening gyre" (1989, 195–96).

Vivitur Ingenio

The conversation between V and "Madam Justice" in which it is her infidelity that has driven him away, her ruins that transfer his love: "you are no longer *my* justice. You are his justice now. You have bedded another." And so it is to Mistress Anarchy that V turns because, in his words, "she has taught me that justice is meaningless without freedom . . . the flames of freedom. How lovely. How just . . . O Beauty, 'til now I never knew thee" (Moore and Lloyd 1989, 41). It is this transition, the passage to the shadow, the evaporation of the architecture and the statue into a specter, into an idea, that demands attention. All is fulminating, fireworks, explosives, ignition, and light. It is to this emergence out of fire, an old figure of generation, of flaming formation that proffers the principal *détournement* of the treatise. It is in part, as hinted, that the enflaming, the burning and wasting, has a significance, one which was best and most lovingly pursued in Gaston Bachelard's (1972) *Psychoanalysis of Fire*, and other works on reverie and flames. There is a desire hidden in the burning, what Bachelard dubbed the nemesis complex, referencing the erotics of watching death, the desire to see the object consumed, wanting, and so desiring, urging the thing to be over and done and the *novum* will emerge. That, and the reverie of nemesis, of identifying with the combustible object and being complicit in the flickering and the flames that promise transformation.

V emergent is naked, "he had flames behind him" and appears as a shadow in the novel, arms by his side (Moore and Lloyd 1989, 83). Phoenix-like, a bird of Psaphon, a chimerical and inchoate birth in flames all signify, like the emblematic salamander, a figure and idea that does not burn and will not die. The body emerges, naked, in outline or shadow, as a faceless form, an adumbration, an outline or sketch of any person. What emerges is an idea, a beyond of death, a future that is more structural than temporal: *vivitur ingenio* meaning wit lives on is here represented in the spectral and unformed shadow of a body. The impersonal lives on through mutation, change of form, adaptation to environment, synchrony with circumstance. It is again an emblematic figure, a mark of something more, *plus ultra*, as sign of something final, that cannot be gone beyond, that survives and is transferable, an image or mask even, that lives through and on. *Vivitur ingenio*, wit lives on in incorporeal form as the collectivity of thought, the shared intellect symbolized in early images in the clasped book with a sign of eternity, a circle, atop. By the same token, when later in the narrative detective Finch, seeking to understand his protagonist, returns to Larkhill, he too experiences a second birth, a passing on of V for *vie*, and subsequently for *Evey*, for free, for life. Finch strips naked, emerges poetically "vaulting, veering, vomiting up the values that victimized me, feeling vast, feeling virginal . . . Was this how he felt? This verve. This vitality. This vision. *La voie. La vérité . . . La vie*" (Moore and Lloyd 1989, 216). Arms raised toward a sun emerging through the pillars of Stonehenge, Finch is V—*vivitur, vita—redivivus*, or a version of the antique legal maxim *vividae rationes*—vivid, embodied, enacted reasons. Finch becomes V, both *nemesis* and creator, a vestige that will become a valediction, the burning of a path, a phoenix—an idea—from the ashes. The inversion is much stronger in the novel than in the film because it is the law, the policeman, the detective hunting for V who finds V inside himself, is transformed, liberated, reborn and set on his path. The idea of V, the versus, the vice versa upends the norm and frees the law from within itself. It is not V, and it is more than V that emerges, the no more one, more than one that Derrida declares of hauntology, of death, but also a proliferation, transformation, and versification in the classical sense of poetics, creation through the zodiac of wit (Derrida 1994, 2).

The detective dances, gesticulates, sings out, and this is the *détournement*, the shift of law into the metadiscourse of anarchy as a freedom that signals most distinctively the libertarian thematic of the work. The next scenario shows V in the Shadow Gallery and reiterates that V is unknown in the sense of unrecognized, his face a mask and so ever capable and often performing a pluralization that is possible precisely because "you must never know my face" (Moore and Lloyd 1989, 248). What cannot be recognized, what lacks an identity cannot be killed. Is that not the point of the mask? It is a counter-*dispositif*, an anti-apparatus, it is the face as anonymity, a hiding of the "fair aspect" that "puts apparel on my tottered loving . . . then may I dare to boast how I do love" (Shakespeare, "Sonnet XXVI"). The mask is mobile, meaning that it is an ambulant, visible, painted critique of the person as the unit of subjection and subjugation. There can be no *dispositif* or *dispositor*, meaning no disposition or hierarchical arrangement of subjects, no capture of governed souls, no market or commodification, without the *personae* or social presences and identifying marks to which the apparatuses, the modes of disposition, placement or subtraction, can attach.[9] What is left is only demographics, only principles, communality as the deflection of interpellation, the mask as mark of community stores an interiority of knowledge, freedom as an ontology of knowing that exists everywhere and nowhere, as collective thought, and as resistance. The mask as anti-apparatus or nonface signals V's equivalent of the King's two bodies, an impersonal physical presence is pure symbol, the visage as virtuality, a faceless *pharmakon*, a reeling relay of the real as collective thought. It is thus in the constant dance of a communal and popular identity, in the impersonality of the mask that the authorities become confused and deranged and turn in effect upon themselves: every time a mask is removed, the subject unveiled, it is the wrong subject, it is *facies altera*, another face of the administration excoriating itself. It is never V that is unmasked, never the amorphous narrative or plot of insurrection that is disturbed, never the subject that is being sought by the authorities, but rather and most emblematically, it is the Norsefire broadcaster—Roger Dascombe—dressed up as V who in an act of poetic justice is killed by his own security team. It is always V and it is never V, an aspect that makes of the mask and the masquerade a constant revel, a dance of identities, a sudden freedom and trajectory as formulated in the film, though not in the novel, through Shakespeare:

> I prethee (and I'le pay thee bounteously)
> Conceal me what I am, and be my aid.
> For such disguise as happ'ly shall become
> The form of my intent. (*Twelfth Night*, Act 1, Scene 2)

Disguise, no guise, and thus dis-guy, Guy's loss of faith, in which the face is both designation and denunciation, and the mask is transformed into its opposite in the trajectory of the unfinished. The mask is something donned, put on as the form of a collective self—a man or a woman, who cares?—a feature of "The Vanishing," after the dance scene in the Shadow Gallery, it is time to lose *persona* again, as V takes up his theatrical and so social garb and Evey, in mimicry, as the sign of joining, of becoming a collective being, an anarchist in the making, a volunteer for freedom, puts on a blindfold, a minor and historically a comedic mask, the royal headband that slipped over the eyes (Goodrich and Hayaert 2015), as she follows V through an open door. She moves here from darkness to light, to a new beginning, an *incipit novum* or advenience of novelty (figure 11.4). The mask as *persona*, as identifier of another character being played, here hides what Esposito elaborates as the key feature of impersonality. The person, as a legal category, as both status

Figure 11.4: *Incipit novum*. From *V for Vendetta*. Alan Moore and David Lloyd, 1989, 98. © DC Comics.

and power, identifies and captures or in Althusser's cold term interpellates the subject. Once there are persons, then there can be nonpersons and indeed the class of person—as subject, as bearer of rights, as islander or citizen—exists precisely so as to distinguish included and excluded. For there to be persons there have to be nonpersons. It is against this major concept of juridical recognition that the minor and mutating character of the mask is pitched: "the impersonal does not refer to the homogeneity of the undifferentiated but to the heterogeneous mobility of difference" (Esposito 2015, 197).

Video et rideo begins to take on a sense of relief, of laughter not as denigration but as relinquishment and exodus: to cast aside the identity and the inclusive exclusion of the person is suddenly to free the subject—V, Finch, Evey—from a preconstituted, formed and finished place and role, law and restraint. The masquerade is the collectivity and impersonality of thought as such, as a communal, social enterprise of thinking, philosophy as an office and way of life. This is the meaning of the famous line, relayed in the novel when Finch shoots V and the latter responds: "There, did you think to kill me? There's no flesh or blood within this cloak to kill. There's only an idea. Ideas are bullet proof. Farewell" (Moore and Lloyd 1989, 236). This paradoxical scene—*ave atque vale*—occurs, significantly enough, just after the Leader—Adam James Susan—has been shot and so at one level the symbol of sovereignty and that of sovereign resistance coalesce in death but with

Figure 11.5: *Imago, id est quod figurat*. From *V for Vendetta*.
Alan Moore and David Lloyd, 1989, 121. © DC Comics.

the difference that V chooses to die, allows Finch to shoot him, so as to perpetuate the cause of freedom, so as to become an idea, whereas the Leader's
demise is neither chosen nor a passage to anything, as he is unelected, feared,
lacking in either concept or motion, now but a missing face.[10]

The sign of transition, the idea transmitted in the novel, is that of the mask
as a veil and a domino, an item in a chain disclosing a general and substitutable form of *perpetuum mobile* or constant change. The mask is the threat,
as signaled when Finch insists that any mistake with "*HIM*," represented
directly by the mask, is fatal (figure 11.5). The face that represents faceless-
ness is precisely the intimation of destruction of the established order, the
insignum of anarchy, freedom to choose a way of life, a structure, and like
many structures it also goes unnoticed, repressed. Thus, after the ferocious
signal that this is the threat, that the "inhuman" V is the terrorist to be feared,
Finch lets the mask drop as if it were a simple covering, a reticule (figure 11.6).
The structural sign, the inventive and driving force of an idea made visible
is too much for the detective to hold on to, but is dropped, let go, forgotten,
and thus becoming unconscious, morphoses a greater force.

This discarding is no *vis inertiae* but rather the marking of that which
escapes the apparatus and at the same time eludes apprehension. Can thought
be collective, intellect without property? The mask is thus an invariant yet

Figure 11.6: Counter-*dispositif*. From *V for Vendetta*. Alan Moore and David Lloyd, 1989, 121. © DC Comics.

variable presence of collective possibility, it is glimpsed in corners, reposing in cupboards, appearing on screen, as evidence, hanging at the bottom of the page, looming in shadows, on stage, in mirrors, and covering one face and then another and another.[11] It is at the feet of Evey, as the rumor of V's death is announced too often and too soon, that the mask is glimpsed below the stairs, waiting, present impersonal (figure 11.7). It is this ironic representation of impersonality as the generic plurality of visages, as *vividae rationes*, that performs the transition into the life of the idea, the vaudevillian vault from the person into the collective and transferable process of thought as the transmission of ideas. The mask is in this sense a mode of becoming a figure of invention, a vice and device that divines an idea, that drives the sense, both the appeal and the threat of the narrative of freedom, that we are all the same, collective and connected beings, participants in the tradition and communality of thought. The masquerade, the freedom of playing a part in a carnival or dance of unidentified impersonalities, liberates the ideas from being the property of identity or the reified and owned belongings of the person. The idea—the mask of thought—can be put on or taken off, relayed from one to another, singularized or pluralized but always with the identity of the wearer as a made-up character, the figure of the dancer, an invention

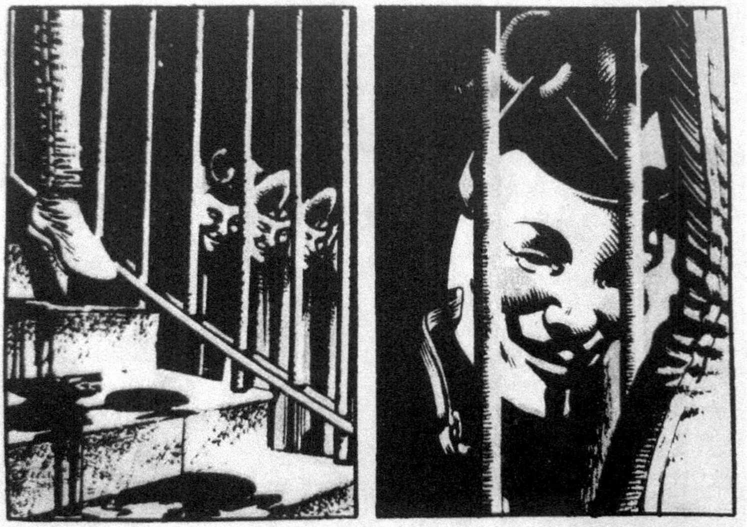

Figure 11.7: How strange the change from major to minor. From *V for Vendetta*. Alan Moore and David Lloyd, 1989, 247. © DC Comics.

of rhythm, an idea and not an identity, a movement between rather than a singular instance, unique author, or solipsistic conception.

V represents, encrypts, and symbolizes a perdurance, not simply the Nietzschean paradox of the necessity of freedom but the overcoming of the self in the exchangeability and replication of the mask as device, as the means of apparition in the social. It does not matter who speaks, what signifies is what appears, the comedy and the speech, delivery and elocution, illocution and enactment. Far from being the prisoner of the body, the idea—*anima* or soul—is precisely what escapes, exceeds, and transcends the limited tellurian space and housing of the person en route for impersonality, for collectivity, for the body of thought or *corpus idearum*. In the old language this was treated in terms of *de umbris idearum*, the shadow and better the cloud of ideas, the satirical impersonality of *nebulo nebulonum*, that escapes death simply by lacking temporality and physicality. Thus V gets shot to prove the impersonality of the idea, the no more one, more than one that constitutes the collectivity of thought and renders into comic form the emblematic motto that so appealed to Walter Benjamin, *vivitur ingenio*—wit, lives on (*notitiam feræ posteritatis habet*) (Schoonhove 1618, 89). This is visible in the image of Evey reacting to the presence of gelignite, the proximity of death, as V walks on, the scene a prelude to transition, and to the side, too visible to be noticed perhaps, a row of masks, already seen from different angles, awaiting, laterally, their similitude and role. The city turns to rubble, buildings fall to ruin, the great architectural monuments, the various theatrical stages, proscenia, statues return to dust but wit and wisdom in the heteroglossia of discourse, in the monuments and images of artistic invention, in the collectivity of ideas, live on. Once released, sketched, spoken, printed, screened, externalized, the thought escapes any individuality, and the idea forms beyond all inchoate possession. It is conceived, now a concept, the ultimate figure of impersonality, the skeleton of *vivitur*, V as an idea that circulates in the vast host of ideational alliterations and the forward movement of the poetics of a thought of the social as the sociality of thought. The mask remains in place "lest interview annul a want that image satisfies" (Dickinson 1924, xxviii).

To Occupy: V for [in]Version

The story, the technics of the mask have been traced in the history of the *imago*, the death ceremonies and morbid casts of ancestors, but less often in the transitivity and theatricality of the comedy of the social and the play of offices and roles (Goodrich 2012). The referent of the mask, however, continues to retain a certain sense of atemporality and of inheritance as well as of taking on, picking up, playing with, and promulgating. The question in relation to *Vendetta* is that of whether the vivid identification of a mask that is the face, a mask with no person, a pure symbol changes our understanding of the masquerade, the role of an impersonal advocacy of freedom, the place of an imprint of a nonvisage, a scream, in the movement and progress of an idea. Part of the answer, an immediate and political expression of V—as mask, as vendetta, and as symbol—comes in the pluralization of the wearing of the image in the global antiglobalization and occupy movements.

Trace where V has been after the delayed release of the film in 2005. From graphic novel to silver screen is the first moment of progress in which our protagonist moves from the Shadow Gallery, from page to film, from comic book sketch to the figuration of sound and motion. Two dimensions become three. Lift off. Recollect that the first encounters were marked by appearance at night, in darkness, umbrageously, as the oneiric figure of freedom and the chance of change emergent. From there, in exponential mode, the comic book mask leaves the page for the screen and then enters the virtual, the collective, politics, life. V becomes an internet meme, a gaming figure, a hacktivist motif, a gif, and then pluralized as a symbol of anonymity and as the costume of protest against corporatism, government overreach, domination in its multiple and global forms. The mask, V's supersession and transmission has appeared in the Arab Spring in Bahrain, Egypt, Saudi, and in the Occupy movement across the world from Thailand to Turkey, Britain to Brazil, India to Iceland, Berlin to Brisbane, Canada to Corfu, Venezuela to Venice, Port Harcourt to Helsinki. A wild array of sites and causes, occupants and expressions that signal the power of the idea of impersonality and the appeal of V as a flag, a living on as the collectivity of resistance, the power of acting differently and owning the nonownership of ideas. V as mask, the vexillological sign is the embodiment of a ventriloquism that allows transmission, a speaking through of the collectivity of the idea, the effacement of the subject in the passage through self to other as the wit that is housed impersonally in thought, as that which speaks through us. The appeal is to plurality, to the minor gesture and to the commons, to the music of protest and that prefigurative being together which signals, as Graeber fondly argues, a new mode of politics, a community now acting as a community to come (Graeber 2004).[12] What does this inversion portend and how does wearing a removable mask, identifying with a generic, minor, substitutable device, an anti-apparatus as a collective ontology, as being in common, signal political change? The answer, insofar as it makes any sense to illate in terms of answers, must begin with the series of inversions that V triggers.

The alliterative character of *Vendetta*, novel and film, *graphos* and *logos*, already signals, as earlier adumbrated, an inversive logic in which the poetic convention of rhyming endings is displaced by the assonance of beginnings, versification here signaling a cadence, both harmony and measure of opening. Rhyme most directly signals the plurality of the word, its conjunction and community, in that no word can rhyme alone, it is its separation and isolation in the lexicon that is its artificiality, its unreal abstraction, because the word is always more than the word, the excess of its singularity. The popularity and viral quality of V, the ventriloquism of the mask, thus inaugurates a novelty which at its boldest inverts and conflates the duality of subject and mask, or as Parsley develops the theme, of natural life and representation of being as *persona*: "the mask, the appearance, is the only self" (Parsley 2010, 31). There is no natural self or pure life, ontology or subjectivity lurking before or behind the mask, save for the collapse and ruin of the visage that the concept of nature sought to deny. The logic of inversion is the exchange of the mask for the face, the relay of the reality of artifice, and thus the *volte-face*, the about face begins as the tragicomedy of *Vendetta*, the appropriation of being as and to the mask that appears, pops up, comedically, comically, sketchily in protests across the globe. The theatricality of being, a play of many players precedes, embraces, and enfolds natural being as the artifice and apparatus of all human life. The first explosion is the destruction of Parliament, the end of representational politics, no more persons as parochial or representational modes of presencing, but rather an inaugural ending, a proleptic beginning in which the expropriation and distancing of the *demos* is viewed from a rooftop, from afar, so as to take back the theater of the political and embody it in the community, in the *physis* of *politeia*, in its appearances, their immediacy and affect.

The inaugural ruin of the political precedes the denunciation and demolition of Justitia, the fulmination and evaporation of the symbol of law and justice, both court and statue, monument and figure. The emphasis on this particular trajectory and progression is one of deepening and cohering the elision—the conflagration and conflation—of the metaphor of representation along with its juridical moment of personality, identity and right, in the fusion of mask and community and the indifferentiation of face and subject, being and body, *corpus* and *iuris*. The comedy of the mask is in *Vendetta* a pure theatricality, a layering that fuses a nonidentitarian subjectivity with the energy and force of the collectivity of flesh, being as being together. *Video et rideo* now has a curiously more direct and immediate meaning: there is appearance, the theater of mask and presence, of face and being, and it is a comedy, a theatrical undertaking, a comic and comical staging of the visages that make up a variable sociality and inconstant, mutable, and plural being. All is performance and the player is continuously smiling, ready to share, a witting part of the collective (see figure 11.8). To see is to perform, and to enact is to laugh, to put into play, to theatricalize, as, for example, when V declaims through tears his loss of faith and the transfer of his affections from Justice to Anarchy, from the abstraction of juridical safekeeping to the gay science of the body and affect of combustion: he bows, and leaves a heart shaped gift at the feet of Justitia and then farewell to the pretense of lawyers, *exeunt*, and in their place precious anarchy: "O Beauty, 'til now I never knew thee" (Moore and Lloyd 1989, 41).

V wonders why Justitia could never look him in the eye. Abstractions don't see. Hence the blindfold, that great mistake of legal history, the misunderstanding of a marker of sovereignty, a purple headband, a royal scarf, a *fascia* that had slipped down over the eyes, to be a sign of impartiality (Goodrich and Hayaert 2015, 16–17).[13] A comedic moment if ever there was, the tragedy of a lack of vision which faces its undoing in the very moment at which V dons his mask: "I'm a funny person, Evey . . . A very funny person indeed,"

Figure 11.8: *Veritas falsa*. From *V for Vendetta*. Alan Moore and David Lloyd 1989, 221. © DC Comics.

rideo, comedy, enactment as the player finally acknowledging their performance and then the prognostication, "you and me against the world. Ha, Ha, Ha! Melodrama, Evey! Isn't it strange how life turns into melodrama? . . . It's everything, Evey. The perfect entrance, the grand illusion. It's everything . . . And I'm going to bring the house down" (Moore and Lloyd 1989, 31). Here V takes up his mask to reclaim a forgotten drama, and moving through vaudeville proclaims in Shakespearean fashion "all the world's a stage," a play of shadows, a tenebrous reclamation in a cabinet of curiosities. The joke, the *jocus* in the *joco-seria*, is that Justice wears a mask.

V can be left at this point as clown, comedian, actor, and symbol of an emergent thought. It is rather the logic of inversion that needs expatiation. The blindfold which masks Justitia has been claimed in inverted and comedic form by the disguise, the *imago*, the nonguy of Guy Fawkes. This transition takes place in the Shadow Gallery, an inversion internal to the political system, against the law, and for the materiality of thought, housed in books (*doctis quæsita libellis*), enacted in music and dance, through the body and the flesh. The figure that represents the entirety of the legal system is inverted into the mask as a symbol of freedom, of value and beauty but nonetheless a figure, a shadow with its gallows humor, a leader of sorts who has to die so as not to lead but rather to give: "That is their task: to rule themselves; their lives, their love and land . . ." (Moore and Lloyd 1989, 245). At that moment V inverts in the sense that death transfers and upends, as Evey, the expansion and inheritor of V, takes up the mask and in never knowing V's face comes to know her own as the visage she puts on, a shared visage, the theatrical, social, resistance of the face. Beyond that, the inversions are manifold, one mask for another, of course, but rubble to blank canvas, ruin to creation, violence—the clamor of insurrection and the din of bombs—to self-determination, law to anarchy, V to Evey, even Finch discovers himself through the ambiguous act of killing and so immortalizing V.

Conclusion

Early in the graphic novel, not long after the demolition of the houses of Parliament and Evey's expostulation, "But that . . . that's against the *Law*" (1989, 14), V introduces his guest to his home, the Shadow Gallery. The sciographic concept is a crucially nebulous one. The shadow is outside the law and extant only as an image, as an ungovernable specter that accompanies and haunts. A face, a word, a sign, a flag that conceals and leads nothing and no one. The Shadow Gallery is precisely a collection of images, trophies in the old sense of architectural and also literary tropes, and most specifically, for V, the wisdom—*ingenio* or genius—of books and bibliophilia, of music and the desire to dance that Legendre dubbed the passion to become an other (Legendre 1976).[14] The shadow is irrefragably not present except as itself, as a tenebrous and changing, mutable, possibility. Thus V appears first as an image on stage marking the opening chapter, "The Villain," and then after his heavily draped encounter with Evey, we see him next on screen in the Eye, in the background, spectral, a looming presence, the mask as news item. His subsequent outing as villain and bogeyman occurs in darkness and the report is that the witness "just sort of caught something moving in the corner of my eye," a black shape. The witness continues: "and it had a face, only not a proper face, see? An it was *smiling*" (Moore and Lloyd 1989, 22). The improper face is impersonal, hidden, and so without identity. The only other sign is the etched or sketched V on the wall of the carriage, the enigma of V but also the encoding of a lexical item, a mark of difference within the alphabet, a sign in a dictionary.

The point is that there is a sense of an ending in the figure of rebirth. In the same spirit, the afterlife of the graphic novel is in the film. There is a certain reverse causality by which the movie moves and changes the novel.

It lives on and gains a second life as the emblem of a multitude of resistance movements, occupations, uprisings, art works, and installations. The comic becomes a *comédie humaine*, the enactment of the revolutionary plot, first time, in 1605, as failure, second time as the seizure of momentary powers, as the symbol of revolt and the making real of the theater of sociality. The *volte-face* or transitional about face of the mask, from killer to liberator, shadow to reality, is most extreme, most plural and pervasive in the film and the spectacular finale, the destruction of the Houses of Parliament. It is this last scene, the inversion of the narrative of the novel, that can provide a last emblem, an envoi in which the movie surpasses the script, inverts its order, so as to end with the opening of the space of politics to plurality and to the populace. The movie, in stricter terms, achieves what the novel argues for, namely *détournement*, the overturning of all established order, the graphic becoming metagraphic, a change of the plot, a flowering of themes and options made possible by the razing of the building, the architecture and architectonic of the established order and its political settlement. It would be strange indeed to argue that the film should follow the novel, that *graphos* should determine and rule *logos* and govern its figures and images, its sound and motion, its unwritten scope and forms. The impersonality of thought, the collectivity of the intellect deprives the author of the graphic novel of any claim to ownership or dictation of use. The film breaks free, it treats the novel as unfinished, it competes, disorders, unmakes. In a curious, which is to say paradoxical, conformity to the graphic narrative and plot, the movie moves on.

Notes

1. For a discussion of the impetus toward utopia, toward the betterment of the world, see Matthew J. A. Green's chapter in the present volume.

2. For more on the concept of heteroglossia in comics reading, see Paul Fisher Davies's chapter in the present volume.

3. On the history of the *imago*, see Dupont 1987; and more broadly on the reception of such rituals and images, see Giesey 1960; Duch 2016; and, for theoretical elaboration, see Marin 1984.

4. For a lucid introduction to such a theme see Hayaert 2019. In magnificent detail, see Hayaert 2008.

5. Jacob Cats 1618, n.p.: "*sciamus omnia æquè levia esse . . . introrsus pariter vana.*"

6. Note also the fine discussion of the technics of the mask in Connal Parsley 2010, 34: "Perfection and collapse, perfection and ruin: the ruin of law's traditions" in the conjunction of nature and mask, ontology and theatrics, person and performance.

7. This theme is well developed in Jacques Derrida 1995; and discussed acutely in Carolyn Steedman's *Dust* 2001.

8. The unfinished gains no mention, consistently enough, in the lengthy introductory essay in the 2016 reissue of *The Politics of Abolition Revisited* (London: Routledge, 2016). There is a comparable energy in Paul Feyerabend 1975, 20: "It is surprising to see how rarely the stultifying effect of the 'Laws of Reason' or of scientific practice are examined by professional anarchists. Professional anarchists oppose any kind of restriction and they demand that the individual be permitted to develop freely, unhampered by laws, duties, or obligations. And yet they swallow without protest all the severe standards which scientists and logicians impose upon research and upon any kind of knowledge-creating and knowledge-changing activity."

9. *Dispositor* is taken from Agamben's essay "What Is a Dispositor?" which is available at https://eclass.upatras.gr/modules/document/file.php/ARCH213/Agamben%20Dispositor.pdf. For further discussion of apparatuses, there is Agamben 2009. The starting point, however, is Louis Althusser on ideological state apparatuses, now available in Althusser 2014. In the context of film, and the close up as *dispositif*, see Noa Steimatsky 2017.

10. For more on the complex relations between the sovereign order and V, see Vladislav Maksimov's chapter in the current volume.

11. Appearing in Moore and Lloyd 1989 at the bottom of page 14 and then and alternately every 8 and 6 pages on; on screen on 112–13; as evidence on 121; glimpsed from the staircase, through bars on page 247. It is the emblematic constant inconstant.

12. See also Graeber 2002, 62: "The very notion of direct action, with its rejection of a politics which appeals to governments to modify their behaviour, in favour of physical intervention against state power in a form that itself prefigures an alternative—all of this emerges directly from the libertarian tradition."

13. For more discussion on the symbolism of Justitia and her blindfold, read in the context of *Daredevil*, see Timothy D. Peters's chapter in the present volume.

14. A brief extract of Legendre 1976 is translated in Goodrich 1996.

References

Agamben, Giorgio. 2009. *What Is an Apparatus? And Other Essays*. Translated by David Kishik and Steffan Pedatella. Stanford, CA: Stanford University Press.

Agamben, Giorgio. 2013. *The Highest Poverty: Monastic Rules and Form-of-Life*. Translated by Adam Kotsko. Stanford, CA: Stanford University Press.

Althusser, Louis. 2014. *On the Reproduction of Capitalism: Ideology and Ideological State Apparatuses*. Translated by G. M. Goshgarian. London: Verso.

Bachelard, Gaston. 1972. *The Psychoanalysis of Fire*. Translated by Alan C. M. Ross. Boston: Beacon Press.

Cats, Jacob. 1618. *Silenus Alcibiadis, sive Proteus, Vitæ Humanæ Ideam, Emblemate Trifariàm Variato, Oculis Subijciens*. Middleburg: Johnnis Hellenij.

Coccia, Emmanuel. 2006. "*Regula et Vita* : Il Diritto Monastico e la Regola Francescana." *Medioevo e Rinascimento* 20 (17): 97–147.

Combe, Thomas. 1610. *Theatre of Fine Devices*. London: Field.

Derrida, Jacques. 1994. *Specters of Marx: The State of the Debt, the Work of Mourning, and the New International*. Translated by Peggy Kamuf. London: Routledge.

Derrida, Jacques. 1995. "Archive Fever: A Freudian Impression." Translated by Eric Prenowitz. *Diacritics* 25 (2): 9–63.

Dickinson, Emily. 1924. *Complete Poems*. Boston: Little Brown.

Duch, Anna M. 2016. *The Royal Funerary and Burial Ceremonies of Medieval English Kings, 1216–1509*. PhD diss., University of York.

Dupont, Florence. 1987. "Les Morts et la mémoire : la masque funèbre." In *La Mort, les morts et l'au-delà dans le monde romain*, edited by Monique Dondin-Payre and Yann Le Boh, 167–72. Caen: Presses Universitaires de Caen.

Esposito, Roberto. 2015. *Two: The Machine of Political Theology and the Place of Thought*. Translated by Zakiya Hanafi. New York: Fordham University Press.

Feyerabend, Paul. 1975. *Against Method*. London: New Left Books.

Giesey, Ralph. 1960. *The Royal Funeral Ceremony in Renaissance France*. Geneva: Droz.

Goodrich, Peter, ed. 1996. *Law and the Unconscious: A Legendre Reader*. London: Macmillan.

Goodrich, Peter. 2012. "The Theatre of Emblems: On the Optical Apparatus and the Investiture of Persons." *Law, Culture and the Humanities* 8 (1): 47–67.

Goodrich, Peter, and Valérie Hayaert. 2015. *Genealogies of Legal Vision*. London: Routledge.

Graeber, David. 2004. *Fragments of an Anarchist Anthropology*. Chicago: Prickly Paradigm.

Graeber, David. 2002. "The New Anarchists." *New Left Review* 13: 61–73.

Hayaert, Valérie. 2008. *Mens Emblematica et humanisme juridique: le cas du* pegma cum narrationibus philosophicis *de Pierre Coustau (1555)*. Geneva: Droz.

Hayaert, Valérie. 2019. "Emblems." In *The Oxford Handbook of Law and Humanities*, edited by Simon Stern et al. Oxford: Oxford University Press.

Herring, Francis. 1641. *Mischeefes Mysterie: Or, Treasons Master-Peece, the Powder-Plot*. London: Hartford.

Legendre, Pierre. 1976. *La Passion d'être un autre*. Paris: Seuil.

Marin, Louis. 1984. *Portrait of the King*. London: Macmillan.

Mathieson, Thomas. 1974. *The Politics of Abolition*. London: Martin Robertson.

McTeigue, James, dir. 2005. *V for Vendetta*. Warner Brothers.

Moore, Alan, and David Lloyd. 1989. *V for Vendetta*. New York: DC Comics.

Parsley, Connal. 2010. "The Mask and Agamben: The Transitional Juridical Technics of Legal Relation." *Law Text Culture* 14: 12–39.

Pynchon, Thomas. 1963. *V.* New York: Lippincott.

Perrière, Guillaume. 1540. *Le Thëatre des bons engins*. Toulouse: Janot.

Schoonhove, Florentine. 1618. *Emblemata. Partim Moralia, Partim Civilia*. Goudae: Burier.

Steedman, Carolyn. 2001. *Dust*. Manchester: Manchester University Press.

Steimatsky, Noa. 2017. *The Face on Film*. New York: Oxford University Press.

12

"So You *Still* Believe in the *Future?*"

Socialist Utopianism and Marxist Critique in
The Red Virgin and the Vision of Utopia

MATTHEW J. A. GREEN

Perhaps indeed we need to develop an anxiety about losing the future which is analogous to Orwell's anxiety about the loss of the past and of memory and childhood. This would be a fear that locates the loss of the future and futuricity, of historicity itself, within the existential dimension of time and indeed within ourselves.

—FREDERIC JAMESON 2007

The third in a trilogy of graphic novels written by Mary Talbot and illustrated by her husband Bryan Talbot, *The Red Virgin and the Vision of Utopia* (2016) explores the intersection of violence, law, and gender, explicitly identifying feminist struggle with revolutionary politics and utopianism. Moreover, through its celebration of "the utopian urge in nineteenth-century literature and politics" (Talbot and Talbot 2016, back cover), *Red Virgin* allows an unprecedented opportunity to explore what can be called the *expository function* of graphic narrative. Drawing on a Marxist tradition of critique embodied in the contemporary philosophical interventions of Frederic Jameson and Slavoj Žižek the current chapter will not only explore the political commitments of this graphic novel, but also provide the first ever exploration of the continuity between Mary Talbot's writing for comics and her academic work in the field of language and gender. Reading the Talbots' work in this way suggests a hitherto untapped direction in critical comics studies, moving away from the sharp division between academic analysis and creative production. The use of critical theory can help to hone the political edge of semiotic analyses which on their own can tend toward abstraction and rigid formalism. Similarly, a philosophically astute and politically self-reflexive investigation of the interrelationship between comics and their contexts helps to foreground the political salience of such historical work. However, while both of these scholarly processes are useful in their own right, each maintains a distinction between the comic or graphic novel as an object of study and the theoretical or methodological apparatuses used to dissect it.

This chapter will suggest that critical comics studies should not only include the critical study of comics but also the study of *critical* comics, i.e., creative texts that perform a scholarly function informed by a larger tradition of critique. While such a claim might appear less controversial in the case of nonfiction or overtly expository comics, the Talbots' work allows for the exploration of a less obvious example by suggesting ways in which graphic novelists can embed an expository function within a larger narrative framework. Beyond yielding insight into *Red Virgin*'s sociopolitical dimensions, therefore, the discussion below will also describe ways in which arguments originating in academic work can be developed and refined through the medium of comics. Such an approach enriches our understanding of the way *Red Virgin* uses a combination of fiction and nonfiction, as well as of text and image, to provide a nuanced contribution to debates concerning utopianism and revolutionary politics within the fields of critical theory and political philosophy.

Red Virgin tells three stories. The main narrative details the life of Louise Michel, a key figure in the Paris Commune, a supporter of anticolonial struggles in Algeria and New Caledonia, as well as a prominent lecturer and writer. This story is embedded within a frame narrative that identifies the narrator of Michel's tale as a young Parisian, Monique, whose mother, Élianne, fought alongside Michel. Monique relates Michel's biography to Charlotte Perkins Gilman, the American writer and lecturer, who arrives in Paris on the day of Michel's funeral procession. Bookending both narratives is an additional frame narrative, which depicts Franz Reichelt designing and testing a wearable parachute after witnessing Louis Blériot's successful flight across the English Channel in 1909. Combined with *Red Virgin*'s particular deployment of elements such as closure and braiding, discussed below, the interweaving of these stories and the distinct ways in which its narrative levels interrelate provide the structural mechanisms for the Talbots to pursue a socialist defense of utopianism within a graphic novel that demonstrates the capacity of comics to contribute to critical debate. It is worth noting in passing that *Red Virgin* engages in a knowing and insightful way with the field of utopian studies and further investigations of that aspect of its scholarly interventions would no doubt prove profitable; however, the focus of the current chapter, in keeping with the theoretical commitments of this collection of essays, rests on the related—but distinct—relationship between what Jameson terms the "utopian impulse" and the broader politics of empowerment undertaken by the Talbots.

The Talbots have consistently asserted the sociopolitical role of art and literature. In her first academic monograph, *Fictions at Work*, drawing on Edward Said, Michel Foucault, and Norman Fairclough, Mary Talbot analyzed the way in which certain types of fiction "denaturalize, contest or in some way put up a resistance to dominant discourses, the subject positions they offer, and the ideologies embodied in them" (1995, 145). *Red Virgin* continues this work, both in terms of its engagement with the emancipatory potential of science fiction, which occupies the final chapter of *Fictions*, and as it engages in "the rediscovery of women's writing" (Talbot 1995, 151) through extensive discussions of, and quotations from, Michel's own writing. Moreover, *Red Virgin* performs another form of rediscovery, providing a historical overview of the literary utopia and demonstrating the relevance of this genre to feminism. *Red Virgin* thus seeks both to mobilize the political potential Talbot attributes to fiction and to develop the theoretical claims staked by her academic work.

Bryan Talbot's previous comics work, which emerged from the UK underground comix scene, similarly articulates a socialist position that incorporates elements of cultural critique. While his engagement with feminism may be less overt than Mary Talbot's, his deployment of strong female characters and frank representations of sexuality in the Luther Arkwright graphic novels (collected in Talbot 2014) suggest that these texts can be considered as feminist science fiction. While these texts do not share the same expository function as *Red Virgin*, both *The Adventures of Luther Arkwright* and *Heart of Empire: The Legacy of Luther Arkwright* are woven of a dense network of literary and visual allusions that demonstrates a critical engagement with source material. *Alice in Sunderland*, moreover, does include an expository strand throughout, engaging in an archaeological project that unearths aspects of Lewis Carroll's biography that have been largely effaced (Bryan Talbot 2007). This archaeological project necessarily involves a revisionary stance, which is incorporated within a much larger political project. As I have argued previously, "*Sunderland* recoups the political force embodied in the Menippean tradition . . . by seeking to wrest British history and the Union Jack from the allegedly populist discourse of the far right" (Green 2015, 123).

Whereas *Sunderland*'s focus on the working class demonstrates a clear commitment to socialist principles, *The Tale of One Bad Rat* (Bryan Talbot 2010a), dedicated to Mary, engages in a process of consciousness raising clearly situated within a larger feminist politics. The following excerpts from "Rat's Tail," an essay appended to the trade paperback editions, both explain the political motivation of the graphic novel and undertake to inform readers:

> It's been estimated that one in three girls will be molested before they're eighteen. Approximately 90 percent of that abuse is committed, not by the stereotypical stranger . . . , but by a close, male relative. And less than one in twenty of reported offenders are prosecuted.
>
> . . . [B]ecause the media largely ignores it, this abuse can still go on unhindered. It works in a conspiracy of silence.
>
> The more child abuse is discussed . . . in whatever medium, the more likely it is that the victims will realise that it is something that happens all the time, that they can speak out, be believed, and get it stopped. (Talbot 2010b, 125–27)

Prior to Mary Talbot's emergence as a comics writer, *Bad Rat* demonstrates a cross-fertilization between comics and feminist scholarship running between herself and Bryan Talbot. Indeed, if her presence can be felt in the feminism of his previous work and in the scholarly apparatus that supports the expository dimension of *Sunderland*, so too his influence can be perceived in aspects of her scholarship. The most visible, though not the only, example is in the appearance of the rat from *Bad Rat* in *Fictions*, where he peers up inquisitively at a block of Mary's text discussing the representation of rats in James Herbert's *Lair* (Talbot 1995, 132). At issue both in Mary Talbot's reading of *Lair* and in the secondary subject of exposition in *Bad Rat* (the prejudice against rats in western culture) are the cultural presuppositions that transform creatures that "are small furry animals" with "attractive characteristics" into vermin (Talbot 1995, 136). In the passage she analyses from *Lair*, Talbot notes that the rats stand for otherness in general and, specifically, occupy the position of the "cowardly 'Injun' horde" in the traditional Western (Talbot 1995, 135). In *Bad Rat*, meanwhile, the protagonist identifies her sense of social isolation and misrepresentation with the cultural misunderstandings circulating around her pet rat (Talbot 2010a, 4, 35–37, 62–63, 90, 106).

Red Virgin approaches the concept of utopia in much the same way as *Bad Rat* and *Fictions* approach the figure of the rat, which is apt given that today's anti-utopians construct the latter in much the same way as Herbert's novel presents its rats, i.e., "as the ultimate evil" (Mary Talbot 1995, 136). Evil in both cases is equated with the enactment of violence on innocent human bodies: Herbert's mutant rats gorge themselves on human flesh while for John Gray, the most prominent anti-utopian of our moment, "the hope of Utopia spilt blood on a scale that traditional creeds cannot match, and the world is well rid of it" (2008, 295). Significantly, even as it recounts the life of a self-proclaimed anarchist (Michel), the defense of utopianism within *Red Virgin* grounds itself in the socialist politics underpinning not only Bryan Talbot's work in comics, but also Mary Talbot's academic work. For example, *Language and Gender: An Introduction* (1998) combines a social constructionist approach to gender with Critical Discourse Analysis, a sociolinguistic methodology that can be traced back to Karl Marx (Fairclough and Graham 2002). Significantly, Mary Talbot here attributes a formative position to capitalism, with the construction of gender identities "determined by capitalist social conditions and constructed in capitalist social relations" (Talbot 1998, 171). Whereas *Language and Gender* presents socialism and feminism as inextricably linked, the *Red Virgin* initially appears to subsume the former within the latter, presenting the emancipation of women as the hegemonizing signifier capable of uniting socialists and anarchists:

MONIQUE: But she was an *anarchist* and—
GILMAN:—AND I'm an *American socialist?* Both *feminists*, though! Both—*hmhm!—changin'* the *world!* (Talbot and Talbot 2016, 9, emphases in original)

It is, however, important to recognize the polyvocality at work here, for Gilman's comments in the frame-narrative run counter to the politics of the embedded narrative, in which what we might call feminist utopianism becomes inextricably tied to revolutionary socialism, a conjunction which subsequently emerges in Gilman's later comments on the utopianism of socialists like Wells and Bellamy and in the accompanying footnotes.

This link is made most powerfully, however, via the representation of fellow Communard, Paule Minck, whose speeches, stressing the need for nationalization and the abolition of private ownership, are used to represent the political voice of women during the Commune (Talbot and Talbot 2016, 48). In contrast, representations of Michel's revolutionary commitment emphasize a general emancipatory position rather than a specifically anarchist politics: "The *great day* has *arrived*, the *decisive* day for either the *emancipation* or the *enslavement* of the *proletariat*" (52, emphases in original).

In terms of the political argument underpinning *Red Virgin*, the representation of Minck's relationship with Michel is triply significant. Firstly, their depiction together on page 40, amidst the revolutionary crowd, represents both women as more militarily astute and more willing to enact preemptive violence than their male counterparts who are concerned about establishing democratic legitimacy for themselves: "Louise is *right!* If we don't strike now, they'll come back to *kill us all!*" (Talbot and Talbot 2016, 40, emphases in original). Secondly, on page 42, their dialogue contrasts the futility of trusting in elected men with the practical aspects of liberation: opening schools, providing clothing and childcare, as well as organizing food distribution. Finally, the decision to focus on Minck rather than André Léo, another of the female Communards, adds further insight into *Red Virgin*'s celebration of the utopian. As Eichner notes, Minck's political legacy became far more closely aligned with revolutionary Marxism after the Commune:

> Within a year, Minck radically altered her ideological stance, rejecting the idea that socialism would best be attained through a gradual, non-authoritarian approach. Instead, she advocated a centrally planned, radical, violent revolution. . . . Léo, in sharp contrast, remained firmly committed to moderate, collectivist socialism. (2003, 76)

The defense of utopianism can thus be situated within a Marxist politics that underpins not only the Talbots' previous creative and scholarly work, but also identifies utopian violence as a necessary aspect of socialist resistance, a position that similarly emerges in the cultural critiques undertaken by Žižek and Jameson.

While it is essential not to elide the work of the Talbots with that of Jameson or Žižek (Mary Talbot's academic work suggests a closer affinity to the former), they share a common goal of recuperating utopianism and an attention to its role in resisting symbolic and systematic violence. For Žižek, subjective violence denotes "violence enacted by social agents, evil individuals, disciplined repressive apparatuses, fanatical crowds" (2008b, 10), while objective violence refers to the socioeconomic backdrop against which this enactment occurs: "Social symbolic violence at its purest appears . . . as the spontaneity of the milieu in which we dwell, of the air we breathe" (2008b, 31). Žižek's work allows for an understanding of emancipatory violence that identifies genuinely disruptive critique at the level of theory with historical revolutionaries associated with armed struggle and state terror; however, he insists that the defining characteristic of emancipatory violence is the disruption of the status quo rather than simply killing one's enemies: "If one means by violence a radical upheaval of the basic social relations, then . . . the problem with historical monsters who slaughtered millions was that they were not violent enough" (2008b, 183). Žižek's argument that not voting is "a true political *act*" and his rigid insistence on the dichotomization of gender (2008b, 30, 183) are contrary to the spirit of the Talbots' work (see especially Talbot, Charlesworth, and Talbot 2014; Mary Talbot and Alwyn Talbot 2014). Nevertheless, his conceptualization of revolutionary violence as that which disrupts the objective violence structuring social life yields insight into precisely what sort of utopian vision *Red Virgin* defends. In contrast to the type of utopia caricatured at length by anti-utopians, "the utopia of a perfected harmonious social order without antagonisms" (Žižek 2008a, 310), Žižek advocates understanding "utopia in the more radical sense of enacting what, *within the framework of the existing social relations*, appears as 'impossible'" (Žižek 2008a, 310, emphasis in original). *Red Virgin* undertakes an extensive meditation on the conceptualization of utopia as a process of expanding the limits of the possible within a given sociopolitical context as opposed to the absolute eradication of antagonism; however, before exploring this aspect of the Talbots' work in more detail, it is necessary to approach this notion of disruption, and its relationship to traditional articulations of the utopian impulse, from another direction.

Jameson's analysis of utopia suggests a deeper problem for the defense of utopianism than a moral rejection of violence, revealing that all modes of utopia rely upon the same "formal necessity of Utopian closure" (2007, 205), a fact which complicates attempts to realize the utopian dream within history: "closure is initially motivated by secession and the preservation of radical difference (as well as the fear of contamination from the outside and from the past or history)"; in earlier utopias, closure is enacted spatially while with the emergence of "capitalism and historicity, this imaginary no-place migrates from the south seas or the north or south pole to the future" (Jameson 2007, 203–4). Indeed, it is precisely this paradox, that the perfect society requires an absolute secession warranted by extreme violence, which motivates the plots of Iain M. Banks's Culture novels. Moreover, this same limiting function is performed by the Parisian barricades depicted in *Red Virgin*, improvised ramparts that seek to draw a line between the commune and the troops sent to retake the city on behalf of the Versailles government (Talbot and Talbot 2016, 53–5). Jameson's work undercuts in advance the claim made by Gray that utopianism has moved from being "a movement of withdrawal from the world" into "an attempt to remake the world by force"

(2008, 21). At the moment utopia breaches the boundaries of the historical world seeking ingress, it ceases to be utopian as such, a fact which both fails to preserve utopia from contamination by the excessive violence of revolutionary terror (for it is violence alone that maintains this ontological gap) and appears to undermine any sense of its political efficacy. Nevertheless, Jameson appears to solve this problem by reconceptualizing utopia not in opposition to the disruptive violence of closure but in fact as its originary eruption:

> The formal flaw—how to articulate the Utopian break in such a way that it is transformed into a practical-political transition—now becomes a rhetorical and political strength—in that it forces us precisely to concentrate on the break itself: a meditation on the impossible, on the unrealizable in its own right. (2007, 232)

Jameson diagnoses the loss of alternative visions for the future, expressed most often in the self-proclaimed realist's belief that capitalism is the only game in town, as a political problem affecting our own period for which the conceptualization of utopia as disruption offers the solution: "Utopia thus now better expresses our relationship to a genuinely political future than any current program of action, where we are for the moment only at the stage of massive protests and demonstrations, without any conception of how a globalized transformation might then proceed" (232). And yet, there remains something deeply unsatisfying in the concomitant valorization of utopia as instilling a state of expectancy: "a rattling of the bars and an intense spiritual concentration and preparation for another stage which has not yet arrived" (2007, 233).

Red Virgin confronts this problem directly by placing this view of utopia as a process of disruption in a larger literary and historical context stretching back at least to the latter half of the nineteenth century. En route to New Caledonia aboard the transport ship, *Virginie*, Michel reflects on the defeat of the Commune in conversation with Natalie, a fellow communard:

> MICHEL: *Where* did we go wrong, Natalie?
>   We need to *learn*, so we do it right *next* time.
> NATALIE: Next time?
> MICHEL: Yes. But *how* to *awaken* people?
> NATALIE: *Where* we're going, who knows? (69, emphases in original)

As it turns out, Michel does find a way to foster revolutionary acts in the prison colony, welcoming transportees from Algiers as comrades and supporting the rebellion of the indigenous tribes. Moreover, detailing these successive struggles allows *Red Virgin* to expand its emancipatory politics to include anti-imperialism. The graphic novel thus extends what Jameson terms a "new discursive strategy" (231) well beyond our own historical moment, drawing on an analysis of the utopian tradition which parallels that undertaken in the first part of *Archaeologies*. Moreover, the form of the graphic novel is used to explore two different modes of closure, that of the comics form and of the embedded narrative, which demonstrate the ways in which disjunction serves to generate meanings that themselves hold out an emancipatory promise. Finally, *Red Virgin*, in both of its frame narratives, in its embedded narrative and in its epigraphs, explores the importance of failure and reinforces the sense that utopia is best understood as a liminal space. Indeed, the quotations from Oscar Wilde and Samuel Beckett included in the epigraphs serve as an additional frame, informing our own understanding of utopia as we enter the text.

The epigraphs to the graphic novel, which precede the dedication, provide the first sustained engagement with utopia, opening with a definition of the term as "A place of ideal perfection especially in laws, government and social conditions" (1), before immediately deconstructing this meaning through the two subsequent quotations. The first, "A map of the world that does not include Utopia is not even worth glancing at" (1), is taken from Wilde's *The Soul of Man under Socialism* and the endnotes provide the subsequent two and a half sentences from the source text:

> for it leaves out the one country at which Humanity is always landing. And when Humanity lands there, it looks out, and, seeing a better country, sets sail. Progress is the realisation of Utopias. (Talbot and Talbot 2016, 122, quoting Wilde [1891] 2009, 27)

This quotation unravels the hegemonizing clarity and certitude of the opening definition as Wilde's indelible irony presents utopia as a provisional place, not one island but an apparently endless archipelago. Moreover, the closure separating utopia from the present world is both a barrier and a mode of communication. In the very movement of sequestering itself, the utopian space opens up to its own radical alterity that is, in this case, the imperfect world we inhabit. As we will see, this movement which is simultaneously a withdrawal and an intervention replicates the functioning of closure within comics as evidenced by the formal characteristics of *Red Virgin*.

Rethinking Closure and Revaluing Failure

In its reclamation of the utopian impulse, *Red Virgin* asserts the value of failure and imperfection as originary elements in the construction of utopia and it does so by triangulating three distinct senses of closure: within comics, within narrative, and within utopianism. Failure first emerges as a theme in the Talbots' third epigraph:

> "Ever tried. Ever failed. No matter. Try again. Fail again. Fail better."
> Samuel Beckett (Talbot and Talbot 2016, 1, quoting Beckett 2009, 81)

Taken from *Worstward Ho!* this quotation supplements the preceding epigraphs on utopia with the sense of an unwavering commitment to a project bedeviled by repeated failures. Far from bearing a tangential relation to the plot and politics of *Red Virgin*, this dogged determination that defies rationality, a single-mindedness that transforms the human subject into something monstrous or bestial, is central to the Talbots' representation of Michel. Consider, for example, their depiction of an argument she has with her mother, Marianne, upon returning from exile:

> MARIANNE: *Really!* All these *lectures!* All these *ridiculous* public appearances! You've become their pet exotic *animal* on the end of a leash, and they're making you *dance* to amuse the *crowds!*
> MICHEL: That's *right!* I'll go and I'll *dance* and they'll pour money into my hand and then some of the hungry will have a meal.
> MARIANNE: And all these *prison stretches! Louise! What* am I to think of you?
> MICHEL: I *love* it in there! *That's* the only time I get any *peace!* I have to catch up on my *writing* some time! (Talbot and Talbot 2016, 109, emphases in original)

The dialogue details the seemingly absurd nature of Michel's utopianism, which transforms her into a dancing animal whose entertainment value diverts the revolutionary energy she attempts to channel. Michel's situation here is identical with the utopian dreamer of our own day, whose revolutionary position is co-opted in advance by the neoliberal hegemony; her response develops what we might call a dialectic of failure, embracing the latent potential within each demarcation of disaster. The images and page layout add an additional layer of irony that reframes her mother's petty-bourgeois definitions of success as a more fundamental mode of imprisonment, itself symbolized by the comfortable domestic space she inhabits. Across the three horizontal panels on page 109 (figure 12.1), Marianne Michel stands with her back to the window, not only turned away from the light but also oblivious to the window grilles that are here reminiscent of prison bars. The message is clear: Louise Michel's refusal to give up, her Beckettian insistence on trying again and again to the point of absurdity, is directly contrasted with Marianne Michel's acceptance of the status quo.

Beyond its applicability to Michel's own biography and political development, the quotation from *Worstward Ho!* further positions *Red Virgin* in the context of contemporary debates over the value of utopia for current political thought. Very specifically, this epigraph aligns *Red Virgin* with Žižek's *In Defense of Lost Causes*, a book that returns repeatedly to this very quotation: "To paraphrase Beckett's memorable phrase, to which I shall return many times later, after one fails, one can go on and fail better" (2008a, 7). The willingness to risk failure before the event and to embrace it afterward becomes, for Žižek, the very condition of the revolutionary act and he insists that the Beckettian attitude holds more relevance today than ever before:

> The situation is "completely hopeless," with no clear "realistic" revolutionary perspective; but does this not give us a kind of strange freedom, a freedom to experiment? . . . [T]here is always a space to be created for an act—precisely because . . . it is not enough to wait patiently for the "right moment" of the revolution. If one merely waits for it, it will never come, for one has to start with "premature" attempts which . . . in their very failure to achieve their professed goal create the (subjective) conditions for the "right" moment. (2008a, 361, emphases in original)

In a similar vein, *Red Virgin* represents at length Louise's delight in experimentation and her refusal to relinquish the future—most notably in the repeated use of celebratory dialogue and gestures throughout the depiction of her visit to the Universal Exposition of 1889—and it alludes to the concept of the "premature" revolution in its depiction of the Bloody Sunday massacre, which precipitated the first Russian Revolution and occurred on the same day as Louise's funeral, January 22, 1905 (Talbot and Talbot 2016, 116).

The intersection of politics, futurity, and death is explored textually in "The Red Carnations," a poem Michel wrote in Satory prison and which the Talbots quote during two panels depicting Louise's voyage to New Caledonia.

Figure 12.1: From *The Red Virgin and the Vision of Utopia*, 2016, 109. © Mary Talbot and Brian Talbot.

In the first, we see Louise reading aloud: "If I go to the black cemetery, brothers, throw on to your sister, as a final hope, some red carnations in bloom" (71). The final three stanzas are presented in the first panel of the next page, placed within individual caption boxes overtop a scene of the *Virginie* sailing through a storm:

> In the last days of Empire,
> When the people were awakening,
> It was your smile, red carnation,
> That told us all was being reborn.
>
> Today, go blossom in the shadow
> Of black and sad prisons,
> Go bloom by the sombre captive
> And tell him that we love him.
>
> Tell him that through fleeting time,
> Everything belongs to the future,
> That the livid browed conqueror,
> Can die more surely than the conquered. (Michel, as quoted in Talbot and Talbot 2016, 72)

Bryan Talbot's depiction of the funeral procession makes clear that, as per her poem's injunction, Michel's coffin was surrounded by red carnations, and indeed the red flower—either individually or in bunches—provides the most overt example of an iconic motif (Groensteen 2007, 127) throughout the graphic novel. Excluding the endpapers and back cover, the red carnation first appears under the epigraphs and then reappears on pages 3, 78, 106, 107, and 115, where it is used to symbolize both utopian hope and death. Using the image of the carnation in this manner is particularly appropriate as here a symbol of futuricity is used in a technique, braiding, which disrupts the chronological unfolding of story time by participating in the logic of the "series" rather than the "sequence" (Groensteen 2007, 123).

Thierry Groensteen notes that because comics panels are arranged in a network of both linear and nonlinear relations the comics system requires a mechanism for making connections across multiple pages; "braiding" is the name he gives to "the operation that . . . programs and carries out this sort of bridging" (2007, 122). In its ability to leap over the intervening panels and so to facilitate the construction of meanings outside of the linear narrative, braiding can be seen as an unexpected agent of what Scott McCloud calls "closure," the process by which the reader makes connections between successive sequential panels:

> Comics panels fracture both time and space, offering a jagged, staccato rhythm of unconnected moments.
> But closure allows us to *connect* these moments and *mentally construct* a *continuous, unified reality*. (1993, 67, emphases in original)

Just as closure names the process by which readers imagine the connection between two panels, side by side, so too braiding prompts the attentive reader to make connections between panels separated by a greater distance. Groensteen retains the French "ellipse" to describe McCloud's "closure" (2007, 147), reserving "closure" to refer to the framing action of the panel borders, and this suggests precisely the link with braiding that I am proposing, though Groensteen himself does not go so far. For our purposes, however, retaining the term "closure" allows us to triangulate three different processes which, at least initially, can appear completely distinct: comics-specific processes (navigating panel-to-panel transitions as well as braiding), the resolution in narrative fiction, and the divisive break required by utopia. In all of these cases, the break or rupture can be transformed into a medium of communication (it is significant that for Groensteen, the silence between panels "has nothing to introduce, no gap to suture" [2007, 97]), at which point the specter of a totalizing discourse (re)emerges. The preservation of an ongoing rupturing effect is essential to counter what Groensteen calls "the imperialism of braiding" (2007, 130) and by extension the hegemonic imperatives of all modes of closure within the comics medium. While it is tempting to identify readers, in their capacity as cocreators of meaning, as potential sites of this disruption, it is important to recognize that readers can participate in constructing meaning from juxtaposed panels only if they have been initiated—or, more accurately, interpellated—into the comics system.

In this respect, the system of comics functions in the same way as the utopian system in its most terroristic dimension: "It is this seamless closure of the new system that renders it alien and existentially threatening, and which clothes the radically New in the lineaments of sublime terror before which we necessarily pause and hesitate, or draw back" (Jameson 2007, 202). Initially surprising, this link between semiotics and utopianism makes sense given that closure is not only the process that violently inaugurates utopia, but it also participates in the symbolic violence that we can see "embodied in language and its forms" and that "pertains . . . to its imposition of a certain universe of meaning" (Žižek 2008b, 1). In the study of narrative, too, as Mary Talbot has noted in her academic work, closure performs a political function that extends beyond the fictional world:

> Fictional resolutions become narrative formulae, narrative paradigms that transmit a message on their own and strongly influence people's expectations in and outside of fiction. The contradictions that are "solved" are real world phenomena. Fiction and reality are not as clearly distinguishable as we might like to think. (Talbot 1995, 8)

Jameson too devotes considerable attention to ideology and closure in narrative form (1983, see especially 33–34, 37, 98, 140, 153, 194–270). For our purposes, however, we can rely on one particular type of closure as summarized by Mary Talbot: "One way ideology enters narrative is through the provision of the satisfactory sense of closure that comes in the way the sequence of events making up the narrative is rounded off" (1995, 8). The idea that closure across sequential panels in comics often aims at the same sort of resolution as closure in narrative is obvious, but so too the process of creating coherence across a braided series can become ideological, suggesting that the very form of *Red Virgin* could demand a totalizing process analogous to the sort of imposition its account of revolutionary emancipation seeks to resist. Nevertheless, if Jameson is correct that "the effectively ideological is also, at the same time, necessarily Utopian" (1983, 276), then it may be possible to anticipate a genuinely emancipatory disruption at the level of artistic form. Specifically, we can ask ourselves whether it is possible for comics—and specifically for *Red Virgin*—to use the mechanisms that seek to enact closure as a means to disrupt readerly expectations to such an extent that the very act of making sense of the narrative leads readers into twin processes of critique and criticism.

Although intelligibility requires that any signifying system allow at least a minimum degree of closure, the medium of comics offers its own peculiar opportunities for resistance. *Red Virgin* realizes this potential in its representations of utopia as a space that fosters a revolutionary politics precisely because it is staged as a transitionary place (i.e., as Wilde suggests, our landing as readers is always temporary). The graphic novel's representation of Michel's arrival in New Caledonia exemplifies a use of closure that destabilizes both the sequence of the narrative and the series of the braid. The two panels on page 77 (figure 12.2) offer the initial view of the colony, with the top panel more or less equivalent to Michel's perspective (the vantage point is behind and slightly to the right of her) while the bottom provides a view of the ship approaching the landing. The work of closure between these panels involves not only a shift in perspective, from inside to outside the ship, but also a change in direction—the bottom panel depicts a different view of the coastline, one in which the pristine landscape has been polluted by smoke rising from indistinct habitation and intruded upon by the pier extending into the bay. The bottom image thus establishes a relationship of contrariety with the two captions at the top of panel 1: "Then one day what she saw through the gunport was a tropical paradise. / A *Utopian vision . . .*" (77, ellipsis in original). There is a further disjunction opened up by these captions, however, as, belonging to Monique, these words represent a shift from the story world to the frame narrative, which has been absent for ten pages. A final rupture is opened by the third caption on the panel—"New Caledonia. December 10th, 1873."—which provides information from an omniscient narrator speaking from a space beyond the embedded narrative *and* both frame narratives, from, perhaps, the extradiegetic space depicted on page 78, whose single borderless panel depicts a red carnation surrounded by ink splatter such that the flower appears thrown into the white void that surrounds it.

Indeed, the transition effected by the page turn from page 77 to 78 punctuates the narrative with a rupture to narrative time and space. The closure required by the braiding here effectively circumscribes the vision of utopia on the preceding page with a motif, the carnation, that not only recalls the intersection of death and utopian hope throughout the text, but which closely echoes the bunch of carnations depicted with the same coloring, ink splatter, and suggestion of downward trajectory beneath the epigraphs on page 1. The braiding series here resists totalization precisely because the carnation embodies such contradictory impulses—the black void of death coupled with the life-affirming fullness of utopianism.

In fact, though, the utopian vision depicted in *Red Virgin* is structured around the very antagonisms and disjunctures that traditional utopias purportedly resolve. The account of Michel's arrival in New Caledonia resumes on page 90 (figure 12.3), following several different narratives each of which involves a significant chronological disruption, moving from frame narrative to the 1889 Expo to the biography of the young Michel and back to the frame narrative. The resumption of the New Caledonia story line on page 90 reaffirms the contrariety embodied in the symbol of the carnation as the utopian vision from the top panel of page 77 is replaced by the image of a

Figure 12.2: From *The Red Virgin and the Vision of Utopia*, 2016, 77. © Mary Talbot and Brian Talbot.

naked and emaciated child. Though separated by twelve pages, the comparison of these images is suggested on a structural level by the use of the same page layout on both pages—two horizontal panels with the top slightly larger—and by the caption continuing the dialogue from the frame narrative. Here Monique both resumes and refutes the words attributed to her on our first sight of New Caledonia: "Paradise? / That's what she *thought* she saw through the gunport . . ." (89–90). The bottom panel shows us the child from behind as s/he meets Michel, here depicted having just left the boat that ferried her from the *Virginie*. Michel faces us with an expression of dismay, but the red pom-poms on the hats worn by the sailors suggest a glimmer of revolutionary hope (their color and shape are evocative of the carnation). This suggests that pages 77 and 90 do not negate each other, but neither do they stand in a dialectical relation leading to a Hegelian sublimation. Rather, the utopian impulse is itself embodied in the malnourished frame of the child, not as a latent promise to be realized but rather as the sign of work to be done. The subsequent panels depict Michel's unwavering faith in the struggle for egalitarian justice, both for the colonists and for the indigenous people, a fight that will be undertaken both in the improvised classroom of her hut and in the anti-imperial violence of insurrection. Thus, page 101 depicts Michel's symbolic gift of her red scarf from the Commune, which she divides between two Kanakas, who wear the pieces as headbands as they go to war. Even as the Rousseauian vision of a natural utopia represented on page 71 is withdrawn, the reality beneath this ideological curtain is not *anti*-utopian, but *alter*-utopian; the foreclosure of a romanticized utopian space opens the way for an alternative and spectral utopian movement in which the boundaries of capitalist colonialism are repeatedly tested. On a narrative level, then, the manifestation of utopia-as-disruption echoes the uses of braiding and closure within the graphic novel's structure, which simultaneously support and undermine the comics system's generation of meaning through totalization.

A similarly disruptive use of narrative closure is enacted via the frame narratives. The frame in which the narration of Michel's story occurs provides an education in the dialogic dimension of the utopian text. Much could be said on this topic, but for our purposes it is sufficient to note that this frame narrative—and its accompanying endnotes—demonstrate the way in which the anti-utopian negative is incorporated within the utopian. Specifically, and in keeping with its presentation of utopia as a movement through time rather than a location in space, the frame narrative addresses directly the contingency of every utopian vision. For example, *Red Virgin* stages a

Figure 12.3: From *The Red Virgin and the Vision of Utopia*, 2016, 90. © Mary Talbot and Brian Talbot.

feminist critique of H. G. Wells's, via Gilman's identification of the utopian impulse within Michel's emancipatory ambitions: "This is all *fascinating*," she tells Monique; "I would have dearly liked to talk over *Mr. Wells'* new book with her" (Talbot and Talbot 2016, 44, emphases in original). What ensues is one of several instances where *Red Virgin* foregrounds the interconnection between science fiction, natural science, and social science:

MONIQUE: Is it another one of his *scientific romances?*
CHARLOTTE: More of his dubious *social engineering* I would say!
    Dogs and timid women, indeed!
MONIQUE: Pardon?
CHARLOTTE: Oh, the way he writes about *women* makes my *blood boil*
    ... [H]e's a fine writer ... but his *male* perspective stunts his *vision*.
    ... [W]ith his *scientific* habit of mind, it's *unworthy* of him. (44, emphases in original).

The historical basis for this fictional dialogue is identified by the notes, which cite Gilman's review of *Ann Veronica* and *The History of Mr. Polly* and which add depth to readerly appreciation of the knowingly dialogic positioning of their texts: "Wells, for his part, seems to have been something of a fan—on visiting the United States, his first request was to meet [Gilman]" (Talbot and Talbot 2016, 125, citing Eichner 2004, xii). Not only were these works of utopian fiction, science fiction, and political philosophy responding to each other and to their historical contexts, but their authors themselves participated in the cultural life of their period and engaged in dialogue in the flesh as well as on the page. The visual aspect of the comics form reminds readers of the interpersonal and embodied lives of the writers depicted as Bryan Talbot provides evocative depictions of Gilman in conversation with Monique and her mother in a Parisian cafe.

Moreover, in showing the process of intertextuality running in parallel with interpersonal conversation, the ideological tensions that operate as negations of the utopian ideal are brought to life. For example, in the overview of *Herland* provided in the endnotes, Mary Talbot confronts Gilman's own cultural blind spots:

My favourite work of Gilman's is the feminist utopia Herland . . . The book is a critical, and sometimes highly amusing, exploration of gender identities, roles and relationships. It does not advocate separation; rather, Gilman uses the device of an all-female society to show women functioning effectively and independently as full citizens. It's unfortunate that she didn't extend her optimism about the capacities of white women to African Americans, however. (Talbot and Talbot 2016, 122)

This duly critical appraisal of Gilman's racism is later incorporated into the storyworld of the text on two levels—in the racism the former Communards display toward the indigenous population of New Caledonia and in the heated exchange between Gilman and Élianne occasioned by Monique's narration of Michel's support for the Kanaka's revolt:

> CHARLOTTE: You mean, she *helped* the nig—?
>   I mean, she didn't *stick* with her own *kind?*
> ÉLIANNE: Her own *kind?*
>   Her own *kind*, you say. She WAS sticking with her own *kind!*
>   She stuck with the indigenous people, just as she *always* stuck with
>   the *oppressed!* (142, emphases in original)

This passage directly confronts the two most fundamental negations of utopianism, which relate respectively to the ideological content within every utopian text and to the transformation of subjectivity presupposed by the inauguration of each and every utopia. Jameson links the inevitability of such ideological contamination to our "situatedness in class, race and gender, in nationality, in history" (2007, 170). *Red Virgin*, moreover, both supports and puts into practice Jameson's observation that "one of the unique features of the Utopian tradition consists in the way in which the form itself seems to interiorize differences which generally remain implicit in literary history (thereby paradoxically remaining external to the literary works themselves)" (2007, 143).

The pressure such limitations exert on the imagination of the utopian writer herself speaks to both the necessity and the impossibility of transforming consciousness—perhaps even human nature—in order to realize the utopian dream. As Gray puts it, "given the fact of human fallibility the [utopian] model is sure to contain flaws, some of which may be fatal" (2008, 74), but the recognition of this fallability does not require us to join Gray in endorsing a view of human nature as "fixed *and* flawed (2008, 280, emphasis added). One can accept fallibility without necessarily rejecting the possibility of change.

Indeed, as the Talbots' previous book, *Sally Heathcote: Suffragette*, demonstrates, the belief in the fixity and imperfections of women's minds and

bodies was an impediment successfully overcome in part through the suffragette's use of violence. While Gray's argument seeks to accommodate such
extensions of freedom through acknowledging the example of abolition, he
endeavors to distinguish such historical developments from utopian projects:
"A project is utopian if there are no circumstances under which it can be
realized. . . . [It] is enough if it can be known to be impossible under any
circumstances that can be brought about or foreseen" (2008, 28). The problem
here—and it is one that the Talbots acknowledge upfront—is that in many
cases there is no way of knowing with certainty whether something is possible or not. It is here that the representation of failure—and specifically its
appearance in the Reichelt narrative—serves to underpin, even as it threatens
to undermine, the graphic novel's celebration of utopianism.

Whereas the second frame narrative assists in the suturing aspect of
closure by making connections between different contexts, the first frame
narrative—with which the graphic novel opens and closes—more overtly
encourages the disruptive mode of closure which can, as discussed above,
be enacted by the panel frame in comics and by the revolutionary event in
socialist utopianism. In terms of narrative, there are no points of continuity
in plot or character between Reichelt's story and either the second frame
narrative or the Michel biography. The opening scene of the Reichelt narrative (Talbot and Talbot 2016, 3–4) is set in 1909 and the closing one, which
depicts Reichelt's ill-fated decision to test his invention by jumping off the
Eiffel Tower (117–19), on February 4, 1912. Nevertheless, even as at the level
of plot and character there is an absolute break between these two narrative
frames, there are visual markers that suggest a certain conceptual resonance
between them. Most obviously, the similarities in artistic style and page
layout provide a visual link and, while the first person narration, attributed
to Reichelt himself, differs in both voice and point of view from that of the
other narratives, the omniscient narrator who provides the captions giving
spatial and temporal coordinates is consistent across all three narratives, a
fact highlighted by the use of a typewriter font rather than hand lettering
for these panels.[1] Such links bridge the break sufficiently to make braiding
operative, and it is through the interaction between the iconic motif series
and the narrative sequence that the concept of utopianism begins to emerge.

In terms of braiding, the two key motifs are the red carnation, which
appears on a woman's hat in panel 2, page 3, and the depiction of the Eiffel
Tower in panel 1, page 117, which recalls the image of panel 1, page 83. Though
innocuous, these visual cues encourage the reader to undertake the work of
connective closure, cocreating meaning across these disparate narratives. I

would argue that this process of bridging what appears initially—and necessarily—as an unbridgeable break parallels the work of the utopian, not because it allows a transition from one place or time to another (from a lapsarian to a pre- or postlapsarian state), but because it enables us to identify the pursuit of meaning with utopia reconceptualized as disruption. Mary Talbot wryly notes that Reichelt "seems to have been undeterred by previous failures, and injuries, from much smaller jumps, which I reckon makes him a worthy candidate for a Darwin Award" (135); and yet, the resources of tragicomedy do not exhaust the symbolic potential of this narrative. After witnessing the technological marvel of human flight, Reichelt as represented here becomes consumed by a passion for parachutes—it becomes the cause that gives meaning to his life. While to the external observer his acts may appear absurd, the only surefire way of avoiding such descents into folly is a retreat from meaning altogether, a withdrawal that is no less deadly than the attempt to impose a totalized vision of utopia. The final panel of the narrative, a double-page spread empty save for the image of Reichelt caught up in the fabric of his parachute, can also function as a metaphor for the trajectory of the utopian dreamer today. His ambition was not wholly misplaced—parachutes have indeed become an everyday, yet lifesaving, reality for pilots—and his failure is itself part of a larger success story. And yet, Reichelt broke the law—his permit was not for a live test—and his reward was an ignoble death viewed over 8 million times on YouTube but not depicted visually in *Red Virgin*. Indeed, the graphic novel holds Reichelt's end in abeyance; we leave him before his landing, still en route to utopia.

This then is the inescapable aporia with which the *Red Virgin* leaves us. Utopia today is only viable as a process of twofold closure, constituted by an act of separation that enables even as it resists a dialogic construction of meaning. Faced with two discrete states—pre- and postemancipation—the reader is subjected to the injunction to puncture the boundary. To reduce utopianism to yet another in a series of postmodern language games, however, is to shirk our responsibility. The role of writers and artists does not end on the page and as practitioners of critical comics studies we are called upon to subject our own work to the processes of critique that we direct toward objects of scholarly interest and, more significantly, to appreciate and identify opportunities for utopian disruption. Such a nexus of intellectual, aesthetic, and physical commitment to the emancipatory cause is staged in the *Red Virgin*'s representation of the lifelong comradeship that Michel shares with Albert Robida, the satirical artist and writer recruited to the National Guard during the siege that preceded the Commune (Talbot and Talbot 2016,

20–22). The pair meet again in the World Expo of 1889, long after the violent fall of the Commune, which involved mass slaughter as well as the execution or deportation of leading Communards, and after Michel has witnessed the triumphant violence of imperialism in New Caledonia. Robida, whose depictions of futurity have been consistently tinctured with a Menippean hue, here becomes the foil for Michel's commitment to the double movement of withdrawal and return that constitutes the utopian impulse in all of its violent efficacy. Robida asks, with apparent incredulity, "So you *still* believe in the *Future?*" Michel's answer is unequivocal: "*And in the Revolution!*" (83, emphases in original). Subsequently, Robida predicts, "You *will* marvel at the *technology* in the century to come. But it won't be *perfecting* the future, I *assure* you!" (84, emphases in original). This statement allows the text to use Louise's reply to define a vision of utopia based on social change enabled by education: "But 'Perfecting the Future,' Citizen Robida, is *not* about *machines* and *gadgets*. / It's about *children*" (84, emphases in original).

Throughout the graphic novel, Michel's utopianism clothes itself in the raiment of education and domestic economy, relegating not only technology but also systems of government to a secondary status. *Red Virgin* argues for a progressive view not of history nor of humanity, but of utopianism itself, here understood as the disruption of the repressive and exploitative status quo. The future, meanwhile, becomes not an ideal destination in which all antagonisms are eradicated, but rather the locus from which our call to responsibility emanates and the site in which to anchor our hopes. Like language, the desire for Utopia transgresses the void, passing through the generations as it seeks to call into existence a better world from what it steals from the abyss:

> Enough. Sudden enough. Sudden all far. No move and sudden all far. All least. Three pins. One pinhole. In dimmost dim. Vasts apart. At bounds of boundless void. Whence no farther. Best worse no farther. Nohow less. Nohow worse. Nohow naught. Nohow on.
> Said nohow on. (Beckett 2009, 103)

Notes

1. This differentiating use of font was brought to my attention by participants in the Nottingham Does Comics group at our bimonthly meeting of October 26, 2018. I am grateful for this observation and others I have been unable to include here, as well as for the opportunity to test the readings contained above before a live audience.

References

Beckett, Samuel. 2009. "Worstward Ho." In *Company / Ill Seen Ill Said / Worstward Ho / Stirrings Still*, edited by Dirk Van Hulle, 79–103. London: Faber and Faber.

Eichner, Carolyn. 2003. "'Vive la Commune!' Feminism, Socialism, and Revolutionary Revival in the Aftermath of the 1871 Paris Commune." *Journal of Women's History* 15 (2): 68–98.

Eichner, Carolyn. 2004. *Surmounting the Barricades: Women in the Paris Commune*. Bloomington: Indiana University Press.

Fairclough, Norman, and Phil Graham. 2002. "Marx as Critical Discourse Analyst: The Genesis of a Critical Method and Its Relevance to the Critique of Global Capital." *Estudios de Sociolinguistica* 3 (1): 185–229.

Gray, John. 2008. *Black Mass: Apocalyptic Religion and the Death of Utopia*. London: Penguin.

Green, Matthew. 2015. "'I Don't See What Good a Book Is without Pictures or Conversations': Imaginary Worlds and Intertextuality in *Alice in Wonderland* and *Alice in Sunderland*." In *Drawn for the Classics: Essays on Graphic Adaptations of Literary Works*, edited by Stephen Tabachnick and Esther Saltzman, 110–26. Jefferson, NC: McFarland.

Groensteen, Thierry. 2007. *The System of Comics*. Translated by Bart Beaty and Nick Nguyen. Jackson: University Press of Mississippi.

Jameson, Frederic. 1983. *The Political Unconscious: Narrative as a Socially Symbolic Act*. London: Routledge.

Jameson, Frederic. 2007. *Archaeologies of the Future*. London, Verso.

McCloud, Scott. 1993. *Understanding Comics: The Invisible Art*. New York: Harper Perennial.

Talbot, Bryan. 2007. *Alice in Sunderland: An Entertainment*. London: Jonathan Cape.

Talbot, Bryan. 2010a. *The Tale of One Bad Rat*. 2nd edition. Milwaukee, WI: Dark Horse Books.

Talbot, Bryan. 2010b. "Rat's Tail." In *The Tale of One Bad Rat*, 2nd edition, [n.p.]. Milwaukee, WI: Dark Horse Books.

Talbot, Bryan. 2014. *Arkwright Integral*. Milwaukee, WI: Dark Horse Books.

Talbot, Mary. 1995. *Fictions at Work: Language and Social Practice in Fiction*. London: Longman.

Talbot, Mary. 1998. *Language and Gender: An Introduction*. Cambridge, UK: Polity.

Talbot, Mary, and Alwyn Talbot. 2014. "Preparation for Leadership." In *Cross: A Political Satire Anthology*, edited by Lizzie Boyle and Conor Boyle, n.p. N.p.: Disconnected Press.

Talbot, Mary, and Bryan Talbot. 2012. *Dotter of her Father's Eyes*. London: Jonathan Cape.

Talbot, Mary, and Bryan Talbot. 2016. *The Red Virgin and the Vision of Utopia*. London: Jonathan Cape.

Talbot, Mary, Kate Charlesworth, and Bryan Talbot. 2014. *Sally Heathcote Suffragette*. London: Jonathan Cape.

Wilde, Oscar. (1891) 2009. *The Soul of Man under Socialism*. Auckland: Floating Press.

Žižek, Slavoj. 2008a. *In Defense of Lost Causes*. London: Verso.

Žižek, Slavoj. 2008b. *Violence*. London: Profile.

13

The Parable of Bill Ayers

Comics, Allegory, and Critical Legal Thinking

ADAM GEAREY

Another year with nothing to do
—STOOGES 1969

Introduction

To Teach is a collaboration between the comics artist Ryan Alexander-Tanner and the progressive activist/theorist Bill Ayers (Ayers and Alexander-Tanner 2010). The book traces Ayers's path from new left radical to progressive school teacher. We will read *To Teach* as a parable or allegory about the possibilities of critical thinking beyond Critical Legal Studies (CLS).[1] Alexander-Tanner and Ayers's text sets up a "dialectical dance" between text and image, political anxiety and aesthetic playfulness (Ayers and Alexander-Tanner 2010, xv).

There are issues to deal with before we outline our argument in more detail. How is it possible to write about comics? How can we make sense of this strange conjunction of radical philosophy and comics text? Critical comics studies defines an experimental zone where such a reading could be staged. If this thesis is correct, then we need to think in a playful way—for what else is the comic if it is not the dance, the carnival; a summoning of energies of difference, confusion—perhaps even the joyous abandon of a freak out. The etymologies employed in this chapter are an attempt to make words follow the dialectical dance of *To Teach*. How? In the same way that the comics box divides up a stream of images joined and separated by a gutter, the creative deployment of etymologies brings out the semantic energies contained within words. This method is closer to certain understandings of poetic thinking than it is to conventional scholarship or straight philosophy. So, this essay is perhaps a poetic thinking of the comic. It is worth noting that there is nothing ahistorical or acultural in any of these claims. We are simply trying to work through the logics provoked by the comic in the "here and now" of our reading of this text.

Consider the relationship of the dialectic to parable and allegory. Etymologically, the word *parable* (παραβολή, *parabolē*) stems from a verb that carries the sense of throwing things side by side. Allegory derives from words meaning to speak other. Already, it is possible to sense that this complex of terms might provide a description of comic art. Given Alexander-Tanner's description of comic art as a "dialectical dance" we can elaborate our understanding of allegory and parable by thinking about the etymology of *dialectic*. The root of the word (διά, *diá*) has the meaning of "through" (as in the speech *through* which people discourse with each other). Comic art creates its own "through"—its own peculiar mediation of ideas by pictorial forms. The boxes of comic illustration effectively throw things side by side—compelling ideas and events to be read differently.

Our discussion of the gutter (the white space that separates the boxes in comics) furthers this analysis. The gutter gives the comics dance its rhythm. Etymologically the word *gutter* borrows from the sense of "running in grooves" as of water down a pipe or tube. Anyone who has ever listened to the rain coursing down a drain will know that it has its own rhythm. There is a clear resonance between the rhythms of the comics box and the ideas of passage through a medium. A further transformation of these themes takes us to the word *anxiety* whose root meaning refers to the tube of the throat and its restriction under certain intense experiences. Anxiety, then, is at root a description of tightening or even lacing or pulling things together.

We will use this notion of anxiety to help us trace the seam that joins the reading of the comic to the world. The etymology of comics derives from κῶμος (*kômos*, carousal) and thus has links with drunkenness and shouting and roaring—a concern that takes us back to one of the problems of allegory: a semantic excess that keeps on generating new images, new readings. The critical reader thus experiences an anxiety in encountering the comic, asking him/her/its self: "What has this text got to do with my world?" Theory is always "trouble[ed]" in this respect (Kwan 2000, 690). Anxiety is occasioned by inheritances that define the fraught space of contemporary critical thinking. The fissiparous history of the critical legal traditions is well known. The splits are many and various: between a sober leftism and a ludic postmodernism; between opposition to power and reassertions of power despite their disavowal; concerns for race, gender, and sexuality. Must we accept that each critical tendency can only speak for itself or is there a tentative way of working in and between the fragments? Who can speak for critical theory? Whose voice? Whose power and whose authority? Whose roaring? The fundamental point: how to activate the dialectic of anxiety and creativity, authority and plurality, experimentalism and focus.

Thus, our reading attempts to make sense of a comics text in a particular context. Arguably one of the main tensions inherited from CLS (and which CLS, in turn, inherited from the new left) presents itself as the clash between an aesthetic mode of thought associated with postmodernism and strands of engagement that express themselves in terms of identity politics. We will pick up on this theme in more detail below, but for now (and to use a rough short hand) our main concern is with the problem of anxiety and aesthetics. This problem is, for us, at the heart of critical comics studies: how do we find the intellectual resources to further progressive and egalitarian thinking. Of course you can disagree. The particular trajectory of this essay comes out of traditions of aestheticism and postmodernism. We are in pursuit of a something like an anxious, joyous spirit that celebrates tension and sees in critical comics studies a dancing partner and fellow raver.

Engaging with these themes requires a genealogy of critical thought. The genealogy presented in this essay is, of course, as partial as any. While it cannot escape its own implicit and explicit claims to authority, it can at least attempt to make them visible, and, in so doing, work through various troubled legacies. To recount the parable of Bill Ayers is to talk of critical thinking in a particular cultural and historical location.[2] Ayers frames the central question of this essay: how do you live and think in such a way that you do not make "a mockery of your values?" (Ayers 2001, 61). To return to the genealogy: the anxieties of contemporary critical thought can be traced back through CLS to the new left. Critical thinking has received a tradition of radical philosophy focused on two key terms: alienation and reification. The contemporary relevance of these notoriously slippery ideas might, at first, appear obscure. But, we argue that, read sensitively, alienation and reification form a complex that can generate common concerns for different strands of critical thought. How?

Alienation—at root—carries the sense of a relationship with another. The Latin word is related to the Greek word which forms the root of allegory. The root of reification is the Latin *res* or *rem*—a word translated as "thing," but whose semantic web extends to the idea of an assembly or gathering— and thus, perhaps, the sense of people talking to each other. Taking these meanings together we can suggest that they are concerned with social life—a life lived in common with others. Alienation becomes reification when others are turned into things—when the dialectical relationships through which we identify ourselves and others take fetishized forms and we can no longer think or speak allegorically or in other words. Unable to achieve new forms of conviviality or solidarity, we are stuck with ourselves as we are. The parable of Bill Ayers thus helps us to examine how the different themes that animate the post-CLS environment might speak to each other. We want to sketch a spirit of thinking that works between critical race theory, LatCrit, queer theory, feminism, and other congruent currents of legal theory. This is not to propose some general philosophy of alienation that forms a substratum for a reborn CLS. From the parable of Bill Ayers, critical theory learns that it must come to terms with its past and open itself to its own differentiation. Or risk dogmatism and irrelevance.

The Dialectical Dance of the Comic

We need to consider a sequence of images from *To Teach*. Ayers is presented as a radical teacher learning his craft. Before we elaborate our reading of these images, we need to anticipate a peculiar effect of a register of language. There is a joyous life to Alexander-Tanner's images that is often absent from philosophical texts. At the same time, these images do not resist philosophical readings. Perhaps it is a question of spirit—or of tracing the peculiar way in which the comics text both invites, resists, and generates interpretation.

The twelve images in figure 13.1 are spread out like a tarot deck before the inquirer. Alexander-Tanner's boxes set up a visual and semantic field in which a number of themes jostle with each other. The first three boxes set the scene (and, as we will see, echo an argument from a classic CLS essay). We will read these images as an engagement with alienation. What is alienation? It is hard to find a philosophical argument about the "estrangement of humanity from itself" in these boxes (Gordon 1997, 70). We need to join the dance of the images. To be alienated is, first of all, an emotional experience. One feels lost, detached, and separated from a more dynamic sense of life. In place of vitality is the dull repetition of the same thing. Reacting to the endless broadcasts of authority, the Ayers character comes up against disembodied power that articulates itself through rituals of community. Note the way that the Ayers character looks anxiously over his shoulder as he dismantles the loud speaker. At one level, Ayers's anxiety might be the fear of being discovered sabotaging

CREATIVE INSUBORDINATION

FINDING ALLIES

CRITICISM

SELF-CRITICISM

98

Figure 13.1: From *To Teach*, 2010, 98. © William Ayers and Ryan Alexander-Tanner.

school property. More properly, his anxiety is wired up with the meaning of the act of creative destruction itself. This connects with the images of the isolation and loneliness of the imprisoned self. If we leave aside for a moment the caption "finding allies," we can read this sequence as an illustration of the difficulty of taking anxiety upon oneself: anxiety, at this stage in its dialectic, singles out the anxious one who must discover the meaning of an act. If one does find allies, anxiety becomes creative. Alexander-Tanner's image of illumination, a light switched on by Ayers's friend, is a depiction of just such an encounter. We now need to examine the relationship between anxiety, alienation, and reification.

Reification is alienated thinking, or inauthentic thinking incapable of grasping itself. Critical thinking must therefore be self-reflective, aware that it can be captured and disarmed by reification. Without reflexive self-criticism, patterns of fetishized normativity reassert themselves. Ayers swaps places with the figure brandishing a pair of scissors. Although for some this interpretation might be stretching it, Alexander-Tanner's clever repetition of the authority figure illustrates another central feature of both alienation and reified thinking—commodification. We will return to commodification below, but, for the moment, we can see that the most relevant aspect of the social phenomenon of commodification is identity thinking. Just as different commodities can be exchanged for amounts of money, commoditized thinking flattens out the differences of the social world. Different qualities are resolved into featureless quantities. It might be said that all teaching is simply work for wages. There is no point in thinking that one might be able to do things differently. The structures of the professional world assert themselves so that the rebel becomes the bureaucrat, the maverick the arch conformist.[3]

So, reified thinking is thought that cannot understand the hold of power on the world. Thought that seeks to question alienation remains reified if it fails to criticize itself. Reflexive thought must question its own assumptions—retain a form of creative anxiety—and be wary of simply repeating fetishized forms of power and authority that constitute alienation in the first place. This point can be extended. Unless you confront your own self-certainty, you become lost in your own impeccable radicalism. "Creative subordination" becomes a new dogmatism. Thus, the repeated image in Alexander-Tanner's text of the Ayers character plunging or falling has an intriguing ambiguity. The fall—or indeed the anxiety of falling—can be an acceptance of an affirmatory risk, a radical openness to the world, or it could be the collapse into a stifling belief in the correctness of one's own worldview. Being able to recognize one's own errors, to think without becoming dogmatic or distracted, is (to shift the metaphor) the tightrope the critical thinker must walk.

The image of the tightrope walker is also a figure of how the reader reads the comic. In thinking this through, we come across a kind of reflexivity that is central to the comics antidote to reification. If one reads the text in its entirety, the Alexander-Tanner character often appears in dialogue with the Ayers character. They talk things through. In a more extended sense, it is a dialogue with the reader about how one can make use of the lessons of the comics parable. As suggested above, the gap between the boxes can be seen as a pause, a suspension. One's reading has to walk the lines that separate the images. The gutter offers the possibility of different readings of the same images.[4] For instance, the visual metaphor in the final scene is well chosen. The bar that defines the prison of self-certainty becomes transformed into the taught rope and the balancing act of the final image. This is a metaphor—a horizontal line that echoes the white gutter itself (as indeed does the line of the tightrope). These are visual puns—metaphors for a process of aesthetic association invited by the images. Terms like alienation and reification, which insist on analytical capturing and labeling of experience, map onto these puns but belong to a different intellectual register. If nothing else the gutter illustrates the limitations of philosophical language. The aesthetic energy evoked by the image/text may be a better way of indicating something beyond alienated language that is not compromised by reifying thought processes.

Very well, but, as suggested above, the reader's aesthetic thrill in comics allegory runs up against critical anxiety. The delights the comics reader experiences are at best fleeting and at worst an enjoyment of ludic play for its own sake. There are urgent tasks in the real world. One should not be wasting time reading comics. But is it necessary to choose between the comic and the world? Can this tension become creative?

The Comic and the Critical Imagination

Alexander-Tanner provides the perfect figure for "coming to know"—or, the radical confronted by the reification of his/her/its thought. In *To Teach*, the figure for a sudden experience of a profound realization is the Ayers character stopped short, hand to head, aware that it is necessary to start again. We can make reference to Alexander-Tanner's illustration of a notorious image from the dark days of the new left to elaborate this point. In the boxes in figure 13.2,

Alexander-Tanner has taken a celebrated photograph of the student radicals starting out for the Days of Rage in Chicago in 1969. A historical perspective on the new left would suggest that the Days of Rage were a pivotal moment when the idealism of the Students for a Democratic Society began to shift toward the armed struggle of the Weather Underground. This fraught moment is bound up with Bill Ayers's biography. Ayers, along with others (including Bernardine Dohrn whose image also appears in the comic) was a significant figure in the Weather Underground. How can this problematic moment in American history be made part of a useable past?

Alexander-Tanner has incorporated the photograph of the Days of Rage into a compound image whose parts exist in dynamic tension (in the first panel in figure 13.2). In the bottom left of the box is an image of a young Ayers staring in horror at his reflection in a mirror. This image exists alongside another one in which a kindly elder woman teaches a very young Ayers to count (an image repeated later in the book with Ayers as the figure of the teacher). It is, therefore, a question of how one counts—how one reckons with one's self. How can we develop this theme? We need to read two passages from *Fugitive Days* and then return to the comic:

In *Fugitive Days*, Ayers writes:

> I carved a red star rising on my left shoulder, my first real tattoo, a bloody and painful inscription gouged with a needle and India ink, my first little brand of autonomy and my personal declaration of independence. I wanted to make a claim on my body, to fix my shifting identity. I was already a rebel, and I would now become a freedom fighter. (Ayers 2014, 71)

This can be compared with another passage:

> The big red star has fared the worst—faded now to a harmless pink— and the rainbow and lightning bolt between my shoulder blades were wrinkled and sadly dim. My permanent reminders had all proved unreliable.... That's just the way of time—nothing and no one—stays the same. (Ayers 2014, 293)

A carving on the skin. A "brand" (or pact) with the self—a symbol of what one will be—a commitment to the cause. It is intriguing that, etymologically at least, we could link the words character and comics etymologically around the issue of just such scratchings, grooves, or inscriptions.[5] Alexander-Tanner

Figure 13.2: From *To Teach*, 2010, 97. © William Ayers and Ryan Alexander-Tanner.

stresses that any inscription exists against a blank space—a space that might act as a repository for ideas that are yet to be thought and for events that might change interpretations. The intervals around inscription mobilize an open and ongoing dialectic where what is, what is not, and what might be, dance with each other. Ayers's writing concentrates these themes into the figure of the fading tattoo. His teaching practice takes place under the figure of the blurring red star—and the becoming dim of the Weather Underground tattoo ("the rainbow and lightning bolt"). The metaphor of fading is not diminution. It is a figure for a loss of easy certainty—a process of qualification and reflection that prevents you from becoming the kind of person that "[you] once warned others about" (Ayers 2010, 144).

Teaching under the pink star might, therefore, be a metaphor for a self-critical praxis that can work the way out of its own reification. This praxis cannot be learned in any once and for all sense, as it is practiced in situations "never twice the same" (Ayers 2010, 136). There are certainly techniques that can be pressed into services. Ayers refers to Stanislavsky's method acting, where actors do not so much learn lines and move around a stage as find in themselves the personal resonances that allow them to bring their own experience to a role. Ayers also finds Rilke's advice to a young poet helpful: "go into yourself" (Ayers 2010, 137). This, in turn involves a "gap"—the space between "what is" and "what could be"—the division between "hard reality" and personal transformation. One has to "work the gap" or remain within the "contradiction" of what is and what might be.

One particularly relevant exemplification of these themes is a fourteen-box sequence that appears in the center of the book. It is focused on a story told by a high school teacher called Avi Lessing. Lessing's philosophy of teaching is based on the idea that the teacher is "a human being engaged with other human beings." The interaction between students, and students and teachers, determines the "field" in which teaching takes place—an "in between" that puts in play the human dynamic of the classroom (Ayers and Alexander-Tanner 2010, 60). "The field" or the "in between" can thus be understood as the space that opens a dialectical conversation where meanings are arranged and rearranged. Alexander-Tanner's illustration of Lessing's story involves a particularly difficult moment when a presentation by a white student goes dreadfully wrong, leading to accusations of racism by a black student. Lessing lets this event "unfold"—but it leads to uncomfortable self-questioning. Lessing asks himself: "Are some things better left unsaid?" A text box contains the comment that "white privilege is a hidden curriculum throughout our society"—and that while "trials and errors" are "points of investigation" there are "no neat conclusions" (Ayers and Alexander-Tanner 2010, 60). Indeed, the classroom discussion of the incident "moved everyone, but settled nothing." Lessing anxiously questions his own work as a teacher in a conversation with his mother. She tells him that he belongs in the classroom because he is "still able" to "question" himself (Ayers and Alexander-Tanner 2010, 60).

The story of Avi Lessing is an allegory about a way of thinking. The rhythm of the boxes, Alexander-Tanner's organization of the visual space, is key to the articulation of this point. The incident itself, with all its tensions and hostilities, is a sequence of small boxes—classroom group scenes. Lessing's own self-examination occupies two long, oblong boxes that reach across the page. The transition between these two "shapes" of page force the reader to slow down and to deal with the same questions that confront the character. What does it mean to persist with trial and error? The illustration of Lessing's face as he ponders the question of the question is the concluding image of the story. There is no saying that dialogue is possible—that the dialectic will stutter into life and that newness will come into being. But Lessing and the reader are left with the singular importance of the unanswerable question. Of course, the location of this question within the book as a whole does not suggest that one is simply left in perpetual torment. Without an openness to others, it is hard to interrupt the certainties that close the self around its own alienated and alienating monologue.

If CLS repeats something like Ayers's mistakes, how might we use *To Teach* to rework themes that have a continuing importance for critical thought? We can set up the thesis more precisely. If the founding problematic of CLS is a question of how "transformative projects" are possible in legal work, then we need to track the very idea of a transformative thinking that is both serious and playful (Klare 2001, 1073). To sharpen up the question still further, we need to revisit the thinking of the new left, trace its influence on CLS, and examine its legacy for critical legal thinking.

Critical Legal Studies: Law and Alienation

For the new left, alienation was a social effect of commodification. Commodification is the subtle but ultimately banal reduction of complex social, cultural, and political structures to market logics of competition and privatization. Alienation is the internalization of disconnection and deadening routine: the world of "*métro, boulot, dodo*"—an endless round of work, shopping, debt, and exhaustion. The culture of commodification is also marked by a division of labor along racial and gender lines. These social structures sustain forms of dominance that are seen as, if not "natural," part of the way that "things are" and thus unquestionable. The social world is fragmented into antagonistic parts. Hegemonic forms of commodified social life may be powerful, but their dominance is not total. One can awake from alienation. Awakening compels a confrontation with one's place in a social, economic, and political order. As we have suggested, analyzing alienation means engaging with reification. Reification describes the way in which forms of thought become solid, unquestionable, and thinglike. New left philosophies remained reified to the extent that they did not confront their own assumptions.

This problematic was inherited by CLS. Given the depth, range, and intensity of CLS scholarship on alienation, we are forced to engage with the themes outlined in the paragraph above in a somewhat compressed manner. Our focus will be on an essay that served as a major point of reference for CLS thinking. There is another important point that justifies reference to the text in question. The section from *To Teach* analyzed at the beginning of this essay echoes a key moment in Peter Gabel's celebrated discussion of alienation in "The Phenomenology of Rights-Consciousness and the Pact of the Withdrawn Selves." Gabel is trying to rescue a way of thinking that can be traced back to student radicalism before its distortion and collapse in the armed struggle of the Weather Underground.

Gabel's analysis echoes the scene that Alexander-Tanner captures—the singing of the national anthem. Like Ayers and Alexander-Tanner, Gabel is concerned with the way in which reified thought limits our understanding of ourselves. We are already familiar with the image from Alexander-Tanner's illustration in figure 13.1. Ayers describes it as the interruption of his class by "[a] scratchy recording of the star spangled banner" that signified that "our space was not our own" (Ayers 2001, 143). We can relate this scene to a "first grade classroom" scene described by Gabel:

> It is 8:29 and children are playing, throwing food, and generally engaging in relatively undistorted communication. At 8:30, the teacher (who is replacing the father and who, in later years, will be replaced by the judge) calls the class to attention: it is time for the "pledge of allegiance." All face front, all suffer the same social rupture and privation, all fix their eyes on a striped piece of cloth. (Gabel 1980, 26–7)

Go back to Alexander-Tanner's illustration. Gabel captures the reason why Ayers dismantles the loudspeaker. Note also the contrast between "relatively undistorted communication" and the "privation and rupture" of the pledge of allegiance. The argument posits a contrast between relatively unalienated and alienated behavior. Perhaps this contrast is a little too sharp but it provides a powerful opening for an argument that seeks to outline an intellectual ground for CLS. However, for all its subtlety, Gabel's argument does not quite work. Its avowed concern with detailed local description is too quickly generalized into an overarching theory. Gabel presents a technique to be learned from the master. This is not, of course, a "weather fry."[6] Gabel's approach is quite different, but the essay does mandate a way of doing things correctly. These criticisms can be elaborated. Gabel does not concern himself with matters of race, gender, or sexuality. He ignores the very issues that the white new left ignored. The reader does not get the sense that the author is at all anxious about his own authority. Indeed, there is a fetishization of the "anxiety of correct thought" in the phenomenological method itself (Gabel 1980, 1574).

On reading Gabel, the comics crit might come to the conclusion that his philosophy is lacking in self-critique. There is an alternative approach within the CLS canon. We argued in the first section of this essay that the comic evokes an aesthetic energy through metaphor and visual puns. Such playfulness may better evoke unalienated or unreified experiences. This is, of course, the argument of another foundational CLS text. "Roll Over Beethoven" pits Gabel against Duncan Kennedy in a dialogue over the nature and direction of "the movement" (Gabel and Kennedy 1984). The very idea that CLS is a movement echoes the new left's own self-description—and it is not unreasonable to read the piece as a negotiation of inherited intellectual tensions that we are studying. Kennedy presents a form of thinking that sidesteps Gabel's spirit of philosophical gravity. If there are moments when alienation is suspended, or when one glimpses possibilities of other ways of living and being, they are rare gifts. Kennedy's point is that to think about "a beyond" (or limit) of alienation requires an ironic or playful dancing around concepts that risk deadening abstraction. Plotting the philosophical coordinates of alienation is futile. Indeed, the essay might have been better presented as a comic rather than a dialogue. One could imagine what an artist of Alexander-Tanner's talents would make of Gabel and Kennedy and their debate.

We appear to be suggesting that in this dialogue between two "white male heavies" Kennedy fares better than Gabel (Crenshaw 2011, 1293). This is a mistake, as it effectively reasserts a false choice that Kennedy himself struggles to avoid in "Roll Over Beethoven" and other essays as well. In *Legal Education as a Training for Hierarchy* (1982), for example, there is no under-arching theory, dialectical or otherwise, but a sense of how it is possible to engage authentically with a number of ongoing problems that require different ways of working, thinking, and teaching.[7] Philosophy certainly cannot be jettisoned in place of a cult of spontaneous, intuitive action. This problematic informs Kennedy's later affirmation of a distinction between two forms of critical thought in CLS. One approach is aligned with "the ethos of post-ness" and "doubleness." The other is an expression of "post-Marxist systemacity" or "identity politics" (Kennedy 1997, 339). Doubleness is an "aesthetic" category and so could be aligned with comics allegory. Post-Marxist systematicity relates to Gabel's phenomenology, but extends to those forms of identity politics that could be seen as an exemplification of austere essentialism. The risk is that this categorization of different intellectual tendencies leaves us on yet another frozen borderland. In order to free up these tensions—to liberate the play between different frames of thought—we need to be aware that this characterization of forms of thought is "uneasy" and tentative (Kennedy 1997, 178). The worst thing to do would be to fetishize anxiety as a slogan to be woven on a banner. These concerns will help us to negotiate the contemporary realities of critical legal thinking. In the final section of this essay we will examine the various debates within contemporary critical thought before turning to a final evocation of a spirit of critique that borrows from the comic's dialectical dance.

CLS and Critical Legal Thinking

Critics of CLS proposed a form of liberatory theory rooted in "lived experience" and engaged with processes of "self recovery" and "collective liberation" (hooks, 1994). The "post-ness" and "doubleness" of CLS were targets. They reflect the privileges of those who have time to play—the "self-indulgence" of dilettantes (Conaghan 2001, 61, 723). What do we make of these points? Are we not stuck with yet another distinction between identity politics / sober leftism and postmodernist ("pomo") ludism? Before we can weigh up an answer to this question, we need to remember that the critique of CLS has been subjected to further critique. Those calling for a rejection of a certain theoretical voice or style have themselves been criticized for introducing a false choice between modes of thought that are not necessarily in opposition.[8] More broadly, activist scholars have stressed that while an awareness of oppression on the basis of race, sex, and gender remains central to radical thought and practice, it is also necessary to think about how cooperation between diverse groups might be possible (Maeckelbergh 2009, 19–21; Graeber, 2009; Christie 2011).

So, rather than seeing the various tendencies that define cotemporary critical positions as separate and mutually antagonistic, can we not find relations of synergy? Take, for example, the notion of intersectionality. Intersectionality was central to advances in both theory and practice that came out of the critique of CLS. However, intersectionality is itself concerned with relationships between different ways of thinking and the complex ways in which identity is understood (Crenshaw 1991; Combahee River Collective 1979). It would be pointless to posit the priority of an economic over a cultural moment. Furthermore, an intersectional approach is central to contemporary modes of critical thinking that have moved on from the battles of the second and third wave of CLS. These struggles seem less acute to a contemporary generation of scholars whose work does not find an irresolvable tension between theory and praxis, identity politics, postmodernism, and Marxism. Perspectives from critical race theory, feminism, queer theory, and LatCrit compel a further nuancing and reworking of the terms of critical thinking.

Picking up on a central theme of our argument, it may be that an engagement with alienation and reification can provide the locus around which these concerns can come together. In taking alienated and commodified human being as a starting point, critical thought has returned to an examination of the social and psychic costs of markets. We can find contemporary scholarship making use of these ideas in a wide variety of fields. A brief overview would include studies of law and aesthetics (Manderson 1996), taxation (Passant 2015), international law (Korhonen 2015; Varga 2015; Rijswijk 2012), critique of law and economics (McCluskey 2018), law and literature (Glen 2007), technology (Shaw 2015; Neacsu 2014), property theory (Armstrong 1991; Harris 1993; Schlag 2015), critical race theory (Modiri 2012; Peller 2011; Taylor 2014; Kim 2013; van Marle 2001), constitutionalism (Sultany 2014), family law (Rasario-Lebrón 2013) and transgender rights (Green 2012; Ronner 2013).

While these tactical or specific engagements with legal issues are not attempts to produce a general jurisprudence of alienation, there are those who are committed to elaborating an "ongoing project of human liberation from dehumanized (alienated, inauthentic) existence" (Andrews 2004, 899; see also Litowitz, 2000). Angela Harris's work suggests a major advance in this direction. Harris deploys a theory of alienation as a way of articulating a critical account of "emotional labour" and compassion. Concepts of alienation and reification become ways of defining the relationships between "property, animality, humanity, and race"—a concern that extends both concepts in intriguing new directions (Harris 2012, 348). Motro's work also draws on and expands thinking on alienation—developing a notion of inauthenticity to address the scholar as a "compromised academic" in law schools dedicated to the reproduction of alienated forms of legal thought: the dull repetition of the certainties of mainstream law and economic thinking. Ideas that provide a way out of the fly jar are only "wild" and "impractical" to those lost in ideology. In words that echo the images at the beginning of this essay, the isolation and bad faith that comes from "dil[uting] radical views" squander opportunities to build forms of intellectual community that bring together "other colleagues at the margins" (Motro 2015, 118).

How, though, to proceed? Is there a way of articulating shared concerns without collapsing into intellectual imperialism or restrictive distinctions? Possibilities present themselves. Can we reclaim ideas like sympathy and solidarity—parts of progressive vocabulary that are largely absent from critical legal theory?[9] The idea of reflexive thought is central. Reflexivity is a self-questioning that takes into account one's own history and constitution. Authentic self-inquiry must always begin afresh—and it is worth carrying forward the advice of the Ayers character on the tightrope: too much self-criticism produces timidity and powerlessness. The honesty required for such private and public analysis is haunted by the very idea of the "weather fry"—the distortion of a desire for transformation into public humiliation, inflexible thinking and beliefs.

The representative figure here is precisely that provided by Alexander-Tanner: Ayers, the exemplary radical, stopped in his tracks—hand on head—confronting something that he had not previously thought about. In this spirit, critical thinking does not pretend to be an account of interconnectivity "cosynthesis" or multidimensionality (Valdes 1995; Hutchinson 1997; Kwan 2000). It is not as elegant as these theories of identity after intersectionality. Nor is critical thinking anything like a philosophy of humanism, a phenomenology of withdrawn selves craving social connection or a summoning of the intersubjective zap. These terms are, of course, all abstractions. Critical thinking walks the line. The parable of Bill Ayers suggests that if critical thinking is possible, it might be something like risk-taking, reflexivity, and openness. The "trouble" that attends critical thought is the anxious desire that critique should transform its practitioners and the worlds in which they act.

Figure 13.3: From *To Teach*, 2010, xv. © William Ayers and Ryan Alexander-Tanner.

The Juggler and the Magician

This description of the dialectical dance of comic art and critical thinking is no more than a sketch. The red star has become pink and blurred. This is an image of change—a welcome blurring, an opening to play: figure 13.3. These boxes present the spirit of the collaboration, a deflation of seriousness, and a celebration of conviviality. In Alexander-Tanner's playful world of images, people and things become weightless, drift into the air, fall off cliffs, and change places. Chairs, tables, and things dance in an image that recalls Derrida's discussion of the séances that summon the specters of Marx. In these boxes, *To Teach* presents us with an image of disagreement that is not fatal—part of a comics world that is malleable and open to creative reinvention. Alexander-Tanner, Ayers, and Dohrn tease each other about the nature of the text in which they appear—with Dohrn's Oliver Hardy–like glance toward the viewer a fine piece of comic illustration. Dohrn's deflation of seriousness is exemplary of conviviality amongst allies. Argument without crippling anxiety. The question of genre not only relates to the comic but to the entire problematic of how things fit together and thus reminds us of the allegorical energies that the comic lets loose—the energies that makes things spin like stars in the halo of a materialist saint. The world of the comic brings together serious discussion of text, genre, and parable with images of tightrope walkers and jugglers. *Le Bateleur*—fool and magician; the zero, wild card, and summoner of possibilities and transformations. We have joined the dance; opened a new hand . . . becomings . . . funkier grooves, more inventions.

Notes

1. Critical Legal Studies (CLS) is perhaps best conceived of as a left-leaning grouping of scholars based in university law schools. Standard accounts of CLS trace one line of inheritance back to American Legal Realism and the historical context of the New Deal, but this does tend to obscure the relationship between the new left and CLS. Although the first Conference on Critical Legal Studies at the University of Wisconsin did not take place until 1977, CLS was rooted in the radical politics of the 1960s. CLS scholars tended to see law as political; claims to legal autonomy and neutrality effectively concealed law's role in social control and the ideological construction of private property, the market, and bourgeois order. This thesis took a slightly different form in arguments about legal indeterminacy. Not only could legal doctrine be considered fractured and ambiguous, but law itself could never be properly delineated from politics (Duxbury 1995, 432). CLS can also be seen as an important site in which various themes from continental philosophy and social theory were received into legal thinking. In turn, these influenced later postmodernist accounts of law and legal

thinking. CLS thus provides something of a bridge or mediator between legacies of sixties radicalism and more recent currents of thought.

2. Ayers was a leading figure in the radical politics of the 1960s—linked to both the Students for a Democratic Society (SDS) and the Weather Underground. The SDS was one of the most significant new left groups. Ayers's *Fugitive Days* recounts his transformation from a high school rebel to an SDS activist. His fledgling experiences picketing segregated restaurants led him deeper into the antiwar cause. Ayers found his place in the SDS's antiracism, "applied activism," and comradeship. He was involved in a community organizing project in Cleveland, the Community Union—and also with the creation of a community school in a project linked to a program called Radicals in the Professions. In the wake of the Days of Rage, a running battle with police fought on the streets of Chicago, the SDS split. The Weathermen emerged as a faction from the SDS. Later they changed their name to the Weather Underground. After the demise of the Weather Underground, Ayers pursued a distinguished career in early years teaching, becoming a professor at the University of Illinois.

3. The alienated person remains an object—a "spectacle of himself[/herself/itself]"—lacking substantial, self-determined being. The reality of objectification/subjectification is then covered up—or "denied" through a "discourse" that normalizes and makes invisible the effects of commodification that are transmitted through social and cultural institutions (Farley 1997, 464, 475). Farley is particularly concerned with ideologies that articulate the division of labor around supposedly natural distinctions between sexed, gendered, and raced bodies. But consciousness can understand its own commodification through the discovery of its own self-making: "We, the fetish objects who have become aware of ourselves as fetish objects, are, therefore, no longer objects, but subjects" (Farley 1997, 531). In other words, the thinking commodity comes to a limit or a boundary of "what it is" in understanding its own determination as labor in a market (Farley 1997, 531).

4. Scholars of the comic form have identified the polysyntactic way in which the image both separates and unites meanings. Key to the operation of the image, and the play of picture and word, are the energies created by the gutter—the framing space—which both "separates and unites" (Groensteen 2007, 114).

5. The word character comes from the Greek for a stamping tool; a word related to the verb to engrave. Character is thus something marked or engraved (in the sense of tattoo) on the skin. Mark has a different etymology, and can be traced back to the Old English for a trace, the Mercian for a boundary—and further back to the Old Norse and Proto Germanic words of similar meanings—and back further still to the PIE root whose putative meaning is boundary or border. These etymologies suggest that comic illustration, as the creation of marks, border, and boundaries thus has at least some relationship to the study of symbols of commitment and fidelity.

6. The Weather Underground were fixated on the formation of a new character with the "iron will" of the revolutionary: "It was fanatical obedience, we militant nonconformists suddenly tripping over each other to be exactly alike." The so-called "weather fries," endless "criticism-self criticism" exercises, were, as Ayers confesses, hard to "manage" because his own "honest sense of self was disappearing" (Ayers 2001, 154). The openhearted experimentation in ways of living that had characterized an early period of radicalism was replaced

with a political line that knew no deviation: "We were becoming prisoners of our schemes, intoxicated on theory" (Ayers 2001, 159).

7. Kennedy's complex relationship with the radical past can be seen in one of the ur versions of the essay that closes with the claim: "If there is 'revolution' in the air, it is not primarily institutional, but psychic territory which is at stake, or the whole thing is a waste of time" (Kennedy 1970, 1). Revolution appears in scare quotes—an ambiguous qualification of the value of revolution at the same time as it is being asserted. It is not surprising, then, the epigram for the essay is from the Beatles "Revolution," in which John Lennon sang "When you talk of revolution / Don't you know that you can count me out (in)." Lennon's equivocation is itself a subtle comment on the tormented world of the new left. Kennedy is careful to distinguish his approach from dogmatic Marxism. It is open, based on "study" of philosophy and politics. In other words, it is nondoctrinaire and—"not at all revolutionary." But it is not "reformism" because it borrows from the "rebellion" of the new left (Kennedy 1982, 611).

8. Intersectional thought is itself open and provisional—"yet to take theoretical shape" (Bartky 1982, 130). It would be wrong to write it off as doctrinaire. Moreover, intersectional thinking is worth celebrating as it reorientates "classical" and rather limited accounts of alienation to feminist thinking. Feminism did not accept the narrowness of the Marxian accounts of alienation (or those available in social theory). For instance, feminism focused on rethinking the notion of labor to include various forms of affective work. One important lesson we can learn from feminist writing concerns that relationship between narcissism and alienation. The fundamental point is that the alienated one is narcissistic in the sense that de Beauvoir (1976) articulated: trapped in ideas of the self that are inherited and limit possibilities of being. Looking inward, the narcissist is unable to criticize what s/he has become. The road out of the alienation passes alongside that of those who recognize themselves differently.

9. Certainly these themes do appear in both the legal and the feminist literatures (Fejfar 1996, 605–6; Bartky 2002).

References

Andrews, Rhonda V. Magee. 2004. "Racial Suffering as Human Suffering: An Existentially-Grounded Humanity Consciousness as a Guide to a Fourteenth Amendment Reborn." *Temple Political and Civil Rights Law Review* 13 (2): 891–926.

Armstrong, George M., Jr. 1991. "The Reification of Celebrity: Persona as Property." *Louisiana Law Review* 51 (3): 443–68.

Ayres, Bill. 2001. *Fugitive Days.* New York: Penguin.

Ayers, Bill, and Ryan Alexander-Tanner. 2010. *To Teach: The Journey, In Comics.* New York: Teachers College Press.

Bartky, Sandra Lee. 1982. "Narcissism, Femininity and Alienation." *Social Theory and Practice* 8 (2): 127–43.

Bartky, Sandra Lee. 2002. *Sympathy and Solidarity.* Lanham: Rowman and Littlefield.

Christie, Isham. 2011. "Possibility, Universality, and Radicality: A Universal Chorus for Emancipation." *Tidal: Occupy Theory, Occupy Strategy* 1: 19–21.

Combahee River Collective. 1979. "A Black Feminist Statement." *Women's Studies Quarterly* 42 (3–4): 271–80.

Conaghan, Joanne. 2001. "Wishful Thinking or Bad Faith: A Feminist Encounter with Duncan Kennedy's Critique of Adjudication." *Cardozo Law Review* 22 (3–4): 721–46.

Crenshaw, Kimberlé. 1991. "Mapping the Margins: Intersectionality, Identity Politics, and Violence against Women of Color." *Stanford Law Review* 43 (6): 1241–300.

Crenshaw, Kimberlé. 2011. "Twenty Years of Critical Race Theory: Looking back to Move Forward." *Connecticut Law Review* 43 (5): 1253–354.

De Beauvoir, Simone. 1976. *The Ethics of Ambiguity.* New York: Citadel Press.

Duxbury, Neil. 1995. *Patterns of American Jurisprudence.* Oxford: Clarendon.

Farley, Anthony Paul. 1997. "The Black Body as Fetish Object." *Oregon Law Review* 76 (3): 457–74.

Fejfar, Anthony J. 1996. "An Analysis of the Term Reification as Used in Peter Gabel's *Reification in Legal Reasoning*." *Capital University Law Review* 25 (3): 579–612.

Gabel, Peter. 1984. "Phenomenology of Rights-Consciousness and the Pact of the Withdrawn Selves." *Texas Law Review* 62 (8): 1563–600.

Gabel, Peter, and Duncan Kennedy. 1984. "Roll Over Beethoven." *Stanford Law Review* 36 (1–2): 1–56.

Glen, Patrick. 2007. "The Deconstruction and Reification of Law in Franz Kafka's *Before the Law* and *The Trial*." *Southern California Interdisciplinary Law Journal* 17 (1): 23–66.

Gordon, Lewis R. 1997. *Existence in Black: An Anthology of Black Existentialist Philosophy.* London: Routledge.

Graeber, David. 2009. *Direct Action: An Ethnography.* Oakland: AK Press.

Green, Jamison. 2012. "If I Follow the Rules, Will You Make Me a Man: Patterns in Transsexual Validation." *University of La Verne Law Review* 34 (1): 23–88.

Groensteen, Thierry. 2007. *The System of Comics.* Jackson: University Press of Mississippi.

Harris, Cheryl I. 1993. "Whiteness as Property." *Harvard Law Review* 106 (8): 1707–91.

Harris, Angela P. 2012. "Compassion and Critique." *Columbia Journal of Race and Law* 1 (3): 326–52.

hooks, bell. 1991. "Theory as Liberatory Practice." *Yale Journal of Law and Feminism* 4 (1): 1–12.

Hutchinson, Darren Lenard. 1997. "Out Yet Unseen: A Racial Critique of Gay and Lesbian Legal Theory and Political Discourse." *Connecticut Law Review* 29 (2): 561–645.

Kennedy, Duncan. 1970. "How the Law School Fails: A Polemic." *Yale Review of Law and Social Action* 1 (1): 71–91.

Kennedy, Duncan. 1982. "Legal Education as Training for Hierarchy." *Journal of Legal Education* 32 (4): 591–615.

Kennedy, Duncan. 1997. *A Critique of Adjudication.* Cambridge, MA: Harvard University Press.

Kim, Janine Young. 2013. "Postracialism: Race after Exclusion." *Lewis and Clark Law Review* 17: 1063–140.

Klare, Karl. 2001. "The Politics of Duncan Kennedy's Critique." *Cardozo Law Review* 22 (3–4): 1073–104.

Korhonen, Outi. 2015. "Deconstructing the Conflict in Ukraine: The Relevance of International Law to Hybrid States and Wars." *German Law Journal* 16 (3): 452–78.

Kwan, Peter. 2000. "Complicity and Complexity: Cosynthesis and Praxis." *DePaul Law Review* 49 (3): 673–92.

Litowitz, Douglas. 2000. "Reification in Law and Legal Theory." *Southern California Interdisciplinary Law Journal* 9 (2): 401–42.

Maeckelbergh, Marianne. 2009. *The Will of the Many: How the Alterglobalisation Movement Is Changing the Face of Democracy.* London: Pluto Press.

Manderson, Desmond. 1996. "Beyond the Provincial: Space, Aesthetics, and Modernist Legal Theory." *Melbourne University Law Review* 20 (4): 1048–71.

McCluskey, Martha T. 2018. "Are We Economic Engines Too? Precarity, Productivity and Gender." *University of Toledo Law Review* 49 (3): 631–56.

Modiri, Joel M. 2012. "The Colour of Law, Power and Knowledge: Introducing Critical Race Theory in (Post-)Apartheid South Africa." *South African Journal on Human Rights* 28 (3): 405–36.

Motro, Shari. 2015. "Scholarship against Desire." *Yale Journal of Law and the Humanities* 27 (1): 115–56.

Neacsu, Dana. 2014. "Technology, Alienation, and the Future of Litigation-Based Social Change." *Temple Political and Civil Rights Law Review* 24 (1): 155–84.

Passant, John. 2015. "Some Basic Marxist Concepts to Help Understand Income Tax." *Journal Jurisprudence* 27: 263–312.

Peller, Gary. 2011. "History, Identity, and Alienation." *Connecticut Law Review* 43 (5): 1479–502.

Rasario-Lebrón, Aníbal. 2013. "For Better and for Better: The Case for Abolishing Civil Marriage." *Washington University Jurisprudence Review* 5 (2): 189–256.

Rijswijk, Honni van. 2012. "Towards a Feminist Aesthetic of Justice: Sarah Kane's *Blasted* as Theorisation of the Representation of Sexual Violence in International Law." *Australian Feminist Law Journal* 36: 107–24.

Ronner, Amy. 2013. "Let's Get the Trans and Sex out of It and Free Us All." *Journal of Gender, Race and Justice* 16 (3): 859–916.

Schlag, Pierre. 2015. "How to Do Things with Hohfeld." *Law and Contemporary Problems* 78 (1–2): 185–234.

Shaw, Julia J. A. 2015. "From Homo Economicus to Homo Roboticus: An Exploration of the Transformative Impact of the Technological Imaginary." *International Journal of Law in Context* 11 (3): 245–64.

Stooges, The. 1969. "1969." *The Stooges.* New York: Elektra.

Sultany, Nimer. 2014. "Religion and Constitutionalism: Lessons from American and Islamic Constitutionalism." *Emory International Law Review* 28: 345–424.

Taylor, George. 2014. "The Object of Diversity." *University of Pittsburgh Law Review* 75 (4): 653–78.

Valdes, Francisco. 1995. "Sex and Race in Queer Legal Culture: Ruminations on Identities and Inter-Connectivities." *Southern California Review of Law and Women's Studies* 5 (1): 25–74.

Varga, Csaba. 2015. "Koskenniemi and the International Legal Argument as Founded in the Law's Ontology." *Hungarian Yearbook of International Law and European Law,* 331–56.

van Marle, Karin. 2001. "Reflections on Teaching Critical Race Theory at South African Universities/Law Faculties." *Stellenbosch Law Review* 12 (1): 86–100.

CONTRIBUTORS

PAUL FISHER DAVIES gained his PhD with the thesis title "Making Meanings with Comics: A Functional Approach to Graphic Narrative" in the school of English at the University of Sussex, where he has also been an associate lecturer. He teaches English language and literature at East Sussex College in Lewes, UK.

LISA DETORA is associate professor and director of STEM Writing at Hofstra University, New York. A founding member of the International Comparative Literature Association's Graphic Narrative Research Group, her publications also extend into the domains of medicine, biomedical publication ethics, medical humanities, and technical communication.

YASEMIN J. ERDEN is senior lecturer in philosophy at St Mary's University. Her research interests range from interdisciplinary (with science and technology) to philosophy of identity, language, and aesthetics. Her most recent publications include topics in agency, recognition, and dialogue. She is a realist who dreams of an existential renaissance.

ADAM GEAREY is a professor of law at Birkbeck College, University of London. His most recent publication is *Lives That Slide out of View: Poverty Law and Legal Activism* (Routledge 2018). His research interests are in the areas of political philosophy, the critique of political economy, and legal aesthetics.

THOMAS GIDDENS is lecturer in law at the University of Dundee, Scotland. He founded the Graphic Justice Research Alliance, and recently published *On Comics and Legal Aesthetics: Multimodality and the Haunted Mask of Knowing* (Routledge 2018). His research focuses on critical, comics, and cultural legal studies, with particular interests in aesthetics, epistemology, and visuality.

PETER GOODRICH is professor of law and director of law and humanities at Cardozo Law School in New York, as well as being executive editor of the journal *Law and Literature*. He has written extensively in legal history and theory, law and literature, and semiotics. His most recent book is *Schreber's Law* (Edinburgh University Press 2018).

MAGGIE GRAY lectures in critical and historical studies at Kingston School of Art, Kingston University. She researches the history, aesthetics, and politics of

British comics, and their relationship to modes and practices of performance. She is author of *Alan Moore, Out from the Underground: Cartooning, Performance and Dissent* (Palgrave 2017).

MATTHEW J. A. GREEN is a trade unionist and associate professor at the University of Nottingham. An avid *aikidoka* (*Yoshinkan*) and erstwhile Augustinian Buddhist, he has published widely on William Blake and comics and is currently completing a monograph on the graphic novels of Bryan Talbot.

VLADISLAV MAKSIMOV completed his undergraduate studies at NYU Abu Dhabi in political science, specializing in legal studies. He is currently a master's student of international security at Paris School of International Affairs, Sciences Po, with research interests in international law and governance.

TIMOTHY D. PETERS is senior lecturer in law, USC Law School, University of the Sunshine Coast, an adjunct research fellow, Law Futures Centre, Griffith University, and president of the Law, Literature and the Humanities Association of Australasia. His research examines the intersections of legal theory, theology, and popular culture.

CHRISTOPHER PIZZINO is associate professor of contemporary US literature at the University of Georgia, where he teaches comics and contemporary literature, film, and television, among other topics. His current research concerns the relation of comics to theory of the novel and to image theory.

NICOLA STREETEN lectures in critical and theoretical studies at London College of Communication, University of the Arts London, and Kingston School of Art, Kingston University. Her research area is women's comics and cartoons and the use of humour as a feminist strategy. Her expertise is on work in Britain. Her most recent publication is *UK Feminist Cartoons and Comics: A Critical Survey* (Palgrave Macmillan 2020). https://www.streetenillustration.com/.

LYDIA WYSOCKI is a research associate in education at Newcastle University. Her research interests include critical education, representation, microaggressions, and visual research methods. She founded Applied Comics Etc, making and using comics for specific purposes. She is pursuing her PhD (ESRC/NEDTC funded), exploring readers' readings of specific British comics 2010–2017.

INDEX

Adorno, Theodor, 127, 130

Agamben, Giorgio, 200–201, 202–5, 207, 210, 212, 213, 227, 228, 231, 245, 261. *See also* biopolitics

Alexander-Tanner, Ryan, 288, 289, 291, 293, 294–95, 296–97, 299, 300, 303, 305. See also *To Teach* (2010)

Alice in Sunderland (2007), 265–66. *See also* Talbot, Bryan

alienation, 117, 290–94, 298, 302–3, 307; Arts Lab Press and, 129–30; Ar:Zak and, 117, 120, 125, 129–30; commodification and, 298–99; Critical Legal Studies and, 290, 299–300; pledge of allegiance and, 299–300; reification and, 290–94, 299, 302. *See also* anxiety; Marxism

alternative press, 185; Arts Lab Press and, 113–14; Ar:Zak and, 115–16, 125. *See also* print

Althusser, Louis, 251, 261

anarchy, 196, 241, 245, 267; abolitionism and, 246; freedom and, 246; law and, 257; V and, 245–46; *V for Vendetta* and, 249, 257. *See also* revolution

antihero, 56–57; Deadpool as, 57, 61, 68, 69; existential, 58, 68, 69; hero and, 56

anthropological machine: Giorgio Agamben, 226–27, 229–30, 231, 233; and Mara, 232

anxiety, 290, 291–93, 301; critique and, 293, 303. *See also* alienation

apparatus, 212, 227, 231, 234, 238–39, 241–42, 249–50, 252, 256–57, 261, 268; mask and, 249–50; person and, 241. *See also* biopolitics

Arkwright, Luther, 265

Arts Council of Great Britain (ACGB), 112, 120

Arts Lab Movement, 109–11; autonomy and, 110–11; capitalism and, 110, 125,

129–30; the Covent Garden Arts Lab and, 109–11; the New London Arts Lab and, 111. *See also* Arts Lab Press (ALP); Birmingham Arts Lab, the

Arts Lab Press (ALP), 108, 109, 111, 113–14, 116–17, 122; alienation and, 129–30; alternative press and, 113–14; capitalism and, 120–21, 125, 129–30; cultural production and, 120. *See also* Arts Lab Movement; Ar:Zak; Birmingham Arts Lab, the

Ar:Zak, 108, 109, 111, 114–30; alienation and, 117, 120, 125, 129–30; alternative comics and, 115; alternative press and, 115–16, 125; cultural production and, 120, 123–24, 125–26; organization of, 115–17, 121–25. *See also* Arts Lab Press (ALP); Emerson, Hunt; *Streetcomix*; Varty, Suzy

autonomy: Arts Lab Movement and, 110–11; Deadpool and, 62–63, 69–70; freedom and, 64; Jean-Paul Sartre and, 59, 62–63, 64, 66; Ludwig Wittgenstein and, 63; Marxism and, 108; uncertainty and, 61–64. *See also* freedom

Ayers, Bill, 288, 290–91, 295, 297, 299; in *To Teach*, 291, 293, 303. See also *Fugitive Days* (2014); *To Teach* (2010); Weather Underground, the

Bachelard, Gaston, 248

Bakhtin, Mikhail, 137, 140, 152, 159–60, 164–65. *See also* Vološinov, Valentin

"Ball Boy," 139; class in, 142; race in, 139–41. See also *Beano*

bare life: biopolitics, 200–202, 203, 210, 226, 227; and Evey, 205–7, 211; and V, 202, 211

Barker, Martin, 147

"Bash Street Kids, The," 142; class in, 142–44; race in, 142

www.ingramcontent.com/pod-product-compliance
Lightning Source LLC
Chambersburg PA
CBHW071836270326
41929CB00013B/2012